OWN IT! 4

B1+ Preliminary test content in *Own It!* Level 4 has been checked by Cambridge Assessment English for accuracy and level.

TEACHER'S BOOK
WITH DIGITAL PACK

Garan Holcombe

CAMBRIDGE UNIVERSITY PRESS

CAMBRIDGE
UNIVERSITY PRESS & ASSESSMENT

Shaftesbury Road, Cambridge CB2 8EA, United Kingdom

One Liberty Plaza, 20th Floor, New York, NY 10006, USA

477 Williamstown Road, Port Melbourne, VIC 3207, Australia

314–321, 3rd Floor, Plot 3, Splendor Forum, Jasola District Centre, New Delhi – 110025, India

103 Penang Road, #05-06/07, Visioncrest Commercial, Singapore 238467

José Abascal, 56–1°, 28003 Madrid, Spain

Cambridge University Press & Assessment is a department of the University of Cambridge.

We share the University's mission to contribute to society through the pursuit of education, learning and research at the highest international levels of excellence.

www.cambridge.org
Information on this title: www.cambridge.org/9781108726610

First published 2020

20 19 18 17 16 15 14 13 12 11 10 9 8 7 6 5 4 3

Printed in Great Britain by Ashford Colour Press Ltd.

A catalogue record for this publication is available from the British Library

ISBN 978-1-108-72661-0 *Own it!* Teacher's Book with Digital Pack Level 4
ISBN 978-84-9036-132-0 *Collaborate* Teacher's Book Level 4

Additional resources for this publication at www.cambridge.org/ownit/resources

Contents

Welcome to *Own It!*

'It's your world, so OWN IT!'

Welcome to *Own It!*; the course which ensures your students are confident and future-ready through a combination of global topics, collaborative projects and strategies to develop learner independence.

While developing *Own It!* we spoke with teachers and students around the world to identify their top priorities in the Secondary classroom ...

> I'd like to do project work with my students, but it can be too time-consuming to plan.
> *Merve, Turkey*

Project Work

Collaboration is a key strand of this course. *Own It!* includes a CLIL project in every even-numbered unit of the *Student's Book* and a *Culture Project* for every odd-numbered unit available in the *Teacher's Resource Bank* online. These are accompanied by a *Project Book* with step-by step guides and practical tips for teachers.

For more information: Pages 6, 7 and 25

> I want my students to become more independent learners.
> *Maria, Spain*

Learn to Learn

The *Learn to Learn* feature of the course is designed to introduce students to vital learning strategies and techniques which will help them become more independent learners, all aligned to the *Cambridge Life Competencies Framework*.

For more information: Pages 6, 7 and 24

> I want my students to feel that they belong to the world; that they are global citizens.
> *Itana, Brazil*

Global topics

Own It! has a global, cultural focus, with topics from traditional dress to unique festivals. The documentaries and the *Around the World* pages bring these global topics to life, exposing students to different countries, and asking questions which encourage students to think about the differences between their culture and other cultures.

For more information: Page 23

> I want a variety of videos that will help me to engage my students with the topic and see the language being used in a meaningful way.
> *Antonio, Mexico*

Teen-friendly videos

Own It! includes four to five videos per unit made especially for this course. As well as documentaries, there are *Language in Action* and *Everyday English* videos designed to appeal to the teenage learner.

For more information: Page 26

> I need resources and support to manage students of different levels in the same class.
> *Andrés, Ecuador*

Mixed-ability support

In *Own It!* there is extensive support for teachers with mixed-ability classes, including:

- graded *Workbook* activities
- suggestions for differentiated activities
- an entire *Project Book* guiding teachers through each project
- graded grammar and vocabulary worksheets

For more information: Page 27

Cambridge Life Competencies Framework

How can we prepare our students to succeed in a world that is rapidly changing? We need to help students develop transferable skills, to work with people from around the world, to think creatively, to analyse sources critically and communicate their views effectively. How can we teach these skills alongside language?

In response to these questions, we have developed the *Cambridge Life Competencies Framework*. This Framework underpins the syllabus for the *Learn to Learn* pages and the collaborative project work in *Own It!*, helping teachers recognise and assess the many transferable skills that the course develops.

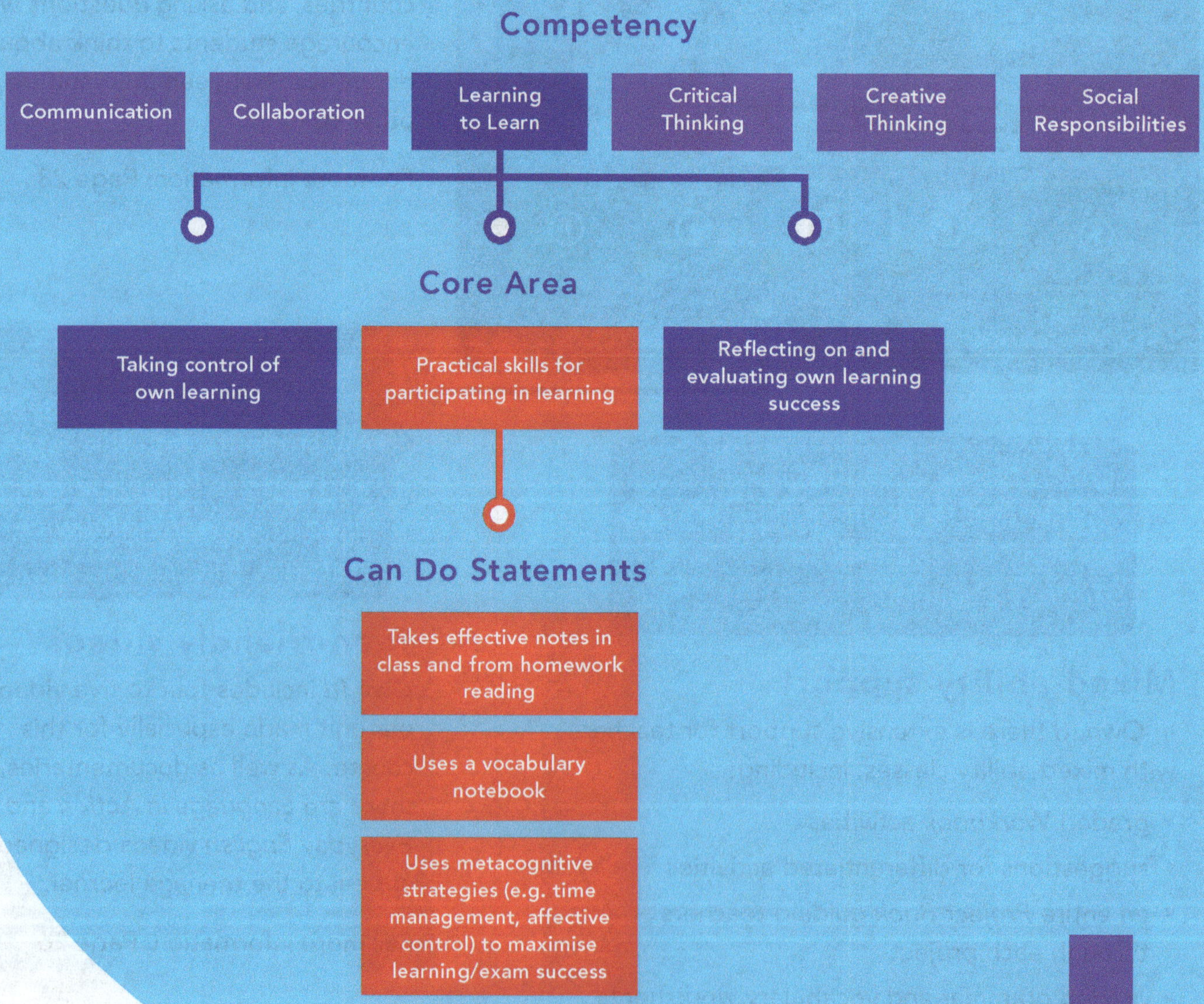

Learn to Learn

These core areas are developed in the *Learn to Learn* feature which appears throughout the unit and on the *Learn to Learn* page at the end of each unit.

This page from Level 1 Unit 1 helps students organise their notebook by encouraging them to look at an example of a notebook, compare it with their own, and finally, reflect on how theirs could be improved.

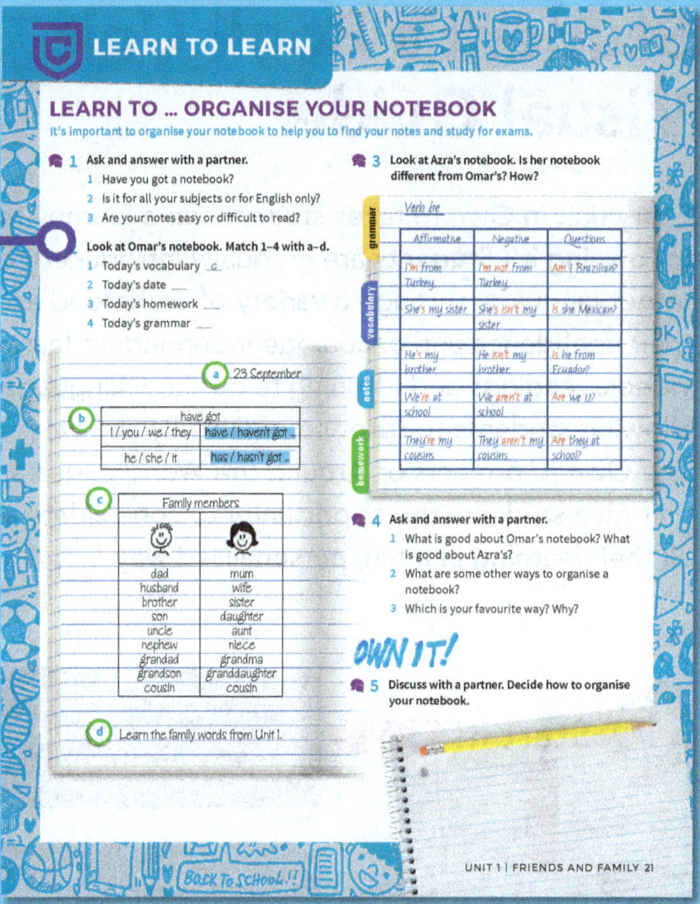

LEARN TO LEARN

LEARN TO ... ORGANISE YOUR NOTEBOOK

It's important to organise your notebook to help you to find your notes and study for exams.

1 Ask and answer with a partner.
1 Have you got a notebook?
2 Is it for all your subjects or for English only?
3 Are your notes easy or difficult to read?

2 Look at Omar's notebook. Match 1–4 with a–d.
1 Today's vocabulary _c_
2 Today's date ___
3 Today's homework ___
4 Today's grammar ___

a 23 September

b

have got	
I / you / we / they	have / haven't got ...
he / she / it	has / hasn't got ...

c

Family members	
dad	mum
husband	wife
brother	sister
son	daughter
uncle	aunt
nephew	niece
grandad	grandma
grandson	granddaughter
cousin	cousin

d Learn the family words from Unit 1.

3 Look at Azra's notebook. Is her notebook different from Omar's? How?

grammar / vocabulary / notes / homework

Verb be

Affirmative	Negative	Questions
I'm from Turkey	I'm not from Turkey	Am I Brazilian?
She's my sister	She's isn't my sister	Is she Mexican?
He's my brother	He isn't my brother	Is he from Ecuador?
We're at school	We aren't at school	Are we 12?
They're my cousins	They aren't my cousins	Are they at school?

4 Ask and answer with a partner.
1 What is good about Omar's notebook? What is good about Azra's?
2 What are some other ways to organise a notebook?
3 Which is your favourite way? Why?

OWN IT!

5 Discuss with a partner. Decide how to organise your notebook.

UNIT 1 | FRIENDS AND FAMILY 21

Project Work

The *Collaboration* competency of the *Cambridge Life Competencies Framework* also plays a huge part in the course, through projects in the *Student's Book* and in the *Teacher's Resource Bank* online. All of which have extensive support and guidance in the *Project Book*.

This project from Level 1 Unit 6 asks students to analyse some of the key features of a model project before planning and creating their own. Finally, they can evaluate other groups' tasks.

THE PE PROJECT

An information leaflet

1 Look quickly at the leaflet. Circle its purpose.
1 to give directions to a sports club
2 to give information about a sport
3 to give transport times

2 Read the leaflet and make notes on the ideas in the box.

What? When? Where? Who? Equipment One of the rules One of the benefits

3 Read the leaflet again. Are the sentences *T* (true) or *F* (false)?
1 You need some special equipment to play streetball. _F_
2 There are sometimes ten players in a game of streetball.
3 You can't touch the ball with your hands in streetball.
4 Some sports are more expensive than streetball.

How to design a leaflet

4 Read the tips about designing a leaflet. Circle the ones you think are good pieces of advice.
a Use serious colours, not bright ones.
b Use photos and a map.
c Make sure the people are not smiling in the photos.
d Include contact details.
e Choose a clear font (if you're using a computer) or write neatly.
f Include everything you know about the sport.

5 Listen to the advice and check your answers to Exercise 4.

78 SPORT FOR LIFE | UNIT 6

STREETBALL

WHAT IS IT?
It's outdoor basketball in your local area.

WHERE AND WHEN?
We meet every Tuesday at 5.30 pm at the West Avenue basketball court. Come along and join us.
Find us here:

West Avenue

WHO?
Everyone is welcome! You don't need to belong to a team and you don't need special training.

Equipment
We've got a basketball and nets. Just bring yourself and your trainers!

Teams
- A team can play with only two players but there are never more than five.

Rules
Different streetball games have different rules, but these are ours:
- Players can bounce, throw and catch the ball.
- When you score, your team gets one point.
- After you score, your team keeps the ball.
- A team wins when they score 7 points.

BENEFITS
- It's free!
- It's a great way to get fitter and healthier!
- The matches are faster and more exciting than normal basketball.
- It's great fun!

WHY NOT COME ALONG AND MAKE NEW FRIENDS?

Any questions? Contact Greg at gregscott@jmail.com

OWN IT!

FACT
Bucharest is the unofficial streetball capital of the world! Every year more than 1,000 streetball players travel to the Romanian capital city and play in a streetball competition.

PLAN
6 Work with a group. Choose a street sport or another sport and find out information about it. Complete the steps below.
- Decide on the information you want to include.
- Decide and choose the photos and illustrations to include.
- Draw a rough plan of the layout of the leaflet.
- Make a first draft of your leaflet.
- Discuss how you can improve your first draft.

PRESENT
7 Prepare your final leaflet and present it to the class. Remember to include facts about your sport, photos, illustrations and maps, and the tips in *How to* design a leaflet.

CHECK
8 Look at your classmates' leaflets and complete the notes.
Which sport is the most interesting?
Which leaflet has the best design?
Which sport do you want to try? Why?

UNIT 6 | SPORT FOR LIFE 79

For more information about how *Own It!* correlates to the *Cambridge Life Competencies Framework*, go to pages 28 and 29.

Student's Book Unit Visual Guide

Every unit in *Own It!* takes students on a journey from 'starting it' to 'owning it'! Students are gradually introduced to the topic and target language through a variety of scaffolded activities that build their confidence and encourage independent learning. Vibrant videos, readings and listening texts show language in context, allowing students to respond personally and work collaboratively. The *Own It!* projects or *Around the World* pages at the end of the unit give students the opportunity to consolidate and demonstrate all their learning in a fun, personalised way.

Start it! → Activate prior knowledge
Get students interested in the topic
Provoke critical thinking

Explore it! → Develop research skills
Extend learning beyond the classroom

Use it! → Practise target language in a personalised, controlled activity

Voice it! → Allow students to respond personally to the topic

OWN IT! → Demonstrate topic knowledge and language learning in a collaborative project or on the *Around the World* pages

The unit journey is underpinned by the *Learn to Learn* strand which supports the development of vital learning skills, and the *How to …* feature which provides useful tips for completing project work successfully. These features support students on their journey from *Start it!* to *Own It!*

Learning outcomes clearly show unit aims at a glance.

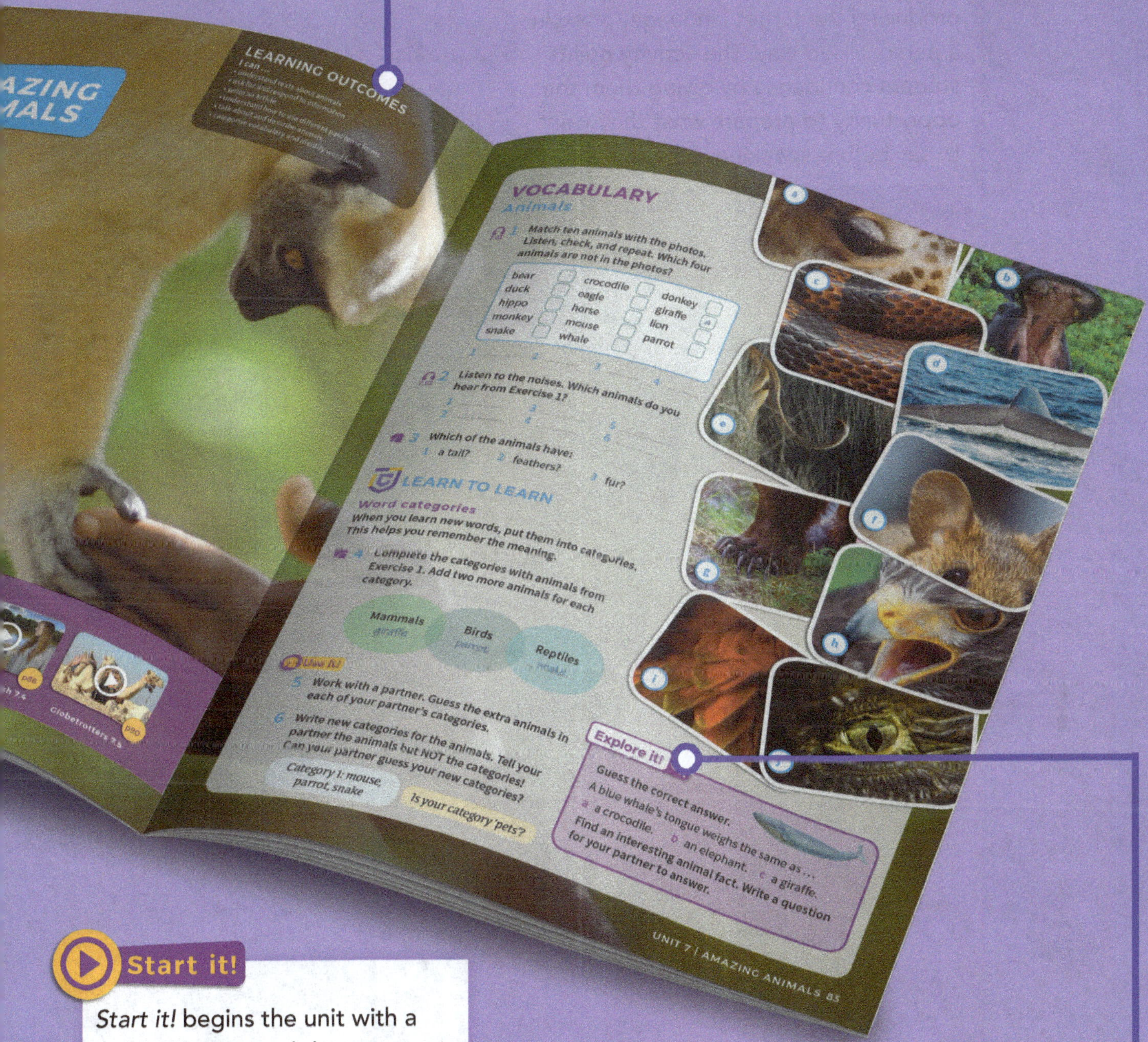

Start it!

Start it! begins the unit with a striking image and documentary. The questions provoke curiosity, activate prior knowledge and get students thinking critically.

Explore it!

Explore it! is a guided activity to help students develop research skills and extend their learning beyond English.

Use it!

Use it! gets students practising and producing the target language, often in a personalised way. The activity builds student confidence by giving them the opportunity to prepare what they want to say before speaking.

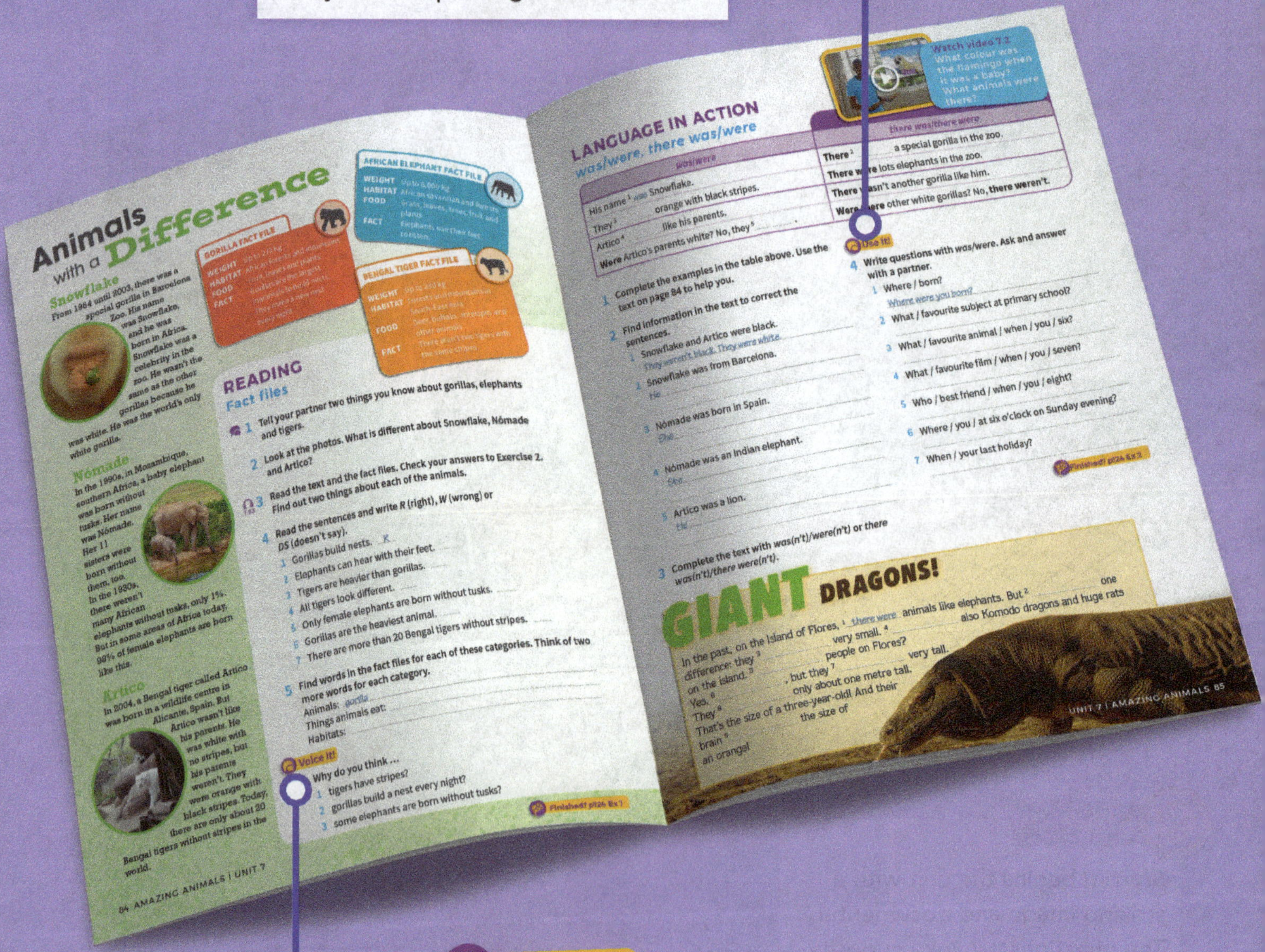

Voice it!

Voice it! is a thought-provoking speaking activity which asks students to give their personal response to a reading or listening text, encouraging critical thinking.

LANGUAGE IN ACTION VIDEOS

These videos show teenagers using the target language in context, in a teen-friendly vlog-style, plus an interactive grammar presentation, perfect for flipped classrooms.

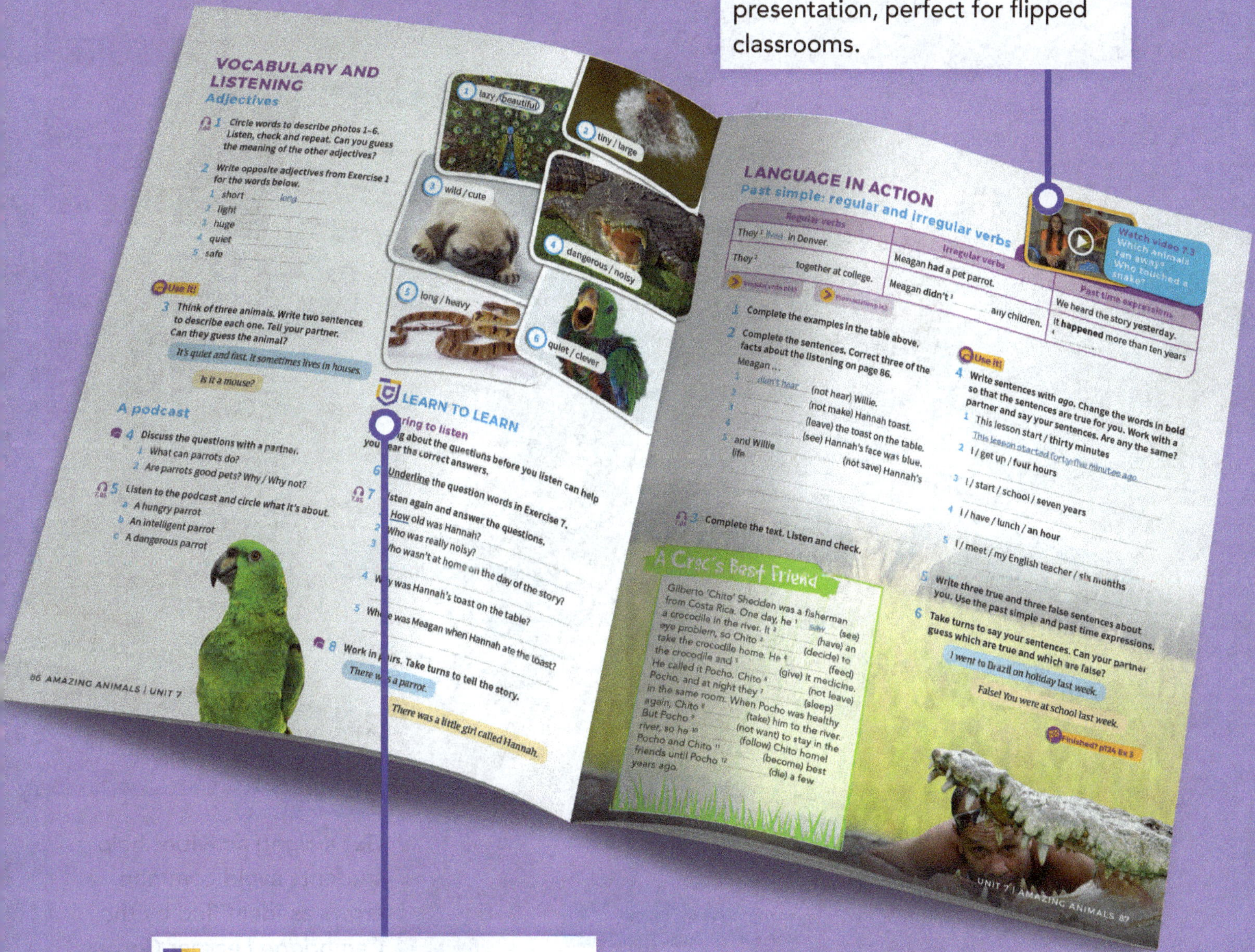

LEARN TO LEARN

Learn to learn introduces students to vital learning strategies and techniques, which will help them become more independent learners, all aligned to the *Cambridge Life Competencies Framework*.

Plan, Write and Check

The scaffolded approach of the speaking and writing pages builds students' confidence by giving them time to prepare before they speak and write. The *Check* stage encourages self-assessment, a key step towards learner independence.

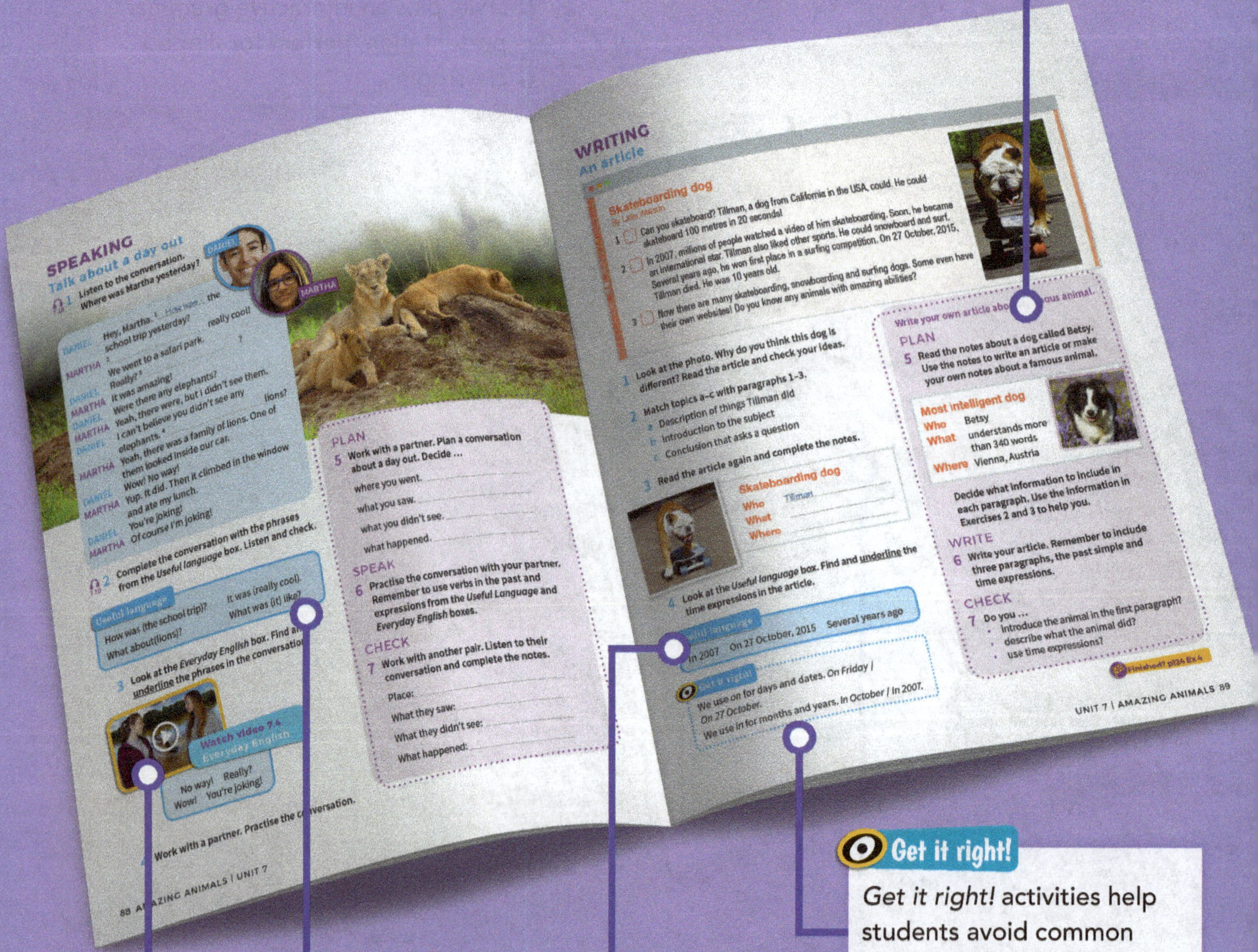

Get it right!

Get it right! activities help students avoid common errors as identified by the *Cambridge Learner Corpus*.

Useful Language

Useful language boxes appear throughout the unit, highlighting genre-specific target language.

Everyday English

In every unit there's a fun vlog-style video to teach students the meaning, form and use of the *Everyday English* from the conversation on the speaking page.

AROUND THE WORLD

The *Around the World* pages, which appear in Units 1, 3, 5, 7 and 9, introduce students to different people and cultures from around the world, encouraging critical thinking and raising cross-cultural awareness.

Globetrotters

These documentaries are thematically linked to either the topic of the unit or the *Around the World* pages. They contextualise the grammar and/or vocabulary of the unit and engage students' interest in the topic.

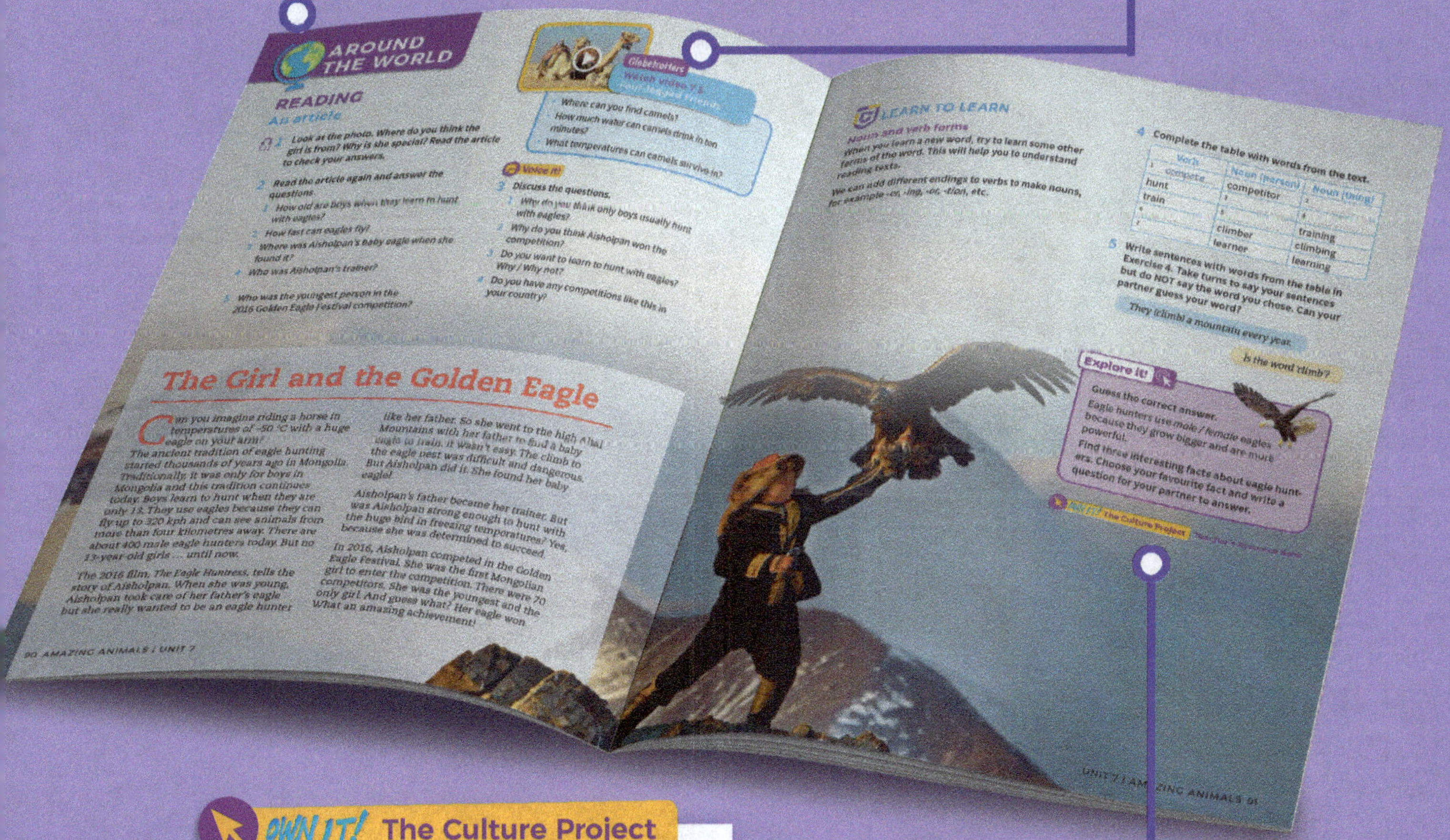

OWN IT! The Culture Project

Extend the page and get students to 'own' their language and topic knowledge with an optional culture project available in the *Teacher's Resource Bank* online, with teacher's notes available in the *Project Book*.

THE CLIL PROJECT

The *CLIL project* pages appear in Units 2, 4, 6 and 8. They encourage students to 'own' the language and topic knowledge they have gained throughout the unit in an individual or collaborative project.

Plan, Present and Check

The step-by-step guide helps students work through the project without the need for constant supervision by the teacher, promoting peer-learning and student autonomy.

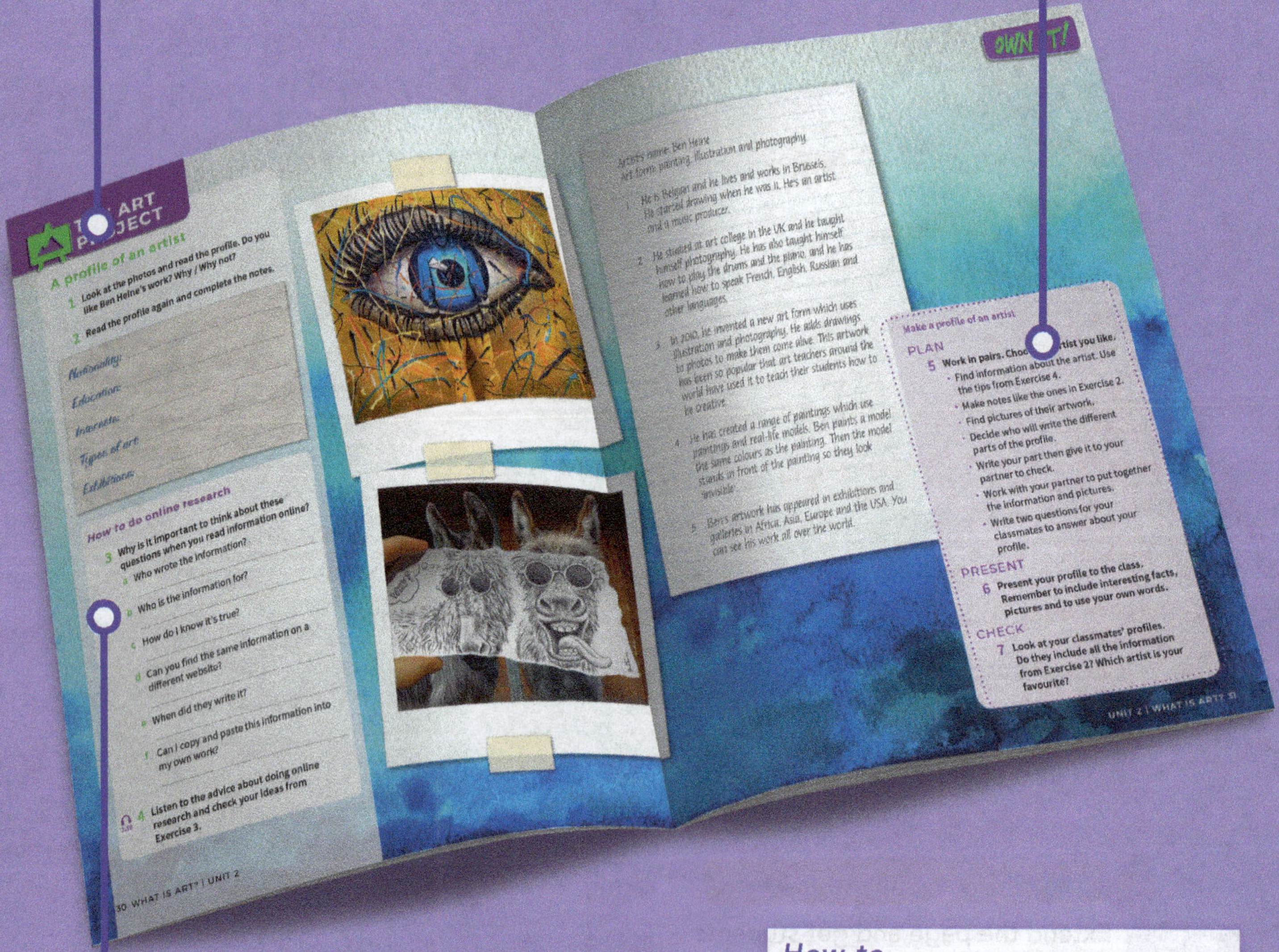

How to …

These practical tips help students complete the project by raising their awareness of the particular skills required to carry it out.

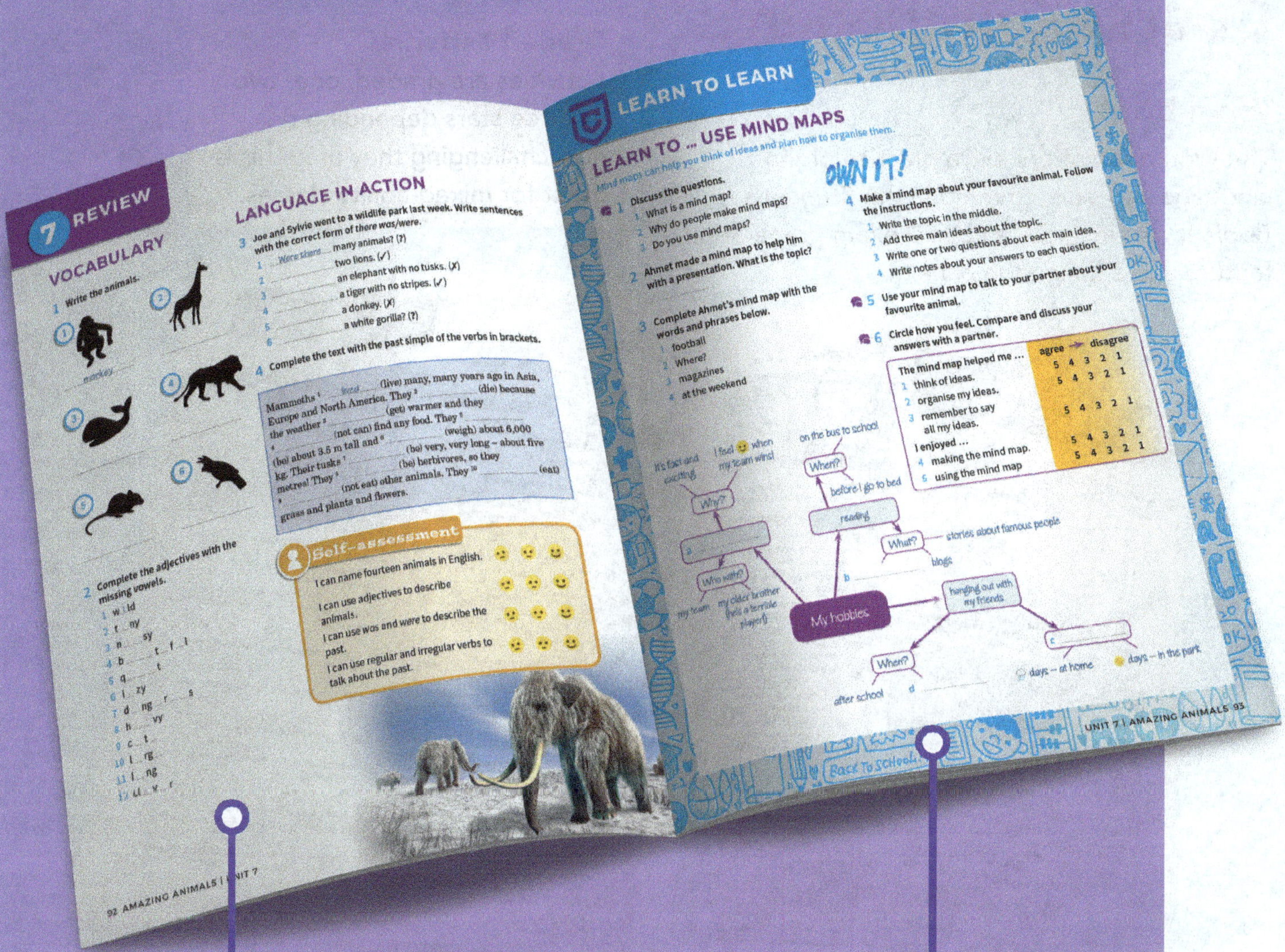

Review

Revise the language from the unit in these useful review pages, which include a self-assessment task, encouraging students' self-awareness.

LEARN TO LEARN

The *Learn to learn* pages focus on developing core areas from the *Cambridge Life Competencies Framework*. Students have the opportunity to 'own' their learning by putting the new skill into practice.

Course Components

Workbook

The Workbook offers extra practice of the language and skills covered in the *Student's Book*. It also includes a special exam-preparation feature and a *Language bank*.

Graded activities

Activities are graded, one, two or three stars depending on how challenging they are. This is great for mixed-ability classes.

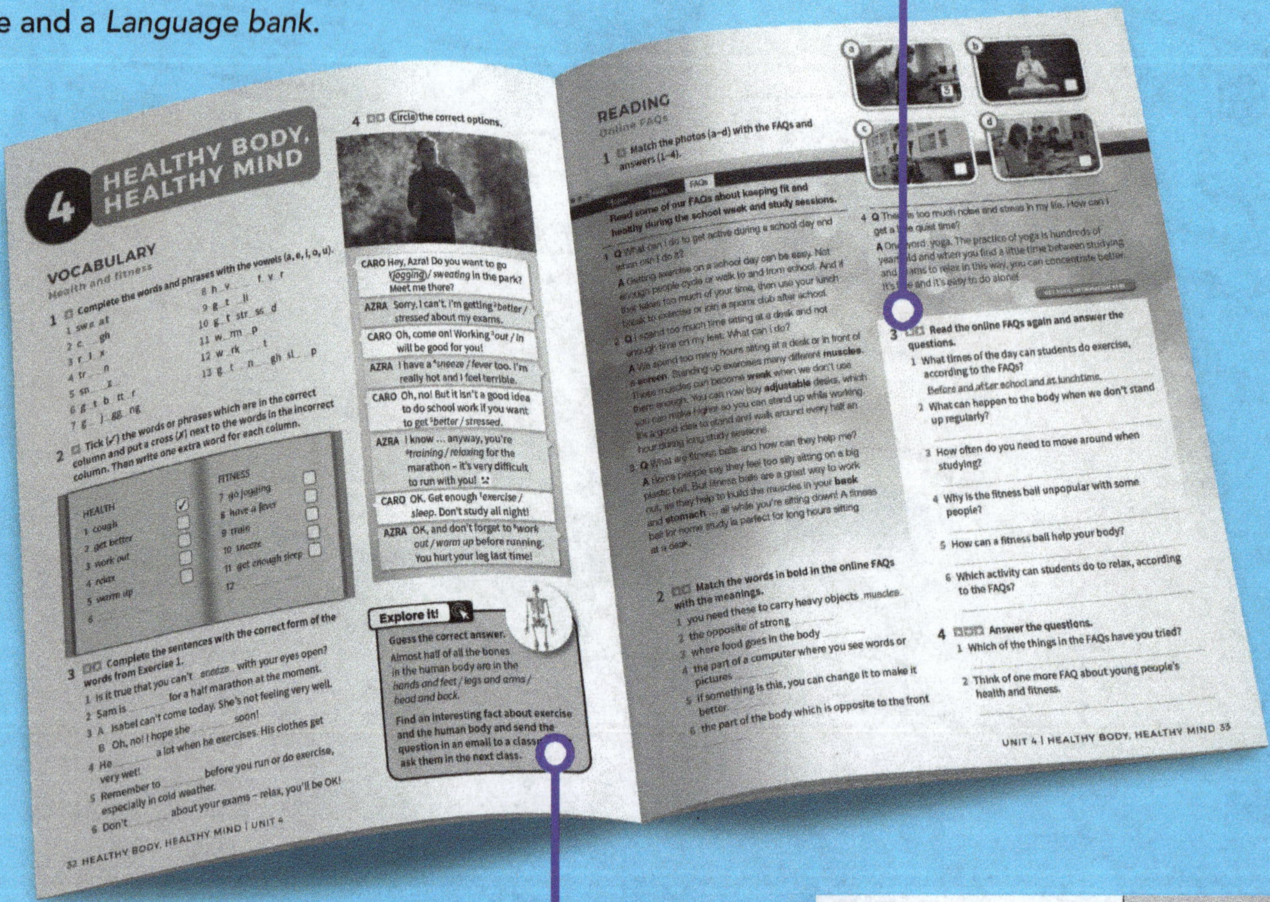

Explore it!

The *Explore it!* feature extends learning beyond the classroom and helps students develop the research skills that are vital for learner independence.

Exam Tips

The exam preparation pages at the end of the *Workbook* provide useful tips and practice to help students prepare for international exams.

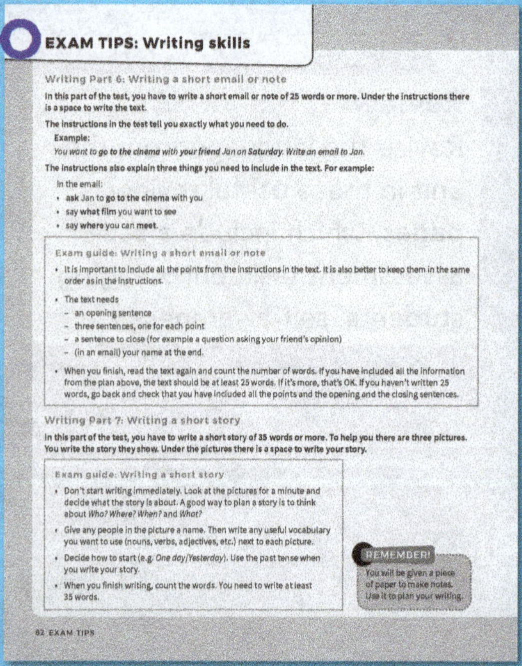

OWN IT! Digital Tools

All your digital tools together in one place!

With *Own It!* everything you need is at your fingertips, including *Presentation Plus*, audio and video, additional practice, games, *Test Centre* and an innovative digital collaboration space for students.

Presentation Plus

- *Student's Book* and *Workbook* with interactive exercises
- games
- accessible online and offline

Teacher's Resource Bank

- Online teacher's resource area with culture projects, graded grammar and vocabulary practice worksheets, video worksheets, communication worksheets, writing template worksheets, video worksheets, speaking extra activities, and more!
- *Test Centre*, including end-of unit, term and year tests, and exam practice tests.

Digital Collaboration Space

- Students can collaborate digitally online and offline in the collaboration space, where teachers can set, track and assess students' work.
- Students can also archive and share their work as well as comment on each other's projects.

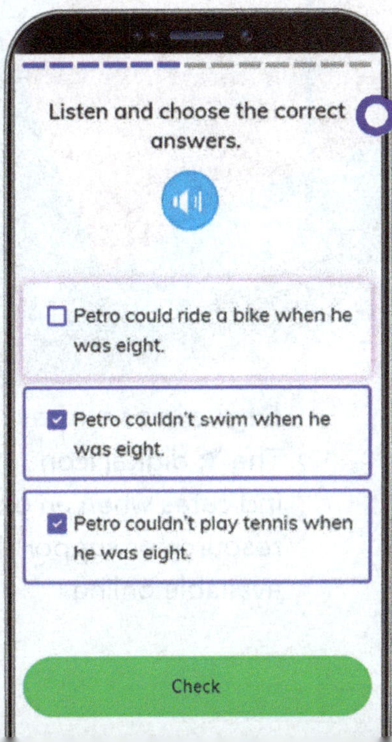

Practice Extra

- mobile friendly platform and content
- bite-sized learning activities
- online speaking tasks with audio and video
- performance tracking and gamification

For the most up-to-date information on, *Own It!*'s Digital Tools, visit www.cambridge.org/ownit/digital or use this QR code:

How to use the Teacher's Book

Warmer
Engaging ideas for introducing students to the topic of the unit and activating their prior knowledge.

Class challenge
Get students interested in the topic and extend their learning beyond language, using this quiz-style question.

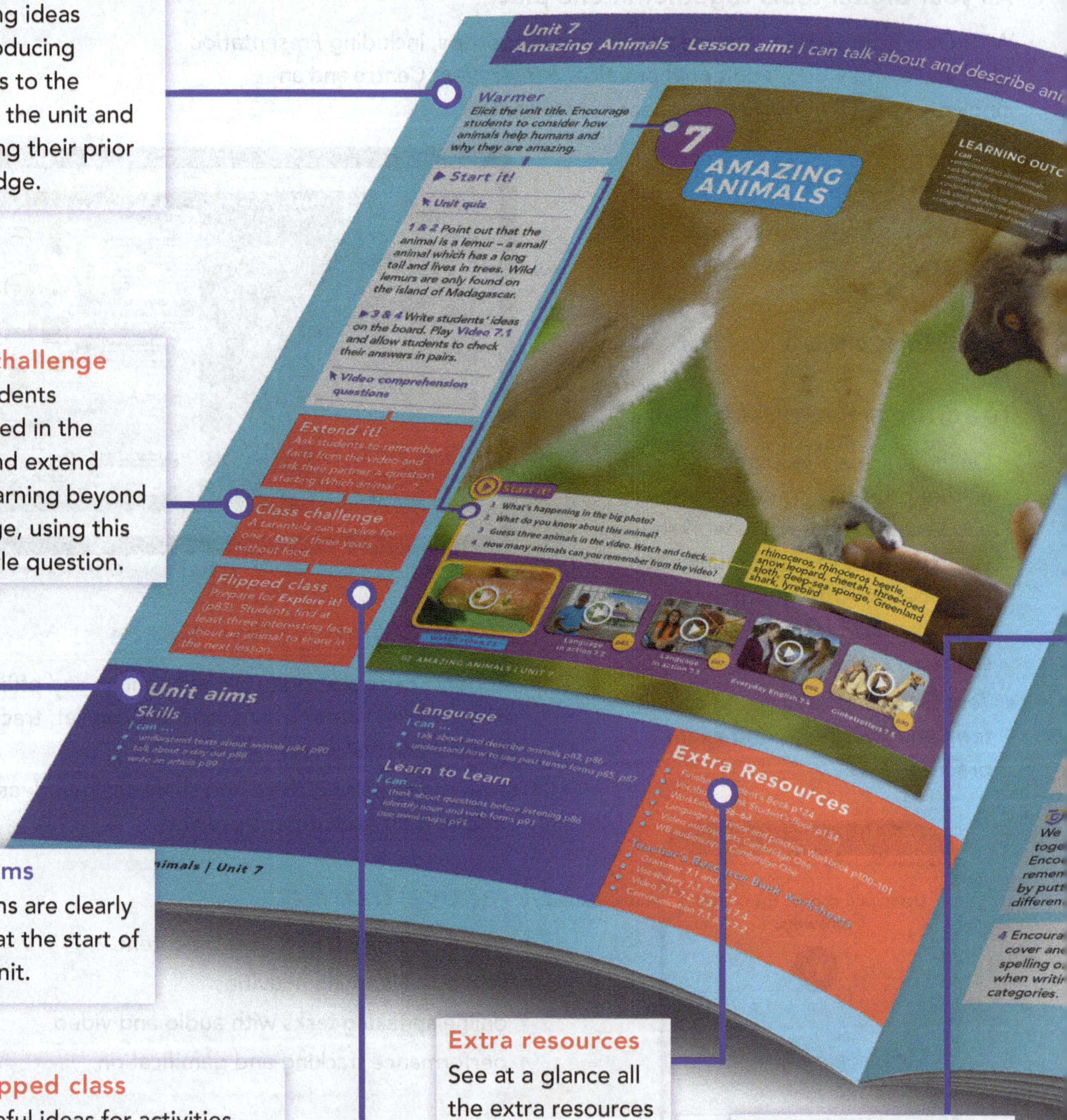

Unit aims
Unit aims are clearly shown at the start of every unit.

Flipped class
Useful ideas for activities that students could do at home to consolidate in-class learning and encourage independent study.

Extra resources
See at a glance all the extra resources available for teachers to use with this unit.

Digital resources
The digital icon indicates when an extra resource or support is available online.

Graded activities

Some activities are graded with one or three stars. One star activities show ideas for providing more support to students and three star activities show ideas for providing extra challenge – great for mixed-ability classes!

Pronunciation

Find pronunciation for all target vocabulary easily.

Integrated answers

Find all of the answers in place on the page for quick access.

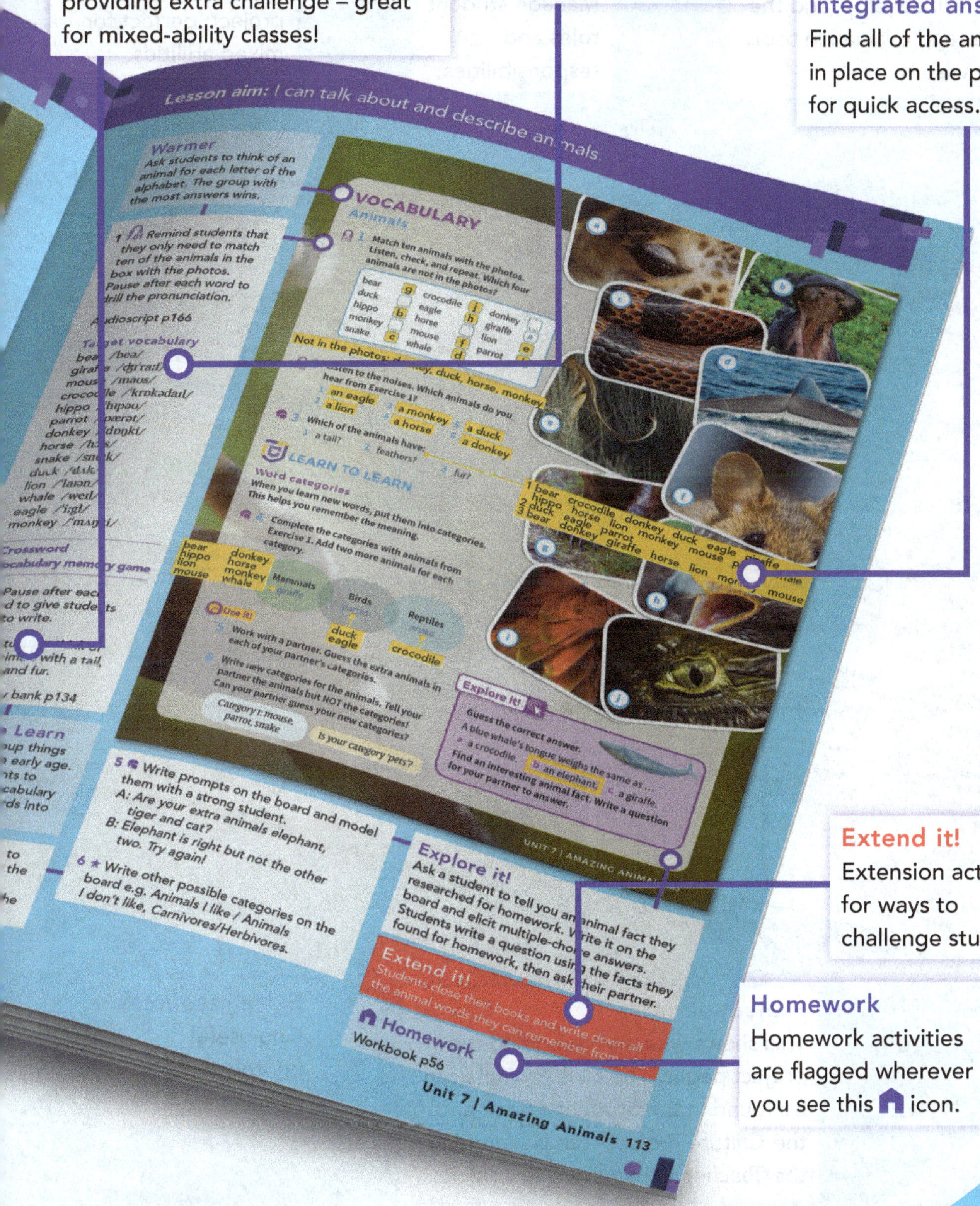

Extend it!

Extension activity for ways to challenge students.

Homework

Homework activities are flagged wherever you see this icon.

How to use the Project Book

Learning outcomes

See learning outcomes at a glance, as well as the skills students will develop, and the resources and evaluation tools you may wish to use.

Student roles

Manage student roles and responsibilities.

Mixed-ability tips

Get ideas for extra differentiated practice in each project; perfect for mixed abilities.

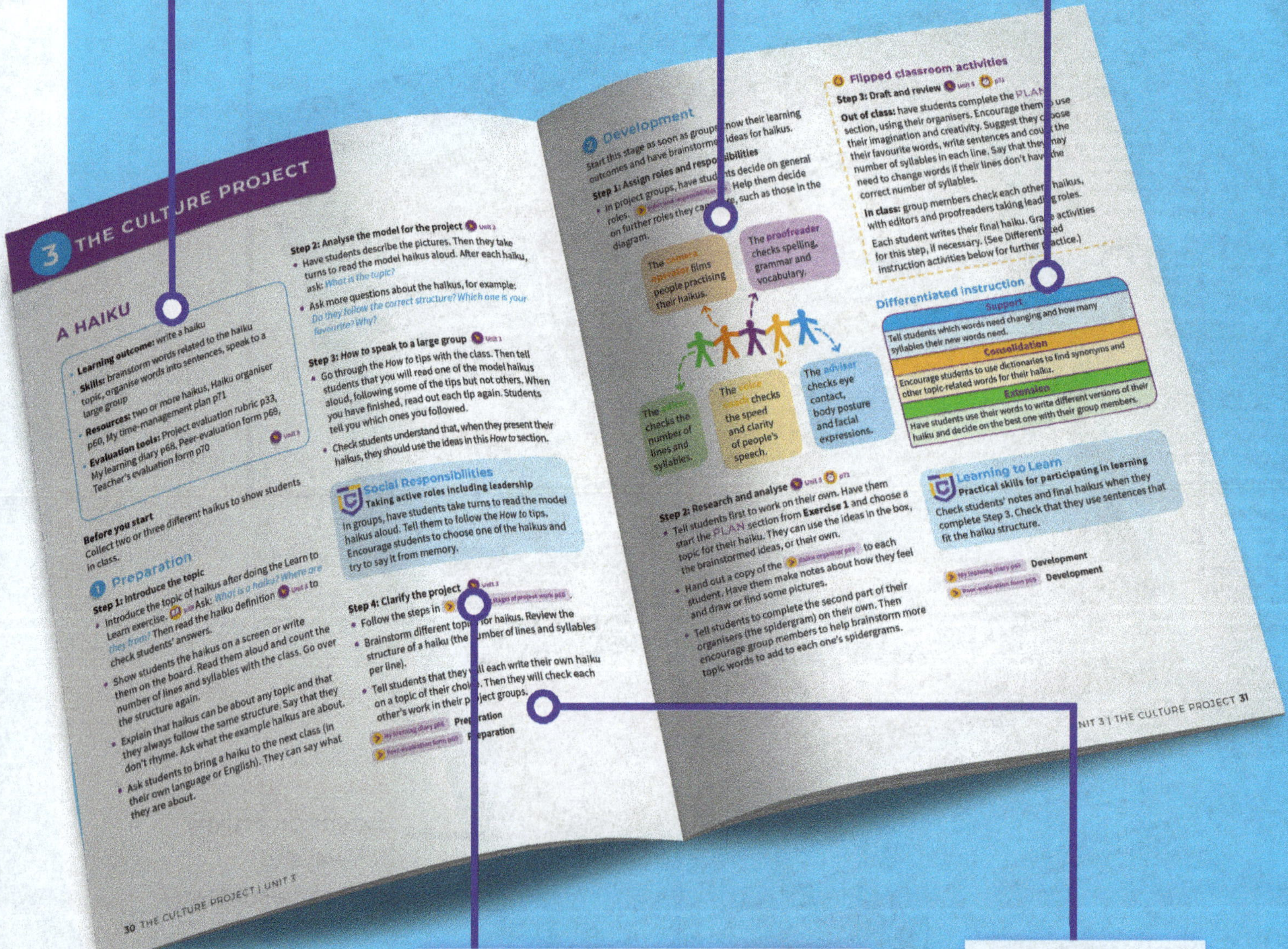

Project pages

This shows where you can find the project pages. The *CLIL Projects* can be found in the *Student's Book* and the *Culture Projects* can be found in the *Teacher's Resource Bank* online.

Extra resources

Find useful photocopiable resources.

Digital collaboration space
Students can work together on their projects in the digital collaboration space and teachers can track and assess their work. Students can also share and comment on each other's work via their digital portfolio.

Evaluation guidelines
See clear guidelines for identifying and assessing student performance.

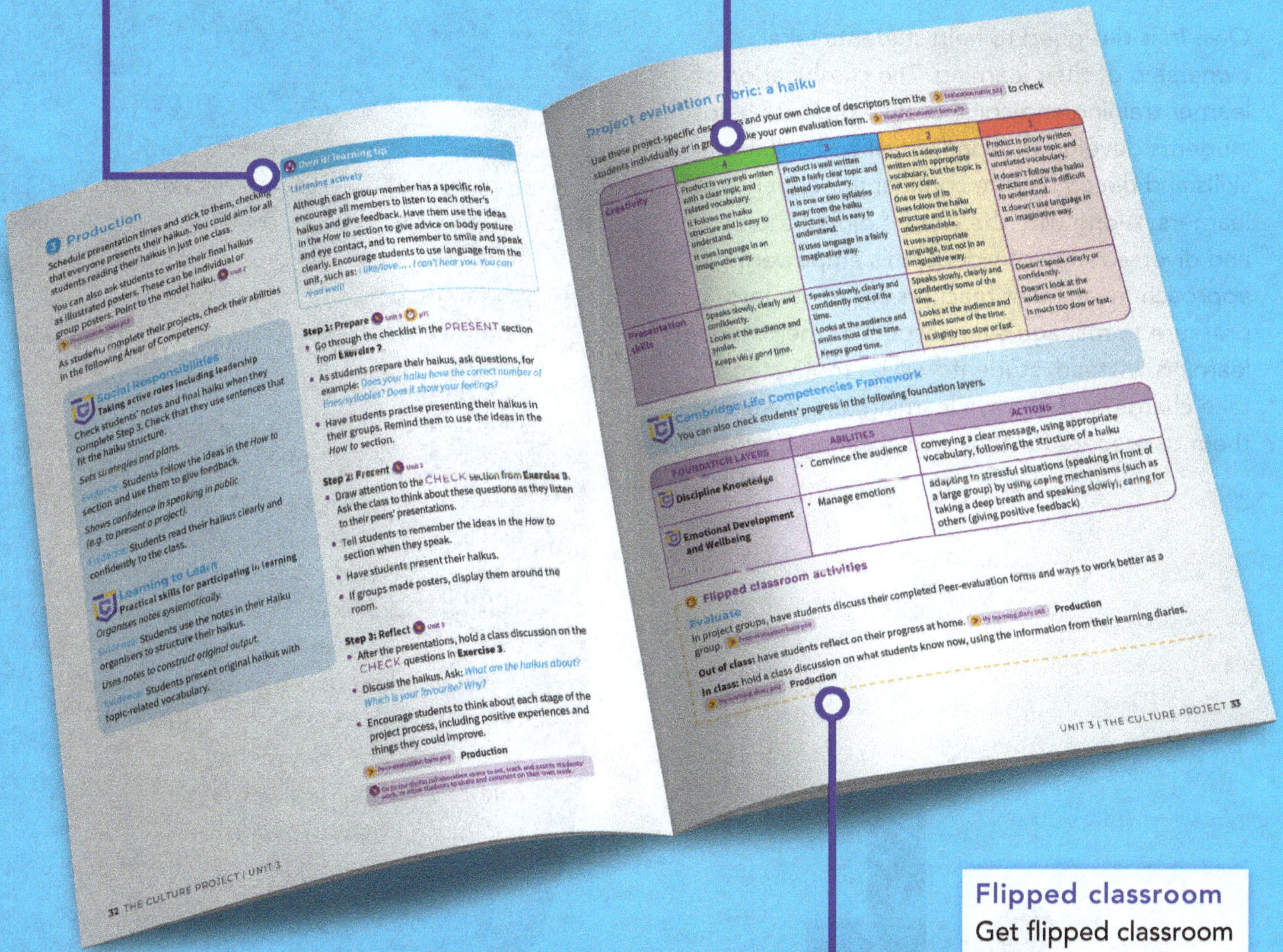

Flipped classroom
Get flipped classroom ideas for carrying out the activities both in and out of class.

Course Research and Rationale

We at *Cambridge University Press* have an unparalleled reputation for English Language courses underpinned by the latest language and pedagogical research. Here are some insights into how *Own It!* is informed by this, as well as feedback from teachers and learners from around the world.

Own It! is designed to help students take ownership of their learning. The combination of learner training and collaborative projects helps students develop their individual and collaborative skills and become more confident, independent learners. Along with the vibrant global topics and diverse range of videos, this empowering approach means that teachers are under less pressure to manage every aspect of their students' learning. Instead, students will be motivated to take charge of their own learning, empowering them to prepare for their own exciting future.

You spoke. We listened.

I want my students to feel that they belong to the world; that they are global citizens.
Itana, Brazil

Global cultural topics

Own It! includes a variety of global topics, with a dedicated *Around the World* page in every other unit. This helps students broaden their understanding of other people and places, preparing them for life in a diverse, multi-cultural environment.

Learners of English now outnumber speakers of English as a first language. Students are therefore far more likely to use English to communicate with people whose first language is not English. This has significant implications for traditional English teaching because an understanding of the language is now only part of successful communication and we cannot underestimate the role of cross-cultural understanding in communication.

Schema theory suggests that as humans learn, we create mental shortcuts by organising information into categories. These categories, or schemata, enable our brains to deal with most 'typical' scenarios without too much effort, since we can base our responses on our expectation. Students who are told they are going to hear a conversation at a train station can reasonably expect to hear certain language: train times, platform numbers and ticket types. Their expectations about these scenarios help them listen more effectively.

However, schemata can also work against a student's ability to understand. Their expectations are heavily influenced by their culture.

Teachers will be aware that their students are already interacting with globalised media. From watching international TV shows to playing online video games, teenagers are already encountering English being used by both native and non-native speakers from different cultural and social backgrounds. This interconnectedness is only going to increase, so it is vital that students develop the skills they need to communicate effectively.

That's why *Own It!* has a global, cultural focus, alongside documentaries in every unit, all of which encourage students to think about the differences between their culture and other cultures.

You spoke. We listed.

> I want my students to become more independent learners.
> *Maria, Spain*

Learn to learn

When students reach secondary school, they are expected to start taking more and more responsibility for their own learning, and once they reach school leaving age, they should have acquired the ability to learn independently. The rapid rate of technological advance means that many jobs in the near future may become automated. To give the next generation the best chance in life, they need to be able to acquire new skills and knowledge throughout their lives, making them adaptable to whatever the future holds.

Yet teachers often find that their students do not know how to learn, and lack basic learning techniques like taking notes, categorising information, and assessing their strengths and weaknesses, particularly in the first year of secondary school. To address this, the *Learn to learn* feature appears throughout each unit, extended by a dedicated full-page at the end of every unit.

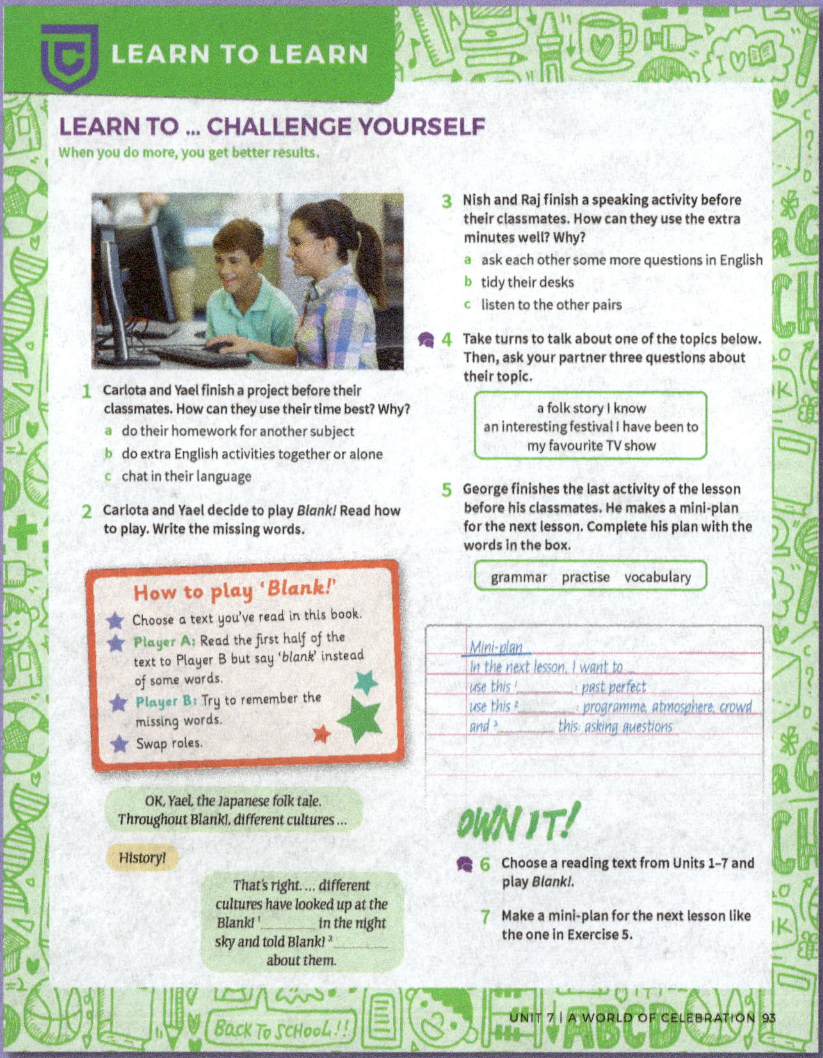
LEARN TO LEARN

LEARN TO ... CHALLENGE YOURSELF

When you do more, you get better results.

1 Carlota and Yael finish a project before their classmates. How can they use their time best? Why?

a do their homework for another subject
b do extra English activities together or alone
c chat in their language

2 Carlota and Yael decide to play *Blank!* Read how to play. Write the missing words.

How to play '*Blank!*'

- Choose a text you've read in this book.
- Player A: Read the first half of the text to Player B but say '*blank*' instead of some words.
- Player B: Try to remember the missing words.
- Swap roles.

OK, Yael, the Japanese folk tale. Throughout Blank!, different cultures ...

History!

That's right. ... different cultures have looked up at the Blank! ¹_______ in the night sky and told Blank! ²_______ about them.

3 Nish and Raj finish a speaking activity before their classmates. How can they use the extra minutes well? Why?

a ask each other some more questions in English
b tidy their desks
c listen to the other pairs

4 Take turns to talk about one of the topics below. Then, ask your partner three questions about their topic.

a folk story I know
an interesting festival I have been to
my favourite TV show

5 George finishes the last activity of the lesson before his classmates. He makes a mini-plan for the next lesson. Complete his plan with the words in the box.

grammar practise vocabulary

Mini-plan
In the next lesson, I want to ...
use this ¹_______: past perfect
use this ²_______: programme, atmosphere, crowd
and ³_______ this: asking questions

OWN IT!

6 Choose a reading text from Units 1–7 and play *Blank!*.

7 Make a mini-plan for the next lesson like the one in Exercise 5.

UNIT 7 | A WORLD OF CELEBRATION 93

The *Learn to learn* sections cover three broad areas of learner training:

1 practical skills for participating in learning
2 taking control of own learning
3 reflecting on and evaluating own learning success

After each *Learn to learn* tip, students practise them immediately in an activity. This helps students incorporate these techniques into their learning routine.

You spoke. We listened.

> I'd like to do project work with my students, but it can be too time-consuming to plan.
> *Merve, Turkey*

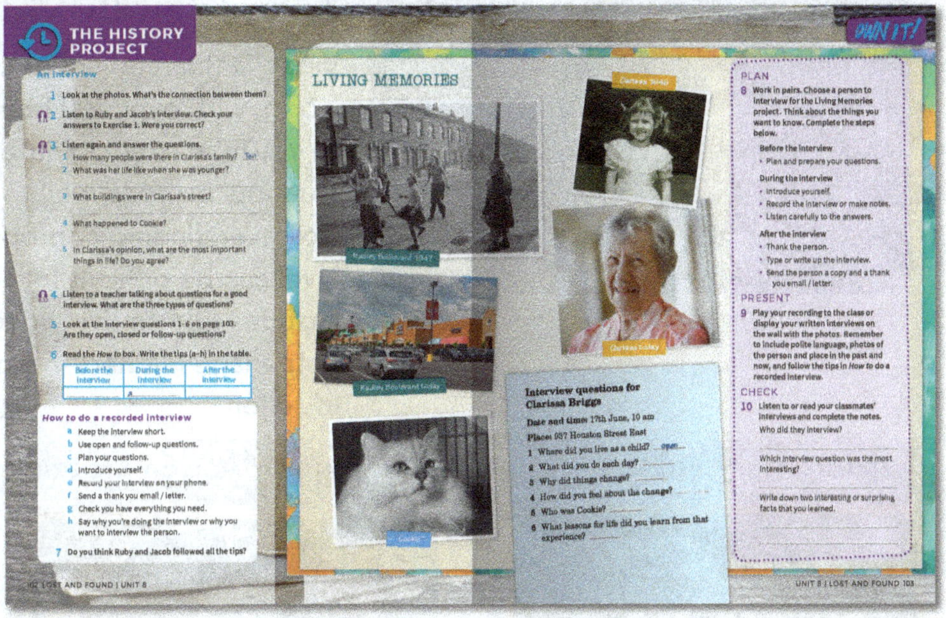

Project work

Collaboration is an effective way of empowering students. *Own It!* includes a project in every other unit of the *Student's Book* with more available in the online *Teacher's Resource Bank*, as well as an accompanying *Project Book* which offers extra support and practical tips for teachers. In addition, students can work together on their projects in the digital collaboration space and teachers can track and assess their work there.

Project work allows students to …

- build collaborative skills, such as communication, teamwork and leadership;
- acquire practical, transferable skills associated with different types of projects, like doing research and making presentations;
- choose and explore areas that they are interested in, thereby increasing their motivation;
- engage with the real-world issues as projects are often interdisciplinary and based on real world scenarios.

However, preparing project work can be very time-consuming for teachers. That's why *Own It!*'s projects are aligned to the topic of the unit, with a step-by-step guide and practical tips for students, plus a full teacher's guide in the *Project Book*. This is project work made simple!

In response to teacher feedback, the projects in the *Student's Book* have a cross-curricular approach, covering topic areas like Science, Art, Music and Maths, giving students the opportunity to improve their subject knowledge whilst exploring a wide variety of topics in English. The *Around the World* pages also have an optional double page project available online which allows students to further explore the cultural theme of the unit.

All of the projects develop competencies from the *Cambridge Life Competencies Framework*.

You spoke. We listened.

> I want a variety of videos that will help me to engage my students with the topic and see the language being used in a meaningful way.
> *Antonio, Mexico*

Teen-friendly videos

Video is the medium of communication in the modern world, with over 300 hours of video being uploaded to YouTube every minute! So, it is not surprising that students respond well to video content being used in class. However, finding appropriate videos at the right language level can be difficult for teachers. That's why *Own It!* includes four to five videos per unit specifically aimed at teenage learners in which they can see the language in action.

Documentary videos

Documentaries appear at the beginning of every unit. They get students thinking about the unit topic and activate any prior knowledge and language.

Globetrotters documentaries also appear on the *Around the World* pages in every other unit. These contextualise the grammar and vocabulary of the unit and are linked to the topic of the reading.

Teachers can use the video lesson in the downloadable video worksheets in the *Teacher's Resource Bank*.

Language in Action videos

Language in Action videos appear on every grammar page of the unit. These fun vlogs feature teenagers using the target language in context and an animated presentation of the grammar. They are designed to make teaching and learning grammar more meaningful, and give the teacher the option of using a flipped classroom model by getting students to watch the video before class.

Teachers can also use the downloadable video worksheets in the *Teacher's Resource Bank*.

Everyday English videos

Everyday English videos appear on the speaking pages. Teachers often find that students love learning the latest colloquial words and real phrases in English, and these videos are a great way of presenting this. They feature teenagers using authentic English from the speaking dialogue, and give students the chance to try out these phrases for themselves.

You spoke. We listened.

> I need resources and support to manage students of different levels in the same class.
> *Andrés, Ecuador*

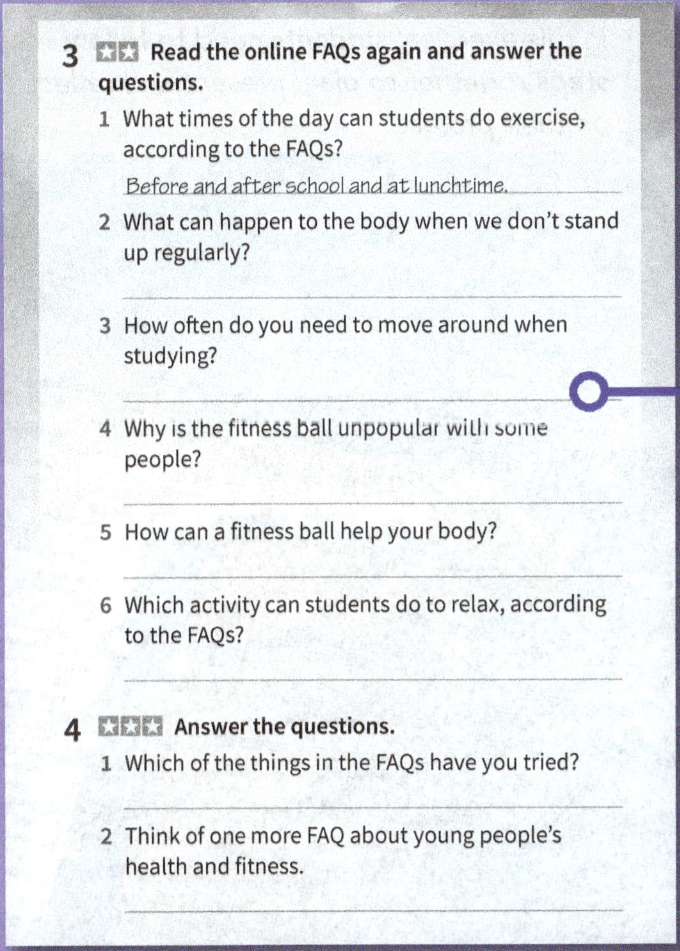

3 ★★ **Read the online FAQs again and answer the questions.**

1 What times of the day can students do exercise, according to the FAQs?

Before and after school and at lunchtime.

2 What can happen to the body when we don't stand up regularly?

3 How often do you need to move around when studying?

4 Why is the fitness ball unpopular with some people?

5 How can a fitness ball help your body?

6 Which activity can students do to relax, according to the FAQs?

4 ★★★ **Answer the questions.**

1 Which of the things in the FAQs have you tried?

2 Think of one more FAQ about young people's health and fitness.

Mixed-ability support

The average English class will have students with a variety of different language abilities, not to mention different interests, levels of motivation and learning preferences. In *Own It!* there is extensive support for teachers with mixed ability classes, including the following:

- On the *Student's Book* page, *Finished?* icons direct fast finishers to fun extra practice at the back of the book to ensure all students are challenged.
- *Workbook* activities are graded one, two or three stars to indicate their difficulty level. This means that students can start at the easiest level and move onto more difficult activities when ready. Alternatively, teachers can set different activities for different students according to their ability.
- *Teacher's Book* notes provide suggestions for grading activities to different students' abilities.
- *Project Book* teacher's notes provide specific suggestions for differentiated instruction. These cater for students who need more support, as well as students who would benefit from more challenge.

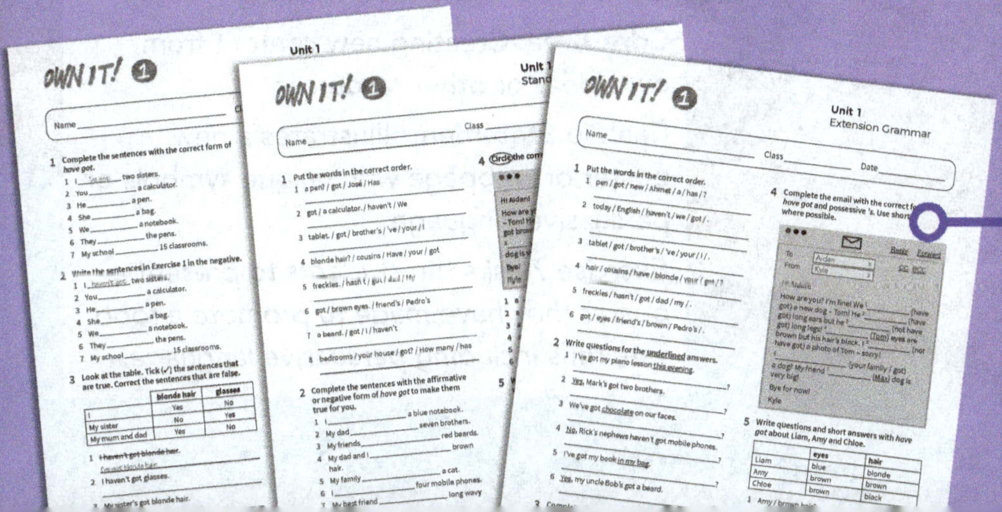

- Graded grammar and vocabulary worksheets at three different levels can be found in the online *Teacher's Resource Bank*.

Own It! and the Cambridge Life Competencies Framework

Although *Own It!* focuses on both the *Learning to Learn* and the *Collaboration* competencies in the *Cambridge Life Competencies Framework*, all of the six Life Competencies are explored throughout the course.

The table on page 29 shows, at a glance, where you can find an activity which concentrates on a particular Core Area. There is also a link below that table where you can download the comprehensive guide of how each level of *Own It!* correlates to the *Framework*.

Here are a few examples of how activities can help your students develop particular Can Do Statements:

Competency: Collaboration

Core area: Managing the sharing of tasks in a project

Can do statement: Works with others to plan and execute class projects

In this exercise, students need to follow steps together to plan, present and reflect on their project.

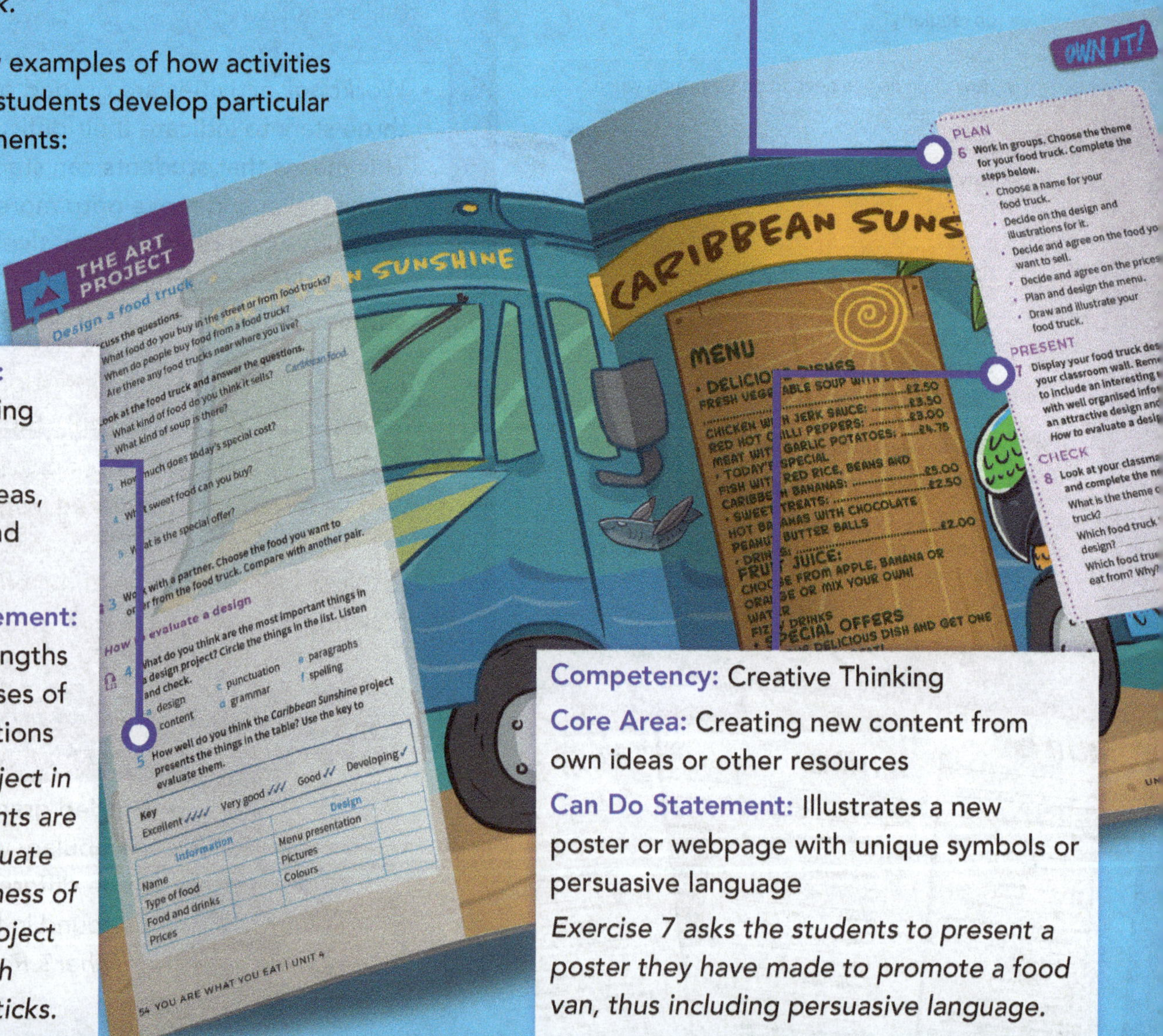

Competency: Critical Thinking

Core Area: Evaluating ideas, arguments and options

Can Do Statement: Assesses strengths and weaknesses of possible solutions

In the art project in Unit 4, students are asked to evaluate the effectiveness of the model project by giving each element 1–4 ticks.

Competency: Creative Thinking

Core Area: Creating new content from own ideas or other resources

Can Do Statement: Illustrates a new poster or webpage with unique symbols or persuasive language

Exercise 7 asks the students to present a poster they have made to promote a food van, thus including persuasive language.

Competency Area	Competency	U0	U1	U2	U3	U4	U5	U6	U7	U8	U9
Creative Thinking	Participating in creative activities		✓	✓		✓		✓			
	Creating new content from own ideas and other resources			✓		✓		✓		✓	✓
	Using new content to solve problems and make decisions						✓		✓	✓	
Critical Thinking	Understanding and analysing links between ideas			✓		✓	✓	✓			✓
	Evaluating ideas, arguments and options	✓	✓	✓	✓		✓	✓	✓	✓	
	Synthesising ideas and information	✓		✓		✓	✓			✓	
Learning to Learn	Practical skills for participating in learning	✓	✓	✓	✓	✓	✓	✓	✓	✓	✓
	Taking control of your own learning		✓		✓			✓		✓	✓
	Reflecting on and evaluating own learning success		✓	✓	✓	✓		✓	✓	✓	✓
Communication	Using appropriate language/ register for context	✓				✓	✓	✓			✓
	Managing conversations	✓						✓			
	Participating with appropriate confidence and clarity			✓	✓	✓		✓		✓	
Collaboration	Taking personal responsibility for own contributions to a group task			✓		✓		✓		✓	
	Listening respectfully and responding constructively to others' contributions			✓		✓		✓	✓	✓	
	Managing the sharing of tasks in a project		✓	✓		✓		✓		✓	
	Working towards a resolution for a task			✓		✓		✓		✓	
Social Responsibilities	Understanding personal responsibilities as part of a group and in society, including citizenship		✓		✓		✓		✓		✓
	Taking active roles, including leadership			✓		✓		✓		✓	
	Understanding and describing own and others' cultures		✓		✓		✓		✓		✓
	Understanding and discussing global issues – environmental, political, financial and social		✓		✓		✓		✓		✓

OWN IT! Level 4

Skills Overview

Skill	Learners will be able to:
Listening	understand the main points of clear standard speech on familiar matters; understand the main point of many radio or TV programmes on current affairs or topics of interest when the delivery is relatively clear.
Reading	understand texts that consist mainly of high frequency language; understand the description of events and feelings in personal letters.
Speaking	deal with most situations likely to arise whilst travelling in an area where the language is spoken; enter unprepared into conversation on familiar topics; connect phrases in a simple way in order to describe experiences and events; briefly give reasons and explanations for opinions and plans; narrate a story or relate the plot of a book or film and describe their reactions.
Writing	write personal letters describing experiences and impressions; write straightforward connected texts on topics which are familiar or of personal interest.

Skills in Detail

How the goals of the CEFR are realised in *Own It!* Level 4

LISTENING

At B1+, learners are expected to be able to understand speech that is clearly articulated and delivered relatively slowly, and concerns familiar topics.

OVERALL LISTENING COMPREHENSION
Can identify both general messages and specific details.
Can follow short narratives.

Starter	Unit 1	Unit 2	Unit 3	Unit 4	Unit 5	Unit 6	Unit 7	Unit 8	Unit 9
6 (video)	10 (video)	22 (video)	34 (video)	46 (video)	58 (video)	70 (video)	82 (video)	94 (video)	106 (video)
7	11	23	37 (video)	49 (video)	61 (video)	73 (video)	85 (video)	97 (video)	109 (video)
8 (video)	13 (video)	25 (video)	38	50	62	74	86	98	110
	14	26	39 (video)	51 (video)	63 (video)	75 (video)	87 (video)	99 (video)	111 (video)
	15 (video)	27 (video)	40	52	64	76	88	100	112
	16	28	40 (video)	52 (video)	64 (video)		88 (video)	100 (video)	112 (video)
	16 (video)	28 (video)	42 (video)		66 (video)		90 (video)	102	
	18 (video)								

UNDERSTANDING INTERACTION Can generally follow the main points of extended discussion around them.									
Starter	Unit 1	Unit 2	Unit 3	Unit 4	Unit 5	Unit 6	Unit 7	Unit 8	Unit 9
	11	23	40	50	64	76	86	97 (video)	112
	16	28	40 (video)	52			88	100	112 (video)
	16 (video)	28 (video)		52 (video)			88 (video)	100 (video)	

LISTENING TO MEDIA & RECORDINGS Can understand the main points of TV and radio programmes, including news bulletins and interviews.									
Starter	Unit 1	Unit 2	Unit 3	Unit 4	Unit 5	Unit 6	Unit 7	Unit 8	Unit 9
6 (video)	10 (video)	22 (video)	34 (video)	46 (video)	58 (video)	70 (video)	82 (video)	94 (video)	106 (video)
8 (video)	13 (video)	25 (video)	37 (video)	49 (video)	61 (video)	73 (video)	85 (video)	97 (video)	109 (video)
	14	26	38	50	63 (video)	74	87 (video)	98	110
	15 (video)	27 (video)	39 (video)	51 (video)	64 (video)	75 (video)	88 (video)	99 (video)	111 (video)
	16 (video)	28 (video)	40 (video)	52 (video)	66 (video)		90 (video)	100 (video)	112 (video)
	18 (video)		42 (video)					102	

LISTENING TO ANNOUNCEMENTS & INSTRUCTIONS Can understand simple technical information, such as operating instructions for everyday equipment. Can follow detailed directions.									
Starter	Unit 1	Unit 2	Unit 3	Unit 4	Unit 5	Unit 6	Unit 7	Unit 8	Unit 9
		28		38					
				40					

READING

At B1+, learners can read and understand to a satisfactory level straightforward factual texts and texts about familiar subjects.

READING CORRESPONDENCE Can understand the description of events, feelings and wishes in personal letters well enough to correspond regularly with a pen friend.									
Starter	Unit 1	Unit 2	Unit 3	Unit 4	Unit 5	Unit 6	Unit 7	Unit 8	Unit 9
9							89		

READING FOR ORIENTATION Can scan longer texts to find specific or relevant information in everyday material, such as letters, brochures and short official documents.									
Starter	Unit 1	Unit 2	Unit 3	Unit 4	Unit 5	Unit 6	Unit 7	Unit 8	Unit 9
		24		54		78			
		30							

READING FOR INFORMATION & ARGUMENT Can identify the main conclusions in clearly signalled argumentative texts. Can recognise the line of argument in the treatment of the issue presented, though not necessarily in detail. Can recognise significant points in straightforward newspaper articles on familiar subjects.									
Starter	Unit 1	Unit 2	Unit 3	Unit 4	Unit 5	Unit 6	Unit 7	Unit 8	Unit 9
5	12	29	36	48	60	72	84	96	108
	17	30	41	53	65	77	90	101	113
	18		42	54	66				114
	21								

SPEAKING

Overall Spoken Interaction

At B1+, learners can communicate with some confidence, but may struggle to understand non-standard accents, rapid or extended speech, and idiomatic usage.

CONVERSATION

Can enter unprepared into conversations on familiar topics.
Can express and respond to feelings such as surprise, happiness, sadness, interest and indifference.

Starter	Unit 1	Unit 2	Unit 3	Unit 4	Unit 5	Unit 6	Unit 7	Unit 8	Unit 9
	10	22	34	46	58	70	82	94	106
		23			64	76	88		

INFORMAL DISCUSSION (WITH FRIENDS)

Can express thoughts on more abstract, cultural topics such as films, books, music, etc.
Can give or seek personal opinions and give brief comments on the views of others.
Can express belief, opinion, agreement and disagreement politely.
Can make their opinions understood when discussing problems or practical questions of where to go, what to do, who or which to choose, how to organise an event (e.g. an outing), etc.

Starter	Unit 1	Unit 2	Unit 3	Unit 4	Unit 5	Unit 6	Unit 7	Unit 8	Unit 9
5	10	24	34	48	58	70	82	94	106
7	12	26	36	52	60	72	84	95	108
	14	31	43	55	61	73	88	96	115
	16		45		62	74	91	98	117
					64	75	93	100	
					66	76		103	
						79			
						81			

GOAL ORIENTED CO-OPERATION

Can explain why something is a problem, discuss what to do next and compare and contrast alternatives, giving brief reasons and explanations.

Starter	Unit 1	Unit 2	Unit 3	Unit 4	Unit 5	Unit 6	Unit 7	Unit 8	Unit 9
		31		55		79	93	103	

INFORMATION EXCHANGE

Can exchange, check and confirm information.
Can describe how to do something, giving detailed instructions.
Can summarise a short story, article, talk, discussion interview, or documentary and answer further questions of detail.
Can ask for and follow detailed directions.

Starter	Unit 1	Unit 2	Unit 3	Unit 4	Unit 5	Unit 6	Unit 7	Unit 8	Unit 9
4	11	22	35	46	59	71	83	97	109
6	13	25	37	51	63		85	98	110
8	15	26	39	57	69		86	99	111
	19	27	40				87		117
		28							

INTERVIEWING AND BEING INTERVIEWED Can provide concrete information required in an interview/consultation (e.g. describe symptoms to a doctor) but with limited precision. Can use a prepared questionnaire to carry out a structured interview, with some spontaneous follow-up questions.									
Starter	**Unit 1**	**Unit 2**	**Unit 3**	**Unit 4**	**Unit 5**	**Unit 6**	**Unit 7**	**Unit 8**	**Unit 9**
	13								

Overall Spoken Production

At B1+, learners can give straightforward monologues on familiar subjects.

SUSTAINED MONOLOGUE: DESCRIBING EXPERIENCE Can give detailed accounts/descriptions of • experiences, describing feelings and reactions. • unpredictable occurrences, e.g. an accident. • events (real or imagined), dreams, hopes and ambitions. Can relate the plot of a book or film and describe their reactions. Can narrate a story.									
Starter	**Unit 1**	**Unit 2**	**Unit 3**	**Unit 4**	**Unit 5**	**Unit 6**	**Unit 7**	**Unit 8**	**Unit 9**
				47	64		93		107
				49	69				112
				50					
				52					

WRITING

At B1+ learners can convey information and ideas on abstract as well as concrete topics, and get across the points they feel are important.

OVERALL WRITTEN PRODUCTION Can write straightforward connected texts on a range of familiar subjects within their field of interest, by linking a series of shorter discrete elements into a linear sequence.									
Starter	**Unit 1**	**Unit 2**	**Unit 3**	**Unit 4**	**Unit 5**	**Unit 6**	**Unit 7**	**Unit 8**	**Unit 9**
9	17	29	41	53	65	77	89	101	113
		31		55		79		103	
		33							

CORRESPONDENCE Can write personal letters and emails asking for or giving simple information, giving news or expressing thoughts.									
Starter	**Unit 1**	**Unit 2**	**Unit 3**	**Unit 4**	**Unit 5**	**Unit 6**	**Unit 7**	**Unit 8**	**Unit 9**
9						89			

CREATIVE WRITING Can write a description of an event, a recent trip (real or imagined). Can write accounts of experiences, describing feelings and reactions in some detail. Can narrate a story.									
Starter	**Unit 1**	**Unit 2**	**Unit 3**	**Unit 4**	**Unit 5**	**Unit 6**	**Unit 7**	**Unit 8**	**Unit 9**
	17		41		65				113

COHERENCE Can link a series of shorter, discrete simple elements into a connected, linear sequence of points.									
Starter	**Unit 1**	**Unit 2**	**Unit 3**	**Unit 4**	**Unit 5**	**Unit 6**	**Unit 7**	**Unit 8**	**Unit 9**
		29				77			

Lesson aim: I can talk about travel, music and theatre.

Warmer

Elicit students' ideas about travelling. Ask: *Do you like going to other places? What sort of holidays do you enjoy?*

1 S.01 Before playing the recording, focus students' attention on the pictures. Ask: *What can you see in the photos?*

Audioscript p158

Target vocabulary
accommodation /əkɒmə'deɪʃən/
backpacking /'bækpækɪŋ/
holiday resort /'hɒlədeɪ rɪ'zɔːt/
sightseeing /'saɪtsiːɪŋ/
tourist attractions /'tʊərɪst ə'trækʃənz/
trip /trɪp/

2 S.02 ★ Encourage students to use the context to help them complete the gaps. For example, we can guess that *sightseeing* goes in the first gap because the text goes on to refer to Big Ben.

Audioscript p158

Vocabulary Bank SB p127

Learn to learn

Explain to students that *personalising* vocabulary means to connect it in some way to themselves, their experiences or things and people they know.

3 ★★★ Students write their own gapped sentences for their partner to complete using vocabulary from Exercise 1.

4 S.03 ★★★ Encourage students to think of personalised contexts for each word, e.g. when they were last a member of an audience or a part they played in a school play. Students can then discuss these contexts in pairs.

STARTER

WELCOME!

VOCABULARY

Travel

1 S.01 **Match the words in the box with the photos. Listen, check and repeat.**

accommodation	4	backpacking	6
holiday resort	3	sightseeing	1
tourist attractions	5	trip	2

2 S.02 **Complete the comments with the words in Exercise 1. Listen and check.**

Where did you go on holiday this summer?

London. It's a great city for [1] *sightseeing* because there are so many [2] tourist attractions. My favourite was Big Ben.

To a [3] holiday resort in Greece. The [4] accommodation was amazing – a beautiful hotel right next to the beach.

I went [5] backpacking in Mexico this summer – just me, my bag, and a paper map. It was the best [6] trip of my life.

LEARN TO LEARN

Personalising vocabulary

Writing sentences helps you to remember words.

Use it!

3 **Write true sentences about your holidays with the words in Exercise 1.**

Music and theatre

4 S.03 **Match the nouns in the box with the definitions. Listen, check and repeat.**

audience lines part ~~rehearsal~~ scene show

1 When people practise a play *rehearsal*
2 live performance in a theatre show
3 the words actors say lines
4 a character in a play part
5 the people who watch audience
6 a part of a play scene

Use it!

5 **Complete the questions with words in Exercise 4. Discuss the questions.**

1 Have you ever been in a *show* at school? What part did you play? How did you learn your lines? Did you have any rehearsals before the show?
2 How is the audience at the theatre and cinema different to at a concert?
3 If you were in a film, would you like to appear all the way through the film, or be in one big, important scene?

Explore it!

Guess the correct answer.

What films do these lines come from?

a 'To infinity and beyond!' *Toy Story*
b 'Just keep swimming.' *Finding Nemo*

Write other famous lines from English films. Can your partner guess the film?

4 STARTER UNIT

Audioscript p158

Target vocabulary

audience /'ɔːdiəns/	rehearsal /rə'hɜːsəl/
lines /laɪnz/	scene /siːn/
part /pɑːt/	show /ʃəʊ/

Extra vocabulary practice

5 Give students two minutes to complete the questions. Encourage them to ask follow-up questions to develop their conversations.

Vocabulary Bank SB p127

Explore it!

If appropriate, allow students to use their smartphones to look up films and other famous lines.

Homework

Workbook p4, Exercises 1–3

Warmer

Ask students if they ever read interviews on websites or in magazines. If yes, ask: *Who have you read about recently? Was it interesting? Why / Why not?*

Background information

In the UK, in the long summer holidays, young people can attend workshops (which are sometimes called camps) for a week or more, where they can concentrate on their interests (e.g. drama, sports, science, music, etc.).

1 S.04 Elicit answers from the class as a whole. You could write students' ideas on the board.

2 ★★★ Challenge students to find the answers quickly by setting a one-minute time limit.

3 ★★★ Challenge students to think of what the words could be before they look for the words in the article.

Extra vocabulary practice

4 Read out the two questions. Give students a minute to think through their answers before discussing them in pairs.

Extend it!

Students design their own summer camp. They give their camp a name, come up with a theme for it (e.g. sport, music, theatre) and design a short programme of activities. Students present their idea to the class, which then votes for the best ones.

READING

An interview in a school magazine

S.04 **1** **Look at the photo. What do you think the boy is doing? Read the interview and check your answer.**

Now that we're back to school, everybody's talking about what they did in the summer. Some of you probably stayed in a holiday resort or went sightseeing with your family, and most of you probably spent time at the pool with friends. But not Joshua Wills. His summer was very different. Let's find out why.

Joshua, you didn't have a normal summer holiday this year, did you? What did you do?

No, I didn't. I took part in a theatre camp for teenagers. Our teachers were real actors from the theatre and TV. They taught us all about acting – you know, how to develop a character, how to project your voice and use your body. It was lots of fun.

Did you put on a show?

We put on a musical about a detective. I played the part of the detective's assistant. We had one rehearsal every day for a week, and then three performances. Lots of my friends and family came.

How did it go?

It was great, but on the first night, in the final scene, I forgot my lines. Everything was going really well and then suddenly I couldn't remember anything! Everyone in the audience was looking at me, thinking, 'What's wrong? He's not speaking. He's not even moving!'

Were you panicking?

I wasn't panicking. I was just frozen! But in the end I remembered the lines and it was all OK.

Do you want to do more theatre?

Definitely! I don't want to stop. In fact, I'm writing a play. It's more difficult than I expected, but I'm really enjoying it. I want to put it on at school.

Are you looking for any actors?

Of course! Why? Do you want to join us?

Maybe! It sounds like fun!

2 **Read the interview again and answer the questions.**

1. Why was Joshua's summer holiday unusual? *He took part in a theatre camp.*
2. What did the theatre camp participants learn? *Acting, how to develop a character, how to project your voice, how to use your body.*
3. How often did the group practise their play? *Seven times (once a day for a week).*
4. What problem did Joshua have? *He forgot his lines.*
5. How did the audience react to the problem? *They looked at him, wondering why he wasn't speaking or moving.*
6. Why is Joshua looking for actors now? *He's writing a play.*

3 **Find words in the interview that mean:**

1. speak loudly and clearly (phrase) *project your voice*
2. somebody who helps someone do their job (n) *assistant*
3. unable to move (adj) *frozen*
4. 100% yes! (adv) *definitely*

Voice it!

4 **Discuss the questions.**

1. Joshua's teachers were real actors. What is good about this?
2. Have you ever acted or spoken in front of a big group of people? How was it?

STARTER UNIT 5

Flipped class

▶ Ask students to watch **Video S.1** and do the **Video worksheet** in the *Teacher's Resource Bank*.

Homework

Workbook p4, Exercises 4–5

Lesson aim: I can use the present and past simple and continuous.

Warmer

▶ Play **Video S.1** if it was not set for homework and elicit that the speaker studied every day, and now he's playing basketball on the school team.

1 Elicit the general difference between the present simple and continuous (actions we do regularly versus actions happening now). Then explain the past simple and continuous (a completed action at a specific time in the past versus an action in progress in the past). Elicit that we can also use the present simple for things which are generally true and that we do not usually use the present continuous with verbs of feeling (e.g. *love*, *hate*) and senses (e.g. *sound*, *smell*).

2 S.05 ★ Tell students to look for words and phrases which help them decide the correct form of the verb, e.g. *didn't*, *last week*, *right now*.

Audioscript p158

3 ★ Tell students to use the context to decide the correct form of the verb. For example, for gap 2, we know a past form is needed because the previous sentence begins with *Yesterday* … .

Extra grammar practice

4 & 5 Ask some students to tell the class what their partner said in response to the questions.

LANGUAGE IN ACTION

Present and past simple and continuous

Watch video S.1
What did he do every day?
What's he doing now?

Present simple	Present continuous	Past simple	Past continuous
It **sounds** like fun.	I [1] **'m** **writing** a play.	We **had** one rehearsal every day.	Everybody in the audience [2] **was** **looking** at me.
I [3] **don't** **want** to stop.	He **isn't speaking**.	You [4] **didn't** **have** a normal summer holiday this year.	I [5] **wasn't** **panicking**.
[6] **Do** you **want** to try?	[7] **Are** you **looking** for actors?	What [8] **did** you **do**?	**Were** you **panicking**?

1 Complete the examples in the table above with the correct form of *be* or *do*. Use the interview on page 5 to help you.

2 S.05 Complete the sentences with the correct form of the verbs in brackets. Listen and check.

1. Mike *goes* (go) sightseeing every year.
2. Amalia **didn't learn** (not learn) her lines until the night before the first show.
3. A Where's Harry? B He **'s reading** (read) in his room.
4. You didn't like the play, did you, Emir? You **were sleeping** (sleep) during it!
5. I'm so happy we **weren't staying** (not stay) in that holiday resort last week when the terrible storm came.
6. Ana's not at the rehearsal because she **'s not feeling** (not feel) well right now.

3 Complete Esma's blog with the correct form of the verbs in the box.

begin do get up go ~~have~~ not finish not forget practise start think

Hi, everyone. Yesterday we [1] *had* our last rehearsal for the musical. I [2] **were** practising until 11 pm, and when I [3] **went** to bed, some of the others [4] **didn't finish** still **practising**. The first show [5] **starts** at 7.30 tonight. I didn't feel nervous when I [6] **got up** this morning, but I [7] **'m beginning** to feel nervous now – I hope I [8] **don't forget** my lines. But I'm also really excited. I [9] **think** it's going to be a great night. Anyway, [10] **are** you **doing** anything this weekend? Why don't you come and see me?

Use it!

4 Write the questions.

1. what / you / do / at nine o'clock last night
   What were you doing at nine o'clock last night?
2. what time / you / get up / today
   What time did you get up today?
3. during the summer / you / prefer to go sightseeing or go to the beach
   During the summer, do you prefer to go sightseeing or go to the beach
4. what time / you / usually / get up / when you're on holiday
   What time do you usually get up when you're on holiday
5. speak English to anyone / last week
   Did you speak English to anyone last week?
6. what / you / wear / at the moment
   What are you wearing at the moment?

5 Ask and answer the questions.

What were you doing at nine o'clock last night?

I was watching some videos online.

Grammar game

Put students into small groups. Write gapped questions (using the grammar structures from the lesson) on the board, e.g. *Where __ you go yesterday?* The first group to complete each question and come up with a grammatically correct answer wins a point.

Homework

Workbook p5, Exercises 1–3

Lesson aim: I can talk about different ways of communicating.

1 S.06 Ask students to describe what actions they can see in the emoticons before looking at the words in the box.

Audioscript p158

Target vocabulary
describe /dɪˈskraɪb/
greet /griːt/
post /pəʊst/
shake hands /ʃeɪk hændz/
shout /ʃaʊt/
smile /smaɪl/
translate /trænzˈleɪt/
wave /weɪv/
whisper /wɪspə/

Extra vocabulary practice

2 S.07 ★ Before playing the recording, elicit definitions for each pair of communication words.

Audioscript p158

3 Students can work in pairs to complete the table.

Vocabulary Bank SB p127

Learn to learn

Drill the pronunciation of *gesture* /ˈdʒestʃə/. Check understanding (a gesture is a movement of the body to show the meaning of something).

4 Elicit how students defined the words in the box or the gestures they used.

5 Give students a minute to prepare for this activity.

6 S.08 ★ Before students listen to Mateo, ask them to say which tips they think are best and why.

Audioscript p158

VOCABULARY AND LISTENING

Ways of communicating

1 S.06 Match the verbs in the box with the emoticons 1–9. Listen, check and repeat.

describe	9	greet	7	post	8
shake hands	1	shout	5	smile	4
translate	6	wave	3	whisper	2

2 S.07 Listen to the dialogues and circle the correct words in Exercise 1.

1 whisper / shake hands
2 translate / smile
3 post / shout
4 greet / translate
5 wave / describe

3 Do we express the verbs in Exercise 1 with actions or words? Complete the table.

Actions	Words
shake hands post smile wave	*describe* greet shout translate whisper

LEARN TO LEARN

Describing words you don't know with other words or a gesture

When you don't know a word, use words you do know to describe it or use gestures to express what you mean.

4 Express or explain the words in the box with other words or gestures.

accommodation cry dance film frozen sing stand up tourist attraction

It's a place where you can stay. *Accommodation?*

Use it!

5 Use gestures or tell your partner *I do this when …*. Can they guess the verb?

A talk

6 S.08 Listen to Mateo and tick (✓) the tips that helped him learn English.

a Describe a word with other words ✓
b Do a language course ☐
c Don't worry about making mistakes ✓
d Listen to music ☐
e Talk as much as possible ✓
f Translate words and make them sound English ✓
g Watch TV ✓

7 S.08 Listen again and complete each sentence with one word.

1 Mateo is studying translating at university.
2 He didn't understand the family at first because they spoke so fast.
3 When he doesn't know a word, he describes it, translates it or makes a word in English similar to the Spanish word.
4 Lots of things were different for him, but he liked the people best.

Voice it!

8 Discuss the questions.

1 Which of Mateo's tips do you use?
2 Which tips would you like to try?

STARTER UNIT 7

7 S.08 Elicit the type of word needed to complete each gap (e.g. a verb). Then ask students if they can remember any of the words which fill the gaps. Play the audio again for students to check.

8 ★★★ Encourage students to think of other tips to help someone learn English, e.g. read books and articles in English.

Flipped class

▶ Ask students to watch **Video S.2** and do the **Video worksheet** in the *Teacher's Resource Bank*.

Homework

Workbook p5 Exercises 4–6, p6 Exercises 1–4

Lesson aim: I can use the present perfect and past simple.

Warmer

▶ Play **Video S.2** and elicit that the girl went to a summer camp in Spain to learn Spanish last summer and that she has never studied Turkish.

1 Elicit the difference between the present perfect (used for experiences and actions which began in the past and continue to the present) and the past simple (used for finished actions at a definite time in the past).

Get it right!

Explain that *since* does not go with the present simple because it refers to a time or situation which began in the past.

2 ★ Encourage students to use the examples in the table in Exercise 1 to help them complete the rules.

3 S.09 ★★★ Challenge students to explain their choice of verb form in each case. Students can then practise reading the conversation in pairs.

Audioscript p159

4 Ask students to read the gapped text through once before they choose the options. Ask: *Where did the writer work last summer?* (in a Mexican restaurant.) *What has the writer done since then?* (He/She has been to Spanish classes.)

Extra grammar practice

5 Encourage students to ask follow-up questions using the past simple.

LANGUAGE IN ACTION

Present perfect and past simple

Watch video S.2
Where did she go last summer?
Which language has she never studied?

Present perfect	Past simple
I've been at university now for three months.	I **started** my course in October.
I **haven't stopped** ¹ since I was there! I've ² never **been** to London.	I **met** lots of people in the first few weeks.
Have you ³ ever **been** to London?	**Did** you **go** to London last year?

1 Complete the examples in the table above with *ever*, *since* or *never*.

Get it right!

We don't use the present simple with *since*.

*We've been here **since** Tuesday.*

NOT ~~*We are here since Tuesday.*~~

2 Look at sentences a–d. Circle the correct options to complete the rules.

a Last year I **spent** six months in London.

b I **didn't understand** the kids because they **spoke** fast.

c I've **watched** every episode of *The Big Bang Theory.*

d I've **stayed** in contact with people I **met** in London.

1 Use the *present perfect* / *past simple* (circled) for things that happened in a finished time period, e.g. last year.

2 Use the *present perfect* (circled) / *past simple* for things that happened in the past in an unfinished time period, or when the exact time of the action is not important.

S.09 **3** Circle the correct words. Listen and check.

BEN ¹*Have you ever been* (circled) / *Did you ever go* to a music festival?

JESSIE Yeah, ²*I've been* / *went* (circled) to one this summer. It was great.

BEN Where ³*has it been* / *was it* (circled)?

JESSIE Near the town where we ⁴*have been* / *went* (circled) on holiday. ⁵We*'ve stayed* (circled) / *stayed* in the town lots of times but this was our first time at the festival.

BEN What ⁶*have you liked* / *did you like* (circled) best?

JESSIE The Night Owls ⁷*have had* / *had* (circled) some amazing dancers and ⁸*have sounded* / *sounded* (circled) incredible.

BEN ⁹*I've never heard* (circled) / *didn't hear* of them.

JESSIE Oh, they're great! ¹⁰*I've liked* (circled) / *liked* them for ages.

4 Complete the text with the past simple or present perfect.

I ¹ have never been (be) to Mexico, but last summer I ² got (get) a job in a Mexican restaurant. I ³ 've met (meet) loads of people since I ⁴ started (start) working there and I ⁵ 've made (make) friends. At first they ⁶ spoke (speak) to me in Spanish, but I ⁷ didn't understand (not understand). Since then I ⁸ 've been (go) to Spanish classes and I ⁹ 've learned (learn) lots. Our teacher ¹⁰ has taught (teach) us how to describe things when we don't know the exact word.

Use it!

5 Discuss the questions.

1 How many cities in your country have you visited?

2 How long have you know your best friend?

3 Have you ever been to a festival?

I've been to three cities. I went to the capital last month, but there are some cities I've never been to.

8 STARTER UNIT

Grammar game

Students write five experiences they think their partner has never had, e.g. *You've never been to New York. You've never ridden a horse.* In pairs, students show each other their ideas. The student with the most correct guesses wins.

Homework

Workbook p6, Exercises 5–7

Warmer

Write *informal email* on the board. Elicit that we use an informal style when writing to family or friends or if you want to appear close to someone (rather than distant). Elicit words and phrases commonly used in informal emails, e.g. *Hi, How's it going? Love.*

1 & 2 Set a one-minute time limit for students to read Azra's email and find the answers.

3 ★ Check students understand the meaning of the word *recipient* (a person who receives something) before they do the matching task.

4 Explain that the phrases in the *Useful language* box are commonly used in informal emails. Point out that we don't use exclamation marks in formal emails in English. Ask students to highlight Azra's use of exclamation marks (Paragraph 1: ... *so kind!*, Paragraph 2: ... *words to the songs!*; Paragraph 3: *I hope you like it!*).

Extra Useful language practice

5 ★ With the class as a whole, brainstorm ideas for fun activities an English-speaking visitor could do in your country. Write these ideas on the board.

6 Point out that an email ought to be well-organised into paragraphs. Encourage students to use Azra's email as a model to follow when writing their own.

7 As well as checking their own work, encourage students to check each other's work and look for ways to improve it.

WRITING

An informal email

1 Look at the photos. What can you see? Read Azra's email and put the photos in the correct order.

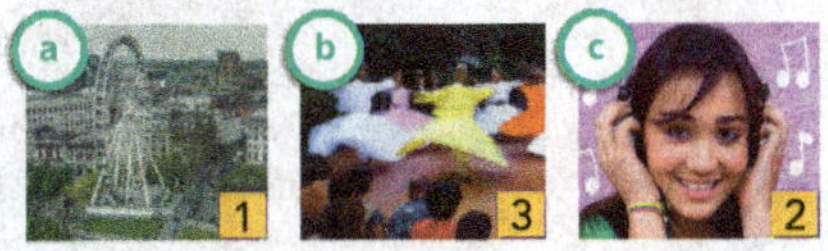

a 1 b 3 c 2

2 Read the email again. Why did Azra write the email? What did she enjoy about her visit?

She is writing to thank Gaby and her family for her visit. She enjoyed meeting Gaby's friends and family, and visiting Manchester.

[1]From:	azra.kara@myemail.com
[2]To:	gaby.bates@myemail.com
[3]Subject:	Thank you

[4]Hi Gaby,

[5]How are things? [6]I just wanted to say thank you for a great visit to Manchester. I had an amazing time and your family are so kind!

I loved meeting your friends and visiting the city. There's so much to see! I learned so much about the UK that I didn't know before. I've listened to the playlist you made me lots of times since I got back home and I know all the words to the songs!

I've told my friends all about my trip and they're really looking forward to meeting you next month. I can't wait to take you sightseeing in Istanbul to show you all the tourist attractions and introduce you to my friends and family. We've bought tickets to go and watch a Turkish dance show while you're here – I hope you like it!

[7]Write back soon,

[8]Love Azra

3 Match the letters a–h with the parts of the email 1–8.

- a Address of the recipient **2**
- b Address of the sender **1**
- c Ending and your name **8**
- d First sentence **5**
- e Last sentence **7**
- f Reason you are writing **6**
- g Beginning and name **4**
- h Topic of the email **3**

4 Complete the *Useful language* box with phrases from the email.

Useful language

Starting and ending an informal email

Start + name: Hello Gaby / [1] Hi Gaby

First sentence: How are you? / Thanks for your email / [2] How are things?

The reason you are writing: I'm writing to / [3] I just wanted to say

Last sentence: See you soon. / Bye for now. / [4] Write back soon.

End + name: Take care, Azra / [5] Love, Azra

Write your own informal email to a friend.

PLAN

5 Imagine you are doing an exchange with someone in an English-speaking country. You have visited their country and they are going to visit yours. Make notes about these things.

where you went ______

what you did ______

what you liked about your visit ______

what you are going to do when they visit you ______

WRITE

6 Write your email. Remember to include language and vocabulary from this unit, phrases from the *Useful language* box, the parts of the email in Exercise 3 and the ideas in Exercise 5.

CHECK

7 Do you ...

- start and end the email correctly?
- give the reason why you are writing?
- say what you are going to do when your friend visits?

STARTER UNIT 9

Class challenge

The 'e' in *email* stands for exciting / extra / **electronic**.

Class challenge

Prepare for Unit 1. Ask students to think of what fashion means to them and find out about fashion in the 1960s.

Homework

Workbook p7

Lesson aim: I can give my opinions about fashion.

Warmer

Write *trendsetters* on the board. Elicit its meaning (a trendsetter is someone who makes something fashionable, e.g. an item of clothing, new technology, an idea). Ask students if they can name any young trendsetters.

▶ Start it!

Unit quiz

1 Discuss this question with the class as a whole. Write key words and phrases on the board (e.g. *cool, colourful, casual, informal, teenagers*) as necessary.

2 & 3 ▶ Students were asked to think about these questions for homework. They can now share their ideas in pairs. Play **Video 1.1** and allow students to check their answers.

4 Encourage students to compare their opinions in groups. Do students share a taste in fashion? Do they like and dislike the same styles?

Video comprehension questions

Flipped class

In preparation for **Explore it!** (p11), students find out about a well-known clothes designer whose designs they like.

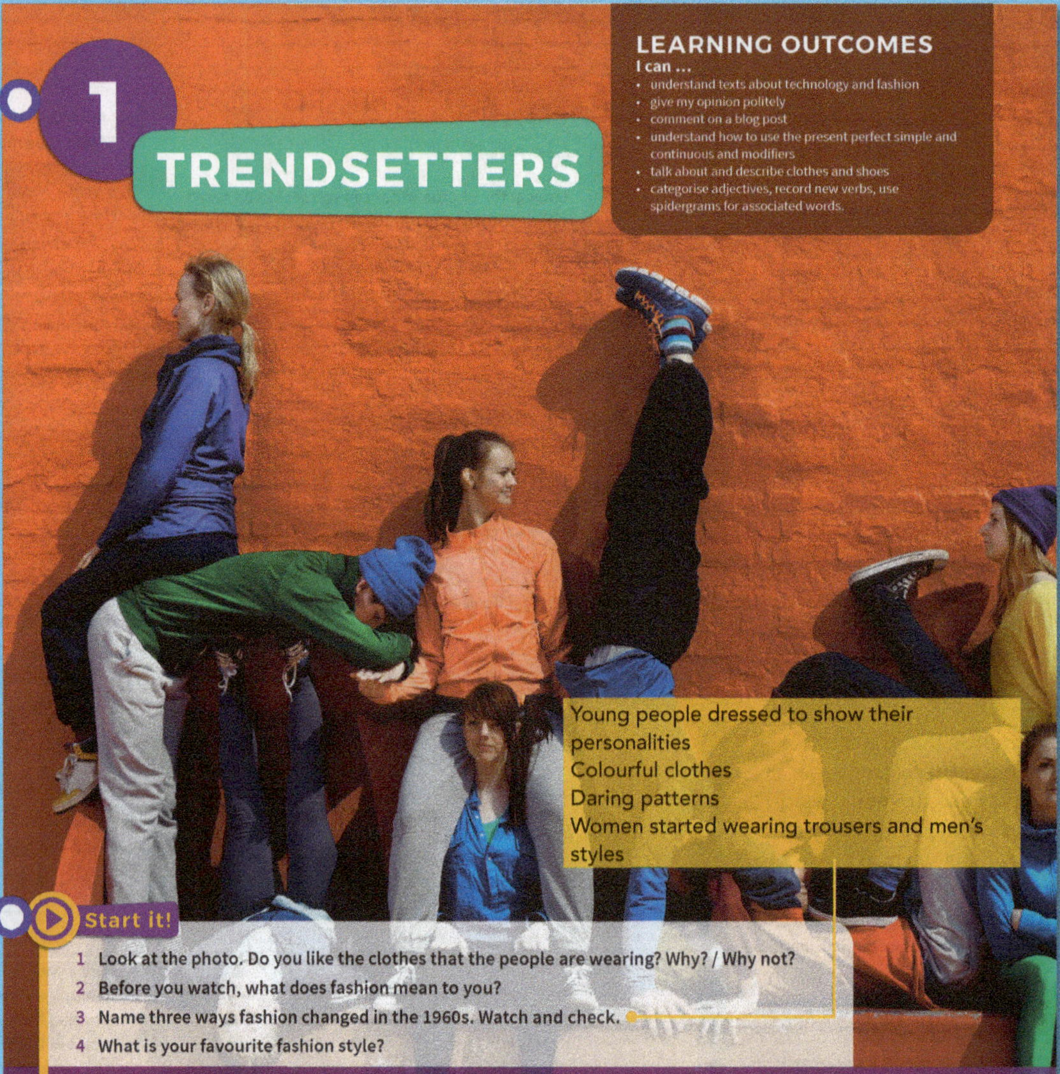

1 TRENDSETTERS

LEARNING OUTCOMES
I can ...
- understand texts about technology and fashion
- give my opinion politely
- comment on a blog post
- understand how to use the present perfect simple and continuous and modifiers
- talk about and describe clothes and shoes
- categorise adjectives, record new verbs, use spidergrams for associated words.

Young people dressed to show their personalities
Colourful clothes
Daring patterns
Women started wearing trousers and men's styles

▶ Start it!

1 Look at the photo. Do you like the clothes that the people are wearing? Why? / Why not?
2 Before you watch, what does fashion mean to you?
3 Name three ways fashion changed in the 1960s. Watch and check.
4 What is your favourite fashion style?

Watch video 1.1 | Language in action 1.2 (p13) | Language in action 1.3 (p15) | Everyday English 1.4 (p16) | Globetrotters 1.5 (p18)

Unit aims

Skills

I can ...
- understand a text about fashion and technology p12
- give my opinion politely p16
- write a blog comment p17
- understand a text about traditional Scottish dress p18

Language

I can ...
- describe clothes and shoes p11
- understand how to use the present perfect simple and continuous p13
- use verbs related to clothes and shoes p14
- understand how to use modifiers p15

Learn to Learn

I can ...
- put adjectives into categories p11
- record new verbs p14
- use spidergrams p19
- write different kinds of example sentences p21

Extra Resources

- *Finished?* – Student's Book p118
- *Vocabulary Bank* – Student's Book p128
- Pronunciation – Student's Book p141
- Workbook p8
- *Teacher's Resource Bank* on *Cambridge One* for tests package, Cambridge Exam practice, word-lists, differentiated worksheets and many other extra resources.
- *Practice Extra* and *Digital collaboration space*

Warmer

Ask: *Do you like the clothes in the photo on page 11? Why? Why not?* Students can discuss these questions in pairs.

1 1.01 Ask students, in pairs, to take turns saying an adjective and writing it down, to practise pronunciation and spelling.

Audioscript p159

Target vocabulary

baggy trousers /ˈbægi ˈtraʊzəz/
checked shirt /tʃekt ʃɜːt/
denim skirt /ˈdenɪm skɜːt/
flat shoes /flæt ʃuːz/
flowery dress /ˈflaʊəri dres/
high-heeled boots /haɪˈhiːld buːts/
long-sleeved dress /lɒŋsliːvd dres/
plain cotton T-shirt /pleɪn ˈkɒtən ˈtiːʃɜːt/
spotted shoes /ˈspɒtɪd ʃuːz/
striped T-shirt /straɪpt ˈtiːʃɜːt/
tight jeans /taɪt dʒiːnz/

Extra vocabulary practice

2 1.02 ★ Point out that both speakers mention items of clothing that they don't end up buying. Students should only note down the items the speakers decide to buy.

Audioscript p159

Vocabulary Bank SB p128

Learn to learn

Explain that while we hardly ever put three or more adjectives together we often put two together. Point out that in English, it sounds odd if we say *The cotton plain T-shirt* rather than *The plain cotton T-shirt*.

VOCABULARY
Describing clothes and shoes

1.01 **1** Match the adjectives in **bold** with the numbers in the photos. Listen, check and repeat.

baggy trousers	9	**checked** shirt	5
denim skirt	3	**flat** shoes	10
flowery dress	6	**high-heeled** boots	8
long-sleeved dress	7	**plain cotton** T-shirt	2
spotted shoes	11	**striped** T-shirt	4
tight jeans	1		

1.02 **2** Juan and Rosa are shopping for clothes for a school party. Listen to the conversation. Which things in Exercise 1 do they buy?

checked shirt, baggy trousers, long-sleeved dress, flat shoes

LEARN TO LEARN
Categorising

When we use lots of adjectives to describe one thing, we use this order: shape, colour, pattern, material.

3 Complete the table with the adjectives in Exercise 1.

Shape	Pattern	Material
baggy, flat, high-heeled, long-sleeved, tight	checked, flowery, plain, spotted, striped	cotton, denim

4 Write three sentences describing the clothes in Exercise 1. Use at least two adjectives in each sentence.

She's wearing a white cotton T-shirt.

1 ______
2 ______
3 ______

5 Read your sentences in Exercise 4. Can your partner guess which photo you are describing?

Use it!

6 Discuss the questions.

1 Which clothes in Exercise 1 do you have?
2 Can you describe the clothes you are wearing?
3 Which shapes, patterns and materials do you usually wear? Which do you never wear?

Explore it!

Guess the correct answer.

Some celebrities wear special 'anti-paparazzi' scarves. What do you think these scarves do?

a make their faces more beautiful
b make the photos go black
c make the celebrities look ugly

Find out about a clothes designer. Write a question for your partner to answer.

UNIT 1 | TRENDSETTERS 11

3 Ask students to compare tables with a partner.

Choose the correct order

4 Give students two minutes to write their sentences.

5 ★★★ Ask students to describe clothes people are wearing in the class. Their partner guesses who is being described.

6 Give students three minutes to discuss the questions.

Explore it!

Students use the facts they researched about designers.

Homework

Workbook p8

Background information

The adjective *smart* means 'well-dressed' or 'intelligent', but has come to be used to describe not only objects, but places which are enhanced by technology, which is why we talk of 'smartphones' and 'smart cities'.

Warmer

Write *smartphone and smart TV* on the board. Elicit that *smart* in this context refers to objects which have been designed to perform some of the functions of a computer. Ask: *How can clothes be smart?* Elicit students' ideas.

Fashion & technology

CONNECTED CLOTHES

Anyone who has been reading my blog for a while knows that I'm a huge fan of technology in fashion. Here are my latest discoveries.

A We've all seen watches that measure how much we move or sleep, but what about a T-shirt? Over the last few years, scientists have been developing clothes which can record information about our heart rate or breathing and which can help us stay healthy. Most people have a denim jacket. But have you ever seen a denim jacket that can play music or send instant messages? Well, scientists have designed one that can. You just have to touch the sleeve and your music starts playing!

B Scientists have also created clothes with sensors that take our body temperature and circulate warm or cool air through the material so that we never feel too hot or too cold. Special clothes for astronauts or emergency service workers have been using this technology for years, but now companies have created similar materials for everyday clothing and shoes. Great! No more hot, sweaty feet!

C Now there are even smart clothes that produce energy while we're wearing them! Scientists in South Korea have created a material that turns movement into electricity. So, you can charge your phone while you're doing exercise or just walking around! That's smart!

D Finally, if you haven't been following my updates on 3-D printing, check out these trendy designs. My favourite is the high-heeled shoes. I love the fact that each design is individual and that one day we'll be able to design and print our own patterned or plain clothes and shoes at home.

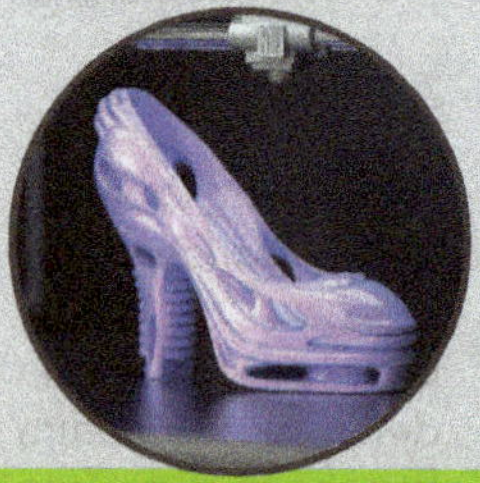

READING
A blog post

1 Look at the pictures. How do they combine technology and fashion?

The sweatshirt includes lights that light up a message, in this case the word 'hola'; the T-shirt and trousers have sensors to calculate heartbeat, breathing etc.; the shoe is 3-D printed.

2 1.03 Read the blog post. Match headings 1–4 with paragraphs A–D.

1 3-D printed clothes D
2 Clothes that change temperature B
3 Connected clothing A
4 Energy-producing clothes C

3 Read the blog post again and answer the questions.

1 How can we watch our health with connected clothing?
It can record and tell us information about our heart rate and breathing.
2 How does the denim jacket in the text play music?
You touch the sleeve.
3 What's good about creating electricity with clothes?
You can charge your phone while you're doing exercise or walking.
4 What does the blogger predict about 3-D printed clothes?
We will be able to design and print our own at home in the future.

4 Find words in the blog that mean:

1 the part of clothing that covers your arm (A) sleeve
2 to move around something (B) circulate
3 to put electricity into a device like a phone (C) charge
4 the latest information (D) update
5 to produce something with a printer (D) print

Voice it!

5 Discuss the questions.

1 Would you like to have any of the smart clothes in the blog?
2 What other things would you like clothes to do in the future?
3 Do you think smart clothes are important? Why / Why not?

Finished? p118 Ex1

12 TRENDSETTERS | UNIT 1

1 Do this task with the class as a whole. Elicit students' ideas about the pictures and write those ideas on the board.

2 1.03 Read out the four headings. Ask students to predict the sort of content they would expect to appear under each of those headings, e.g. how 3-D technology works, an example of 3-D clothing, what the author thinks of the technology.

3 Ask students if they can answer any of the four questions without looking back at the blog post.

4 ★★★ Before students look for the words in the text, read out the definitions and ask students if they can guess what words are being defined. Challenge students to write sentences using these four words from the text.

Match the clothing to the people

5 Give students time to think and make notes before they begin discussing anything.

Extend it!

In groups, students think about how to make an item of clothing 'smart', listing the things it can do. Groups present their ideas to the class.

Finished?

Students turn to SB p118 and do Exercise 1.

Flipped class

▶ Ask students to watch **Video 1.2** and do the **Video worksheet** in the *Teacher's Resource Bank.*

Homework

Workbook p9

Lesson aim: I can use the present perfect simple and continuous.

Warmer

▶ Play **Video 1.2.** Elicit that Tara's been knitting for a few years and that no one has bought Patrick's shoes yet.

1 Elicit the form of the present perfect simple (*have/has* + participle) and the present perfect continuous (*have/has* + *been* + participle).

2 Once students have completed the rules, ask: *What have you done today?* and *What have you been doing in the last ten minutes?* Elicit answers.

3 Ask students to make use of the irregular verb list on SB p143 when doing the activities on this page.

4 🎧 1.04 ★ Tell students to first read through the gapped text to get an idea of its content, then to choose the correct verb for each gap.

Audioscript p159

5 🎧 1.05 Ask students to compare their answers in pairs, discussing any differences, before playing the audio to check.

Audioscript p159

Extra grammar practice

6 & 7 Before students start speaking, check the completed questions in Exercise 6. Give students a few minutes to discuss the questions in pairs.

LANGUAGE IN ACTION

Present perfect simple and present perfect continuous

Watch video 1.2
How long has Tara been knitting?
How many people have bought Patrick's shoes?

Present perfect simple	Present perfect continuous
Scientists [1] have also **created** clothes with sensors.	Over the last few years, scientists [2] have **been developing** clothes which can record information.
He [3] hasn't **bought** any 3-D printed clothing yet.	If you [4] haven't **been following** my updates on 3-D printing, check out these trendy designs.
[5] Have you ever **seen** a jacket that can play music?	How long [6] have you **been reading** my blog?

1 Complete the examples in the table above with the correct form of *have*.

2 Complete the rules with *simple* or *continuous*.

1 In present perfect simple sentences the focus is on the result of an activity.

2 In present perfect continuous sentences the focus is on how long the activity is.

3 Put the words in the correct order to make sentences.

1 lots of / I've / blog posts / written
I've written lots of blog posts.

2 since / a fashion blog / writing / She's been / January
She's been writing a fashion blog since January.

3 made / Have you / your own clothes / ever / ?
Have you ever made your own clothes?

4 been / He's / two years / designing / for / clothes
He's been designing clothes for two years.

🎧 1.04 **4** Complete the text with the present perfect continuous form of the verbs in the box. Listen and check.

help make not practise ~~try~~ watch work

Recently I [1] *'ve been trying* to learn how to knit. It's really difficult! I [2] 've been watching lots of videos online, but I [3] haven't been practising very much. I [4] 've been making a scarf for a few days now, but it's full of holes and looks awful. My mum [5] 's been helping me too, but she [6] 's been working all week and hasn't really got much free time.

🎧 1.05 **5** Complete the sentences with the present perfect simple or continous form of the verbs in brackets. Listen, check and repeat.

1 How long *has* he *been designing* clothes? (design)

2 Have you ever learned to knit? (learn)

3 She has never worn high-heeled shoes. (wear)

4 I 've been walking in these shoes all morning and my feet really hurt! (walk)

Use it!

6 Imagine you are a fashion designer. Make questions with the present perfect simple or continuous. Then think of your answers.

1 What / designed?
What have you designed?

2 Who / worn your designs?
Who has worn your designs?

3 How long / designing clothes?
How long have you been designing clothes?

7 Ask and answer the questions. Which designer makes the most interesting clothes? Why?

I've designed a coat which changes colour when it gets wet!

Finished? p118 Ex 2

Grammar game

In pairs, students take it in turns to say something, e.g. *I can't find my keys. / My hair is wet.* Their partner guesses the reason, e.g. *Has someone stolen them? / Have you been walking in the rain?* Students get a point for a correct guess.

Finished?

Fast finishers can turn to SB p118 and do Exercise 2.

Homework

Workbook p10

Lesson aim: I can use verbs related to clothes and shoes.

Warmer

Ask students what new items of clothing they would like.

1 1.06 Tell students to read through the fashion forum first to get a general idea of what it is about. Then ask: *Who says it's difficult to find clothes of the right size?* (Gisela.)

Target vocabulary

do up /duː ʌp/
fit /fɪt/
fold /fəʊld/
go out of fashion /gəʊ aʊt əv ˈfæʃən/
go with /gəʊ wɪð/
hang up /hæŋ ʌp/
match /mætʃ/
suit /suːt/
undo /ʌnduː/
wear out /weə aʊt/

Audioscript p159

Vocabulary Bank SB p128

Extra vocabulary practice

Learn to learn

Encourage students to make a note of other words a verb is used with. Does the verb take an object?

2 ★ Elicit the meaning of the verbs in the box before students do the task.

Get it right!

Elicit other items of clothing which are always used in the plural form, e.g. *jeans*, *glasses*.

3 After students have asked and answered the questions, ask some students to tell the class what they found out about their partner.

VOCABULARY AND LISTENING

Verbs related to clothes and shoes

1 1.06 **Read the fashion forum and match the verbs in bold with the definitions. Listen, check and repeat.**

ARE YOU A FOLLOWER OF FASHION?

MARIA I don't buy many clothes because they **go out of fashion** so quickly. I usually buy things that **go with** other clothes I already have. I like wearing green clothes because they **match** my eyes!

GISELA I'm really tall so it's difficult to find clothes that **fit** me, especially jeans! I wear jeans so much they **wear out**! Lots of clothes don't **suit** me, because they haven't been designed for tall people.

EDU I love fashion and I work in a clothes store on Saturdays. It's great because I get to try on loads of clothes. The worst part is the changing rooms. People leave clothes on the floor and I have to **hang up** the jackets and trousers and **fold** all the T-shirts. It takes forever!

IRINA Today I had a complete fashion disaster. I was trying on a dress in a shop. I managed to **do up** the zip! But when I tried to take the dress off I couldn't **undo** it. How embarrassing!

1 be the right size *fit*
2 not popular any longer go out of fashion
3 wear something so much it looks old wear out
4 make someone look good suit
5 look good together go with
6 be similar or the same colour/type match
7 close buttons or zips on clothes do up
8 open buttons or zips on clothes undo
9 put clothes on a coat hanger hang up
10 bend clothes so that one part lies on another part fold

LEARN TO LEARN

Recording new verbs

Make sentences with new verbs so that you can remember how to use them.

2 **Complete the sentences with the correct form of the verbs in the box and the words in brackets.**

do up hang up not go with suit ~~wear out~~

1 You never *wear out your shoes*. They always look new. (your shoes)
2 That colour suits you. It looks good. (you)
3 This top doesn't go with my skirt. They're different styles. (my skirt)
4 Do up the zip on your jacket. It's cold. (the zip)

Get it right!

The word *clothes* is always plural.
Your new clothes look great!

Use it!

3 **Discuss the questions.**

1 Which clothes fit you well?
2 Which ones suit you?
3 Which ones have you worn out?

An interview

4 1.07 **Listen to an interview with Carla. Where does she get her clothes from?**

She makes new clothes from old ones, prints her own designs on T-shirts and tops, and gets her clothes from second-hand shops.

5 1.07 **Listen again and complete the text.**

Carla started looking at fashion designs online when she was [1] *12*. She enjoys upcycling – creating [2] something new from something that exists. She also decorates [3] plain T-shirts and tops with her own designs. She knows that people buy fast fashion because the clothes are [4] cheap and that ethical fashion is [5] more expensive than fast fashion but ethical fashion thinks about the people who [6] make the clothes.

Pronunciation p141

14 TRENDSETTERS | UNIT 1

4 1.07 Before students listen to the interview, elicit where Clara might get her clothes from, e.g. a clothes store, a second-hand shop.

Audioscript p159

5 1.07 Check understanding of the following ideas before listening: *upcycling* – creating a new product from one that exists already; *fast fashion* – clothing produced quickly and sold cheaply in the big clothing chains; *ethical fashion* – helping people in the communities where clothes are produced and minimising the impact on the environment.

Pronunciation

Students can do the activities on p141, practising the pronunciation of the letters *ea*.

Flipped class

Prepare for **Video 1.3** (p15). Students think of their top three fashion mistakes.

Homework

Workbook p11

Warmer

▶ Play **Video 1.3.** Elicit that the mistakes are: dressing like everyone else, trying too hard, and having a messy bedroom. The problem with a messy bedroom is that you can't find anything to wear. After the video, ask students to discuss their own fashion mistakes.

1 On the board, write *I am absolutely obsessed with fashion*. Elicit that *absolutely* is an example of a modifier, that is, a word or phrase which adds to the meaning of another part of the sentence.

2 ★ Guide students to the answers by focusing on the important elements in the sentences, e.g. In 4, identify *longer* as a comparative adjective, then elicit that *a lot* is used in front of such a word to show a big difference.

Extra grammar practice

3 1.10 Tell students to read through the text first, then ask: *What is the text about?* (Answer: making clothes from materials which are good for the environment.)

Audioscript p160

4 Read out the example. Check that students understand what to do. Students can work alone to do the task.

5 Give students a couple of minutes to complete the sentences. Monitor and help as necessary.

6 Once students have done this guessing game, find out if anyone in the class managed to get all five right.

LANGUAGE IN ACTION
Modifiers

Watch video 1.3
What are the top three fashion mistakes? What's the problem if your bedroom is totally messy?

I've been [1] totally obsessed with fashion since I was a child.	a extremely / absolutely / totally / really
They look [2] pretty good.	b quite / rather / fairly / pretty
These clothes are [3] a bit more expensive …	c a bit / a little
but they last [4] a lot longer.	d a lot / far

1 Complete the examples in the table above with *a bit, a lot, pretty* and *totally*. Use the same words in each line.

2 Which words (a–d) do we use before …
1 comparative adjectives to show a big difference? d
2 comparative adjectives to show a small difference? c
3 strong adjectives? a
4 adjectives to mean more than *a little* but less than *very*? b

3 1.10 Circle the correct words. Listen and check.

Making materials like cotton or denim can be [1] extremely / *a lot* damaging for the environment. That's why it's [2] absolutely / *far* essential we create new materials from natural products that are [3] *fairly* / a lot better for the planet. Some materials like bamboo have been [4] fairly / *a little* successful. Others are still being developed, like a material from the rice plant, which is [5] quite / *a bit* similar to cotton, and one made from chicken feathers, which is [6] pretty / *a bit* warm, like wool. Technology has also made it [7] *really* / far easier to recycle materials like plastic bottles into clothes such as leggings and T-shirts, which is [8] really / *a lot* good news for the environment!

4 Complete the sentences with the words in brackets.
1 I feel quite tired today. I need to sleep well otherwise I'll be extremely tired tomorrow. (extremely / quite)
2 The shopping centre in our town is quite good, but the one outside town is far better. (far / quite)
3 He creates totally amazing designs, which are a lot more fun than ours. (a lot / totally)
4 I'm fairly good at art, but there are people in my class who are far more talented than me. (far / fairly)
5 This coat is absolutely beautiful and it's only a bit more expensive than the other one. (a bit / absolutely)

Use it!

5 Complete the sentences so they are true for you.
1 I am pretty good at ______.
2 I feel quite sad when ______.
3 A subject I find a lot easier than before is ______.
4 I'm a bit more interested in ______ than before.
5 I think it's absolutely amazing that ______.

6 Guess what your partner wrote in their sentences. Score one point for each correct guess.

Did you say, 'I am pretty good at English'?

No, I didn't. I said, 'I'm pretty good at art'.

Finished? p118 Ex 3

Grammar game

In pairs, students write gapped sentences, *I think pink T-shirts are absolutely …* Their partner has to guess the missing adjective. A correct guess wins a point.

Finished?

Fast finishers can turn to SB p118 and do Exercise 3.

Homework

Workbook p12

1 1.11 On the board, write *retro clothing*. Elicit the meaning (clothing that uses a fashion style from a particular period in the past).

Audioscript p160

2 1.11 ★★★ Ask students to cover the *Useful language* box. Students then listen to the recording, and fill in the conversation with the phrases they hear.

Useful language practice

▶ Play **Video 1.4** and encourage students to repeat the *Everyday English* phrases with the same intonation.

3 Students think of situations in which they could use the *Everyday English* phrases. For example, A: *Check out my new jeans.* B: *You're such a fashion victim!*

4 Encourage students to make notes here rather than write a full description. The idea is to develop students' fluency rather than ask them to follow a script.

5 Ask students to practise the conversations until they feel comfortable enough to not rely on their notes. Encourage them to improvise a little.

6 As well as answering the three questions about the other pair's conversation, students can give each other feedback on their speaking, focusing on things like use of language, pronunciation and intonation.

SPEAKING

Giving your opinion politely

Diego doesn't like the clothes that Dana has bought.

1 1.11 **Listen to the conversation. Does Diego like the things?**

DIEGO Hey, Dana. How's it going?
DANA Hi Diego. I've been shopping all morning. I've bought some great stuff. Do you want to see?
DIEGO Yeah, sure.
DANA I got this striped jacket from Zaps, that new store they've just opened.
DIEGO Oh right. Wow! [1]That's … er … different!
DANA I know! It's totally out there!
DIEGO Mmm, [2] I'm not a huge fan of yellow and blue together, but the blue matches the colour of your eyes.
DANA Thanks! And check out these trousers.
DIEGO Flowery trousers! Wow! Very retro!
DANA I know! They fit really well. What do you think?
DIEGO Well, [3] They're not exactly my style but I can see why you like them.
DANA Do you think they suit me?
DIEGO Yes, I guess so.
DANA I think I might wear them to go out later, with the jacket.
DIEGO Mmm, [4] I don't know if I'd wear them together. [5] I think maybe the trousers would go better with a plain top.
DANA No, patterns are totally in this year.
DIEGO You're such a fashion victim, Dana!

2 1.11 **Complete the conversation with the phrases from the *Useful language* box. Listen and check.**

Useful language

I don't know if … | I'm not a huge fan of … | I think maybe … | That's … er … different! | They're not exactly my style.

Watch video 1.4
Everyday English

check out | fashion victim | in | out there

3 Match the phrases in the *Everyday English* box with the words and phrases 1–4.

1 someone who follows fashion fashion victim
2 fashionable in
3 different out there
4 look at check out

PLAN

4 Write about the clothes in the photo:

What clothes are they?
Who bought them and why?
What do they look like?
Why do you like or not like them?

SPEAK

5 Practise the conversation with your partner. Remember to use the present perfect simple and continuous, modifiers, the vocabulary from this unit and phrases from the *Useful language* and *Everyday English* boxes.

CHECK

6 Work with another pair. Listen to their conversation and complete the notes.

Who bought them and why? ______
______
What do they look like? ______
______
Do the other pair like them? ______
______

Extend it!
In groups, students design an item of clothing, which they illustrate, describe and present to the class.

Class challenge
London, Paris, Milan and **New York** / Los Angeles / San Francisco are seen as the world's big four fashion capitals.

Flipped class
Prepare for the **Writing** lesson (p17). Students research what is meant by the term *fashion footprint*.

Warmer

Write *blog* on the board. Elicit that a blog is a website, usually maintained by one person or a small group of people, featuring posts, regularly uploaded, on a particular topic.

1 Ask students to share what they found about the idea of a fashion footprint, before they read the blog post (*Fashion footprint* refers to the effect on the environment of the manufacture of the clothes you buy.)

2 Split students into two groups. Ask one group to read Carlos's comment and the other Amie's comment. In pairs, students then discuss the questions and share what they found out about Carlos and Amie.

3 ★★★ Challenge students to think of similar phrases to use for when they enjoy reading a post, learn something from a post, and change behaviour as a result of a post.

Useful language practice

4 ★ Help students by brainstorming ideas for other ways to cut down on their fashion footprint, e.g. make their own clothes, buy clothes from second-hand shops, wear clothes for longer before replacing them, repair old clothes.

5 Give students up to 15 minutes to write their posts. Monitor and help as necessary.

6 Ask students to check each other's work and offer suggestions for improving it.

Four steps to reduce your fashion footprint

Here are some ideas you can try!

- Have a clothes swap party. Swap clothes you don't want with your friends.
- Save energy. Wash clothes less often, dry clothes naturally, don't iron!
- Give old clothes to second-hand shops. Don't throw them away!
- Buy fewer, better quality new clothes.

Comments

Great post! It got me thinking about how to reduce my fashion footprint. I talked to my parents and we decided to try and reduce the amount of energy we use on our clothes. Usually we wash all our clothes every time we wear them, even when they're still pretty clean, but this month we've been washing clothes less often, and we haven't ironed anything. My parents have saved money and I've been much better at hanging up my clothes! Carlos

Thanks for sharing! I had no idea that I throw so many clothes away! I had a clothes swap party last week. I got a great denim jacket that I absolutely love! I also got two long-sleeved tops and some cool high-heeled boots for free! I was absolutely amazed that we swapped everything! Since reading your post I've decided to buy far fewer new clothes in the future. Amie

WRITING
A blog comment

1 Look at the blog post. How can people reduce their fashion footprint? *have a clothes swap party, wash clothes less often, buy fewer clothes*

2 Read the blog comments. Answer the questions.

1. Were the ideas that Carlos and Amie tried successful? How do you know? *Yes. Carlos's parents saved money; Amie got a great jacket.*
2. What does Amie want to do in the future? *Buy far fewer new clothes.*

3 Find the phrases from the *Useful language* box in the blog comments. Which phrases can you use when you …

1. enjoy reading a post? *Great post!, Thanks for sharing!*
2. learn something new from the post? *It got me thinking about … I had no idea that …*
3. change your behaviour because of the post? *We decided to … Since reading your post I've …*

Useful language

Great post!	We decided to …
I had no idea that …	Since reading your post I've …
It got me thinking about …	Thanks for sharing!

Write your own blog comment.

PLAN

4 Look at the ideas in the blog post and make notes about which one to write about.

Which ideas will you try out? ______

Do you think it will go well? Why? / Why not? ______

What other ideas would you like to try in the future? ______

WRITE

5 Write your blog comment. Remember to include the present perfect simple and continuous, modifiers, vocabulary from this unit and phrases from the *Useful language* box.

CHECK

6 Do you …

- explain why an idea might or might not work well?
- explain what you would like to try in the future?

Finished? p118 Ex 4

UNIT 1 | TRENDSETTERS 17

Extend it!

Students can read each other's blog posts and then write an extra comment in response.

Finished?

Fast finishers can turn to SB p118 and do Exercise 4.

Flipped class

Prepare for **Around the World** (pp18–19). Students research a fact about traditional Scottish dress.

Homework

Workbook p13

Lesson aim: I can understand a text about traditional Scottish dress.

Background information

Scotland is a country in the north of Great Britain, which, with England, Wales and Northern Ireland, forms the United Kingdom. Before the kingdoms of Scotland and England were unified in 1707, Scotland was an independent country. It has a population of over five million and has its own education and legal systems.

Warmer

Write *Scotland* on the board. Elicit what students know about the country.

▶ **Video 1.5** develops the theme of clothing. Play the video, then put students into small groups to discuss the questions. Elicit that a *deel* is a long-sleeved coat, it allows for easy movement and protects the body. Also elicit what the following colours represent for the Masai: blue (sky and rain), white (milk), green (the land), yellow (the sun), orange (kindness).

Video comprehension questions

1 1.12 Before students do the true/false task, elicit that a travel guide is a reference book for people travelling to specific destinations. It contains practical information such as listings of hotels, restaurants and transport links, as well as special sections with background cultural information likely to be of interest to the traveller.

AROUND THE WORLD

READING
A travel guide

Globetrotters
Watch video 1.5
What we wear and why

- Why do we wear clothes and what do they show about us?
- What is a *deel* and why do Mongolian people wear it?
- What do the colours blue, white, green, yellow and orange represent for the Masai people?

1 1.12 **Are the sentences about the kilt true or false? Read the travel guide and check your answers.**

1. Kilts are only worn by men. F
2. Kilts have not always been made of tartan. T
3. Tartans today indicate where people live. F
4. Scottish dress is different for men and women. T
5. Tartan patterns are popular outside Scotland. T

Traditional Scottish dress

You have probably seen photos of Scotland's most famous piece of clothing, the kilt. But did you know that Scottish men have been wearing kilts for centuries? A kilt used to be an extremely long piece of heavy plain or checked material that men from the Scottish Highlands wore every day. They wrapped the material around their waist and over one shoulder or their head to protect them from the cold wind or rain. Nowadays, the design of the kilt is totally different. It is knee-length and made from wool, with a pattern of vertical and horizontal stripes in different colours called tartan. Tartan designs used to indicate the area where people lived and were far less colourful than they are today. Since the 18th century, people have been wearing tartan designs that represent their family name or clan (group of families) and today there are over 4,500 designs! The kilt forms part of the traditional Highland dress, which is quite different for men and women.

MEN:
- tartan kilt and a kilt pin
- leather belt
- sporran – a small leather or fur bag that hangs from the belt. There are no pockets in a kilt!
- plain or tartan socks
- kilt knife – a small knife kept in one sock
- ghillies – plain, flat leather shoes with long laces

WOMEN:
- long or knee-length tartan kilt
- tartan shawl – a piece of material worn over your shoulders
- plain or tartan socks
- ghillies

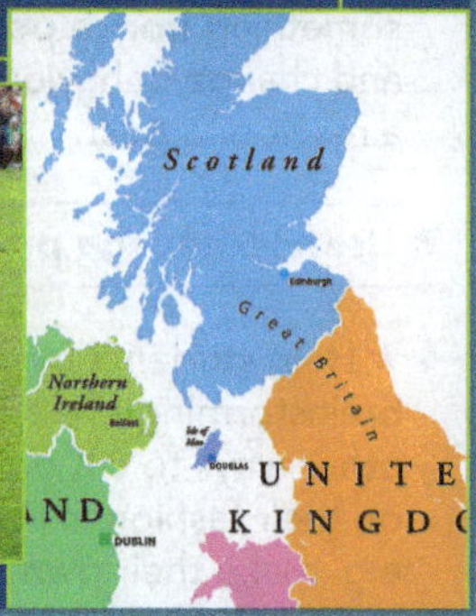

18 TRENDSETTERS | UNIT 1

Class challenge
The famous Scottish musical instrument shown in the picture on p18 is called the windbag / **bagpipes** / airbag.

Lesson aim: I can understand a text about traditional Scottish dress.

Background information

In the 18th century, King George II of the United Kingdom didn't want Scotland to have its own identity, so it was illegal for Scottish people to wear tartan. Only the military could wear tartan kilts. However, Scottish people wore kilts in protest because they were part of their identity and they were proud of it.

2 Read out the example. Encourage students to read the text carefully to identify the information required to complete the rest of the table. Monitor and help as necessary.

3 ★ Read out the nouns in the box. Ask: *Do you know the meaning of any of them?* In pairs, students look at the context the words are used in in the text on traditional Scottish dress. This will help them choose the correct definition.

Crossword

Learn to learn

Explain that using spidergrams can help form associations between words. Encourage students to use spidergrams when recording words which can be linked together in the same way.

4 & 5 Students work alone to complete their spidergrams before comparing their words with a partner.

2 Use the travel guide to complete the table.

Kilts in the 18th century	Kilts in the 21st century
One long piece of cloth worn around waist and over shoulder	Knee-length, made from wool, tartan design. Over 4,500 different colourful tartan designs.
Highland dress for men	**Highland dress for women**
(As listed in the text)	(As listed in the text)
Who wears traditional tartan clothes?	**Who wears modern tartan clothes?**
Men at weddings, funerals and parties. Women for traditional Scottish dancing.	People around the world including celebrities. Designers have designed many types of clothes and shoes in tartan.

Highland dress is extremely popular in Scotland for special occasions such as weddings, funerals or parties, particularly for men. Women often wear kilts to do traditional Scottish dancing at sports and cultural events. Nowadays, tartan isn't just used for traditional dress in Scotland. Fashion designers around the world use tartan to create modern designs such as tartan trousers or tartan shoes and celebrities from Rihanna to Shawn Mendes have been photographed wearing tartan. Even though people have worn tartan for centuries, it is still popular today and looks like it's not going to go out of fashion any time soon.

3 Find the nouns and match them with the definitions.

dress funeral laces pin shawl

1 a ceremony when a person dies funeral
2 a combination of clothes worn together for a particular situation dress
3 a small piece of metal to attach clothes pin
4 a large piece of cloth worn over your shoulders or head shawl
5 string used to fasten shoes laces

LEARN TO LEARN

Using spidergrams

Spidergrams can help you remember words that have a link with other words.

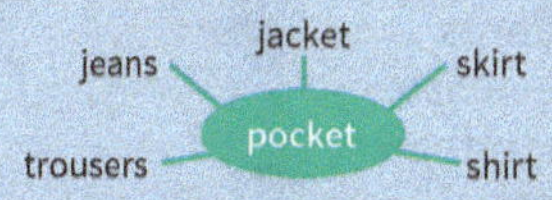

4 Make a spidergram of clothes and shoes which have laces, a zip, buttons or sleeves.

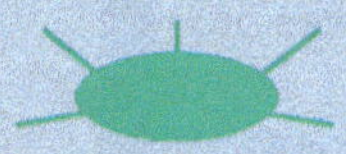

5 Which words did you both write? Add any new words to your spidergrams.

Voice it!

6 Discuss the questions.
1 What is traditional dress in your country?
2 When do people wear it?

Explore it!

Guess the correct answer.
It was illegal to wear tartan in the middle of the 18th century in Scotland. True or false?
a true b false

Find another fact about traditional Scottish dress. Write a question for your partner to answer.

The Culture Project Teacher's Resource Bank

UNIT 1 | TRENDSETTERS 19

6 After students have discussed the questions, encourage students to reflect on their own traditions and cultural practices, and to learn about traditions and cultural practices in other parts of the world. Explain that awareness and appreciation of other cultures helps us develop our understanding of others.

Students can collaborate digitally online and offline in the collaboration space, where teachers can set, track and assess students' work. Students can also share and showcase their work as well as comment on each other's projects.

Culture Project

See Project Book p22 for further information and activities.

Explore it!

To write their questions, students use the information about traditional Scottish dress that they researched for homework.

Flipped class

Prepare for the **Review** lesson (p20). Students revise the grammar and vocabulary from Unit 1.

Lesson aim: I can review what I have learnt and reflect on my progress.

The aim of this review page is for students to revise the grammar and vocabulary from the unit. You can either do it in class, as a timed progress test or set it for homework.

Vocabulary

1 Turn this task into a class competition. Put students into small groups to decide which are the odd words out and why. The first group to complete the task successfully wins.

2 ★★★ After students complete this exercise, challenge them to think of further sentences (personalised if possible) using the verbs in bold. Write these sentences on the board.

Language in action

3 Ask students to explain the difference between the form and meaning of the present perfect simple and continuous. Students can look back at p13 to remind them of these forms.

4 Before students complete the exercise, elicit the modifiers which were introduced on p15. Ask students to sort the modifiers into groups as on p15.

Unit quiz review

1 REVIEW

VOCABULARY

1 Circle the odd word out.

1	baggy	tight	spotted
2	cotton	long-sleeved	denim
3	flowery	flat	plain
4	cotton	striped	checked
5	plain	flat	high-heeled

2 Match 1–5 with a–e.

1 **Hang up** your clothes, e
2 I can't **undo** my jacket, c
3 These jeans are **worn out** a
4 This T-shirt **doesn't fit** me any more, b
5 Your glasses really **suit** you, d

a because I've had them for ages.
b it's too small.
c the zip's broken.
d they look great!
e they're all over the floor.

LANGUAGE IN ACTION

3 Complete the text with the present perfect simple or continuous form of the verbs in brackets.

16-year-old Moziah Bridges [1] ________ (design) ties since he was nine. His grandmother taught him to make bow ties and since then he [2] ________ (own) his own business. The designer [3] ________ (appear) in magazines and on TV and [4] ________ (make) a collection of ties for basketball teams in the USA. Mo is still at school but [5] ________ (work) in the evenings. It [6] ________ (not be) easy, but his mum helps him and he [7] ________ (employ) more people as his business [8] ________ (grow). Mo often gives talks to other people who [9] ________ (think) about starting a business.

1 has been designing
2 has owned
3 has appeared
4 has made
5 has been working
6 hasn't been
7 he's employed
8 has grown
9 have been thinking

4 Circle the correct modifier to complete the sentences.

1 It takes *a little* / *quite* longer to fold your clothes, but then you don't have to iron them.
2 Where did you get that jacket? I *far* / *absolutely* love it!
3 The second film in the series was *a bit* / *pretty* better than the first one, but not much.
4 I speak *a lot* / *fairly* good Chinese, but I can't write it.
5 I'm *far* / *totally* confused by his explanation. I don't understand it at all.
6 Have you seen this video? It's *really* / *a lot* funny.
7 That T-shirt is *far* / *really* nicer than the other one, but it's *quite* / *a lot* expensive.

Self-assessment

I can use words to describe clothes and shoes.
I can use verbs to talk about clothes and shoes.
I can use the *present perfect simple* and *present perfect continuous*.
I can use modifiers.

Self-assessment

After doing the self-assessment, ask students to write *I don't understand this* or *I need more practice* next to their ☹ statements. Encourage them to ask you for extra homework on any of the vocabulary or grammar from Unit 1, if necessary.

Homework

Workbook pp14–15

Lesson aim: I can learn to write different kinds of example sentences.

Example sentences give students a chance to record new vocabulary in a way that is memorable to them. By this stage, students should be experimenting with different ways of doing this, such as the ones featured in Ela's blog.

Warmer

Elicit different ways of remembering new vocabulary, e.g. writing the word in a notebook, writing a definition of the word, translating the word into your own language, asking friends to test you on the meaning and use of a word. Point out that all these ways are fine as long as they help students memorise the items.

1 Ask students to read the first part of Ela's blog. Elicit the three kinds of example sentence that Ela refers to as well as her reasons for using them. With the class as a whole, discuss Ela's ideas. Do students have a favourite kind of example sentence?

2 Students can work alone on this task before comparing answers with a partner.

OWN IT!

3 ★ With the class as a whole, write three example sentences with *baggy*. Put these examples on the board so students have a model to follow. Give students ten minutes to complete the task. Monitor and help as necessary.

4 Encourage students to give each other feedback. Are the examples clear and easy to understand? Could they be improved in any way?

LEARN TO LEARN

LEARN TO ... WRITE DIFFERENT KINDS OF EXAMPLE SENTENCES

You can write different kinds of example sentences to help you understand and remember new words.

1 Read Ela's blog. Why does she recommend using the different kinds of example sentences to remember new words? It helps the words stay in the memory, and can make the meaning clearer.

Ela's English learning BLOG

Today's tip: example sentences

Hi everyone! Today we're looking at a great way to learn vocabulary: example sentences. When I learn new words, I often use them in sentences to help me learn and remember them. There are different types of example sentences you can use. They're all good for different reasons.

- **a** sentences about you, your family or your friends – when you use words in sentences about things people you know have done, the words are easier to remember
- **b** funny sentences – a funny image can help the word stay in your memory
- **c** sentences that explain the word – these make the meaning clear, like the examples in dictionaries

Here are some of my latest examples. Can you guess which types they are?

1. I prefer **plain** T-shirts to ones with writing or pictures on them.
2. Your skin gets **sweaty** when you're hot or exercise a lot.
3. My baby brother always wipes his nose on his **sleeve**.
4. The giraffe couldn't **do up** the zip on his jacket because it was too long!
5. A **checked** pattern is a pattern of squares of different colours.
6. I thought I saw a zebra – but it was a horse in a black and white **striped** T-shirt.

So ... that's all from me today. Don't forget to share some example sentences of your own. You can post them below!

2 Match Ela's examples 1–6 with types a–c.

1	a	4	b
2	c	5	c
3	a	6	b

OWN IT!

3 Choose five words from the box and write an example sentence for each one. Use all of Ela's types a–c at least once.

baggy	charge
fashion victim	flat
hang up	high-heeled
laces	not go with
spotted	updates

1 ______________________

2 ______________________

3 ______________________

4 ______________________

5 ______________________

4 Tell your partner your sentences from Exercise 3. Which types a–c are they? Which sentences are your favourites and why?

Flipped class

Prepare for **Unit 2.** Students research the way their town or city has changed over the last 50–100 years.

Lesson aim: I can talk about how cities change over time.

▶ Start it!

Unit quiz

1 Elicit answers to the question. Write key words and phrases on the board, e.g. *lizard, chameleon, change colour*.

2 ★★★ Help students here by giving them some prompts. On the board, write *population, buildings, transport*. Elicit students' ideas about how these and other things change in cities over time.

3 ▶ Play **Video 2.1** and allow students to check their answers. Students can also complete the Start it! **video worksheet** in the *Teacher's Resource Bank*.

4 Students share the ideas they were asked to think of for homework at the end of Unit 1.

Video comprehension questions

Flipped class

Prepare for **Explore it!** (p23). Students find out about international students in their country.

2 CHANGES

LEARNING OUTCOMES

I can ...

- understand texts about international exchanges and a mystery object
- explain how to use something
- write an opinion essay
- understand how to use *used to* and *would* for past habits, the past simple, and the past perfect with *never, already, by (then), by the time*
- talk about changes and parts of objects
- practise learning new words by using them in different situations and identifying key words to understand audio texts
- make a history exhibition.

The animal is a chameleon, which can change its skin colour.

Start it!

1 Look at the photo. Do you know what this animal is, and how it changes?
2 Before you watch, how do you think cities change over time?
3 Which two events changed the city of Seoul? Watch and check.
4 How has your town or city changed?

Hosting the Olympic Games and the football World Cup.

Watch video 2.1 | Language in action 2.2 p25 | Language in action 2.3 p27 | Everyday English 2.4 p28

22 CHANGES | UNIT 2

Unit aims

Skills

I can ...

- understand a text about international exchanges p24
- explain how to use something p28
- write an opinion essay p29
- understand a text about retro fashion, technology and music p30, p31

Language

I can ...

- talk about changes in life p23
- understand how to use *used to, would* and past simple p25, 27
- talk about parts of objects p26
- understand how to use past perfect with *never, already, by (then), by the time* p27

Learn to Learn

I can ...

- use words in different situations p23
- identify key words p26
- learn to help my partner improve their writing p33

Extra Resources

- *Finished?* – Student's Book p119
- *Vocabulary Bank* – Student's Book p129
- CLIL – Student's Book p137
- Pronunciation – Student's Book p141
- Workbook p16
- *Teacher's Resource Bank* on *Cambridge One* for tests package, Cambridge Exam practice, word-lists, differentiated worksheets and many other extra resources.
- *Practice Extra* and *Digital collaboration space*

1 Elicit further examples with each phrasal verb to check students' understanding of it. e.g. *Could you do without chocolate?*

Target vocabulary

do without /duː wɪˈðaʊt/
end up /end ʌp/
go back /gəʊ bæk/
go through /gəʊ θruː/
look forward to /lʊk ˈfɔːwəd tuː/
move out /muːv aʊt/
move to /muːv tuː/
settle down /ˈsetəl daʊn/
sign up /saɪn ʌp/
turn down /tɜːn daʊn/
turn out /tɜːn aʊt/
try out /traɪ aʊt/

2 2.01 Elicit example sentences with the phrasal verbs to check students' understanding.

Audioscript p161

Extra vocabulary practice
Correct the questions

3 2.02 ★★★ Challenge students to complete the sentences with the phrasal verbs in Exercise 1 (or at least predict which phrasal verb could fit) before they listen to the recording.

Audioscript p161

Vocabulary Bank SB p129

VOCABULARY
Phrasal verbs: changes

1 Which of the phrases a–l describes picture 1? Which phrase describes picture 2?

a **settle down** in a new school
b **look forward** to the weekend
c **sign up** for French lessons
d **try out** a new restaurant
e **turn out** well
f **move out** of a house
g **move to** a new school
h **go back** to the beginning
i **end up** in the wrong place
j **go through** a hard time
k **do without** the Internet
l **turn down** an invitation

2 2.01 Match definitions 1–12 with the phrasal verbs a–l in Exercise 1. Listen, check and repeat.

1 feel happy about something in the future — b
2 not have something — k
3 finally be in a place/situation — i
4 experience — j
5 stop living in a particular place — f
6 try something new — d
7 start to feel happy in a new place/situation — a
8 return — h
9 join an organised activity — c
10 say no to something — l
11 have a particular result — e
12 change to — g

3 2.02 Listen to six conversations and complete the sentences using the phrases in Exercise 1.

1 Mr Smith decides to sign up ______ for French classes.
2 Molly is looking forward to ______ the baseball game. Ben turns down the invitation to the game.
3 Tom is going through a hard time ______ at the moment. He has settled down in his ______ new school.
4 Jo asks Ed to go back to ______ the beginning.
5 The girls are going to try out a new ______ restaurant.
6 In the end, Leila's party turned out well.

LEARN TO LEARN
Using words in different situations

Using new words in different situations helps you to remember them.

4 Think of different situations for the phrasal verbs in Exercise 1.

What can you look forward to?

A party … the end of exams …

Use it!

5 Think of questions using the phrasal verbs in Exercise 1. Ask and answer.

Have you tried out a new restaurant recently?

Yes. We went to a great Italian restaurant last week.

Explore it!

Guess the correct answer.
Where do most international students come from?
a USA b China c India

Find out a fact about students in your country. Write a question for your partner.

UNIT 2 | CHANGES 23

Learn to learn
Point out that phrasal verbs can be used in some contexts but not others. For example, you can ***go through*** a hard time, but you can't *go through a nice time with friends* (despite 'go through' meaning 'experience').

4 Students can do this task in small groups. With the class as a whole, discuss the contexts the groups came up with, making sure they are correct.

5 Give students a few minutes to think of their questions.

Vocabulary Bank SB p129

Explore it!
Students use the facts they researched.

Homework
Workbook p16

Lesson aim: I can understand a text about international exchanges.

Warmer

Write *international student exchanges* on the board. Ask: *Would you like to study in another country? Why? Why not?*

1 Elicit what students know about Finland and Mexico, then ask students to identify those countries in the photos. Discuss the question about life in those countries with the class as a whole.

2 2.03 ★ Encourage students to predict the sort of information they'll be looking for, e.g. to answer question one they'll be looking for two things: a period of time longer than six months and a text written by someone who is still in the country being described.

3 ★★★ Extend the activity by asking students to write their own sentences with these five words.

4 In pairs, students read the sentences and discuss whether they think they are true or false, or whether the text doesn't say. Then, they check in the text.

Comprehension questions

5 Before students discuss the questions, give them time to think about their answers and to make notes.

ACE EXCHANGES – DISCOVER A NEW WORLD AND A NEW YOU!

Student testimonials

LUCY

I love school here – it's so different to the USA. Students have almost no homework and very few exams. At my school, we don't even have school subjects. We study topics and do projects instead. It's a great way to learn.

This experience has really helped me to become more confident. I didn't use to be adventurous, but I've tried lots of new things since I arrived here eight months ago. For example, I went on a reindeer safari on my birthday, and I've been going ice-swimming every Saturday. Plus, I've made lots of friends. Finns are very cool people.

It hasn't all been easy. Winter is very hard because it's really dark – there are only three or four hours of light every day. The good thing is that you can see the beautiful Northern Lights.

If you get the opportunity to study abroad don't turn it down, especially not if you can come to Finland!

Finland

BEN

Last year I spent six wonderful months in Mexico. I used to dream about living in a different country, so when I discovered Ace Exchanges I signed up immediately. It was an absolutely incredible experience. I loved the mix of local, European and African cultures, and the people were really outgoing.

Of course, I went through some ups and downs at first, especially dealing with a different school system. For example, many Mexican schools have two timetables. Some students start school at 7.30 am and some – like me – start at 2 pm. We would finish at 8 pm! Also, I didn't speak much Spanish when I arrived, so it was quite difficult to follow lessons. But my classmates would always help me, and I improved a lot.

I felt a bit homesick from time to time, but now I feel like I have two homes. In fact, I've decided to go to university there. I'm really looking forward to going back.

Mexico

READING

A brochure

1 Look at the photos. Which show Finland? Which show Mexico? What do you think it is like to live there?

2 2.03 Read the brochure. Write *L* (Lucy) or *B* (Ben).

Which person …

1. has been abroad for more than half a year? L
2. found the country's education system difficult? B
3. has changed in a positive way? L
4. found part of the year difficult because of the light? L
5. likes the variety of cultures? B
6. can do something better than they used to do? B

3 Find words in the brochure that mean:

1. happy to try new things (Lucy) adventurous
2. from the nearby area (Ben) local
3. friendly and sociable (Ben) outgoing
4. a mix of good and bad experiences (Ben) ups and downs
5. missing your family (Ben) homesick

4 Read the sentences and write *T* (true), *F* (false) or *DS* (doesn't say).

1. In Finland, students never do exams. F
2. Students have long breaks in Finland. DS
3. Lucy has been ice-swimming more than once. T
4. Ben never wanted to leave the USA. F
5. Mexican students don't all finish school at the same time. T
6. Ben wants to go back home soon. F

Voice it!

5 Discuss the questions.

1. Can you think of a country you would like to go on an exchange to?
2. Why would you like to visit that country?
3. What do you think would be difficult about living there?

Finished? p119 Ex 1

24 CHANGES | UNIT 2

Extend it!

In small groups, students discuss the question of what exchange students coming to live in their country would learn from the experience.

Class challenge

The country of Finland has a population of 5.5 million, and 5.5 million / **8.8 million** / 10 million people live in the capital city of Mexico.

Finished?

Fast finishers can turn to SB p119 and do Exercise 1.

Flipped class

▶ Ask students to watch **Video 2.2** and do the **Video worksheet** in the *Teacher's Resource Bank*.

Homework

Workbook p17

Lesson aim: I can understand how to use *used to*, *would* and past simple.

Warmer

▶ Play **Video 2.2** if it wasn't set for homework. Elicit that the grandmother used to write on a typewriter. Outdoors, she used to ride her bike and play.

1 Elicit that the example sentences show different ways of talking about situations and actions in the past.

Pronunciation

Students can do the activities on p141, practising the pronunciation of *used to*.

2 Point out that if we say *I used to/would go swimming every Sunday* it means that we don't do it any more.

3 Students can do this task individually before comparing answers with a partner.

Get it right!

Point out that we use *used to* for past situations. For example, we say *I used to be good at chess* not ~~*I would be good at chess*~~.

4 ★ Tell students to first decide if a sentence is about an action or situation, then to make their choice of *would* or *used to* (or both).

5 ★ Tell students to decide if the sentence needs a positive or a negative verb, then to think about whether it describes an action, a habit or something that wasn't a habit.

Ask and answer questions about Mary's life

6 & 7 Monitor throughout, checking that students are pronouncing *used/use to*.

LANGUAGE IN ACTION

used to, *would* and past simple

Watch video 2.2 What did her grandmother use to write on? What did she use to do outdoors?

used to / would	Past simple
I [1] used to dream about living in a different country.	I **went** on a reindeer safari.
I **didn't** [2] use **to** be adventurous.	I **didn't speak** much Spanish.
Did Lucy [3] use **to** be adventurous?	**Did** Ben **learn** a lot of Spanish?
My classmates [4] would always help me.	

Pronunciation p141

1 **Complete the examples in the table above with one word in each gap. Use the brochure on page 24 to help you.**

2 **Complete the rules with *used to/would* or the past simple.**

1. We use *used to/would* to talk about situations that continued and actions that happened more than once in the past.
2. We use *the past simple* to talk about things that happened only once.

3 **Complete the text with *used to* and the verbs in brackets.**

My grandfather's childhood was different to mine. When he was a boy, he never [1] *used to have* (have) many toys, but he [2] *used to have* (have) a lot of time. He [3] *used to love* (love) playing outside. Sometimes, his friends [4] *used to play* (play) outside all day – they [5] *used to go* (go) out early and then they [6] *used to come* (come) home late at night. I think it [7] *used to be* (be) safer for children then.

Get it right!

We don't use ***would*** with past situations, only repeated actions.

*We **used to** live in Murcia.*

NOT ~~*We would live in Murcia.*~~

*We **used to / would** play tennis at school.*

4 **Circle the correct words. Sometimes both are possible.**

1. More people *would* / *(used to)* live in the countryside than in cities. Now it's the opposite.
2. In the past, TV channels *(would)* / *(used to)* stop at night.
3. Some people *(didn't use to)* / *(wouldn't)* smile in photos because their teeth were bad.
4. Many people *would* / *(used to)* think that the Earth was flat.

5 **Complete the sentences with *used to*, *didn't use to* or the past simple and the verbs in brackets.**

1. For his birthday, Aidan *got* (get) a new bike. He loved it.
2. Ada *didn't use to like* (like) apples much, but now she does.
3. I *ended up* (end up) in the wrong place yesterday because I didn't have a map.
4. When Bill was younger, he *turned down / used to turn down* (turn down) invitations all the time because he was so shy.

Use it!

6 **Write questions for a partner about their parents' lives with *used to* or the past simple.**

1. what toys / play with *What toys did your parents use to play with?*
2. study English / at school *Did they use to study English at school?*
3. how / meet *How did they meet?*

7 **Ask and answer the questions.**

What toys did your parents use to play with?

I think they used to play with wooden toys, and they would often play outside.

Finished? p119 Ex 2

Grammar game

Students write five sentences about what they used to do when they were younger, but don't do any more. Two should be false. Their partner must decide which are true and which false, winning a point for each correct guess.

Finished?

Fast finishers can turn to SB p119 and do Exercise 2.

Homework

Workbook p18

1 Talk about the objects with the class as a whole. Do any students have any of the objects at home?

Target vocabulary
button /ˈbʌtən/
cable /ˈkeɪbəl/
cover /ˈkʌvə/
display /dɪˈspleɪ/
handle /ˈhændəl/
key /kiː/
lens /lenz/
lid /lɪd/
plug /plʌg/
strap /stræp/

2 2.08 When playing the recording, pause after each word to drill the pronunciation.

Audioscript p161

3 2.09 Encourage students to explain their choice in each case, e.g. 'strap' is correct in number 1 because backpacks are carried using straps not cables.

Audioscript p162

Find the matching pairs

4 Encourage students to ask follow-up questions so they can develop conversations about the objects.

Vocabulary Bank SB p129

5 2.10 Before you play the recording, elicit the sort of thing that people might say about each of the objects in Exercise 1.

Audioscript p162

VOCABULARY AND LISTENING

Parts of objects

1 **Look at the photos. Which objects do you recognise?**

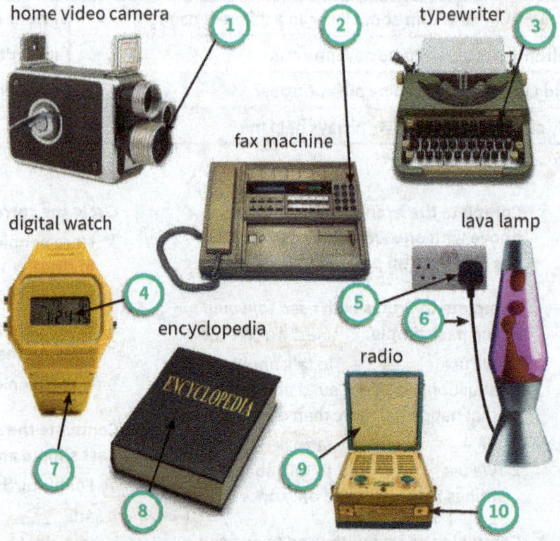

2 2.08 **Match the words in the box with parts of the objects 1–10. Listen, check and repeat.**

button 2	cable 6	cover 8	display 4	handle 10
key 3	lens 1	lid 9	plug 5	strap 7

3 2.09 **Circle the correct words. Listen and check.**

1 When you carry a backpack, do you use one *strap* / *cable* or both? Why?
2 Do you always put the *handle* / *lid* back on the toothpaste after using it?
3 How often do you clean the *key* / *lens* of the camera on your phone?
4 Without looking, can you remember what is on the *cover* / *display* of this book?
5 Can you name six objects that have an on/off *plug* / *button*?
6 Do you take your phone charger *cable* / *display* with you when you go out?

Use it!

4 **Ask and answer the questions in Exercise 3. Are your answers similar or different?**

A quiz show

5 2.10 **Listen to a quiz show about retro objects. Which three objects in Exercise 1 are mentioned?**

a digital watch, a fax machine, a lava lamp

LEARN TO LEARN

Identifying key words

Identifying key words before you listen can help you understand what you hear.

6 **Read the questions and the options and underline the key words.**

1 Joey pushes the buzzer too early because he …
 a can't wait to play.
 b doesn't understand the rules.
2 Nicola guesses the first object correctly because she …
 a has seen one before.
 b has heard of it before.
3 People had fax machines …
 a in their houses.
 b in their workplaces.
4 People used lava lamps …
 a instead of lightbulbs.
 b because they were attractive.

7 2.10 **Listen again and answer the questions in Exercise 6.**

Voice it!

8 **Discuss the questions.**

1 Do you know any retro objects that have come back into fashion?
2 What do you think of them?

Learn to learn

Students should take practical steps to help themselves with listening tasks. One such step is identifying key words, which will help them decide what information they need to listen out for, and make it clearer what their purpose is when listening.

6 Before students do this task, point out that key words are usually verbs, nouns, adjectives and adverbs.

7 2.10 Before you play the recording, remind students to focus on the key words they underlined in Exercise 6.

8 ★ Brainstorm answers to question 1 (e.g. vinyl records, record players, Polaroid cameras, digital watches) with the whole class. Students can then do question 2 in pairs.

Flipped class

▶ Ask students to watch **Video 2.3** and do the **Video worksheet** in the *Teacher's Resource Bank*.

Homework

Workbook p19

Lesson aim: I can use the past perfect with *never*, *already*, *by (then)*, *by the time*.

Warmer

▶ Play **Video 2.3**. Elicit that the girl went on a school trip to a university and that 3-D printers were first developed in the 1980s.

1 Write *the past perfect* on the board. Elicit the form (*had* + past particle) and the use (for giving information about actions or situations before those described by the past simple).

2 & 3 Once students have completed both tasks, check their understanding of the past perfect by writing *Before I ..., I had never ...* on the board and eliciting ways to complete it: e.g. *Before I went to secondary school, I had never learnt French.*

Extra grammar practice

4 2.11 Tell students to read the gapped text quickly. Then ask: *What had the writer learnt before she went to Russia?* (the Russian alphabet). Students should then read the text more slowly to decide on the correct form for each verb, using the irregular verb list on p143 to help them.

Audioscript p163

5 Before students ask and answer the questions, check that they have formed the four questions correctly.

LANGUAGE IN ACTION

Past perfect with *never*, *already*, *by (then)*, *by the time*

Watch video 2.3
Where did she go last week?
When were 3-D printers first developed?

This was before anyone **had** [1] ever **heard** of printers.
I'**d heard** of fax machines before, but I'**d** [2] never **seen** one.
They'**d** [3] already **gone** out of fashion **by the time** you were born.
I **hadn't started** yet.
Had you [4] ever **seen** a digital watch before then?

1 **Complete the examples in the table above with *already*, *ever* or *never*.**

2 **Circle the correct words to complete the rules.**

1 *Already*, *never* and *ever* come (before) / after the main verb.
2 *By the time* means (before) / after something happened.

3 **Answer the questions with the past perfect.**

1 How did you know what would happen in the film? (already / read / the book)
Because I had already read the book.
2 Why did you get lost? (never / be / there before)
Because I'd never been there before.
3 Did you get a ticket for the concert? No, (by the time / I went online / they / sell out)
by the time I went online they had sold out.
4 How was the party? (already / finish / when we got there)
It had already finished when we got there.

4 2.11 **Complete the text with the past simple or the past perfect. Listen and check.**

Last year I [1] *went* (go) on an exchange to Moscow. I [2] had never travelled (never / travel) alone before, so I [3] felt (feel) nervous at first. Before I [4] went (go), I [5] 'd already learned (already / learn) to read the Russian alphabet, although I [6] hadn't practised (not practise) speaking Russian. By the time I [7] left (leave), I [8] had improved (improve) a lot. Everybody in Moscow [9] was (be) really kind and friendly, but it [10] wasn't (not be) easy to deal with the cold weather. I [11] hadn't packed (not pack) enough warm clothes, so I had to buy some after I [12] arrived (arrive). Anyway, I can't wait to go back. I [13] hadn't expected (not expect) to enjoy it much before I actually [14] got (get) there, but in the end I really [15] did (do)!

Use it!

5 **Ask and answer the questions about the topics below. Use the past perfect.**

1 hear of / connected clothing?
2 see / a picture of 3-D printed clothes?
3 hear of / ice-swimming?
4 see / a picture of the Northern Lights?

Before you started using this book, had you ever heard of connected clothing?

No, I'd never heard of it, but now I want to know more! / Yes, I had. I'd already read about it online.

Finished? p119 Ex 3

Extend it!

Students retell the story in Exercise 4 in the third person. For example, *Last year she went on an exchange trip. She'd never travelled alone before ... .*

Grammar game

In pairs, students take it in turns to talk about things which went wrong for them in the past, e.g. *I got to the station, but I couldn't catch the train.* The partner guesses the reason, e.g. *Had you forgotten your ticket?* If they are correct they win a point.

Finished?

Fast finishers can turn to SB p119 and do Exercise 3.

Homework

Workbook p20

Warmer

Tell students to imagine that you've never used a smartphone. Ask them to explain how to use one.

1 🎧 2.12 Read out the question, then ask students to answer it before you play the recording for them to check their answers.

Audioscript p163

2 🎧 2.12 ★★★ Ask students to cover the *Useful language* box. Students then listen to the recording, and fill in the conversation with the phrases they hear. In pairs, students can act out the conversation from Exercise 1.

Useful language practice

▶ Play **Video 2.4**. Encourage students to copy the intonation used by the presenter.

3 ★★★ Challenge students to think of further contexts for the phrases in the *Everyday English* box. Elicit their ideas, check they are right, then write those ideas on the board.

4 ★ To help students, brainstorm ideas with the whole class about how to use the objects on p26.

5 Ask students to practise their explanations until they feel comfortable enough to not rely on their notes.

6 Encourage each pair to give feedback to the other. Was the explanation clear enough? In what ways could it be improved?

SPEAKING
Explaining how to use something

🎧 2.12 **1 Listen to the conversation. Which of the things in the box does the typewriter have?**

cable display ink keys plug speaker

YUSUF	What's that? [1] Is it some kind of computer?
MERI	No, it's my grandad's old typewriter.
YUSUF	Where's the display?
MERI	There isn't one, and there's no plug or cable.
YUSUF	That's so old-school! How did it work?
MERI	The paper would move as you typed. [2] What you do is, you press the keys hard, but not too fast or they get stuck. Try it out!
YUSUF	[3] Like this you mean?
MERI	That's it. Just imagine – people used to type books on these things!
YUSUF	No way! I can't even find the letters I want.
MERI	You need to sign up for typing classes! They're in the same place as an ordinary keyboard.
YUSUF	Oh no! [4] I've messed it up. How do I go back? There's no 'delete' key.
MERI	[5] You'll have to start all over again.
YUSUF	No, thanks! Anyway, how come your grandad had this?
MERI	He used to need it for work, but after a while he ended up buying a computer.
YUSUF	I'm not surprised! I'm glad they'd invented computers by the time I started school! I'd hate to do my homework on this!

🎧 2.12 **2 Complete the conversation with the phrases from the *Useful language* box. Listen and check.**

Useful language

Is it some kind of ...? I've messed it up.
Like this, you mean? What you do is, you ...
You'll have to ...

Watch video 2.4
Everyday English

all over again
I'm not surprised.
old-school That's it.

3 Complete the sentences with the phrases in the *Everyday English* box.

1 Barry's not here yet. I'm not surprised – he's always late.
2 A Do I press this button here?
B That's it.
3 Your new jacket's so old-school. My dad used to have one like that.
4 Oh no! I've lost my homework! I'll have to do it all over again.

PLAN

4 Choose one of the objects on page 26. Make notes on how to use it.

SPEAK

5 Practise the explanation with your partner. Remember to use past tenses, vocabulary from this unit and phrases from the *Useful language* and *Everyday English* boxes.

CHECK

6 Work with another pair. Listen to their explanation and complete the notes.

How does the object work? ______

Do you understand how to use it? ______

28 CHANGES | UNIT 2

Extend it!

In pairs, one student explains how to use an object (this could be any household object, e.g. a TV, a kettle, a microwave), while the other tries to guess the object being described. Students then swap roles.

Flipped class

Prepare for the **Writing** lesson (p29). Students think about how life has changed for teenagers in the last 30 years.

1 With the class as a whole, discuss the question of whether life for teenagers has changed for the better or worse. Guide students to the idea of being stressed and the causes of stress in a typical teenager's life.

2 ★★★ Read out the title of the essay, then set a two-minute time limit for this task.

Highlight *used to*, past simple and past perfect in the opinion essay

3 Point out that an essay should include 'signposting' language such as this to help the reader understand the writer's thoughts.

4 Once students have completed the text, either discuss the ideas in it with the class as a whole or ask students to discuss the ideas in pairs.

5 ★ Brainstorm ideas in response to the statement. Write these ideas on the board, dividing them into two categories: those which agree with the statement and those which disagree.

6 Remind students to use four paragraphs, organised in the following way: 1 introduction, saying whether you agree or disagree; 2 reason 1; 3 reason 2; 4 summary of your opinion. Give students up to 15 minutes to write their essays. Monitor and help as necessary.

7 ★★★ After checking their work, students can then respond to their partner's essay, saying whether they agree or disagree with the points made in it, and why.

WRITING
An opinion essay

1 In what ways has life changed for teenagers in the last 30 years?

2 Read the essay. Does it mention any of your ideas in Exercise 1?

Are teenagers today more or less stressed than previous generations?

The world has changed a great deal in the last few decades, especially for teenagers, and not always in a positive way. In particular, people of my generation are a lot more stressed than teenagers in the past.

Firstly, we are under enormous pressure to do well in exams. This means that we spend a lot of time studying. Young people didn't use to study as much because it wasn't always necessary to go to university. Therefore, they had more time to relax and hang out with friends.

Secondly, previous generations didn't have online profiles to worry about. In fact, young people 20 or 30 years ago hadn't even heard of 'followers' and 'likes' because social media hadn't been invented yet. For people of my age, it is almost impossible to do without social media. In addition, it can become extremely addictive.

In conclusion, I would say that teenagers today have more stressful lives than our parents did.

3 Complete the table with the linkers from the *Useful language* box. Look at the linkers in the essay to help you.

Order of ideas	Connection between ideas
firstly in conclusion secondly	in addition therefore this means that

Useful language

firstly in addition in conclusion secondly therefore this means that

4 Complete the essay with the linkers from the *Useful language* box. Do you agree with the writer? Sometimes there is more than one possible answer.

Some people think that online games are worse for you than traditional games, because they are addictive and don't involve physical exercise, but is this always true?

In my opinion, online games have many good points. [1] Firstly, they improve your memory and your problem-solving skills. [2] Secondly you can make friends. [3] In addition, you play with people from around the world. [4] Therefore, you often have to communicate in English and [5] this means that your English improves. However, it's important to spend time with your friends offline. [6] In conclusion, online games can be unhealthy, but only if you spend all your time playing them.

Write an opinion essay.

PLAN

5 Look at the statement and make notes.

> Teenagers today have more freedom than in the past.

Do you agree or disagree with the statement?
Write two reasons for your opinion.
Give a summary of your opinion.

WRITE

6 Write your opinion essay. Remember to include, *used to*, the past simple and past perfect and phrases from the *Useful language* box.

CHECK

7 Do you …
- give your opinion?
- give reasons for your opinion?
- summarise your opinion?

Finished? p119 Ex 4

UNIT 2 | CHANGES 29

Extend it!
Discuss the following question with the class as a whole: *Social media is a waste of time.*

Finished?
Fast finishers can turn to SB p119 and do Exercise 4.

Homework
Workbook p21

Lesson aim: I can understand a text about retro fashion, technology and music.

Warmer

Ask students the following questions, and encourage a class debate: *Why is history important? What can the past tell us about the present? Why do fashions change from one period of history to another?*

Project Book

For more information and activities, see the Project Book, p26.

1 Focus students' attention on the photos. Brainstorm words and phrases to describe them (writing these on the board). Then, in small groups, students discuss which period of history the photos show. Make sure students don't read the text at this point.

2 2.13 ★ Check students' understanding of *exhibit* (an item in an *exhibition)* and *label* (a description of an exhibit). Before students read, you may also want to explain these phrases from the texts: *come back into fashion, teenage identity.*

3 Either complete this table as an activity with the whole class, or ask students to work in pairs to complete it.

Class challenge

The first time people could buy personal computers to use at home was in 1946 / **1971** / 1995.

THE HISTORY PROJECT

1 FASHION

Fashion is always changing, and old styles often come back into fashion, although few people look forward to seeing 1970s fashion again. If you watch TV shows from that decade, you will see that people used to wear trousers that were tight at the top and wide at the bottom, flowery dresses, a lot of tight cotton T-shirts or shirts with big collars, and plenty of big round glasses. During the early 1970s, bright colours were extremely trendy, but by the end of the decade they had almost completely disappeared. Black, white, grey and brown had replaced them, although people still wore enormous glasses.

2 TECHNOLOGY

It is hard to imagine dealing with the ups and downs of modern life without computers and smartphones. However, in the 70s there were very few computers, and the ones that existed were a lot bigger than those we have today. They were far slower, with simple displays and enormous buttons. Compared to the devices we use today, they also had very little memory. In fact, the computers on the Apollo spaceships that took men to the moon had less memory than some modern toasters. By the beginning of the 1970s, some companies had started to use computers in their offices, but it was extremely rare to see a computer in a house. In fact, most people had never used one, and some people had never seen one.

A retro museum exhibition

1 Look at the photos. What period in history do you think they are from?

2 Read the exhibit labels. Which one do you find most interesting? Why?

3 Complete the table about exhibits 2 and 3.

	1	2	3
Area	fashion	technology	music
Period	1970s	1970s	1970s / 1990s / now
Examples	trousers (tight at top, baggy at bottom), flowery dresses, big glasses, bright colours	computers were slower, had less memory than modern toasters, companies started to use computers	people used to go to shops to buy music, record covers were important, many were famous
Changes over time	black, white, grey, brown became more popular	computers have become smaller, faster and have more memory	CDs became more popular than records in 1990s, records have come back into fashion

4 Read out the four steps. Then put students into small groups and give them ten minutes to choose their period, areas to focus on, and who in their group is going to research and write about which exhibit. When students have finished this, decide with the students how long they will have to complete the project. It is then for the students to decide how long to spend on each of the four stages in the *How to* schedule section.

How to schedule

At this level, students should be learning how to carry out a number of tasks within a given period of time. This involves identifying the most important tasks, estimating the time required to complete each task, and matching different people with different tasks.

5 ★ Before students present their exhibits, encourage them to check their work one final time. Have they included the right information and is everything clear and easy to follow? Help each group by asking them to do a bit of their presentation in front of you. Offer any tips you think will help each group improve its presentation.

6 Encourage students to make note of interesting things in their classmates' presentations. Discuss with the class as a whole, what students learn from the different presentations.

7 Encourage students to give each other feedback. Are the examples clear and easy to understand? Could they be improved in any way? Is their language clear?

OWN IT!

3 MUSIC

Music has always been an important part of teenage identity, but in an age of streaming and downloading it's easy to forget that it hasn't always been as available as it is today. In the 1970s young music fans would spend hours in record shops looking for new music to buy. It wasn't only the music that was popular. The record covers were also important, and many of them became famous for their artwork. By the middle of the 1990s, CDs had become more popular than records. Nevertheless, people continued to collect records and DJs still used to play them at discos. Recently, they have come back into fashion, as many people prefer the sound of a record to the sound of a digital file.

How to schedule

4 **Ask your teacher how long you have to complete the project. Then decide together how long to spend on each of these stages:**

1 looking for information and photos
2 writing draft texts for the labels
3 checking and correcting the drafts
4 writing the final labels and putting them on a poster with the photos.

PLAN

5 **Work in groups. Complete the steps below.**

- Decide which period in history you want to concentrate on (for example, the 19th century, the 1980s).
- Choose three areas you want to focus on.

entertainment	fashion	food and drink
house and home	school life	
technology/communication	toys and games	

- Decide who is going to research and write about which exhibit.

PRESENT

6 **Present your history exhibition on the wall of your classroom. Remember to include a title for each label, vocabulary from this unit, *used to*, the past simple and past perfect and the tips in *How to* schedule.**

CHECK

7 **Read the other groups' history exhibitions. What areas are they focusing on? Which group's exhibition is most interesting?**

UNIT 2 | CHANGES 31

Students can collaborate digitally online and offline in the collaboration space, where teachers can set, track and assess students' work. Students can also share and showcase their work as well as comment on each other's projects.

For more work on History, students can turn to SB p137. See p153 for teaching notes.

Extend it!

Students think about which period of history they would like to go back to and why. They can discuss this in pairs or in small groups.

Flipped class

Prepare for the **Review** lesson (p32). Students revise the grammar and vocabulary from Unit 2.

Lesson aim: I can review what I have learnt and reflect on my progress.

The aim of this review page is for students to revise the grammar and vocabulary from the unit. You can either do it in class, as a timed progress test or set it for homework.

Vocabulary

1 Elicit the phrasal verbs from p23. Write them on the board, then put students into small groups. The first group to complete the six gaps with the correct phrasal verbs wins.

2 ★★★ Extend the challenge by asking students to define each of the words they didn't circle in the exercise.

Language in action

3 Before students complete the text, elicit example sentences with *would* and *used to*. Students can look back at p25 to remind themselves.

4 Encourage students to use the irregular verb list on p143 to help them with this task. Students can compare answers in pairs, and discuss any differences before checking answers as a class.

Unit quiz review

Self-assessment

After choosing the appropriate options, encourage students to ask you for extra homework on the language they had the most problems with. You can then assign them additional exercises to do from the Workbook.

2 REVIEW

VOCABULARY

1 Complete the conversation with the correct form of a phrasal verb.

A How was your bike trip? Where did you go?

B Well, we wanted to [1] try out a new route. We were planning to cycle to this old village near the sea, but we got lost and [2] ended up on a farm!

A Didn't you have a map with you?

B No, but the farmer helped us, so it [3] turned out OK in the end. We found the village!

A Was it nice there?

B Beautiful. I'd love to go back one day. How was your weekend?

A Not great. I was sick. My friends wanted me to go a concert. I'd said yes, and I [5] was looking forward to it, but in the end I had to [6] turn down them.

2 Circle the correct words.

Did you know ...?

- The [1] (lids) / covers of plastic water bottles are made from a different plastic to the bottle.
- If you change the [2] lens / (display) on your phone to black and white, it can become less addictive.
- On old trains, you couldn't open the doors with a [3] (button) / plug. You had to use a [4] strap / (handle), like a normal door.
- Every second, 600,000 people around the world press the space [5] cable / (key) when they're on a computer.

LANGUAGE IN ACTION

3 Complete the text with *used to*, *would* or the past simple and the verb in brackets. Sometimes there is more than one possible answer.

My dad's a writer now, although he [1] didn't use to be (not be). He [2] used to be (be) a diplomat, so when I was small, my family [3] used to / would move (move) countries all the time. Once, we [4] lived (live) in three different countries in two years! I remember when I [5] moved (move) to the school where I am now, in Rio de Janeiro. I [6] didn't know (not know) any Portuguese at first, so the first week [7] was (be) difficult. I used to take my lunch to the playground and then I [8] used to / would eat (eat) it alone. However, Brazilian people are really friendly, so after a few days my classmates [9] started (start) to invite me to eat with them and I quickly [10] made (make) lots of friends. We've been living here for many years now, and I'm really happy.

4 Complete Ben's message to Tom with the past perfect.

Tom, I'm so sorry I missed the wedding! I decided to take the car to the airport, but because I [1] 'd never driven (never / drive) there before, I got lost. Just the night before, I [2] 'd thought (think), 'I must fix the GPS!', but then I completely forgot! Anyway, I got to the airport around two o'clock. The plane [3] hadn't taken off (not taken off), but by the time I finished checking in, the gate [4] had closed (close). I tried to buy a ticket for the next flight, but they [5] 'd already sold out (already / sell out)!

Self-assessment

I can use phrasal verbs to talk about changes.

I can use words to talk about parts of objects.

I can use *used to*, *would* and the past simple.

I can use the past perfect with *never*, *already*, *by (then)*, *by the time*.

32 CHANGES | UNIT 2

Homework

Workbook pp22–23

Lesson aim: I can learn to help my partner improve their writing.

Point out that we regularly ask other people to take a look at something we have done to see if they can think of ways of improving it. It's good training for students to spot areas for improvement in other people's work.

Warmer

On the board, write *What makes a good piece of writing?* Elicit students' ideas, e.g. imaginative use of vocabulary, correct grammar, a clear structure.

1 Read out the information about the writing task. Give students a few minutes to read and correct Edison's writing. In pairs, students compare their answers.

2 ★★★ Extend the task by discussing ways to improve Edison's writing, e.g. *Could the opening and closing sentences be more interesting? Should he have used paragraphs?* For example, use more interesting adjectives, make the writing more personal, begin with a memorable opening sentence. Also encourage students to check each piece of writing they produce, looking for ways to improve their use of grammar, vocabulary and structure.

OWN IT!

3 Give students time to think about the toy or game they would like to write about. Set a 15-minute time limit for the writing task. Monitor and help as necessary.

4 & 5 Make sure you give students enough time to check and discuss each other's work. Encourage students to both explain their reasons for liking or disliking something and offer practical ways to improve their written work.

LEARN TO LEARN

LEARN TO ... HELP YOUR PARTNER IMPROVE THEIR WRITING

When you write something, ask your partner to check it. You can improve your writing this way.

1 Read the instructions for the writing task. Correct Edison's mistakes to help him improve.

WRITING TASK

Write about a favourite toy or game from your childhood.

- Write between 100 and 130 words.
- Use language from this unit.

Don't forget to use punctuation and check your spelling!

When I was little, I [1]~~use~~ used to play with Lego® bricks all the time. I would [2]building build all kinds of things – cars, [3]airplaynes airplanes houses. I even built a computer with keys and a display. After I finished one thing, I would keep it and then try out something else, but I once [4]used to build built a ship that I kept for weeks. [5]I've I'd never built anything like it before. However, I remember my mum [6]would be was really angry with me one day because I played with it in the bathroom and ended up damaging the sides of the bath. I've still got a photo of it somewhere [7] .

Number of words: 107

2 Answer the questions in the checklist. Has Edison completed the task in Exercise 1?

Checklist

	Edison's writing	W
Has he/she ...		
1 written about the topic?	(Yes) / No	Yes / No
2 written between 100 and 130 words?	(Yes) / No	Yes / No
3 used phrasal verbs for changes and words for parts of objects?	(Yes) / No	Yes / No
4 added details to make it interesting?	(Yes) / No	Yes / No
How well has he/she used ...		
5 the past simple?	☹ 😐 ☺	☹ 😐 ☺
6 *used to* and *would*?	☹ 😐 ☺	☹ 😐 ☺
7 the past perfect?	☹ 😐 ☺	☹ 😐 ☺
8 punctuation?	☹ 😐 ☺	☹ 😐 ☺
9 correct spelling?	☹ 😐 ☺	☹ 😐 ☺
Other comments?	*I enjoyed the part about your mum being angry!*	

OWN IT!

3 Do the writing task in Exercise 1.

4 Answer the questions in the checklist for your partner's writing.

5 Tell your partner what you like and what they can improve.

Flipped class

Prepare for **Unit 2**. Students research how food has changed in the last 100 years.

 Lesson aim: I can talk about the future of food.

Warmer

Explain that *food for thought* is a common idiom in English and that it is used to describe something that is worth serious consideration.

▶ Start it!

Unit quiz

1. Elicit answers to the questions. Write key vocabulary on the board, e.g. *spaghetti, pasta, multi-coloured food, food colouring.*
2. Ask students to share the information about how food has changed that they researched for homework.
3. ▶ Elicit students' ideas, then play **Video 3.1** and allow students to check their answers. Students can also complete the Start it! **Video worksheet** in the *Teacher's Resource Bank.*
4. Brainstorm ideas with the class. Write them on the board.

Video comprehension questions

Flipped class

Prepare for **Explore it!** (p35). Students find out some facts about traditional food from their country or another.

3 FOOD FOR THOUGHT

LEARNING OUTCOMES

I can ...

- understand texts from an online forum and a cooking show
- give cooking instructions
- write a listicle
- understand how to use different future forms
- talk about cooking and quantities
- make adjectives from verbs, use diagrams, and understand words from context by using the rest of the text.

Start it!

1. Look at the photo. Would you like to eat this food? Why? / Why not?
2. Before you watch, how do you think food has changed in the last 100 years?
3. What two foods will we eat more of in the future? Watch and check. — algae oil and seaweed
4. Are there other ways that our eating habits may change in the future?

Watch video 3.1 | Language in action 3.2 p37 | Language in action 3.3 p39 | Everyday English 3.4 p40 | Globetrotters 3.5 p42

34 FOOD FOR THOUGHT | UNIT 3

Unit aims

Skills

I can ...

- read an online forum p36
- give instructions p40
- write a listicle p41
- understand a text about food in Australia p42

Language

I can ...

- talk about cooking p35
- understand how to use future tenses p37
- talk about quantities p38
- understand how to use the future continuous and future perfect p39

Learn to Learn

I can ...

- form adjectives from verbs p35
- use diagrams p38
- understand words from context p43
- learn to set and achieve learning goals p45

Extra Resources

- *Finished?* – Student's Book p120
- *Vocabulary Bank* – Student's Book p130
- Pronunciation – Student's Book p141
- Workbook p24
- *Teacher's Resource Bank* on *Cambridge One* for tests package, Cambridge Exam practice, wordlists, differentiated worksheets and many other extra resources.
- *Practice Extra* and *Digital collaboration space*

Warmer

Elicit the food that students like to eat, then ask: *Do you ever cook for your family? What dishes do you make?*

1 3.01 Ask students, in pairs, to take turns saying a word and writing it down, to spelling.

Audioscript p163

Target vocabulary

bake /beɪk/
chop /tʃɒp/
fry /fraɪ/
grate /greɪt/
grill /grɪl/
heat /hiːt/
overcook /əʊvəˈkʊk/
peel /piːl/
roast /rəʊst/
season /ˈsiːzən/
slice /slaɪs/
spread /spred/

Extra vocabulary practice

2 3.02 Encourage students to give a reason for their choices.

Audioscript p163

3 ★★★ Ask students to name food that links to the verbs not chosen (*spread*, e.g. *butter*).

4 When checking answers, drill the pronunciation of the adjectives.

5 ★★★ Challenge students to think of verbs without looking back at Exercises 1 or 4.

Learn to learn

Explain that *-ed* is a suffix which can be used to form adjectives. Ask students to use this suffix to form adjectives from the verbs *cook* and *boil*. Point out how adjectives such as these are usually used in a sentence, e.g. *I like grilled chicken* rather than *I like chicken that is grilled*.

VOCABULARY

Cooking verbs

1 3.01 **Match the verbs in the box with photos 1–12. Listen, check and repeat.**

bake	1	chop	2	fry	3
grate	4	grill	5	heat	12
overcook	6	peel	11	roast	7
season	8	slice	9	spread	10

2 3.02 **Circle the correct verbs to complete the instructions to make a homemade pizza. Listen and check.**

[1]*Spread* / *Peel* the tomatoes and [2]*chop* / *overcook* them. Then [3]*bake* / *heat* them in a pan and [4]*slice* / *season* with salt and pepper. [5]*Grill* / *Roast* some bread. Then [6]*fry* / *spread* the tomatoes on the bread and [7]*grate* / *season* some cheese on top. [8]*Fry* / *Bake* in the oven, but only for a few minutes – you don't want to [9]*overcook* / *slice* it!

3 **Circle the verb which does not go with each food.**

1 pepper: chop fry spread
2 bread: bake roast slice
3 chicken: heat overcook grate
4 fish: peel grill season

LEARN TO LEARN

Wordbuilding: adjectives from verbs

Learn the adjective form of new verbs. Sometimes the form is similar, for example *bake* (v) *baked* (adj).

4 **Write the adjective form of the verbs in Exercise 1.**

bake	baked	overcook	overcooked
chop	chopped	peel	peeled
fry	fried	roast	roast(ed)
grate	grated	season	seasoned
grill	grilled	slice	sliced
heat	heated	spread	spread

5 **Which verbs in Exercise 1 usually go with the foods in the box?**

apple bread cheese chicken chocolate
egg jam meat tomato pepper

Grate ... You can have grated apple, cheese, chocolate, egg, tomato and pepper.

Use it!

6 **Discuss the questions.**

1 Do you usually eat grilled, fried, baked or roast foods? Which are your favourites?
2 What can you cook?
3 Is it important to know how to cook? Why?

Explore it!

Guess the correct answer.

During the Chinese mid-autumn festival, people traditionally bake mooncakes. Which ingredient is baked inside them to symbolise the moon?

a chicken egg b ostrich egg c duck egg

Find another fact about a traditional food. Write a question for your partner.

Pronunciation p141

UNIT 3 | FOOD FOR THOUGHT 35

Complete the sentences

6 Encourage students to ask follow-up questions to develop their conversations.

Vocabulary Bank SB p130

Explore it!

Students use the facts they researched about food.

Pronunciation

Students do the activities on p141 to practise pronouncing the letters *ch*.

Flipped class

Prepare for the **Reading** lesson (p35). Students research the sort of food that we might eat in the future.

Homework

Workbook p24

Lesson aim: I can understand a text about future food.

Warmer

Ask: *What's the most unusual food you have ever eaten? Did you enjoy it?*

1 ★ Students may not know the vocabulary to describe all of the pictures, so be prepared to explain that A shows tarantulas, B shows a hamburger made in a 3-D printer, C jellyfish and E food prepared in a laboratory.

2 3.05 Encourage students to scan the text to look for key words which help with the task, e.g. *jellyfish, tarantulas*. Set a time limit of one minute. When checking answers, ask students to read out the part of the text which gave them their answer.

3 ★★★ Before students re-read the forum, ask them to read the information in Exercise 3 carefully. Can they match any of the of the future food solutions with the reasons without looking again at the text?

4 ★★★ Challenge students to write their own sentences using this new vocabulary. Monitor and help as necessary.

Reading comprehension questions

5 Give students time to think about their answers, and make notes, before they discuss the questions in pairs. Turn question 2 into a debate with the whole class.

READING

An online forum

1 What types of food can you see in the photos? Which ones would you eat?

2 3.05 Read the forum and match comments 1–5 with photos A–E.

1 C 3 D 5 A
2 E 4 B

3 Read the forum again and match the future food solutions 1–5 with the reasons a–e.

Future food solution	Why it solves the problem
1 Jellyfish	a cheap and already eaten in many parts of the world
2 Lab food	b can make new food from old
3 Smart fridges	c better for the environment
4 3-D printers	d help us use the food we already have so we don't buy food we don't need
5 Insects	e a new food and we need to find more of these

4 Match the words in **bold** in the forum with the meanings.

1 another possibility alternative
2 the taste of something flavour
3 not real artificial
4 something special and good to eat delicacy
5 cooking instructions recipe

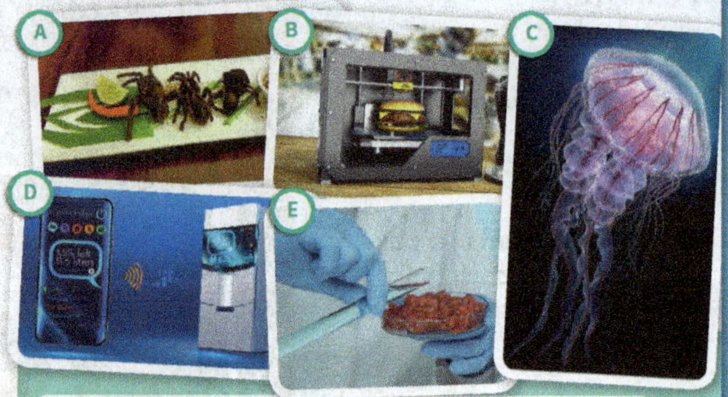

CLASS 4C STUDY ROOM

Read the article about future food and add your comments. Professor Jones is coming to Friday's class and we're going to discuss your ideas.

1 There isn't going to be enough food for everyone in the future because the population is growing, so we're going to need to be more adventurous and find new foods. I read that we could actually eat jellyfish, although many people won't like the idea. Jellyfish probably doesn't have much **flavour**, but if you season it and roast it, it might be quite tasty! *Abi*

2 We may eat **artificial** fish or meat grown in a laboratory in the future. I think the idea sounds disgusting, but scientists say it will be better for the planet. I'm definitely not going to eat lab burgers! *Ben*

3 We throw away far too much food, often because we buy more than we need. I read about these cool apps that will tell us what's in the fridge and suggest **recipes** with the food we already have so we don't waste so much. I think they'll be really popular. *Dana*

4 One thing I'm not sure about is 3-D printed food. The idea that a printer will produce our food is a bit strange. But people say we'll be able to print snacks from food we're going to throw away, so 3-D printers might help reduce food waste. *Marco*

5 Experts say that meat will be far more expensive in the future, so we're going to have to eat **alternative** types of food. Insects are cheaper than farm animals, so they may be a solution. Grilled grasshoppers are a popular snack in Mexico and fried tarantulas are a **delicacy** in Cambodia. In fact, lots of cultures eat bugs, so why can't we? *Emma*

Voice it!

5 Discuss the questions.

1 Which of the ideas in Exercise 3 are your most and least favourite. Why?
2 What other future food solutions can you think of?

Finished? p120 Ex1

36 FOOD FOR THOUGHT | UNIT 3

Extend it!

In small groups, students brainstorm food that's normal to eat and food which is not normal to eat. With the class as a whole, discuss the question of why certain things might seem strange to eat.

Flipped class

▶ Ask students to watch **Video 3.2** and do the **Video worksheet** in the *Teacher's Resource Bank*.

Finished?

Fast finishers can turn to SB p120 and do Exercise 1.

Homework

Workbook p25

Warmer

▶ Play **Video 3.2** if it was not set for homework. Elicit that the school is having a food festival and that he might go to the science-with-cooking workshop. Ask students to talk about their plans for tomorrow or next week, then elicit the language they used to talk about the future.

1 ★★★ Challenge students to complete the example sentences without checking p36.

Extra grammar practice

2 ★★★ Once students have completed the conversation, ask them to talk with a partner about the reason for their choice of verb in each case.

Get it right!

Explain that while these two forms can be interchangeable, we often prefer the present continuous when a future plan has become an arrangement, i.e. we know when and where something is to happen.

3 ★★★ Challenge students to complete the example sentences without looking back at the online forum.

4 Read out the information in the leaflet. Check understanding of the phrase *total darkness*, i.e. so dark that nothing can be seen. After students have completed the conversation, they can practise reading it in pairs.

5 Before students ask and answer the questions, check that they have formed the questions correctly.

LANGUAGE IN ACTION

Future tenses

Watch video 3.2
What's happening this Saturday?
Which workshop might he go to?

Present tenses and *be going to* for future plans and intentions
Friday's class **starts** at nine o'clock.
Professor Jones [1] **is** ______ **coming** to Friday's class.
We**'re** [2] **going to** discuss your ideas on Friday.

1 **Complete the examples in the table above. Use the online forum on page 36 to help you.**

2 **Circle the correct words to complete the conversation.**

A [1]*Do you* / *Are you going to* watch the final tonight?
B Yeah. Kate [2]*comes* / *is coming* to my house to watch it.
A What time [3]*does it start* / *is it starting*?
B 8 pm, but she [4]*comes* / *is going to come* at 7 pm.

Get it right!

We often use the present continuous or *be going to* to talk about the future.
John's cooking later. **OR** *John's going to cook later.*

Predictions with *be going to*, *will* and *may/might*
The population is growing, so we [1] ______ need to find new foods. (a future prediction based on evidence) **'re going to**
We [2] **may/might** eat artificial fish or meat. (a future prediction we are not sure about)
Experts say that meat [3] **will** ______ be far more expensive. (a prediction we are sure about)

3 **Complete the examples in the table above. Use the online forum on page 36 to help you.**

4 **Read the leaflet. Complete the dialogue with the present simple, present continuous, *be going to*, *will* or *may/might* form of the verbs in brackets.**

Come and have dinner in total darkness Tuesday to Saturday 8–10 pm. Use your other senses to taste the food. Try new, unknown foods and guess what you're eating.

LUCAS Hey Milena, [1] *are* you *coming* (come) to Abi's birthday tomorrow?
MILENA Where [2] **are** ______ you **going** ______ (go)?
LUCAS To 'Dining in the Dark'. We [3] **'re going to have** ______ (have) dinner in darkness!
MILENA That's strange. Abi [4] **might/may not like** (not like) it!
LUCAS I'm sure she [5] **'ll love** ______ (love) it! It [6] **'ll be** ______ (be) different to anything she's done before.
MILENA But you [7] **won't be able to** ______ (not be able to) see the food. You [8] **might/may eat** (eat) something you don't like.
LUCAS I know! We [9] **'re going to have to** ______ (have to) guess what we're eating!
MILENA What time [10] **does** ______ it **start** ______ (start)?
LUCAS At eight o'clock.
MILENA I'm not sure. I [11] **might come** ______ (come). I [12] **'ll tell** ______ (tell) you later.

Use it!

5 **Write the questions. Use future tenses. Ask and answer.**

1 What / you / do / tomorrow?
What are you going to do tomorrow?
2 How old / you / be / in 2050?
How old will you be in 2050?
3 What foods we / eat / in the future?
What foods might/will/are we going to eat in the future?
4 When / your next class / start?
When does your next class start?

What are you going to do tomorrow?

I'm not sure. I might go to the beach.

Finished? p120 Ex 2

Extend it!

Students discuss the idea of eating food in total darkness. Ask: *What do you think of the idea? Why?*

Grammar game

In pairs, students use *going to* to make predictions about their partner's plans for the weekend, summer holidays, and such like. For example, Student A says, *I think you're going to go to England this summer.* Student B says, *Yes, that's right. / No, that's wrong.*

Finished?

Fast finishers can turn to SB p120 and do Ex 2.

Homework

Workbook p26

Lesson aim: I can talk about quantities.

Warmer

Write *breakfast*, *lunch* and *dinner* on the board. In pairs, students talk about what they eat for those meals.

1 3.06 Before students choose the photo, ask them to look through the recipe and underline the 'quantity' phrases.

Audioscript p163

Target vocabulary

a chunk of /ə tʃʌŋk ɒv/
a cup of /ə kʌp ɒv/
a splash of / ə splæʃ ɒv/
a spoonful of / ə 'spuːnfʊl ɒv/
a handful of /ə 'hændfʊl ɒv/
a packet of /ə 'pækɪt ɒv/
a piece of /ə piːs ɒv/
a pinch of /ə pɪntʃ ɒv/
a slice of /ə slaɪs ɒv/
a sprinkle of /ə 'sprɪŋkl ɒv/

2 Before students complete the sentences, ask them to decide whether the gaps need a singular or plural noun.

Extra vocabulary practice

Learn to learn

Not all students will enjoy diagrams, but they can be useful, and introducing them gives students the chance to explore the many possible ways to record new words in an organised way.

3 Before students complete the diagram, check their understanding of the three categories.

4 Give students time to think about this before they describe food they like in pairs.

Vocabulary Bank SB p130

LISTENING AND VOCABULARY

Quantities

3.06 **1** Read the recipe and choose the correct photo 1–3. Listen and repeat.

1 

2 

3  ✓

How to make your own fruity cereal

Mix the following ingredients in a bowl:

- a cup of cereal, like oats
- some pieces of strawberry
- some slices of banana
- some chunks of pineapple
- a handful of blueberries
- a packet of nuts
- a pinch of cinnamon
- a sprinkle of brown sugar

Serve with a spoonful of yoghurt or a splash of milk.

Nutritious and delicious!

2 Complete the sentences with quantities in Exercise 1 in the singular or plural form.

1 I have two *slices* of toast for breakfast and ___ coffee with ___ milk.
2 If your throat hurts, have ___ honey.
3 Season the pasta sauce with ___ salt and pepper.
4 I'm going to have a ___ of crisps for lunch.
5 I love cookies with big ___ chocolate!
6 I make the best Greek salad. I put in ___ of olives, some ___ of feta cheese and ___ oregano on top.

Answers: a cup of, a splash of, a spoonful of, a pinch of, packet of, chunks of, a handful of, pieces of, a sprinkle of

LEARN TO LEARN

Using diagrams

Use diagrams to help remember new phrases.

Solids	Both	Liquids
piece, chunk, handful, packet, pinch, slice, sprinkle	cup, spoonful	splash

3 Add quantities in Exercise 1 to the diagram.

Use it!

4 Think of a food you like and tell your partner the ingredients.

A pancake … You need two cups of flour …

A recipe

3.07 **5** Listen to the cooking show and write the quantities.

Pear smoothie	Ant tacos
[1] a cup of orange juice	[6] half a cup of ant larvae
[2] pieces of chopped pear	[7] a cup of chopped tomatoes
[3] a large spoonful of cricket flour	[8] a handful of chopped chillies
[4] chunks of mango and pineapple	[9] a pinch of salt and pepper
[5] a splash of lime juice	[10] a sprinkle of chopped coriander

3.07 **6** Listen again and circle the correct answers.

1 Both of Anton's dishes … .
(a) contain insects b are spicy c are Mexican
2 By 2030 there will be … billion people in the world.
a 5.5 b 6.5 (c) 8.5
3 Cricket flour will add … to the smoothie.
a fruit flavour b vitamins (c) protein
4 Anton is going to … the ant larvae.
(a) fry b heat c roast

38 FOOD FOR THOUGHT | UNIT 3

5 3.07 Check understanding of *smoothie* and *tacos*, and give students time to look at the table, before playing the recording.

Audioscript p163

6 3.07 ★★★ Challenge students to complete as many of the sentences as you can before you play the recording.

Flipped class

▶ Ask students to watch **Video 3.3** and do the **Video worksheet** in the *Teacher's Resource Bank*.

Homework

Workbook p27

Lesson aim: I can use the future continuous and future perfect.

▶ Play **Video 3.3** if it was not set for homework. Elicit that robots will be making our food in the future. Chocolate chip cookies were invented by accident.

1 On the board, write the form and use of the future continuous (*will/won't be doing* – to refer to an action in progress at or around a time in the future) and future perfect (*will/won't have done* – to refer to an action finished by a particular time in the future.) Students can then complete the table.

2 Students can work alone to complete the sentences.

3 ★★★ After students have completed the sentences, ask them to discuss the prediction in item 1. Do they agree? Why/Why not?

4 3.08 Ask students which form thinks about a future time and looks back from that (future perfect); and which thinks about a situation in the future that lasts for a long period (future continuous). Students then work in pairs to complete the conversation, after which they can practise reading it.

Audioscript p164

Extra grammar practice

5 Give students a few minutes to write their sentences.

6 Make sure that students understand that they must make some of the sentences they wrote in Exercise 5 false. Students then play the guessing game.

LANGUAGE IN ACTION

Future continuous and future perfect

Watch video 3.3
Who will be making our food in the future? What food was invented by accident?

Future continuous	Future perfect
I [1] will be **making** a pear smoothie.	We [2] will have **seen** and **tasted** some very unusual dishes.
We [3] won't be **eating** a lot of meat in the future.	He [4] won't have **finished** by the end of the programme.
What [5] will you be **making**?	[6] Will you have **finished** by the end of the programme?

Future continuous

1 Complete the examples in the table above with *will/won't be* or *will/won't have*.

2 Complete the sentences with the future continuous form.

eat · not see · stay · ~~sleep~~

1 Don't ring me at 8.30. *I'll be sleeping.*
2 Where will they be staying while they're on holiday?
3 I've got exams next week. I won't be seeing my friends.
4 Will we be eating insects in 30 years' time?

Future perfect

3 Complete the sentences with the future perfect form.

1 I think scientists *will have found* (find) life on other planets by 2060.
2 I won't have finished (not finish) my exams by the end of May.
3 They won't have started (not start) yet. It's only 7.30.

4 3.08 Complete the conversation with the future continuous or perfect form of the verbs. Listen and check.

ZOE How [1] *will* restaurants *have changed* (change) by 2030?
SAM I think they [2] will have become (become) more automatic. Instead of human chefs, machines [3] will be cooking (cook) your food and human waiters [4] won't be serving (not serve) the tables, robots will.
ZOE So humans [5] won't be working (not work) in restaurants?
SAM That's right, but I think we [6] will have designed (design) robots that look like humans by then.

Use it!

5 Write sentences about your future. Use the future continuous or perfect.

In one years' time …
In 2050 …
On my 21st birthday …
By the end of this year …
By 2030 …
By the time I'm 25 …

In 2050 I'll be living in my own house.
By the time I'm 25 I'll have learned how to drive.

6 Tell your partner your sentences about the future, but change some so that they are false. Can they guess which sentences are true and which are false?

In 2050 I won't be living in my own house.
False?
Yes, it's false.

Finished? p120 Ex 3

Grammar game

In pairs, students write down three important future dates, e.g. 1st July, 2nd January. Their partner guesses why the date is significant, e.g. *Student A: 1st July. Student B: You'll be celebrating your birthday? Student A: No! Student B: You'll have finished all your exams?*

Extend it!

In pairs, students discuss the predictions about restaurants from Exercise 4. Do they agree with them? Do they have any predictions of their own?

Finished?

Fast finishers can turn to SB p120 and do Ex 3.

Homework

Workbook p28

Lesson aim: I can give instructions.

1 🎧 3.09 Look at the photo with students and elicit what they can see (a Spanish omelette). Then ask students to work in pairs and brainstorm the ingredients (and quantities if possible) needed to make a Spanish omelette before they listen and check.

Audioscript p164

Class challenge

The word *omelette* came into English from the Spanish / Farsi / **French** language.

2 🎧 3.09 Ask students to read along with the conversation as they complete it with the phrases. With a partner, students can then act out the conversation.

Useful language practice

▶ Play **Video 3.4** and encourage students to copy the intonation used by the presenter.

3 Students can complete the task in pairs, and then think of situations in which they could use the phrases from the *Everyday English* box. For example, *A: Is it hard to make a pizza? B: No, it's a piece of cake!*

4 ★ Give students time to choose a recipe. If a student knows a dish they'd like to write about, but not its ingredients, they can look online if they have access to the internet or ask you for help.

A Spanish omelette. It is made with potatoes, eggs, salt, oil and an onion.

SPEAKING

Giving instructions

🎧 3.09 **1** **What can you see in the photo? What ingredients do you need to make it? Listen and check your answers.**

🎧 3.09 **2** **Complete the conversation with the phrases from the *Useful language* box. Listen and check.**

ROB Can you give me the recipe for your yummy Spanish omelette? I'm going to make it for the picnic tomorrow. It won't take ages, will it?

EVA No, it's a piece of cake! [1] *You'll need* half a kilogramme of potatoes, five eggs, salt, oil and an onion.

ROB OK. Is that it?

EVA Yep, so [2] start by ____ peeling and slicing the potatoes. [3] ____, Once that's done chop the onion.

ROB OK. Then what?

EVA Heat a cup of oil in a pan and fry the potatoes and onions.

ROB That's a fair amount of oil!

EVA Yeah, I know! [4] While that's ____ frying, mix the eggs in a bowl. Then put everything together and add a pinch of salt. Heat a spoonful of oil in a smaller pan and pour in the mixture. Once the bottom part has cooked, [5] ____ flip the omelette with a plate and cook the other side. don't forget to

ROB OK, I'll try.

EVA It's delicious! Your friends will all be asking for the recipe! Will you still be there at four?

ROB Yeah, but we'll have finished the omelette by then!

Useful language

Don't forget to … (+ verb)	While that's … (+ -*ing*)
Once that's done, …	You'll need …
Start by … (+ -*ing*)	

3 **Match the phrases in the conversation with the meanings. How do you say these phrases in your language?**

1 something that's easy a piece of cake ____
2 delicious yummy ____
3 Is that everything? Is that it? ____
4 quite a lot a fair amount ____
5 a long time ages ____

Watch video 3.4
Everyday English

a fair amount ages a piece of cake
Is that it? yummy

PLAN

4 **Write about a recipe and the ingredients you need.**

____

SPEAK

5 **Practise explaining the recipe to your partner. Remember to use future tenses, vocabulary from this unit and phrases from the *Useful language* and *Everyday English* boxes.**

CHECK

6 **Work with another pair. Listen to their conversation and complete the notes.**

What was the recipe for? ____

What ingredients do you need? ____

Would you like to eat this food? ____

40 FOOD FOR THOUGHT | UNIT 3

5 Give students five minutes to plan their conversations. If appropriate, they can use their smartphones to record themselves explaining their recipes, listening back to check they're using the language from the unit.

6 Tell students not to mention the dish whose recipe they are going to describe. This gives the students listening a greater incentive to listen. Encourage students to respond to what they've heard. Ask: *Do you think the recipe was easy to follow?*

Background information

A *listicle* is a combination of the words *list* and *article*. These texts often come with a title featuring a number, e.g. *The Five Best Recipes From Italy*.

1 Elicit descriptions of the food shown in the photos, then give students a couple of minutes to read and think about the predictions. In pairs, they can share their responses to the predictions, giving reasons for either agreeing or disagreeing with Megan's ideas.

2 ★★★ Students can work alone to complete the task. Extend the activity by asking students if they ever read listicles online and what makes a listicle interesting.

3 Students can work alone on this task, comparing their answers in pairs before you check answers with the class as a whole.

4 ★★★ Challenge students to complete the phrases without looking back at Megan's listicle.

Useful language practice

5 Ask students to discuss these questions in small groups, noting down their ideas.

6 Tell students to write four things in their listicle (following the four questions in Ex 5) and to follow the model text in Ex 2. Give students around ten minutes to write their listicle.

WRITING
A listicle

1 What food can you see in the photos? Read Megan's listicle. Which of her predictions do you agree with?

dairy products (milk, cheese and eggs), fish and chips, pizza, crisps and peanuts

2 The following are features of a good listicle. Which ones are in Megan's listicle?

1. an interesting title
2. a number in the title
3. short texts about the title, one for each number
4. some interesting predictions
5. photos

all of them

FIVE FOODS WE'LL ALL BE EATING IN 2070!

1 If there's one thing we'll still be eating in 50 years' time, it's pizza!
We've been eating pizza since the 19th century, so we're not going to stop now! In the future toppings will change for sure, but pizza isn't going anywhere!

2 Tasty meat alternatives
With more humans on the planet, we'll need alternative sources of protein such as insects. What could be tastier than a sprinkle of roast ants on your salad?

3 Classics that will never die out!
Some classic British dishes, like fish and chips, will be around forever, although the fish will probably come from fish farms instead of the sea.

4 Printed snacks
By 2070 we'll be printing most of our snacks with a 3-D printer. Impossible? Watch this space …

5 Veggies and vegans
Vegetarian food is here to stay! In 2070 being veggie or vegan, and avoiding eggs, milk and cheese, will be the norm!

3 Read Megan's listicle again and make two lists.

Food that will be the same	Food that will be new
pizza fish and chips vegetarian food	pizza toppings insects 3-D printed snacks

4 Complete the *Useful language* phrases with the words in the box. Check in Megan's listicle.

anywhere forever norm space stay

Useful language

is here to [1] stay
isn't going [2] anywhere
Watch this [3] space
will be around forever
will be the [5] norm

Write your own listicle.

PLAN

5 Look at the questions and make notes.

1. What will people still be eating in 50 years' time?
2. What might we start eating in the future?
3. Which dishes will be around forever?
4. What food is unusual now but will be normal in the future?

WRITE

6 Write a listicle about your future food predictions. Remember to include future tenses, vocabulary from this unit and phrases from the *Useful language* box.

CHECK

7 Do you …

- explain what we will or might be eating in the future?
- explain what will be normal in the future?
- make any other predictions?

Finished? p120 Ex 4

UNIT 3 | FOOD FOR THOUGHT 41

7 Students can check each other's work, and then comment on the content. Ask: *Do you agree with your partner's predictions?*

Finished?
Fast finishers can turn to SB p120 and do Ex 4.

Flipped class
Prepare for the **Around the World** lesson (p42). Students find out some facts about Australia and Australian food.

Homework
Workbook p29

Warmer

▶ **Video 3.5** develops the theme of language. Before you play it, make sure students understand that only the second question relates to the video. Ask students to discuss the other questions in groups.

Video comprehension questions

Write *Australia* on the board. Elicit what students know about the country, e.g. places, people, weather. Has anyone in the class been to the country? Would anyone like to go?

1 3.10 Ask students what they can see in the photos. Write key words on the board, e.g. *kangaroo, beach, fish, grub, greenhouse, dim sum.* With the class as a whole, elicit what the photos tell us about food in Australia. Write students' ideas on the board. Before students read the text, teach the meaning of the Australian-English phrase *bush tucker*. *Bush* refers to the uninhabited and uncultivated areas of Australia. *Tucker* means food. *Bush tucker* is the sort of food traditionally eaten by aboriginal Australians (the original inhabitants of the country).

AROUND THE WORLD

READING
An article

You can see: a kangaroo, a grub, dim sum, grilled fish, a greenhouse and a carrot

1 3.10 Look at the photos. What can you see? What do they tell you about food in Australia? Read the article and check your ideas.

Globetrotters
Watch video 3.5
Food in Japan

- What food is usually associated with your country or culture?
- Can you explain what *kaiseki* and *wagashi* are?
- How is Western food influencing Japanese food traditions?

Kaiseki is a traditional meal with many different courses. *Wagashi* are Japanese sweets.

More people are eating sweets and fast food so are consuming more sugar and salt.

A TASTE OF

Australia

A country's food is influenced by its inhabitants, geography, climate and wildlife, and Australia is no exception.

Traditional Australia

For thousands of years, the indigenous people of Australia have eaten plants and animals from the land or sea. Traditional Aboriginal food, or 'bush tucker', includes crocodile, emu and snake. Examples that are still eaten today include kangaroo, macadamia nuts and witchetty grubs. These tasty insect larvae are roasted on the fire or grilled on the barbecue!

Multicultural Australia

Since the first Europeans arrived in Australia over 200 years ago, people have been moving to the country from all over the world. As a result, Australian cuisine is multicultural and includes British, Italian, Greek and Asian food. Popular dishes are fish and chips, roast lamb and dim sum as well as traditional favourites such as kangaroo, seafood pizza and fried shark. The warm, sunny climate means plenty of fresh fruit and vegetables, and barbecues to grill meat or fish outside.

Tomorrow's Australia

Desert food

Australia has built the first farm in the world that can grow fruit and veg in a desert. The enormous solar-powered greenhouse only needs sunshine and seawater to work and Australia has plenty of both. The solar panels create enough energy to transform the salt water into fresh water which is used to water the tomato plants. It's strange to think that in the future we might be eating food which is grown in the desert.

Ugly food

Around a quarter of fruit and vegetables around the world is thrown away before it gets to the supermarkets because people believe it's too 'ugly' to sell. However, some Australian supermarkets are trying to sell this food. They tell their customers that even though the food looks odd, it tastes exactly the same as perfectly formed fruit and veg. There are lots of advantages to eating this ugly food. It's cheaper for customers, farmers sell more of their produce and we reduce food waste.

The witchetty grub and kangaroo are examples of bush food first eaten by the indigenous people of Australia and still eaten today.

Dim sum is an example of food that has come to Australia from another culture.

The barbecue refers to popular food in Australia today.

42 FOOD FOR THOUGHT | UNIT 3

Class challenge

Kangaroos eat meat / **plants** / meat and plants.

Explain that context and meaning in language are linked, which means that the meaning of a word can change depending on the context in which it is used. Encourage students to work out the meanings of new words from context as much as they can.

2 Ask students to work in pairs to complete the rest of the table. When checking answers, challenge students to think of example sentences with the new words.

3 Students can compare answers in pairs before you check answers with the class as a whole.

Reading comprehension questions

4 ★ Elicit the type of word students need to find in each case, e.g. a noun, an adjective.

5 Give students time to think of their answers to the questions before they discuss them with a partner. With the class as a whole, discuss the importance of being open-minded. If we are willing to consider ideas and opinions that are new or different from our own, (i.e. by trying new types of food which seem strange to us) we can learn more about the world and our own place in it, understanding that how we behave and what we like is shaped by the culture into which we are born.

LEARN TO LEARN

Understanding words from context

When you see new words, use the rest of the sentence to help you understand them. Guess what the new word means and then check it in a dictionary.

2 **Find the words in the article and guess the meaning. Check in a dictionary or with your teacher.**

New word	What the other words tell me	What I think it means
1 indigenous	*It's an adjective that describes people who have lived in Australia for a long time.*	*original, first*
2 witchetty grubs		
3 multicultural		
4 shark		
5 solar-powered		
6 greenhouse		

The greenhouse refers to a project run in Australia to grow tomatoes in the desert, which could help solve future food shortages.

The misshapen carrot refers to the campaign to eat ugly fruit and veg.

3 **Read the article again and find examples of how these things influence Australia's food.**

Indigenous people

They have always eaten food from the land and sea and some is still eaten today, e.g. macadamia nuts and witchetty grubs.

Wildlife

People eat plants and animals from the land and sea, e.g. kangaroo, lamb, shark and macadamia nuts.

People from other cultures

Immigration to Australia from other countries has meant that food from other cultures has become part of everyday Australian cuisine, e.g. fish and chips and dim sum.

Climate

Australia is warm so people can grow and eat vegetables and grill meat or fish on a barbecue. It has hot desert areas, and it's possible to develop solar-powered greenhouses that can grow food in desert areas.

Food waste

Australian supermarkets are telling people about the advantages of eating 'ugly' food to reduce food waste.

4 **Find words in the article that mean:**

1 something not included in a group (introduction) exception
2 delicious (traditional Australia) tasty
3 cooking (multicultural Australia) cuisine
4 a short word for vegetable (desert food) veg
5 strange (ugly food) odd

Voice it!

5 **Discuss the questions.**

1 Which foods from other cultures have become popular in your country?
2 Australia is adapting to changes by eating 'ugly' food. How else can we adapt what we eat or drink?

Explore it!

Guess the correct answer.

What will you not find on a pizza in Australia?

a emu b kangaroo c koala d crocodile

Find a fact about Australian food. Write a question for your partner to answer.

NAIL IT! The Culture Project Teacher's Resource Bank

UNIT 3 | FOOD FOR THOUGHT 43

Students can collaborate digitally online and offline in the collaboration space, where teachers can set, track and assess students' work. Students can also share and showcase their work as well as comment on each other's projects.

Explore it!

To write their questions, students use the facts about Australian food they researched for homework.

Culture Project

See Project Book p30 for further information and activities.

Flipped class

Prepare for the **Review** lesson (p44). Students revise the grammar and vocabulary from Unit 3.

Lesson aim: I can review what I have learnt and reflect on my progress.

The aim of this review page is for students to revise the grammar and vocabulary from the unit. You can either do it in class, as a timed progress test or set it for homework.

Vocabulary

1 Put students into small groups to circle the correct verbs. Add an extra challenge by asking students to explain their choice in each case. Turn the task into a game by telling students that the first group to finish successfully wins.

2 Extend the activity by asking students to say the food in the pictures, e.g. 1 = slices of onion; 2 = a spoonful of sauce.

Language in action

3 Do this task with the class as a whole. In each case, elicit not only the answer, but a reason, e.g. *are you going* is correct in number 1 because the question is about a future plan rather than a scheduled event. Students can then practise reading the conversation.

4 Before students complete this exercise, ask them how the future continuous and the future perfect are formed and how they are used. Students can look back at p39 to remind themselves. They can also look at the irregular verb list on p143. Discuss the predictions with the class as a whole.

Unit quiz review

3 REVIEW

VOCABULARY

1 Circle the correct verbs.

1 *Season* / ***Peel*** the orange before you eat it.
2 Is there any butter to ***spread*** / *grate* on my toast?
3 Let's ***roast*** / *fry* a chicken in the oven.
4 Can I borrow a knife to *grill* / ***slice*** the tomato?
5 Sam ***bakes*** / *chops* his own bread. It's great!

2 Match the quantities with the photos. Then think of another example for each quantity.

chunk	9	______	cup	7	______
handful	4	______	packet	8	______
piece	10	______	pinch	3	______
slice	1	______	splash	6	______
spoonful	2	______	sprinkle	5	______

44 FOOD FOR THOUGHT | UNIT 3

LANGUAGE IN ACTION

3 Circle the correct words to complete the conversation.

IVAN What [1]*do you* / ***are you going*** to do this afternoon?
ANDREA We [2]***'re going*** / *will go* to the cinema. Juan and Ali [3]*come* / ***are coming*** too.
IVAN What film [4]***are you going to*** / *will you* see?
ANDREA *The Scream Factor.*
IVAN But you hate horror films!
ANDREA I know! [5]*I'm not enjoying* / ***I'm not going to enjoy*** the film, but Ali wants to see it.
IVAN It [6]***might be*** / *is* OK. Who knows, you [7]*won't* / ***may*** enjoy it.
ANDREA We'll see. Anyway, I have to go. It [8]*will start* / ***starts*** in 45 minutes.

4 Complete the predictions with the future continuous or perfect of the verbs in brackets. Which predictions do you agree / disagree with?

In 10 years' time …
1 African cuisine ______ (become) extremely popular. — will have become
2 most people ______ (stop) eating meat. — will have stopped
3 we ______ (not buy) 'ugly' fruit and veg. — won't be buying
4 we ______ (not go out) to restaurants. We ______ (order) food online to eat at home. — won't be going out; will be ordering

Self-assessment

I can use verbs to talk about food.
I can use words to talk about quantities.
I can use future tenses and *may/might*.
I can use the future continous and future perfect.

Self-assessment

Students look back through the unit in the Student's Book and reflect on how well they can do these things. They then discuss their opinions with a partner.

Homework

Workbook pp30–31

Lesson aim: I can set and achieve learning goals.

Students should be independently able to set their own short- and long-term learning goals and use those goals to help them focus and work effectively.

1 After students have answered the questions, ask: *Will Ada really find it a piece of cake to achieve her learning goal? Why? Why not?*

2 ★★★ Students can work in pairs to complete Ada's action plan. When they have completed it, ask them what they think of the plan and whether they can add anything to it.

3 Read Enzo's learning goal out to the class. Elicit Enzo's answers to the first two action-plan questions, then ask students to write those answers (and the questions) in Enzo's plan.

4 Students discuss the advice in pairs, giving a reason for their choice of the best advice.

5 Students work in pairs to complete questions 3, 4 and 5 of Enzo's action plan. (Note that these questions can be found in Ada's plan in Exercise 2.)

OWN IT!

6 Give students up to ten minutes time to think of a learning goal and complete the action plan.

LEARN TO LEARN

She wants to learn enough English for travelling in New Zealand. She hasn't achieved her goal yet.

LEARN TO ... SET AND ACHIEVE LEARNING GOALS

When you know what your English learning goals are, you can take steps to achieve them.

1 Read what Ada says about her learning goal. What is it? Has she achieved it yet?

In three weeks' time I'm going to New Zealand with my brother. He doesn't speak English so I'll need to book the hotels, order food and ask directions. My goal is to learn enough travel English to do this. I've bought a book with useful phrases for tourists, and I've downloaded episodes of a podcast about New Zealand. I'm going to listen to one episode every week. I'm also going to learn one useful phrase from the book every day. Piece of cake!

2 Write Ada's answers to questions 2–4.

Action plan		NAME: Ada
1	What do I want to do?	learn enough travel English to book hotels, order food and ask directions
2	How much time do I have?	three weeks
3	How am I going to do it?	a learn useful phrases from a book b listen to episodes of a podcast
4	How often am I going to do the things in 3?	a every day b every week
5	What's my goal in one sentence?	By the time we go to New Zealand, I'll have learned enough travel English.

3 Read what Enzo says about his learning goal. Write his answers to questions 1 and 2.

One month from now we've got a speaking exam. I want to get a good grade, but I'm not great at speaking – not like my sister. She speaks English really well!

	NAME: Enzo
1	get a good grade in an exam
2	one month
3	a b
4	a b
5	

4 Whose advice should Enzo take?

Why don't you practise with your sister? Ten minutes a day would help. – **Ela**

I'd study lots of vocabulary the night before. And don't sleep! – **Hamid**

Look at the Everyday English phrases in our book. Use three of them every day. – **Olga**

5 Use your answers in Exercise 4 to complete questions 3 and 4 of Enzo's action plan. Write one sentence about his goal for question 5.

OWN IT!

6 Think of an English learning goal. What are your answers to questions 1 to 5?

7 Tell your partner about your learning goal. Use the action plan to help you.

UNIT 3 | FOOD FOR THOUGHT 45

7 Students can give each other feedback on their action plans and make any changes they think are necessary. Make sure students carry out their plan and that you come back to these learning goals after a set period of time, asking students if they stuck to their plan. Point out that this type of planning should be ongoing, not a one-off activity.

Flipped class

Prepare for **Unit 4**. Students research the senses of animals. Do any animals have a special sense?

 Lesson aim: I can talk about the senses of animals.

Warmer

Elicit the five senses (taste, touch, smell, sight, hearing) and write them on the board. Ask: *Do you know any differences between the senses of humans and the senses of other animals?*

▶ Start it!

Unit quiz

1 Elicit ideas from the class and write them on the board.

2 & 3 ▶ Students can discuss their ideas in pairs. You can then play **Video 4.1** and allow students to check their answers. Students can also complete the Start it! **Video worksheet** in the *Teacher's Resource Bank*.

4 Ask students to share the information about the senses of animals that they researched for homework.

Video comprehension questions

Flipped class

Prepare for **Explore it!** (p47). Students find out a fact about the human senses.

4 SENSE AND SENSITIVITY

LEARNING OUTCOMES

I can ...

- understand texts about people who don't feel pain or fear and artists who make sound effects
- make guesses and give clues about unfamiliar objects
- write an encyclopaedia entry
- make deductions and express obligation, prohibition, necessity and advice
- talk about senses and describe how things look, sound and feel, etc.
- brainstorm and use visual clues when listening
- create an infographic.

Start it!

1 Look at the photo. What different senses do you use when you enjoy an ice cream? *taste, smell, sight and touch*
2 Before you watch, what do you think bats, dolphins and submarines have in common? *They use echolocation to know what is in front of them.*
3 Which animal has the best hearing and how does that help them? Watch and check. *The moth. Moths can hear very, very high sounds, which helps them escape before other animals can eat them.*
4 Can you think of any other animals which have special senses?

Watch video 4.1 | Language in action 4.2 p49 | Language in action 4.3 p51 | Everyday English 4.4 p52

46 SENSE AND SENSITIVITY | UNIT 4

Unit aims

Skills

I can ...

- understand a text about people who don't feel fear or pain p48
- understand an interview with a foley artist p50
- make guesses and give clues p52
- write an encyclopaedia entry p53
- write an infographic about animal senses p54

Language

I can ...

- talk about the five senses p47
- make deductions and express possibility p49
- describe texture, sound, taste, etc. p50
- express obligation, prohibition, necessity and advice p51

Learn to Learn

I can ...

- brainstorm ideas p47
- use visual clues when listening p50
- learn to plan homework p57

Extra Resources

- *Finished?* – Student's Book p121
- *Vocabulary Bank* – Student's Book p131
- CLIL – Student's Book p138
- Pronunciation – Student's Book p141
- Workbook p32
- *Teacher's Resource Bank* on *Cambridge One* for tests package, Cambridge Exam practice, wordlists, differentiated worksheets and many other extra resources.
- *Practice Extra* and *Digital collaboration space*

Lesson aim: I can talk about the five senses.

1 Check answers before students ask and answer the questions in pairs.

2 Go through the example with the class, focusing on the key vocabulary in statement a which gives the answer. Students can then complete the task in pairs.

Target vocabulary
feel /fiːl/
feel like /fiːl laɪk/
look /lʊk/
look like /lʊk laɪk/
smell /smel/
smell like /smel laɪk/
sound /saʊnd/
sound like /saʊnd laɪk/
taste /teɪst/
taste like /teɪst laɪk/
touch /tʌtʃ/

Extra vocabulary practice

Learn to learn

Brainstorming involves getting together with other people to suggest ideas. It's particularly helpful for students working with vocabulary as people have different knowledge and experience and so can offer connections between words that others would not have made.

3 Monitor while students do this task, helping if students struggle to think of extra words for each of the categories.

4 ★★★ Students should not only say which category their partner's extra words belong to but also why.

Quiz questions

VOCABULARY

The five senses

1 Match the words in bold with photos A–E. Answer the questions.

Have you ever:

1 seen a **durian**? C
2 touched a **snake**? D
3 played football on **artificial grass**? B
4 heard a **koala**? E
5 eaten a **knickerbocker glory**? A

2 Match the questions in Exercise 1 with statements a–e. Which things did you already know?

a They **look like** friendly teddy bears but when they cry they **sound** really angry. 4
b It's made of plastic but it can often **feel like** the real thing. 3
c It doesn't **sound like** a food but it is! They **taste** really sweet and look really colourful. 5
d They **look** wet and slimy but when you **touch** their skin they **feel** cold and dry. 2
e They **smell** terrible. In fact, they **smell like** dirty old socks and they don't **taste like** fruit, but many people say they're delicious. 1

LEARN TO LEARN

Brainstorming

Brainstorming word groups can help you make vocabulary connections.

3 Complete each line with the words in bold in Exercise 2. Add three or more words or phrases that you associate with them.

a The ears: *sound, sound like, hear, listen to, music*
b The eyes: look, look like
c The hands: feel, feel like, touch
d The nose: smell, smell like
e The tongue: taste, taste like

4 Choose one group of words in Exercise 3. Say your extra words to your partner. Can they guess which group they belong to?

5 Complete the sentences with the correct form of the words in bold in Exercise 2.

1 When my dad sleeps, he snores so much he *sounds like* a trumpet!
2 I tried some crocodile meat once. It tasted like chicken.
3 The milk smelled bad and looked a bit yellow, so she didn't taste it.
4 I love wearing my new winter coat. It feels so soft and warm.
5 A It doesn't look like a painting by Picasso.
B No, but it is.
6 Please don't touch the wall. I've just painted it.

Use it!

6 Talk about the things in the box with the words in Exercise 2. Compare with another pair. Do you have the same descriptions?

fast food graffiti mobile phones new clothes rap music

Explore it!

Guess the correct answer.

Which human sense is the weakest?

a sight b hearing c touch d taste e smell

Find another interesting fact about the human senses. Write a question for your partner to answer.

5 ★ Go through the first item with the class. Ask why the verb *sounds* is in the present tense (the sentence is referring to habitual actions). Remind students that they may need to change the form of the verb.

6 Before students do this task, point out that they need to talk about what each of the things in the box sounds like, tastes like, etc.

Vocabulary Bank SB p131

Explore it!

Ask students to tell you about some of the facts about human senses that they researched for homework.

Homework

Workbook p32

Lesson aim: I can understand a text about people who don't feel fear or pain.

Warmer

Write *fear* and *pain* on the board. Elicit the meanings. Then discuss why people try to avoid experiencing these emotions and feelings (because they are unpleasant).

1 Elicit answers from the class as a whole. Guide students to the fact that we feel pain and fear for good reasons – they alert us to dangers so that we can take action to protect ourselves.

2 4.01 Split students into two groups. Group A reads about Amy Campbell (the left-hand column of the text), Group B reads about Jordy Cernik (the right-hand column). Students from both groups can then work in pairs to share what they found out.

3 ★★★ After completing the activity, challenge students to give a reason for their choices.

4 ★★★ Ask students to write their own sentences with these new words.

Match words with definitions

5 Give students time to think about their answer, and make notes, before they discuss the question in pairs.

READING

A magazine article

1 Imagine you couldn't feel pain or fear. Would your life be better or worse? Why?

4.01 **2** Read the magazine article. Which problems does it mention?

- not knowing when there's a problem when you hurt yourself
- not enjoying or feeling excited about anything

No pain, no fear – NO WAY!

Everybody knows what pain feels like. It's horrible. So imagine never feeling physical pain. You cut your finger – nothing. You break your leg – no pain at all. It must be wonderful, right? Wrong, because pain is the body's way of telling the brain that there's a problem. But some people, like Amy Campbell, can't feel pain. When she was born, Amy looked like an ordinary baby, but after a few months her parents realised something was wrong and thought she had developmental problems. She would chew her tongue and bite her fingers but she never cried. By the time she was a teenager, she had broken both arms and a leg – all without feeling a thing. It also doesn't matter if the air feels hot or cold, Amy can't feel the weather. But, like any young person, she has friends, hobbies (she plays the guitar), dreams and ambitions. She just has to be very careful. You may think her life can't be easy, but Amy is optimistic about her future. She says her condition affects what she can do, but not who she is inside.

Jordy Cernik

When Jordy Cernik tells people he feels no fear, they usually think he can't be serious. Having no fear might sound like a joke but it's not. During his 20s and 30s, Jordy had to have operations to remove his adrenal glands. Some time later, he realised that these operations had had a strange effect – he couldn't feel any fear. He did a parachute jump but didn't feel scared at all. He finds rollercoasters boring. Some people imagine it must be great not to feel fear, but there are disadvantages to not having any adrenaline. Adrenaline is a natural painkiller, so Jordy now feels more pain than ordinary people. It also means he doesn't feel excited about anything. Jordy now does 'scary' challenges to raise money for charity. Doctors think he could be the only person in the world who feels no fear, but knowledge about his condition may help them understand more common problems like anxiety.

3 Read the magazine article again. Write *T* (true), *F* (false) or *DS* (doesn't say).

1. Amy's parents knew there was a problem when she was born. F
2. Amy wears special clothes on cold days. DS
3. Amy doesn't think her condition affects her personality. T
4. Jordy has never been able to feel fear. F
5. Jordy loves rollercoasters. F
6. There are probably many people like Jordy in the world. F
7. Doctors think studying Jordy's condition could be useful. T

4 Find words in the article that mean:

1. to break food into smaller pieces with your teeth. (Amy) chew
2. the things you want to achieve. (Amy) ambitions
3. a chemical produced by the body. (Jordy) adrenaline
4. a chemical or drug that stops pain. (Jordy) painkiller
5. the feeling of being very worried. (Jordy) anxiety

Voice it!

5 Why do people enjoying doing scary things like riding on rollercoasters?

Finished? p121 Ex 1

Finished?

Fast finishers can turn to SB p121 and do Ex 1.

Flipped class

▶ Ask students to watch **Video 4.2** and do the **Video worksheet** in the *Teacher's Resource Bank*.

Homework

Workbook p33

Extend it!

Elicit or explain 'thrill seeking' (taking part in risky but exciting activities such as sky diving, giving people a rush of adrenalin). Ask: *Would you describe yourself as a thrill seeker? Why? Why not?* Students discuss these questions in pairs.

Lesson aim: I can make deductions and express possibility.

Warmer

▶ Play **Video 4.2** if it was not set for homework and elicit that Andy runs, swims and rides a bike despite being blind. He knows he's near the edge of the pool because someone touches him on the back with a pole.

1 Elicit that *deduction* is the act of deciding that something is true using the information that you have about it. Explain that the gapped sentences in the table are to be completed with modal verbs.

Extra grammar practice

2 4.02 ★ Read out the example. Elicit that 'must have lots of sugar' is correct because the second sentence says the drink tastes sweet. Students can complete the task in pairs.

Audioscript p164

3 4.03 ★ Encourage students to look at the context around each gap. When students have completed the dialogue, ask them to read the dialogue in pairs.

Audioscript p165

4 Read out the example. Check students remember the differences between the modal verbs. Students can then write their sentences. They can use their own ideas as well as the ones in the box.

5 Students can do this task in pairs.

LANGUAGE IN ACTION

Deduction and possibility

Watch video 4.2 Why is Andy an amazing athlete? How does he know when he's near the edge of the pool?

100% certain	It [1] must be wonderful. could / may / might	could / may / might
Possible could / may / might	Having no fear [2] ___ **sound like** a joke. He [4] ___ **be** the only person in the world who feels no fear.	Knowledge about his condition [3] ___ **help** them understand.
100% impossible	He [5] can't **be** serious.	

1 **Complete the examples in the table above. Use the magazine article on page 48 to help you.**

2 4.02 **Circle the correct words. Listen and check.**

1 This drink *must* / *can't* have lots of sugar in it. It tastes really sweet.
2 Don't touch that snake! It *might* / *can't* be poisonous.
3 This milk *must* / *can't* be really old. It smells disgusting.
4 It looks like a painting by Monet, but it *may* / *can't* be. It was painted after he died.
5 A What instrument is that? It sounds like a violin.
B Maybe, or it *can't* / *could* be a viola.
6 This jacket *must* / *can't* be very warm in winter. It feels like a blanket!

3 4.03 **Complete the dialogue with *must*, *can't* or *might*. Listen and check.**

OMER What are you listening to? It's so loud!
BRIONY It's Beethoven. I think it's beautiful.
OMER You [1] must be joking! I thought you hated classical music.
BRIONY Well, that's because I hadn't really listened to any before. Did you know Beethoven became deaf when he was still quite young?
OMER Wow, that [2] can't be easy for anyone, but it [3] must be absolutely terrible for a musician. You should turn it down, though. The neighbours [4] might be home.
BRIONY They [5] can't be. The lights are off and their car's not there. Anyway, I'm sure they'd prefer Beethoven to the heavy metal you always play. They [6] must hate that! Every time you put it on they start banging on the wall.

4 **Write sentences about this situation with the verbs and phrases in the boxes. Use *must*, *can't*, *may*, *might* or *could*.**

Marco hasn't come to school yet. He has to give a presentation with his partner, Alice, and all their notes are in Marco's locker.

be come feel have

a cold in bed late nervous soon very relaxed worried

Marco might be in bed. Alice must feel worried.

She can't feel very relaxed. Marco may/might/could have a cold. He might come soon. He might be late.

Use it!

5 **Look at the photos. What do you think they are?**

It could/might/can't/must be …

It looks like (a) …

Finished? p121 Ex 2

UNIT 4 | SENSE AND SENSITIVITY 49

Grammar game

In pairs, students close their eyes, then touch a classroom object their partner has given them, trying to guess what it is, e.g. *It can't be a pencil because it's too big. It might be a marker pen. Is it a marker pen?* Students win a point for each correct guess.

Finished?

Fast finishers can turn to SB p121 and do Ex 2.

Homework

Workbook p34

1 🎧 4.04 Elicit additional examples of things that each of the adjectives in the box could describe.

Target vocabulary
colourful /ˈkʌləfəl/
faint /feɪnt/
rough /rʌf/
sharp /ʃɑːp/
shiny /ˈʃaɪni/
smelly /ˈsmeli/
smooth /smuːð/
sour /saʊə/
spicy /ˈspaɪsi/
transparent
/trænˈspærənt/

Audioscript p165

2 Students work in pairs. Encourage students to define each adjective as they come to it, e.g. *transparent* describes something you can see through, like an umbrella.

Find the matching pairs

3 Give students a few minutes to think of how to describe the things in the box before they do the task in pairs.

4 & 5 🎧 4.05 Check students' understanding of *sound effects* (sounds created and added to a film, e.g. a creaking door in a scary film).

Audioscript p165

6 🎧 4.05 Challenge students to circle the correct option before playing the recording again.

VOCABULARY AND LISTENING

Describing texture, sound, taste, etc.

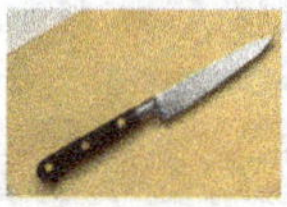
1 a ~~sharp~~ knife

2 transparent umbrella

3 a colourful chameleon

4 smooth skin

5 a spicy chili

6 a rough road

7 a sour grapefruit

8 shiny balloons

9 smelly skunk

10 faint heartbeat

🎧 4.04 **1 Complete the photo labels with the words in the box. Listen, check and repeat.**

colourful faint rough ~~sharp~~ shiny smelly smooth sour spicy transparent

2 Complete the table with the words in Exercise 1.

Feel	Look	Smell	Sound	Taste
rough sharp smooth	colourful shiny transparent	smelly	faint	sour spicy

Use it!

3 Use the words in Exercise 1 to describe the things in the box. Can your partner guess the item?

a cat's tongue a concrete wall a curry a new coin a pencil a whisper lemons stars

It's shiny and gold. *A new coin!*

An interview

4 Foley artists create sound effects for films. What sound effects do you think these items make?

a two coconut halves a horse
b shredded newspaper and a plastic bag someone walking on grass
c cellophane fire
d celery a leg breaking
e rice and a metal tray rain

I think the coconut halves could be the sound of ...

🎧 4.05 **5 Listen to the interview with James Ford, a Foley artist. Check your answers to Exercise 4.**

🎧 4.05 **6 Listen again and circle the correct words.**

1 It's important to (*never*) / *sometimes* have total silence in a movie.
2 The interviewer thinks the second effect is made with (*newspaper*) / *grass*.
3 Foley artists used to make (*more*) / *fewer* sounds.
4 James *made some* / (*didn't make any*) of the explosion sounds in his last movie.
5 To become a Foley artist, formal training is *necessary* / (*unnecessary*).

LEARN TO LEARN

Using visual clues when listening
Use pictures, instructions, etc., to help you understand what you are hearing.

Voice it!

7 Do you think the job of a Foley artist will disappear in the future? Why / Why not?

50 SENSE AND SENSITIVITY | UNIT 4

7 Ask students to talk about a film they've seen recently, say what sound effects it had, and whether those effects made the film more enjoyable.

Flipped class
▶ Ask students to watch **Video 4.3** and do the **Video worksheet** in the *Teacher's Resource Bank*.

Learn to learn
Students often worry about listening tasks. Encourage them to manage this by predicting any topics or details they might hear, using any available information (including visuals).

Extend it!
In groups, students describe how they could make their own sound effects (e.g. an explosion, a car crashing) using everyday objects.

Homework
Workbook p35

Lesson aim: I can express obligation, prohibition, necessity and advice.

Warmer

▶ Play **Video 4.3** and elicit that she is giving advice about how to take a great selfie. She says you should hold the camera up high, you shouldn't ignore the background and you should delete any bad photos.

1 ★★★ Once students have completed the table, check their understanding of the modal verbs, e.g. *What does a teacher mean when she says 'you have to do your homework'?*

Pronunciation

Students turn to the pronunciation exercises on p141 for practise of the weak form of *to*.

2 Ask students to discuss which of the things in the text they do and don't do.

Get it right!

Check students' understanding of this by asking them to put the following sentence into the past: *I must study hard for my exams.*

3 Encourage students to check answers in pairs.

4 4.08 After students have completed the task, ask them to repeat the sentences, paying attention to how *have to* and *had to* are pronounced.

Audioscript p166

5 Students complete the text in pairs, then ask: *Do we take too many photos today?* Students can discuss the question in pairs.

Extra grammar practice

Watch video 4.3
What is she giving advice about?
What three things do you need to do?

LANGUAGE IN ACTION

Obligation, prohibition, necessity and advice

[1] Obligation (present)	[2] Necessity (present)	[3] Prohibition	[4] Advice
They **must** sound natural.	We **need to** experiment a lot.	You **mustn't** speak loudly in the library.	We **should** listen to another one.
These days we **don't have to** do everything.	You **don't need to** have any formal training.		You **shouldn't** do that.
Do you **have to** work hard?			You **ought to** be a creative person.

Pronunciation p141

1 Complete the headings in the table above with *Obligation*, *Prohibition*, *Necessity* or *Advice*.

2 Circle the correct words.

7 TIPS FOR LOOKING AFTER YOUR EYES

1 Most of us [1]*mustn't* / *need to* use computers every day but too much screen time can be bad for your eyes.
2 You [2]*ought to* / *shouldn't* spend more than about 20 minutes looking at a screen without taking a break.
3 You [3]*should* / *shouldn't* avoid using your phone in the dark. If you want to read, you [4]*ought to* / *have to* read a book.
4 Some people [5]*don't have to* / *mustn't* wear glasses, but if you do, you [6]*should* / *ought not* to clean the lenses.
5 Buy a good pair of sunglasses: everybody [7]*needs to* / *mustn't* protect their eyes from bright sunlight.
6 Don't forget about diet either. It [8]*ought to* / *mustn't* include lots of green vegetables and fatty fish.
7 Finally, everybody [9]*doesn't have to* / *should* have an eye test once a year.

Get it right!
We don't use *must* in the past, only *had to*.

Past obligation

In the past, Foley artists [1] had to create all the effects.
I **didn't** [2] have to make those sounds.
[3] Did your parents have to study English at school?

3 Complete the table above with the correct form of *have to*.

4 4.08 Match 1–5 with a–e. Listen and check.

1 She didn't have to study hard for the exam
2 I didn't have to wear a uniform at my last school
3 Billy didn't have to get up early this morning
4 Mia had to go to the dentist
5 I got all the answers wrong

a because it's a holiday.
b so I had to do the exercise again.
c because she had toothache.
d because she's really good at English.
e but I do at the one I go to now.

5 Complete the text with the correct form of *have to* or *should*.

Do your parents have old photos? You [1]should ask them – they might be interesting. In the past, when you took a photo, the people [2] had to stand still. They [3] didn't have to smile but they did. The photographer [4] had to be careful because photos were expensive. Now, you [5] don't have to worry because you can take lots on your phone. Some people think we [6] shouldn't take so many.

Use it!

6 Make notes and compare with a partner.
- something you had to do in the past
- something you ought to do soon

What did you have to do? *I had to visit the dentist last week!*

Finished? p121 Ex 3

6 Give students two minutes to make notes before talking with a partner.

Finished?

Fast finishers can turn to SB p121 and do Ex 3.

Grammar game

On the board, write ideas, some silly, some sensible, e.g. Sentence: *Go swimming in your trousers.* In groups, students compete to be the first to use the most appropriate modal verb in response to the ideas, e.g. *You shouldn't do that!*

Homework

Workbook p36

Lesson aim: I can make guesses and give clues.

Warmer

Ask: *What can we do if we don't know the answer to something?* Elicit that we can make a guess. Then elicit that if we know the answer to something, we can help someone else find an answer by giving them clues.

1 4.09 Elicit students' ideas about the photo. Encourage them to use modals of deduction and possibility, e.g. *It might/could/may be ...*

Audioscript p166

2 4.09 Ask students to cover the Useful Language box, and listen and write the missing phrases. After students have completed the conversation, they can practise reading it in pairs.

Useful language practice

▶ Play **Video 4.4**. Encourage students to copy the intonation used by the presenter.

3 Students think of situations in which they could use the *Everyday English* phrases. For example, A: *Shall we go swimming!* B: *Sure, why not?*

4 ★ Brainstorm ideas with the class. (You may also want to introduce some ideas of your own.) Write the ideas on the board.

5 Give students five minutes to plan their descriptions.

SPEAKING

Making guesses and giving clues

Tabi are Japanese socks that are worn with sandals.

4.09 **1** **Look at the picture. What are *tabi*? Listen and find out.**

4.09 **2** **Complete the conversation with the phrases from the *Useful language* box. Listen and check.**

Useful language

Guess again.
Guess what it is / they are.
I guess they must be …
Perhaps it's something (+ *adjective*)
They're definitely some kind of …

Watch video 4.4
Everyday English

Bingo! I give up! I guess so.
nice and warm/hot, etc. Sure, why not?

AIDAN Hey, do you want to see something cool?
ZOE Sure, why not? Wow! What are those?
AIDAN They're called *tabi*. They're from Japan. [1] Guess what they are.
ZOE Well, they're [2] *definitely some kind* of clothing. They look like gloves, but they can't be, can they?
AIDAN Nope. They're definitely not gloves.
ZOE They're in the shape of an 'L', so I guess [3] *they must be* socks.
AIDAN Bingo!
ZOE But why is the big toe separate from the other toes?
AIDAN I'm not telling you. Try and work it out yourself.
ZOE Hmm. Perhaps [4] *it's something* traditional. Maybe Japanese people wear rings on their big toes?
AIDAN No, that's not it. [5] *Guess* again.
ZOE No, I give up!
AIDAN It's so that they can wear them with sandals with straps. The strap goes between the big toe and the others.
ZOE Oh, that's a clever idea! They must be nice and warm to wear.
AIDAN I guess so. I haven't tried them on yet.

3 **Complete the dialogues with the phrases in the *Everyday English* box.**

1 A Shall we watch a movie? B *Sure, why not?*
2 It's *nice and warm* today. Let's have a picnic!
3 A Is the answer 23? B *Bingo!*
4 A Chinese must be hard to learn. B *I guess so.*
5 A One more guess? B No – *I give up!*

PLAN

4 **Write about something from your country that might be new or strange to a foreigner, for example a food or an item of clothing. How would you describe it?**

SPEAK

5 **Practise describing something from your country to your partner. Remember to use modals, vocabulary from this unit and phrases from the *Useful language* and *Everyday English* boxes.**

CHECK

6 **Work with another pair. Listen to their conversation and complete the notes.**

What did you hear about? ______________

How was it described? ______________

6 ★★★ Extend the activity by asking students to discuss the other pair's conversation. They should consider the following questions: *Do you agree that what was described would be new or strange to a foreigner? Why? Why not?*

Extend it!

Students write up their descriptions in about 100 words.

Lesson aim: I can write an encyclopaedia entry.

Warmer

Write *encyclopaedia* on the board. Elicit the meaning of the word (a set of articles that deal with the whole of human knowledge). Ask students if they have an encyclopaedia at home or if they use websites like Wikipedia.

1 Read out the question. Elicit ideas and write them on the board. (He has a kind of antenna attached to his head which allows him to 'hear' colours as different vibrations.) Encourage students to use modals of speculation and possibility and phrases from the *Useful language* box on p52.

2 Set a one-minute time limit for this task.

3 ★★★ Challenge students to discuss the statements in pairs before they read the text to check. What can they remember?

Comprehension questions

4 Students can work alone to complete the sentences, then compare answers with a partner.

5 If appropriate, students can research these people online and do the writing task in class. If not, set this for homework.

6 If students write their encyclopaedia entry for homework, tell them to leave it for a few hours after they finish it, and to go back to it later for a final check. If they do this, they are more likely to spot mistakes.

7 Encourage students to write a second draft if needed.

WRITING
An encyclopaedia entry

1 **Look at the pictures. What is attached to the man's head? Read the encyclopaedia entry and find out.**

2 **Match titles a–e with paragraphs 1–5.**

a Artwork
b Other information
c Introduction
d Name and date of birth
e Life

1 **d** Neil Harbisson, 27 July 1984

2 **c** Neil Harbisson is known as the world's first cyborg artist. He has been colour blind since birth and has a special antenna connected to his skull that lets him 'hear' colours as different vibrations in his head.

3 **e** Neil was born in Belfast in 1984 and grew up in Barcelona. At the age of 16, he started to make black and white art. In 2004, scientists developed his special camera and attached it to his head. With the camera, Neil can 'hear' 360 colours, including some which are invisible to the human eye. In 2004, when he had to get a new passport, the UK passport office said no at first because he didn't look like a human. However, they finally accepted his application. He must be the only official cyborg in the world.

4 **a** Neil now makes colourful art, including 'sound portraits' of famous people and geometric paintings. He has had exhibitions all around the world.

5 **b** According to Neil, all human skin sounds orange.

3 **Are the sentences *T* (true) or *F* (false)?**

1 Neil has always lived in the same place. **F**
2 Neil doesn't always wear his antenna. **F**
3 Neil can experience colours that ordinary humans can't see. **T**
4 Neil couldn't get a new British passport. **F**
5 People in many countries have seen Neil's art. **T**

4 **Complete the sentences with the phrases from the *Useful language* box.**

1 Stefani Joanne Angelina Germanotta **is known as** Lady Gaga.
2 She **was born on** 28 March 1986 **and grew up in** New York City.
3 **At the age of** four she began to learn to play the piano.
4 She makes energetic pop music, **including** songs like *Bad Romance* and *Alejandro*.
5 **According to** Lady Gaga, you can teach yourself art.

Useful language

According to …	… is known as …
At the age of …	… was born on …
including …	and grew up in …

Write an encyclopaedia entry.

PLAN

5 **These artists all have a physical difference. Choose one and make notes about them.**

photographer Roesie Percy
chef Adam Cole
rapper Sean Forbes

name and date of birth
their life
their artwork

WRITE

6 **Write your encyclopaedia entry. Remember to include five paragraphs, modal verbs, vocabulary from this unit and phrases from the *Useful language* box.**

CHECK

7 **Do you …**

- include information about the person's life?
- include information about the person's artwork?

Finished? p121 Ex 4

UNIT 4 | SENSE AND SENSITIVITY 53

Extend it!

Students display their 'entries' in the classroom. They read each other's entries and make notes. In pairs, they can discuss information about the artists they read about and say who they thought was the most interesting.

Class challenge

The word *cyborg* is formed from the words *cyber* and organisation / **organism** / organ.

Finished?

Fast finishers can turn to SB p121 and do Ex 4.

Homework

Workbook p37

Lesson aim: I can create an infographic.

Warmer

Ask students to share any facts they know about elephants. Elicit any interesting facts from the class.

Project Book

For more information and activities see the Project Book p34.

1 Read out the questions. Elicit the answers, but do not confirm if they are right or wrong at this stage.

2 Before students read the infographic to check their answers, elicit the key information in the questions in Exercise 1: 1) continents; 2) where they are going; 3) strong trunk, long nose; 4) ears. Students can then scan the infographic for words and phrases related to these ideas, and use the symbols in the text, to help them locate the relevant information to check their answers.

How to research

Research is a vital skill, one which students will continue to make use of in school, and will one day make use of in further education and in the work place. Emphasise the importance of evaluating the truthfulness of information. Encourage students to cross-check information by reading from a range of sources.

3 Ask students about how they find information, where it's from, and how they can trust it. Also ask them to discuss how they can tell a fact from an opinion. Students can then work in pairs to complete the task.

THE SCIENCE PROJECT

An infographic on animal senses

1 Work in pairs. Can you answer the questions?

1. Which continents do elephants live in? Africa and Asia.
2. How do they know where they are going? They use their trunks.
3. How strong is their trunk (their long nose)? It has 100,000 muscles in it.
4. What do they use their ears for? As well as hearing they use them to keep cool.

2 Read the infographic and check your answers to Exercise 1.

How to research

3 Which of these things should you do when you research? Tick the correct answers.

1. Decide the main information you want before doing research. ✓
2. Use questions in search engines, e.g. *How well can elephants see?* ✓
3. Read articles from start to finish. ☐
4. Read the contents list of articles or the titles of sections and then decide what you need to read. ✓
5. Make sure the information is fact and not opinion. ✓
6. Only check information on one site. ☐
7. Take notes as you read. ✓

Elephants and

Elephants' eyes are on the side of their head and have three eyelids, one above the eye, one below, like humans, and an almost transparent one they use to keep dust, dirt and water out. However, their eyes aren't very strong. They normally use their trunks to know where they are going. In fact, the leader of a group of elephants is sometimes blind.

Elephants can hear extremely well because they have big ears. They can hear faint sounds, including the calls of elephants up to 1.5 km away. Their ears are about $\frac{1}{6}$ of the size of their bodies. They also use them to keep cool.

Elephants have to move their trunk around and smell the air all the time in order to find water, so they have an excellent sense of smell. They can detect water up to 12 km away.

Elephants use their rough trunks to explore the environment and care for their young. They also use it to fight. The trunk can lift objects that weigh up to 250 kg. They can also sense tiny vibrations in the ground with their feet. Scientists think this must be the reason why many survived the Asian Tsunami of 2004. They felt the vibrations of the earthquake and moved to higher ground.

4 If students do not have access to the internet, put them into groups to choose an animal to research, then set the research task for homework; students can then work on their infographic in the next lesson.

5 Before students give their presentation, encourage them to check their work one final time. Have they included the right information and is everything clear and easy to follow? Students can choose one spokesperson to present their infographic to the class, or they can present it collaboratively, with different students taking responsibility for presenting different facts about the animal to the class.

6 As well as checking one another's work, encourage students to make notes on interesting things in their classmates' presentations. Discuss with the class as a whole, what students have learned from the different presentations.

Students can collaborate digitally online and offline in the collaboration space, where teachers can set, track and assess students' work. Students can also share and showcase their work as well as comment on each other's projects.

For more work on Science, students can turn to SB p138. See p154 for teaching notes.

OWN IT!

their **amazing** senses

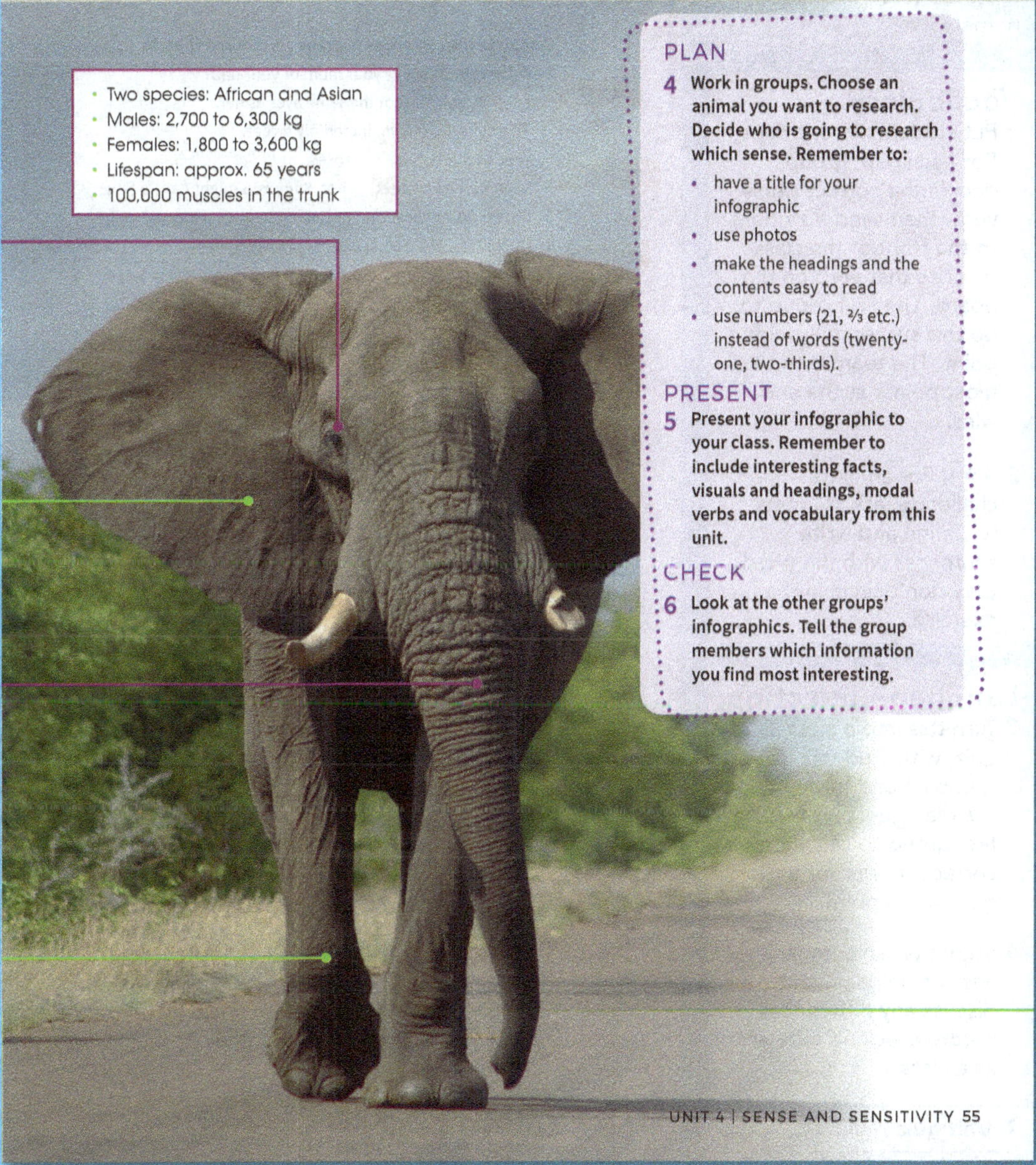

- Two species: African and Asian
- Males: 2,700 to 6,300 kg
- Females: 1,800 to 3,600 kg
- Lifespan: approx. 65 years
- 100,000 muscles in the trunk

PLAN

4 **Work in groups. Choose an animal you want to research. Decide who is going to research which sense. Remember to:**

- have a title for your infographic
- use photos
- make the headings and the contents easy to read
- use numbers (21, ⅔ etc.) instead of words (twenty-one, two-thirds).

PRESENT

5 **Present your infographic to your class. Remember to include interesting facts, visuals and headings, modal verbs and vocabulary from this unit.**

CHECK

6 **Look at the other groups' infographics. Tell the group members which information you find most interesting.**

UNIT 4 | SENSE AND SENSITIVITY 55

Class challenge

The ears of an African elephant are **bigger than** / smaller than / the same size as those of an Asian elephant.

Flipped class

Prepare for the **Review** lesson (p56). Students revise the grammar and vocabulary from Unit 4.

Lesson aim: I can review what I have learnt and reflect on my progress.

The aim of this review page is for students to revise the grammar and vocabulary from the unit. You can either do it in class, as a timed progress test or set it for homework.

Vocabulary

1 Put students into groups. For each gap, groups decide the correct sense verb, then send a student to the front of the class to write that verb on the board. The first group to do this successfully wins a point. The team with the most points at the end wins.

2 ★★★ For an extra challenge, ask students to define and write sentences with the words they don't circle in the exercise.

Language in action

3 Turn this into a class quiz, with students in groups. Read through the dialogue, and the first group to call out the correct answer for each gap wins a point.

4 Students can compare answers in pairs, and discuss any differences before checking answers as a class.

Unit quiz review

4 REVIEW

VOCABULARY

1 **Complete the sentences with the correct sense verb.**

1 A Do you *look like* your mum or your dad?
B My mum – I've got the same eyes as her.
2 This coffee *tastes* incredibly sweet.
3 Your perfume *smells like* roses.
4 Your forehead *feels* hot, Sam. You might have a fever.
5 Listen! Do you hear that noise? It *sounds like* a mouse.
6 Ouch! I *touched* a cactus!
7 I've just started to learn the guitar. I *don't sound* very good yet, but one day I will.

2 **Circle the correct words.**

1 I don't like *spicy* / *smooth* food much – it burns my mouth. (spicy)
2 I heard a very *transparent* / *faint* sound in the distance. (faint)
3 Are they new shoes? They're so *smelly* / *shiny* – I love them! (shiny)
4 Be careful with that knife! It's really *sharp* / *faint*. (sharp)
5 The pictures in that book are really *sour* / *colourful*. (colourful)
6 These glasses are not completely *smelly* / *transparent*. You can't see the eyes of the person wearing them. (transparent)

LANGUAGE IN ACTION

3 **Complete the dialogue with *must*, *might* or *can't* and a phrase in the box.**

be doing that | be right | be studying | be wrong | have football practice | know the answer

A What did you answer for question 10? I put 65.5.
B I put 75.3. We [1] *can't* both *be right*. One of us [2] *must be wrong*.
A Shall we ask Tim? He [3] *might know the answer*. He's good at maths.
B Sure, but where is he?
A I'm not sure. He [4] *might be studying* in the library or he [5] *might have football practice*.
B No, he [6] *can't be doing that*. Football practice is on Tuesday and today is Wednesday.
A OK, let's try and find him in the library then.

4 **Match 1–5 with a–e. Complete the sentences with *have/has to*, *don't/doesn't have to*, *must/mustn't* or *had to/didn't have to*.**

1 Eric got up early yesterday because he *had to* [b]
2 This seat is reserved for old people so you *mustn't* [a]
3 I've got lots to do tomorrow so I really *have to / must* [e]
4 My friend had his car so we *didn't have to* [c]
5 Before visitors enter the exhibition, they *must / have to* [d]

a sit there.
b start work at 7 am.
c take the bus.
d put their bags in a locker.
e go to bed soon.

Self-assessment

- I can use verbs to talk about senses.
- I can use adjectives to describe texture, sound, taste, etc.
- I can use modals of deduction and possibility.
- I can use modals of obligation, prohibition, necessity and advice.

56 SENSE AND SENSITIVITY | UNIT 4

Self-assessment

Students look back through the unit in the Student's Book and the Workbook and reflect on how well they can do these things. They then discuss their opinions with a partner. Encourage them to ask you for extra homework related to the language areas they feel less happy about.

Homework

Workbook pp 38–39

Lesson aim: I can plan my homework.

By this stage, students should be learning how to organise their out-of-school studying, prioritising tasks so as to manage their time and work effectively at home.

Warmer

Write *homework* on the board. Ask students what they think of doing homework. Do they think they have too much? Does homework make them feel stressed?

1 Put students into pairs to ask and answer the four questions in the leaflet. Then give students time to discuss their answers, e.g. If a student often leaves difficult homework until last, do they know why they do this?

2 ★★★ Give students time to read the four pieces of advice in the leaflet. In pairs, they can match the advice to the questions. When you check the answers, challenge students to reflect on the advice given in the leaflet. What do students think of it? Is it good advice? Can students think of any other advice to offer?

3 Elicit that a homework planner sets out a plan for study, setting out things like what homework needs to be done, when it needs to be done by and how long it will take.

OWN IT!

4 Give students ten minutes to produce their homework planner. In pairs, students compare planners, and suggest improvements they can think of. Make sure you revisit the homework planner later in the course, to see if students have found it effective.

LEARN TO LEARN

LEARN TO ... PLAN YOUR HOMEWORK

When you have a lot of homework to do, it's important to decide what order to do it in and when to do it.

1 Ask and answer questions 1–4 in the leaflet with a partner. Are your answers similar or different?

Feeling stressed about homework?
With our useful advice, you don't need to panic!

How often have you ...

1 forgotten what you had to do for homework?
2 handed in a piece of homework late because you didn't start it until too late?
3 not started until you're too tired?
4 done the quick or easy homework first and then not had time for more difficult things?

If you answered 'often' or 'always', then you really need our help!

a Decide when you need to start your homework and give yourself enough time.
b When you ought to start but don't want to, tell yourself, 'I'll just do five minutes'. Once you start, it's easy to continue.
c You should think about how difficult a piece of homework is or how much time it needs.
d When you get your homework, write it down immediately and always in the same place.

Now use our homework planner and start planning!

2 Match advice a–d with the problems in questions 1–4.
1 d 2 b 3 a 4 c

3 Helen is planning her homework. What should she do first and last on Saturday? Why?

Homework Planner **Student's name:** Helen

1 What is the subject and homework task?	2 When do I have to hand the homework in?	3 From 1–5, how easy/difficult is it? 1= very easy, 5= very difficult	4 How much time do I need to do it?	5 What day am I going to do it?	6 On each day, what am I going to do first, second etc.?
Maths, p38 Exercises 6–9	Monday	3	45 minutes	Saturday	
History, essay	Monday	5	1 1/2 hours	Saturday	
Science, p67 Exercises 3 and 4	Monday	4	1 hour	Saturday	
Geography, project	Wednesday	4	2 1/2 hours	Sunday	

OWN IT!

4 Think about the homework you have to do this week. Use the homework planner to plan it.

UNIT 4 | SENSE AND SENSITIVITY 57

Flipped class

Prepare for **Unit 5**. Students research natural wonders such as the Northern Lights, Victoria Falls or Mount Everest and decide which is their favourite.

Lesson aim: I can talk about natural wonders.

Warmer

Ask students to say what the most amazing nature features in their area are, e.g. a mountain, a waterfall.

5 WONDERFUL WORLD

LEARNING OUTCOMES

I can …

- understand texts about smart cities and a virtual reality tour
- express surprise and disbelief
- write a competition entry
- understand how to use the passive, question tags and questions with prepositions
- use verbs related to processes and extreme adjectives
- learn verbs with prepositions, listen for specific information and skim read to understand the general idea.

Start it!

1 Look at the photo of the Northern Lights. What does it look like?
2 Before you watch, can you think of any natural wonders?
3 What does a waterfall in Yosemite National Park look like? Watch and check. fire
4 Which is your favourite natural wonder? Why?

Watch video 5.1

p61 Language in action 5.2

p63 Language in action 5.3

p64 Everyday English 5.4

p66 Globetrotters 5.5

58 WONDERFUL WORLD | UNIT 5

▶ Start it!

Unit quiz

1 Elicit students' ideas and write them on the board. Ask if any students have ever been to see the Northern Lights.

2 In pairs, students can share information about the natural wonders they found out about for homework.

3 ▶ Elicit that Yosemite is a national park in California in the USA. Find out if any students know about its waterfall, then play **Video 5.1**.

4 Students were asked to think of this for homework. In small groups, students can say what their favourite natural wonder is and give reasons for their choice.

Video comprehension questions

Flipped class

Prepare for **Explore it!** (p59). Students find out a fact about birds or insects.

Unit aims

Skills

I can …

- understand an article about smart cities p60
- express surprise and disbelief p64
- write a competition entry p65
- understand a blog about travelling p66

Language

I can …

- talk about processes p59
- understand how to use the passive p61
- use extreme adjectives p62
- understand how to use question tags and questions with prepositions p63

Learn to Learn

I can …

- learn verbs with prepositions p59
- listen for specific information p62
- use a presentation plan p69

Extra Resources

- *Finished?* – Student's Book p122
- *Vocabulary Bank* – Student's Book p132
- Pronunciation – Student's Book p142
- Workbook p40
- *Teacher's Resource Bank on Cambridge One* for tests package, Cambridge Exam practice, wordlists, differentiated worksheets and many other extra resources.
- *Practice Extra and Digital collaboration space*

Warmer

Ask: *Which animals do you find the most amazing? Why?* Elicit students' ideas and write them on the board. Encourage students to think of senses (e.g. owls have excellent hearing) as well as the things that animals produce (e.g. webs, nests).

1 5.01 Ask students to say what they can see in the photos. Elicit the following: *bees, honeycomb, hive, spider, web, steel, crow, traffic lights.*

Audioscript p166

2 Put students into pairs to complete the task. Encourage students to use the context to guess or confirm the answers.

Target vocabulary

attract /əˈtrækt/
collect /kəˈlekt/
communicate /kəˈmjuːnɪkeɪt/
connect /kəˈnekt/
create /kriˈeɪt/
deliver /dɪˈlɪvə/
develop /dɪˈveləp/
measure /ˈmeʒə/
produce /prəˈdʒuːs/
solve /sɒlv/
supply /səˈplaɪ/
waste /weɪst/

Extra vocabulary practice

Learn to learn

When students learn new words, they should learn which other words they usually go with. Doing this helps sensitise students to the interconnected nature of language.

3 Elicit the answers, writing the whole phrase (verbs + preposition) on the board to reinforce the idea that the verbs go together with the prepositions.

VOCABULARY
Processes

1 5.01 Read about three amazing animals. Listen and repeat the words in **bold**.

Bees **measure** distances between new flowers and their hive. They **communicate** this information by dancing for other bees, which then **collect** the nectar and **deliver** it to the hive. Nectar and pollen **supply** the nutrients bees need to live.

Spiders **create** webs to **attract** as well as catch insects. The silk they **produce** is five times as strong as steel, but they have to wait for the wind to **connect** the end of the first line to something nearby. Spiders don't **waste** any silk: they sometimes eat their webs when they have finished with them.

Crows **solve** problems to get food. In some cities they **develop** the ability to read traffic lights; they wait for the red light, place a walnut in the road, then fly up and wait for a car to drive over the nut and break it open.

2 Match the words in **bold** in the text with definitions a–l.

a make something exist *create*
b make something come nearer **attract**
c get a new quality/ability **develop**
d take somewhere **deliver**
e find the size **measure**
f join **connect**
g bring together **collect**
h make something **produce**
i give **supply**
j find the answer **solve**
k share information **communicate**
l use too much **waste**

LEARN TO LEARN
Learning verbs with prepositions

Learn verbs with the prepositions they take. This helps you to use them correctly.

3 Complete each sentence with a preposition (*to* or *with*). Sometimes both are possible.

1 Insects are **attracted** *to* spider webs.
2 Spiders **connect** their webs **to** something nearby.
3 Bees **communicate** **to/with** each other by dancing.
4 Bees collect nectar and **deliver** it **to** other bees.
5 Nectar **supplies** bees **with** nutrients.

4 Circle the correct words.

1 Which puzzle has six sides and is difficult to *solve* / *deliver*?
2 Which North American country *measures* / *supplies* length in inches and feet, not centimetres and metres?
3 Which country *produces* / *attracts* the most films every year?
4 What's the name of the tunnel that *wastes* / *connects* the UK with France?
5 How do dolphins *communicate* / *develop* with each other?
6 Which animals *create* / *collect* nuts for the winter?

Use it!

5 Discuss the questions in Exercise 4.

Explore it!

Guess the correct answer.

Bees beat their wings very fast, but how many times per second?

a 100 b 200 c 300

Find an interesting fact about birds or insects. Write a question for your partner to answer.

UNIT 5 | WONDERFUL WORLD 59

Match verbs to prepositions

4 ★★★ Challenge students to explain their choice in each case. (Students can make use of the definitions in Exercise 1 in order to do this.)

5 If students do not know any of the answers, encourage them to speculate, using *might*, *could* and *may*.

Vocabulary Bank SB p132

Class challenge

Bees have no stomach / one stomach / **two stomachs**.

Explore it!

Students use the facts they researched about birds and insects for homework.

Homework

Workbook p40

Lesson aim: I can read a text about smart cities.

Warmer

Give students, in small groups, one minute to think of the advantages and disadvantages of living in a city. Ask a student from each group to share the group's ideas with the class.

2 5.02 Brainstorm ideas about what a smart city is with the class, write them on the board, and then get students to read and check which idea is closest.

2 ★ Elicit what each of the four headings refers to, e.g. 'soon to become a reality' refers to something which will happen in the near future. Students can then work alone to do the matching task.

3 Put students into pairs. Each pair divides the six questions into two sets of three, then only looks in the article for the answers to those three questions. At the end, students come together and share their answers.

4 ★ Ask students to first read through the definition to work out the type of word they need to look for (verb, noun, etc.). They then scan the relevant paragraph to search for the word, using context to help them.

Reading comprehension questions

5 Give students time to think and make notes before they discuss.

A smart city is a city of the future where everything will be digitally connected to make life better for people living there.

READING

A webzine article

1 5.02 **Look at the photo. What do you think a smart city is? Read the webzine article and find out.**

2 **Match headings a–d with paragraphs 1–4.**

a Soon to become a reality
b Greener streets
c Everything will be connected
d More choices for citizens

3 **Read the webzine article again and discuss the questions.**

1 How will the IOT make urban life better?
2 What will 3-D printers be able to do?
3 How will food be delivered to our homes?
4 How will we be healthier?
5 Why won't electricity be wasted?
6 What percentage of people will be living in rural areas by 2050?

1 It will collect data about information about the weather, traffic, population movement, our health, etc. and use it to make life better.
2 Print something to eat whenever we want it.
3 By drone.
4 Fridges will remind us when to buy food. Wearable devices will measure how fit we are and communicate with a doctor, who will tell us what is wrong.
5 Houses will turn lights off and streetlights will only go on as you walk past them.
6 Less than 30%.

4 **Find words in the webzine article that mean:**

1 the number of people living in a place (paragraph 1) population
2 belong or relating to the city (paragraph 1) urban
3 a small flying machine without a pilot (paragraph 2) drone
4 to stop something happening (paragraph 3) prevent
5 the people who live in a particular place (paragraph 4) inhabitants

Voice it!

5 **Discuss the questions.**

1 What disadvantages might there be to living in a smart city? Think of three ideas.
2 Would you like to live in a smart city? Tell your partner and explain your reasons.

Finished? p122 Ex 1

SMART CITIES OF THE FUTURE

1 c Electric cars, drone deliveries, houses that communicate with you when you're out. Are you attracted by this image of city life? If so, you're not alone. Scientists and engineers around the world are developing a huge digital web called the Internet of Things (IOT) that will make all of this possible. Soon, billions of devices will be connected by the IOT. It will collect all sorts of data – information about the weather, the traffic, population movement, our shopping, the places we visit, even our health. This information will be used to make urban life better for everyone. Welcome to smart cities, the cities of the future.

2 d In smart cities, we'll have more free time. For example, imagine you're feeling hungry on the way home but don't want to cook. All you'll need to do is send a message to your 3-D printer and tell it to print something tasty for you. Or, if you prefer, order a takeaway and within minutes a delicious pizza is delivered by a drone. Smart citizens will be healthier too. Our fridges will remind us when it's time to buy fresh fruit and vegetables, while devices on our bodies will measure our levels of fitness. The data they collect will be supplied to our doctors and we'll be told to visit them as soon as anything is wrong, so we won't be surprised by unexpected health problems.

3 b Smart cities will also be better for the environment, because electricity won't be wasted in them. Imagine you forget to turn the lights off when you go out. Don't worry – your house will do it for you. What's more, streetlights will only be switched on when you walk past them and cars will communicate with traffic lights to prevent traffic jams, saving both time and energy.

4 a When the first cities were built thousands of years ago, their inhabitants couldn't have realised how different urban life would become, but smart cities are nearly here. Will everything and everyone soon be connected by the IOT? Probably not, but by 2050 more than 70% of us will be living in a city, and we'll definitely be even more connected than we are today.

60 WONDERFUL WORLD | UNIT 5

Extend it!

Students work in small groups to suggest how cities could be improved to make them better to live in. Students should think of such things as accommodation, transport, environment, leisure. Then discuss the best ideas with the class.

Finished?

Fast finishers can turn to SB p122 and do Exercise 1.

Flipped class

▶ Ask students to watch **Video 5.2** and do the **Video worksheet** in the *Teacher's Resource Bank*.

Homework

Workbook p41

Lesson aim: I can understand how to use the passive.

Warmer

▶ Play **Video 5.2** if it was not set for homework and elicit that people used to listen to music on CD players. In the future, our clothes will be made by 3D printers.

1 Elicit what students know about the form and use of the passive before doing this task.

2 ★ Go through the example with the class. Point out how the main verb changes to *be* + past participle and how the subject (*bulls*) and object (*moving objects*) change position.

3 ★ Read out the example, then ask: *Why do we need the present simple passive in 1?* Elicit the answer (because the sentence refers to 'every year'). Encourage students to use the words around each gap to help them choose the correct passive form.

4 5.03 Students can practise reading the completed conversation with a partner.

Audioscript p167

Extra grammar practice

5 Give students time to think about the questions before discussing in pairs.

LANGUAGE IN ACTION

The passive

Watch video 5.2
How did people listen to music in the past?
How will our clothes be made in the future?

Present	Past	Future
A pizza [1] _is_ **delivered** by a drone.	The first cities [2] _were_ **built** thousands of years ago.	Billions of devices [3] _will be_ **connected** by the IOT.
Time and energy **aren't wasted**.	Hieroglyphics **weren't understood** until 1822.	We [4] _won't be_ **surprised** by unexpected health problems.
[5] _Are_ you **attracted** by this image of city life?	When **was** the Internet **invented**?	[6] _Will_ everything and everyone soon _be_ **connected** by the IOT?

1 Complete the examples in the table above. Use the webzine article on page 60 to help you.

2 Rewrite the sentences in the present or past with a passive form of the verb in **bold** and *by*.

1. Moving objects **attract** bulls.
   Bulls are attracted by moving objects.
2. Lightning **strikes** men more often than women.
   Men are struck by lightning more often than women.
3. The Romans **didn't invent** Roman letters.
   Roman letters weren't invented by the Romans.
4. Elizabeth Magie **invented** Monopoly.
   Monopoly was Invented by Elizabeth Magie.

3 Complete the text with the verbs in the box in the present and past passive.

build	bury	lift	make
place	pull	use	~~visit~~

The Pyramids of Giza in Egypt [1] *are visited* by millions of tourists every year. When they _were built_, about 5,500 years ago, great kings called pharaohs [3] _were buried_ inside them. What we don't know is how the Pyramids [4] _were made_. More than two million blocks of stone [5] _were used_ for each one, but nobody knows how each stone [6] _was placed_ in the correct position. Clearly, they [7] _weren't lifted_ by hand, because they were too heavy. [8] _Were_ they _pulled_ by ropes or did people push them by hand?

4 5.03 Complete the conversation with the future passive of the verbs in brackets. Listen and check.

A I was reading a blog that said in the future many jobs [1] *will be done* (do) by robots.
B Really? Like what?
A Well, food [2] _will be served_ (serve) by them in restaurants, houses [3] _will be built_ (build) by them – and in some schools, classes [4] _will be taught_ (teach) by them.
B Robot teachers! That will be strange. But [5] _Will_ all humans _be replaced_ (replace) by robots?
A I don't think so. The blog said most operations [6] _won't be done_ (not do) by robots – human doctors and surgeons will still do those.
B What about sports? [7] _Will_ human football players _be replaced_ (replace) completely?
A I don't think so, but who knows?
B I hope not, because that's what I want to be in the future!

Use it!

5 Discuss the questions.

1. Will all lessons be taught in English?
2. Will all shopping be done online?

Some lessons will be taught in English, but not all of them.

Finished? p122 Ex 2

Extend it!

In pairs, students discuss the predictions in Exercise 4. Do they agree? Why/Why not?

Grammar game

In pairs, students write four questions (about history, music, sport, technology, etc.) using the past or present simple passive, e.g. *When was the internet invented?* Students swap questions with another pair. The pair with the most correct answers wins. Avoid encouraging students to make questions with *by* (*Who was … written by?*) because students will learn this structure in a later lesson.

Finished?

Fast finishers can turn to SB p122 and do Exercise 2.

Homework

Workbook p42

Lesson aim: I can use extreme adjectives.

Warmer

Elicit that *virtual reality* (VR) is a computer simulation of an environment accessed using equipment such as a helmet with a screen inside. Find out if any students have used VR.

1 Students may not know any of the places, so make sure that you ask them to describe what can be seen in the photos.

2 5.04 ★★★ Challenge students to not only listen for the names of the places, but for some facts about those places.

Audioscript p167

Learn to learn

Encourage students to make use of the time available to them before they listen to a recording. They should always read through the questions and think about what they might hear.

3 & 4 5.04 Elicit the type of information needed and write it on the board

5 5.04 When playing the recording, pause after each word to drill the pronunciation.

Target vocabulary

boiling /ˈbɔɪlɪŋ/
deafening /ˈdefənɪŋ/
dreadful /ˈdredfəl/
enormous /ɪˈnɔːməs/
fascinating /ˈfæsəneɪtɪŋ/
freezing /ˈfriːzɪŋ/
gorgeous /ˈɡɔːdʒəs/
marvellous /ˈmɑːvələs/
stunning /ˈstʌnɪŋ/
terrifying /ˈterəfaɪŋ/

Audioscript p167

LISTENING AND VOCABULARY

A virtual reality tour

1 Look at photos 1–3. Do you know where these places are?

2 5.04 Listen to the virtual tour and check your answers to Exercise 1.

LEARN TO LEARN

Listening for specific information

Knowing what kind of information we are listening for can help us to hear it.

3 Read the sentences and decide if the missing information is a year, a measurement or a number.

1. There are *seven* New Wonders of the Natural World. *a number*
2. A major sports event took place in South Africa in **2010** . **a year**
3. The top of Table Mountain is **3 km** wide. **a measurement**
4. The biggest Komodo dragons are **3 m** long. **a measurement**
5. There are approximately **1,700** Komodo dragons on Komodo Island. **a number**
6. **275** smaller waterfalls make up Iguazu Falls. **a number**
7. The water falls up to **82 m** . **a measurement**

4 5.04 Listen again and complete the sentences in Exercise 3.

Extreme adjectives

5 5.05 Replace the underlined words in the text with the words in the box. Listen and check.

boiling deafening dreadful enormous fascinating freezing gorgeous marvellous ~~stunning~~ terrifying

The Sahara Desert looks [1]very beautiful *stunning*. I've been learning about it in class. It's [2]very interesting **fascinating** . At 9.2 million km², it's [3]very big **enormous** . The sand dunes are [4]very beautiful **gorgeous** . It would be [5]very good **marvellous** to visit it one day, but it would be [6]very scary **terrifying** to get lost there without water. During the day it's [7]very hot **boiling** , but at night it can be [8]very cold **freezing** . Sometimes there are sandstorms with [9]very loud **deafening** winds. It must be [10]very bad **dreadful** to be caught in one.

Get it right!

We don't use *very* with extreme adjectives, but we can use *really* or *absolutely*.

Use it!

6 Discuss the questions.

1. Where can you find stunning scenery in your country?
2. Which is worse, boiling hot or freezing cold weather? Why?
3. Would you prefer to live in a gorgeous, tiny house or an ugly, enormous house? Why?
4. What's the most fascinating school subject? Why?

There is an enormous waterfall in my country. The noise is deafening when you stand next to it.

Extra vocabulary practice

Get it right!

Explain that this is because extreme adjectives have a strong enough meaning already, i.e. *boiling* already means 'very hot'.

6 Encourage students to ask each other follow-up questions in order to develop longer conversations.

Vocabulary Bank SB p132

Flipped class

▶ Ask students to watch **Video 5.3** and do the **Video worksheet** in the *Teacher's Resource Bank.*

Homework

Workbook p43

Lesson aim: I can use question tags and questions with prepositions.

Warmer

▶ Play **Video 5.3** if it was not set for homework and elicit that she is blogging about Machu Picchu and that she was most impressed by its size and the stones that were used to build it.

1 Explain that we use question tags to check information. Point out that question tags are formed in two ways: a positive sentence + negative tag; or a negative sentence + positive tag. Students can work in pairs to complete the sentences.

Extra grammar practice

2 Read out the example, then ask students to work alone to complete the sentences.

3 ★★★ Challenge students to explain the reason for their answers in each case.

4 Elicit answers from the class, then point out that the preposition goes after the verb or adjective that it is connected to.

5 Elicit the questions and write them on the board. Students can discuss the correct answers with a partner.

6 Elicit answers from the class, but only accept an answer in the form of a question tag, e.g. students say *Don Quijote was written by Cervantes, wasn't it?*

LANGUAGE IN ACTION

Question tags and questions with prepositions

Watch video 5.3
What is her vlog about? What was she most impressed by?

	Positive sentence + negative tag	Negative sentence + positive tag
to be	It**'s** Cape Town, **isn't** it?	It **isn't** Sydney, [1] is it?
auxiliary *have*	The lesson **has** finished, [2] hasn't it?	Ivan **hasn't** arrived yet, **has** he?
modal verbs	The speech **will** be recorded, **won't** it?	You **won't** be eaten, [3] will you?
present simple	You **speak** German, [4] don't you?	They **don't live** here, **do** they?
past simple	Linda **went** home early, **didn't** she?	You **didn't tell** anyone our secret, [5] did you?

Question tags

1 Complete the examples in the table above.

2 Complete the sentences with the correct question tag.

1 That tour was very good, wasn't it?
2 Insects are interesting, aren't they?
3 It's not very hot in here, is it?
4 We can't hear each other, can we?
5 It would be scary to see a ghost, wouldn't it?

3 Match the sentences in Exercise 1 with responses a–e. Complete the responses with the adjectives in the box.

deafening fascinating freezing marvellous ~~terrifying~~

a Yes, it would be terrifying. 5
b No, it's absolutely freezing. 3
c No – the music is deafening. 4
d It was marvellous. 5
e Yes, they're really fascinating. 2

Questions with prepositions

What are we learning [1] about today?	Where are we going [2] to next?
What are you looking [3] at?	What are you scared [4] of?
Who was it won [5] by?	Who do you look [6] like?

4 Complete the examples in the table above with *about*, *at*, *by*, *like*, *of* or *to*.

5 Put the words in the correct order to make sentences. Then circle the correct answers.

1 made / what / Tutankhamen's mask / of / was / ?
What was Tutankhamen's mask made of?
a glass (b) gold c silver

2 to / Apollo 11 / where / did / go / ?
Where did Apollo 11 go to?
a Mars (b) the moon c The International Space Station

3 a compass / what / for / used / is / ?
What is a compass used for?
a making holes (b) drawing circles c cutting paper

Use it!

6 Discuss the questions using question tags.

1 Who was *Don Quijote* written by? Cervantes
2 What is a GPS used for? finding directions
3 What is glass made of? sand (silicon)

Who was Don Quijote written by? *It was written by …, wasn't it?*

Finished? p122 Ex 3

Grammar game

Students work in pairs. They have one minute to use question tags to check things with their partner that they think are true, e.g. *You've got two sisters, haven't you?* They win a point for each correct idea.

Finished?

Fast finishers can turn to SB p122 and do Exercise 3.

Homework

Workbook p44

Lesson aim: I can express surprise and disbelief.

Warmer

Write *Rome* on the board. Elicit what students know about the city and find out if anyone in the class has been there, and what they thought of it.

1 5.06 Elicit that the photo shows the Coliseum in Rome. Find out what students know about it, before they listen to check. We learn that it's where gladiators used to fight each other and animals, such as bears, lions and elephants. They would also fill the stadium with water and have sea battles there.

Audioscript p168

2 5.06 Explain the meaning, and model the pronunciation of each phrase in the box, explaining that we use a rising tone to express surprise or disbelief.

Useful language practice

▶ Encourage students to copy the intonation used by the presenter in **Video 5.4**.

3 ★★★ Challenge students to think of further contexts for the phrases in the *Everyday English* box. Give students two minutes to do this. Elicit their ideas, check they are right, then write those ideas on the board.

4 Give students time to think of a place. This doesn't have to be a place they have been to; it could be a place they'd like to visit and which they know a lot about.

5 Give students five minutes to plan their conversations. If appropriate, they can use their smartphones to record themselves, listening back to their conversations to check they're using the language from the unit.

6 As well as answering the questions about the other pair's conversation, students can give each other feedback on their speaking, focusing on use of language and intonation.

SPEAKING

Expressing surprise and disbelief

5.06 **1** What do you know about the building in the picture? Listen to the conversation. What do you learn about it?

5.06 **2** Complete the conversation with the phrases from the *Useful language* box. Listen and check.

ANGELA So, Ryan, how was your trip to Rome?
RYAN Oh, man, you should go. It's absolutely stunning. There's so much history and so many amazing buildings there. I loved it.
ANGELA Where was your favourite place?
RYAN I'd say it was the Coliseum.
ANGELA That's where the gladiators used to fight, isn't it?
RYAN Got it in one. Sometimes they would fight with animals, too. Bears, lions, elephants.
ANGELA You [1] *can't be serious*. With animals?
RYAN Yep. On one occasion over 10,000 animals were killed in a single day.
ANGELA [2] ___ [Are you kidding] me? That's dreadful!
RYAN And they used to have sea battles there.
ANGELA I find [3] ___ [that hard to believe]. How was that done?
RYAN They would fill the stadium with water from the aqueducts. There were real ships and everything.
ANGELA: [4] ___ [Seriously] ___? That's fascinating.
RYAN Wanna see a photo of me dressed as a gladiator outside?
ANGELA OK, go on. Wow! Is that you? I can't [5] ___ [believe you actually] wore that!
RYAN I look terrifying, don't I?
ANGELA Er, not exactly. You look sweaty. It must've been really hot there.
RYAN It was. It was boiling.

Useful language

Are you kidding me?	Seriously?
I can't believe you actually ...	You can't be serious.
I find that hard to believe.	

3 Complete the dialogues with the phrases in the *Everyday English* box.

1 A What's the best place you've ever been to?
B ___ [I'd say it was] Iceland.
2 A How was the movie?
B [Oh, man], I loved it!
3 A The exam was easy, wasn't it?
B ___ [Er, not exactly]. I think it was quite hard.
4 A Jack's house is enormous, isn't it?
B I know! It's got a pool ___ [and everything].
5 A [Wanna] have a picnic tomorrow?
B I can't, sorry. I'm busy.

Watch video 5.4
Everyday English

... and everything Er, not exactly. I'd say it was ... Oh, man Wanna ... ?

PLAN

4 Write about an amazing place you have been to. Think of three interesting things about it.

SPEAK

5 Practise the conversation. Describe your amazing place and ask your partner about their place. Remember to use the passive, question tags, questions with prepositions and phrases from the *Useful language* and *Everyday English* boxes.

CHECK

6 Work with another pair. Listen to their conversation and complete the notes.

What place did they talk about? ___

What was interesting about it? ___

Would you like to visit it? ___

64 WONDERFUL WORLD | UNIT 5

Class challenge

The Coliseum was built in the year **80** / 150 / 625.

Lesson aim: I can write a competition entry.

Warmer

Give students a minute to note down the most beautiful places they have visited. Students then discuss these places in small groups, explaining why they like them so much.

1 Elicit ideas about the building, then give students two minutes to read the text. In pairs, they can say whether they would like to visit the place and why.

2 ★★★ Students work alone to complete the task. Extend the activity by asking students if they think the writer's description of Petra makes it sound like an attractive place to visit.

3 Students can compare their answers in pairs before you check with the class.

4 ★ Ask the students to use the text to help them match the phrases.

Useful language practice

5 Give students time to choose a place. This could be a place they know, but have not visited.

6 Give students up to ten minutes to write their competition entry.

7 Students can check each other's work. Is there anything they would improve?

Pronunciation

Students can do the activities on p142, practising the pronunciation of letters *mb* and *bt*.

WRITING
A competition entry

the Treasury at Petra in Jordan

1 Look at the photo. What do you think the building is? Read the competition entry and check your ideas.

THE MOST INCREDIBLE PLACE I'VE EVER VISITED

1 [b] I've been to lots of amazing places, but the one that impressed me the most was Petra, an ancient city in Jordan. I visited it last summer with my family. We all loved it.

2 [d] Petra is fascinating. The first buildings were built over 2,000 years ago. At one time it was inhabited by 30,000 people. A lot of it was carved out of the rock of the mountains. In fact, it is sometimes known as 'the Rose City' because of the colour of the rock.

3 [c] The highlight of a visit to Petra is the Treasury. Nobody is sure why it was built, but archaeologists think that a king was buried there or that it was a place for important documents. When the sun shines on the front of the building, it's really stunning. I'm absolutely certain that it will still be visited hundreds of years in the future.

4 [a] I think Petra deserves to win because it is so beautiful, especially the Treasury. Without a doubt, it's one of the most incredible places in the world.

GO GLOBAL
Tell us about the most incredible place you've ever visited to win two air tickets!

2 Read the entry again. Match topics a–d with paragraphs 1–4.

a The reason why the place should win
b Introduction
c Detailed description of part of the place
d General description of the place

3 Discuss the questions.

1 What is unusual about the way Petra was built?
2 What do people think the Treasury was built for?
3 List all the extreme adjectives in the entry.

1 A lot of it was carved out of the rock.
2 To bury a king there or to keep important documents.
3 incredible, amazing, fascinating, stunning, beautiful

4 Match phrases 1–5 with the phrases from the *Useful language* box a–e with a similar meaning.

1 for me, the … that was best was … [d]
2 It's certain that … [e]
3 I'm completely sure that … [b]
4 … should win because … [a]
5 When you go to …, the best part is … [c]

Useful language

a … deserves to win because …
b I'm absolutely certain that …
c The highlight of a visit to … is …
d the … that impressed me the most was …
e Without a doubt …

Write a competition entry.

PLAN

5 Think of the most incredible place you have visited. Find out information about it and write down two reasons why it impressed you.

WRITE

6 Write your competition entry. Remember to include the four paragraphs in Exercise 2, extreme adjectives and phrases from the *Useful language* box.

CHECK

7 Do you …

- give a description of the place?
- say why it impressed you?
- explain why you think the place should win?

Pronunciation p142

Finished? p122 Ex 4

Extend it!

Students read other students' entries in a group. They each nominate a top three, and from that, select a winner.

Finished?

Fast finishers can turn to SB p122 and do Exercise 4.

Flipped class

Prepare for **Around the World** (pp66–67). Students research extreme places on Earth, finding out about the parts of the world that are very cold, hot or wet.

Homework

Workbook p45

Background information

Meghalaya is a state in India, bordering Bangladesh. It is mountainous and 70% of the state is covered in forest. Mawsynram and Cherrapunjee, two villages in the state, are the wettest places in the world.

▶ **Video 5.5** develops the theme of living in extreme conditions. Before students watch the video, ask them to predict answers to the questions.

Elicit that climate, temperature and location can all make a place difficult to live in. The Atacama Desert is very dry as it gets hardly any rain; Siberian winters are extremely cold and can get as cold as -60 degrees C, and there is vegetation for only three months of the year; people live on small islands on Lake Titicaca in houses made from reeds and so they need to be repaired and rebuilt very often. Matera is unusual as it is built into rocks.

Video comprehension questions

AROUND THE WORLD

READING
A travel blog

Globetrotters
Watch video 5.5
Extreme homes

- What can make a place difficult to live in?
- Why is it difficult to live in these places: Atacama Desert, Siberia and Lake Titicaca?
- What's unusual about Matera?

1 Look at the pictures. Where do you think they were taken? Meghalaya, India

2 (5.09) Read Scott's blog for Day 1. Which activities that you can do in Meghalaya does he mention?
go to festivals, explore caves, see waterfalls, visit a bird sanctuary, cross 'living root bridges', go trekking

LEARN TO LEARN

Skimming for gist
Often you want to understand the general idea of a text, not the details. To do this you can 'skim' the text, which means to read it very quickly.

3 Skim the rest of the blog. Which of the activities that Scott mentions in Day 1 of his blog does he not do while he is in Meghalaya?
He doesn't see a waterfall.

66 WONDERFUL WORLD | UNIT 5

SCOTT THE EXPLORER
BLOGGING MY WAY AROUND INDIA

DAY 1
Hi, everyone! This week I'm in Meghalaya in northeast India, the wettest place on Earth. I've only been here for a day but I love the place already. It's really cloudy, but when the clouds lift the scenery is stunning: beautiful mountains covered by gorgeous green forests. The people are really friendly, and there are loads of things to do – you can go to festivals, explore caves, see waterfalls, visit a bird sanctuary, cross 'living root bridges', go trekking and so much more. I can't wait! This blog will be updated while I'm here so make sure you check out my posts!

DAY 2
This morning I went to the marvellous Siju Bird Sanctuary, where lots of endangered birds are protected. I even saw one of the rare peacock pheasants. Check out the photo! After that I tried *jadoh*, a local dish of rice and meat. Rice is traditionally eaten several times a day here, and it was delicious. In the afternoon I wanted to explore the capital, Shillong, where I'm staying, but it started raining heavily, so I stayed inside and relaxed. Tomorrow I'm going to visit the Krem Lymput cave. I'm really excited – I've never been in a cave before!

1 Do this task with the class as a whole. Elicit students' ideas and write appropriate ones on the board.

2 (5.09) Ask students to use the photos to predict the sort of activities that Scott might write about in his post for Day 1 of his trip. They can then read the first paragraph to check.

Learn to learn
Students need to learn a variety of ways of reading, one of which is reading a text quickly to get a general idea of the content. They may already be confident about doing this, so make sure you give students lots of opportunities to practise doing it.

3 ★ Tell students to first highlight the activities that Scott mentions in the *Day 1* section of his blog. They can then read the rest of the blog quickly to locate which of those activities are referred to, highlighting them so as to help them determine which activity Scott doesn't do.

4 5.10 Encourage students to read the text carefully to identify the information required to answer the questions. Monitor and help as necessary.

Reading comprehnsion questions

5 ★ Elicit that an adverb is used to describe a verb or adjective (e.g. *She is* *amazingly good*.) In pairs, students search for the adverbs, using context to help them find the right words.

6 After students have discussed the questions, ask them: *Should boys and girls be treated the same? In which situations should they be treated differently?*

Students can collaborate digitally online and offline in the collaboration space, where teachers can set, track and assess students' work. Students can also share and showcase their work as well as comment on each other's projects.

Extend it!

In pairs, students talk about which country in the world they most like to travel around. They can discuss what interests them about the culture of that country and what activities they would like to do on any trip there.

Class challenge

The capital of India is Mumbai / Kolkata / **New Delhi**.

DAY 3

OK, I've just got back from the cave tour. It wasn't my favourite experience! The guide was great. He explained everything really clearly – how old the cave is, how it was made and so on, and the cave was beautiful, but at times I was really scared. It's over six km long, with some enormous rooms, but most of it was narrow, dark and wet. I had to carry a torch and walk really carefully. It was terrifying! Anyway, I'm safely back in the hostel now. More from me tomorrow!

DAY 4

Today I saw the Nongkrem dance festival. This colourful festival is celebrated by the Khasi people, who are one of the main groups of people in Meghalaya. They have an incredibly fascinating society. Women have a very important role in Meghalaya society. For example, the birth of a boy is not a special occasion but the birth of a girl is celebrated by everyone, children take their mother's surname, and when parents die, the youngest daughter gets their house. It's not the best place to be a boy. The sons don't really get anything!

DAY 5

DAY 6

I'm back! I didn't write anything yesterday because I was trekking in the mountains overnight. I saw some incredible views and finally crossed one of the famous tree root bridges. These bridges are created by hand. People tie the roots of young trees together and help them to grow slowly across rivers. The process takes many years, but eventually the roots are strong enough for people to walk on. Check out the picture I took! Anyway, the time here has gone so fast. I'd love to stay longer but tomorrow I have to leave. Thanks for reading!

4 5.10 **Now read the whole of Scott's blog. Discuss the questions.**

1. What problem did Scott have on Day 2? *It started raining so he couldn't explore Shillong.*
2. Do you think Scott will visit any more caves in the future? Why / Why not? *probably not because he was scared visiting the Krem Lymput cave.*
3. What is unusual about births in Khasi society? *They celebrate the birth of girls but not boys.*
4. Why didn't Scott post anything on Day 5? *Because he was trekking overnight.*
5. How are 'living root bridges' made? *People tie the roots of young trees together and help them grow across rivers.*

5 **Find adverbs in the travel blog that mean:**

1. in a traditional way (day 2) *traditionally*
2. a lot (day 2) *heavily*
3. in a way that is easy to understand (day 3) *clearly*
4. absolutely (day 4) *incredibly*
5. in the end (day 6) *eventually*

Voice it!

6 **Discuss the questions.**

1. Would you like to visit Meghalaya? Why / Why not?
2. Are boys and girls treated the same in your country?

Explore it!

Guess the correct answer.

Meghalaya is the wettest place on Earth, but where is the driest?

a in South America (circled)
b in Africa **c** in Australia

Find another interesting fact about an extreme place on Earth. Write a question for your partner to answer.

Own it! The Culture Project Teacher's Resource Bank

UNIT 5 | WONDERFUL WORLD 67

Explore it!

To write their questions, students use the facts about extreme places that they researched for homework.

Culture Project

See Project Book p38 for further information and activities.

Lesson aim: I can review what I have learnt and reflect on my progress.

The aim of this review page is for students to revise the grammar and vocabulary from the unit. You can either do it in class, as a timed progress test or set it for homework.

Vocabulary

1 Elicit the difference between active and passive forms, writing example sentences on the board. Then put students in groups, and challenge them to be the first to complete each sentence in turn. Groups win a point for each correct sentence. The group with the most points at the end wins.

2 ★★★ Elicit definitions for the adjectives in the box. Then complete the sentences with the class as a whole. Elicit the correct adjective for each gap, then challenge students to say why that adjective is the right one.

Language in action

3 Students can do this task in pairs. Monitor and help as necessary.

4 Elicit the first question and write it on the board. Students can then work alone to complete the dialogue. After you check answers, students can practise the dialogue in pairs.

Unit quiz review

5 REVIEW

VOCABULARY

1 Complete the sentences with the correct form of the verbs in the box.

attract collect communicate connect create deliver develop measure produce solve supply waste

1 The postman **delivered** seven letters to my house this morning.
2 The teacher **will collect** the students' homework next Monday.
3 Scientists **developed** the Internet in the 1970s.
4 Most people **waste** lots of plastic every day.
5 My car engine **produces** a lot of heat.
6 Electric lights **attract** different insects.
7 Walt Disney **created** some of the world's most famous cartoon characters.
8 A stopwatch **measures** time.
9 A young mathematician **solved** the most difficult equation in history a few years ago.
10 Three different companies **will supply** electricity to this city next year.
11 The Channel Tunnel **connects** the United Kingdom with France.
12 Pilots on international flights use English **to communicate** with each other.

2 Complete the sentences with the adjectives in the box.

boiling deafening dreadful enormous fascinating freezing terrifying

1 Turn that music down – it's **deafening**!
2 Can you open the window? It's **boiling** in here.
3 It was a bad movie – the actors were **dreadful**.
4 The Grand Canyon is 446 km long – it's **enormous**.
5 Put your coat on. It's **freezing** today.
6 I'm scared of spiders. They're **terrifying**.
7 The book was **fascinating**. I read it twice!

LANGUAGE IN ACTION

3 Rewrite sentences 1 to 5 in Exercise 1 as passive sentences.

1 **Seven letters were delivered to my house this morning by the postman / by the postman this morning.**
2 **The students' homework will be / is going to be collected next Monday by the teacher / by the teacher next Monday.**
3 **The Internet was developed by scientists in the 1970s. / In the 1970s …**
4 **Lots of plastic is wasted every day by most people / by most people every day**
5 **A lot of heat is produced by my car engine.**

4 Complete the dialogue with the correct questions and question tags.

A looking / you / what / for / are
[1] **What are you looking for?**
B My phone charger. It was here somewhere.
A You haven't put it in your bag, [2] **have you**?
B No, I looked there. You don't have an extra one, [3] **do you**?
A Sorry, no. to / you / who / do / to / talk / need
[4] **Who do you need to talk to?**
B My brother. We're going to a rugby match. It starts in 15 minutes.
A He can just wait for you inside the stadium, [5] **can't he**?
B: No, because I've got the tickets!

Self-assessment

I can use verbs to talk about processes.	☹	😐	☺
I can use extreme adjectives.	☹	😐	☺
I can use the passive.	☹	😐	☺
I can use question tags and questions with prepositions.	☹	😐	☺

68 WONDERFUL WORLD | UNIT 5

Self-assessment

Ask students to look back at the exercises in their Workbook to help them complete the self-assessment box. They can then ask you for extra homework for the areas they have least confidence in.

Homework

Workbook pp46–47

Learners should be developing different ways to communicate clearly in English. Planning what they are going to say is an important way of helping them to become more fluent, as well as more accurate.

Warmer

Write *presentation* on the board. Elicit the meaning (a talk on a particular subject given to an audience). Find out if students ever make presentations in their secondary school, and how they feel about them.

1 Ask students to look at the photos. Elicit what students know about the natural phenomena shown before students look at the notes and decide the topic of Kirill's presentation.

2 Elicit the questions to fill each of the gaps. Write the questions on the board.

3 Put students into small groups to work on building on the notes in Exercise 1. Students can then practise doing the final part of the presentation.

OWN IT!

4 Give students time to read about how a rainbow is formed. Make sure that students understand the description, then give them up to fifteen minutes to work on their presentation. Monitor and help students with their plan if necessary.

5 Encourage students to offer each other feedback on their presentations. Can they think of any way to improve their partner's presentation?

LEARN TO LEARN

LEARN TO ... USE A PRESENTATION PLAN

A presentation plan can help you prepare a presentation and make it clear and easy for the listener to understand.

1 Read Kirill's presentation plan notes. What do you think his presentation is about? Circle a, b or c.

a a rainbow

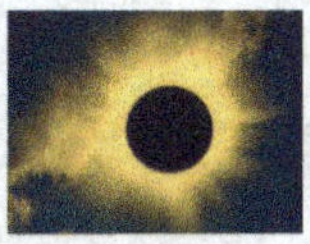

(b) a total eclipse of the sun

c the aurora borealis

Presentation Plan

Introduce the presentation.		Today, I'm going to talk about …
1 *What is it?*		a very special event in the sky!
2 *How does it happen?*		the sun is hidden by the moon, parts of the Earth are covered by its shadow
3 *Where and when can you see it?*	**Where?**	You need to be in the area covered by the moon's shadow.
	When?	about once every year and a half
4 *What other information can I give you?*		Never look directly at it! It's dangerous.
5 *Have I ever seen one?*	**Where?**	Yes, in Russia
	When?	11 August, 2018
	What was it like?	absolutely stunning!

2 Read the beginning of Kirill's presentation. Complete the missing questions.

Good afternoon. Today, I'm going to talk about a total eclipse of the sun. Perhaps you've seen one. [1] What is it? *Well, it's a very special event in the sky.* [2] How does it happen? *It happens when the sun is hidden by the moon and parts of the Earth are covered by its shadow.* [3] Where and when can you see it? *Well, you can only see it …*

3 Imagine you are doing Kirill's presentation together. Use the questions and the notes to do the complete presentation.

OWN IT!

4 Prepare a presentation on how a rainbow is formed. Use the information below to help you.

How is a rainbow formed?

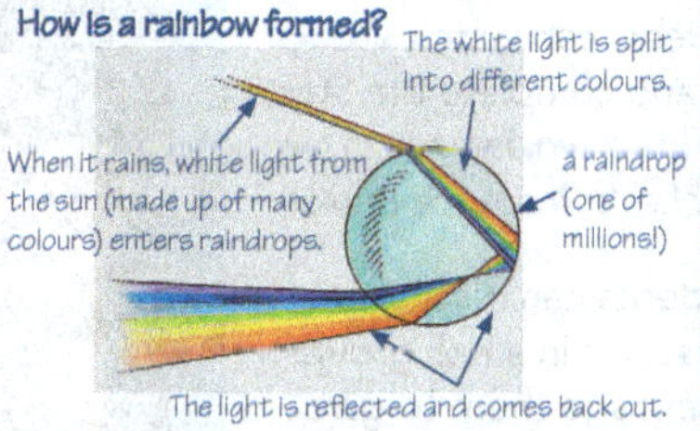

- We see the coloured light from all the millions of raindrops as a rainbow.
- You can see rainbows in the sky opposite the sun.
- Rainbows are really circles, but we only see half.
- If you're lucky, you might see a double rainbow

5 Listen to your partner's presentation and ask a question.

UNIT 5 | WONDERFUL WORLD 69

Flipped class

Prepare for **Unit 6**. Students research extreme sports and think about why people want to do them.

Lesson aim: I can talk about extreme sports.

Warmer

Ask: *What do we mean by extreme sport?* Elicit a definition (any sport involving high risk, e.g. free-solo climbing, bungee jumping), then ask students to say if they have ever done an extreme sport and what they thought of it.

6 NO LIMITS

LEARNING OUTCOMES

I can ...

- understand texts about taking risks and overcoming challenges
- encourage a friend to do something
- write a for and against essay
- understand how to use conditional tenses
- use verb collocations with *get*, *take* and *have*, and talk about inspirations and challenges
- use collocations in sentences, and practise listen and choose questions
- make a leaflet.

Start it!

1 Look at the photo. Would you like to do a sport like this?
2 Before you watch, what extreme sports can you think of?
3 Why do people do extreme sports? Watch and check.
4 Are there any extreme sports you'd like to do? Which ones?

to have a goal in life, be successful at something, to do something that only very few people do, to feel special, to have the feeling of increased energy from adrenalin

Watch video 6.1

Language in action 6.2 p73

Language in action 6.3 p75

Everyday English 6.4 p76

70 NO LIMITS | UNIT 6

▶ Start it!

Unit quiz

1 Elicit the extreme sport shown (snowboarding), then put students into pairs to discuss the question.

2 Students share the extreme sports that they found out about for homework.

3 ▶ Discuss this question with the class. Write students' ideas on the board. Then students can watch **Video 6.1** and complete the Start it! **Video worksheet** in the *Teacher's Resource Bank*.

4 Students can discuss these questions in small groups. Encourage them to give reasons for their answers.

Video comprehension questions

Flipped class

Prepare for **Explore it!** (p71). Students find out a fact about an extreme sport.

Unit aims

Skills

I can ...

- understand a fact sheet about taking risks p72
- encourage a friend to do something p76
- write a for and against essay p77
- understand a text about overcoming challenges pp78–79

Language

I can ...

- use verb collocations with *get*, *take* and *have* p71
- understand how to use the first and second conditional p73
- talk about inspiration and challenge p74
- understand how to use the third conditional p75

Learn to Learn

I can ...

- use collocations in sentences p71
- listen and choose the correct option p74
- learn to take more responsibility for my learning p81

Extra Resources

- *Finished?* – Student's Book p123
- *Vocabulary Bank* – Student's Book p133
- CLIL – Student's Book p139
- Pronunciation – Student's Book p142
- Workbook p48
- *Teacher's Resource Bank* on *Cambridge One* for tests package, Cambridge Exam practice, wordlists, differentiated worksheets and many other extra resources.
- *Practice Extra* and *Digital collaboration space*

Warmer

Write *have breakfast* on the board. Elicit that this is a collocation. Put students into small groups to think of as many other collocations with *have* in two minutes.

1 6.01 Ask students to complete the task by using the context in which the phrases in bold are seen in the sentences.

Audioscript p168

Target vocabulary

get a lot out of /get ə lɒt aʊt ɒv/
get bored /get bɔːd/
get lost /get lɒst/
get on my nerves /get ɒn maɪ nɜːvz/
get to know /get tə nəʊ/
have doubts /hæv daʊts/
have fun /hæv fʌn/
have the chance /hæv the tʃɑːns/
take advantage of /teɪk ədˈvɑːntɪdʒ ɒv/
take an interest in /teɪk ən ˈɪntrəst ɪn/
take pleasure in /teɪk ˈpleʒə ɪn/
take risks /teɪk rɪsks/

Extra vocabulary practice

Pronunciation

Students turn to p142 for practice of stress in multi-syllable words.

2 & 3 Students can compare their results in pairs, giving reasons for either agreeing or disagreeing with them.

Learn to learn

Encourage students to record vocabulary in a variety of ways, such as using an example sentence and highlighting which other words or phrases are used with the new word(s).

VOCABULARY

Verb collocations with *get*, *take* and *have*

1 6.01 Read the quiz. Match the phrases in **bold** with definitions a–l. Listen and repeat the phrases.

a annoy somebody a lot *get on my nerves*
b become unhappy because something is not interesting get bored
c do something that might be dangerous take risks
d enjoy yourself have fun
e be interested in something take an interest in
f feel unsure about something have doubts
g get enjoyment from something take pleasure in
h have the possibility to do something have the chance
i not know where you are get lost
j get a good feeling from something get a lot out of
k spend time with somebody so you learn more about them get to know
l use the good things from a situation take advantage of

1
A I **get bored** when I watch a film I've seen before.
B I **take pleasure in** watching films a second or third time.

2
A I like **taking advantage of** being in unknown places by myself to explore.
B I never walk around new places by myself in case I **get lost**.

3
A I **get a lot out of** extreme sports like skiing or waterskiing.
B I don't like to **take risks** and would never do extreme sports.

4
A I try new foods whenever I **have the chance**.
B I **have doubts** about trying new foods I've never eaten before.

5
A I like **getting to know** people who are exciting and unpredictable.
B People who are unpredictable sometimes **get on my nerves**.

6
A I **take an interest in** all kinds of fun activities, like going on theme park rides.
B I don't **have fun** on theme park rides. They scare me!

Did you choose more As or more Bs?
More As – You enjoy taking risks and like to experience new, exciting situations.
More Bs – You prefer not to take lots of risks and enjoy being in a routine.

Pronunciation p142

2 Read the quiz again. Circle the answers that are true for you.

3 Read the results at the bottom of the page. Do you agree with them?

LEARN TO LEARN

Using collocations in sentences

Collocations with *get*, *take* and *have* have lots of meanings. Record these collocations in a sentence to remember the meaning.

4 Think of true sentences for the collocations in Exercise 1. Use *always*, *usually*, *sometimes*, *hardly ever*, *never*.

I sometimes get bored when I'm at home.

5 Compare your sentences with your partner. What other collocations do you know with *get*, *have* and *take*?

Use it!

6 Write questions with the collocations. Ask and answer the questions.

Have you ever had the chance to try an extreme sport?

Yes, I had the chance to try waterskiing last summer. I had lots of fun!

Explore it!

Guess the correct answer.
How old was the oldest person to skydive?
a 89 b 102 c 110

Find another fact about an extreme sport. Write a question for your partner to answer.

UNIT 6 | NO LIMITS 71

4 & 5 Elicit any other collocations students know with the three verbs and write them on the board.

Order the words

6 Before students ask and answer their questions, check that they have written their questions correctly.

Vocabulary Bank SB p133

Explore it!

Students use the information they researched for homework.

Homework

Workbook p48

Lesson aim: I can understand a text about taking risks.

Warmer

Elicit the meaning of *take a risk* (to do something even though something bad may happen as a consequence). Remind students that *take a risk* is a collocation (we don't say, e.g. *make a risk*). Elicit the sort of activities that involve taking risks, e.g. sky-diving, rock climbing.

1 6.04 Read out the questions. Elicit ideas from the class as a whole, before checking with the text.

2 Students can compare their completed tables in pairs before you go through the answers.

3 ★★★ Challenge students to do this task before reading the text again. In each case challenge students to give a reason for their choice.

Reading comprehension

4 ★ Help students by telling them which paragraph they will find the vocabulary in. (**1** para 2; **2** para 3; **3** para 3; **4** para 4; **5** para 5).

5 Encourage students to ask follow-up questions to develop a conversation.

When taking risks is a *good thing*

Everyone has to take risks sometimes, but many people think risks are negative, especially for teenagers. They connect risk-taking with dangerous behaviour, such as riding a motorbike too fast or looking at your phone while crossing the street. If this sounds like your parents, you might want to explain this to them. Taking risks can also be positive. Sometimes feeling scared or uncomfortable can help us experience new things and learn how to make good decisions. If more people understood this, they might see why teenagers sometimes need to take risks.

What type of risks do you like?

Surprises Would you be happy if your friends planned a surprise party for you? If the answer is yes, then you may enjoy unpredictable things. You get bored very easily and take pleasure in not knowing what's going to happen next.

Danger If you take an interest in activities such as skiing or parkour, you might enjoy danger. If you adore extreme sports or theme park rides, it's because risky situations produce a chemical in the brain called dopamine. Dopamine makes you feel happy and want to repeat an activity again to get the same feeling. That's why you want to go back on a rollercoaster ride as soon as it's finished.

New experiences Alternatively, if you have fun trying new foods or discovering new places, you may be someone who gets a lot out of new experiences. This is important because if you didn't go to new places, you wouldn't learn new things about other cultures.

Healthy risks

How would you feel if you had an audition for the school show? Auditions, selection to get into a school sports team or facing a school bully are situations that might make you feel scared. However, they also help you develop important skills such as how to solve problems, make good decisions and become independent. Just think, you could be the world's best singer, lawyer or volleyball player. But unless you take some risks, you'll never know.

READING

A fact sheet

1 6.04 **How do the people in the photos feel? How would you feel? Read the fact sheet and check your ideas.**

They may feel nervous or scared.

2 Read the fact sheet again and complete the table.

Types of risk taker	1 People who like unpredictable things. 2 People who like danger. 3 People who like new experiences.
Examples of negative risks	Riding a motorbike too fast, crossing the street looking at your phone.
Examples of positive risks	Auditioning for a school show, trying to get into a school sports team, facing a school bully.
Skills you develop when you take risks	How to solve problems, make good decisions and become independent.

3 Read the fact sheet again. Write *T* (true), *F* (false) or *DS* (doesn't say).

1. All risks are dangerous. F
2. Most parents don't want teenagers to take risks. DS
3. Some people like not knowing what will happen. T
4. You have more dopamine in your brain when you feel bored. F
5. Taking risks can teach us about other cultures. T
6. There are advantages to scary situations. T
7. If you don't take risks, you won't solve problems. DS

4 Find words in the fact sheet that mean:

1. something that can change suddenly (adj) unpredictable
2. love (v) adore
3. if something bad could happen (adj) risky
4. another possibility (adv) alternatively
5. choosing someone from a group of people (n) selection

Voice it!

5 Discuss the questions.

1. What type of risk taker is most similar to you? Why?
2. What risky things have you done that aren't dangerous, e.g. having an audition?
3. Can taking risks help solve problems?

Finished? p123 Ex1

72 NO LIMITS | UNIT 6

Extend it!

In pairs, students talk about the riskiest activity they have ever done. First, ask them to make notes on these questions:

- *what is a risky thing that you have done?*
- *how did you feel when doing it?*
- *why you will or won't do it again.*

Then ask them to talk about the subject without stopping for two minutes.

Finished?

Fast finishers can turn to SB p123 and do Exercise 1.

Flipped class

▶ Ask students to watch **Video 6.2** and do the **Video worksheet** in the *Teacher's Resource Bank*.

Homework

Workbook p49

Lesson aim: I can understand how to use the first and second conditional.

Warmer

▶ Play **Video 6.2** and elicit that he tried wakeboarding and that he liked it.

1 ★ Write the following sentences on the board:
1 If I have time tomorrow, I'll go snowboarding.
2 If I had time tomorrow, I'd go snowboarding.
Highlight the form and explain the difference in use (the first conditional is for something that may happen; the second conditional is for something hypothetical or imaginary, i.e. something which won't happen). Students can then complete the table.

Get it right!

Point out that we don't use *unless* with a negative verb, e.g. we don't say ~~*I'll go to the beach tomorrow unless it doesn't rain*~~.

2 Elicit that the activity in the photo is called *parkour*. Ask students if they have ever done it or if they would like to try it.

3 Extend this task by asking students to answer the question and discuss the two statements in pairs.

4 Ask students to read the text quickly to understand it before completing it.

Extra grammar practice

5 Check that students have formed the questions correctly before discussing them in pairs.

LANGUAGE IN ACTION

First and second conditional

Watch video 6.2
What did he try last week?
Did he like it?

First conditional	Second conditional
If this [1] sounds (sound) like your parents, you **might want** to explain this to them.	If you **took** healthy risks, you **could become** more independent.
Unless you [2] take (take) some risks, you'**ll** never **know**.	**If** you [3] didn't go (not go) to new places, you **wouldn't learn** new things about other cultures.
Will you **go** on all the rides **if** we **go** to the theme park?	**Would** you **be** happy if your friends [4] planned (plan) a surprise party for you?

1 Complete the examples in the table above with the correct form of the verbs in brackets. Use the fact sheet on page 72 to help you.

Get it right!

We can use ***unless*** to mean *except if*.
Use a positive verb with *unless*.
I'll go to the beach unless it rains =
I'll go to the beach except if it rains.

2 Put the words in the correct order to make first conditional sentences.

1 you'll / get better at it / If you / a lot, / practise parkour
If you practise parkour a lot, you'll get better at it.

2 from other cultures / if you / You might / try it / enjoy food
You might enjoy food from other cultures if you try it.

3 will you / doesn't rain / go to / If it / the water park / ?
If it doesn't rain, will you go to the water park?

3 Complete the second conditional sentences with the correct form of the verbs.

1 *Would* you *learn* to fly a plane if you *had* the chance? (would / have / learn)

2 If we didn't do crazy things from time to time, life could be boring. (could / be / not do)

3 I wouldn't be frightened if I got lost in a forest at night. (wouldn't / get lost / be)

4 Complete the text with the first or second conditional.

If you [1] *had* (have) the chance, would you risk your life to save someone? If you thought about it carefully, you probably [2] wouldn't put (not put) yourself in danger, but scientists say it's a natural impulse. For example, if we [3] saw (see) someone in the water who couldn't swim, we would save them. In an emergency, unless we [4] stop (stop) and [5] think (think) about it, the human body will react automatically.

Use it!

5 Make questions with *you* in the first or second conditional. Ask and answer.

1 If / not meet / friends / later / might / feel?
If you don't meet your friends later, how might you feel?

2 How / life / different / not have / social media?
How would your life be different if you didn't have social media?

3 What / do this weekend / have some free time?
What will you do this weekend if you have some free time?

4 Which extreme sport / try / could choose?
Which extreme sport would you try if you could choose?

Finished? p123 Ex 2

Grammar game

Write some gapped sentences on the board, e.g. *Life would be boring if ... / If young people never left home ... / If I were rich ...* Students complete these second conditional sentences. In pairs, they then try to guess how their partner completed the sentences.

Finished?

Fast finishers can turn to SB p123 and do Exercise 2.

Homework

Workbook p50

Lesson aim: I can talk about inspiration and challenge.

Warmer
Ask: *We are often inspired by athletes. Why do you think this is?* Elicit students' ideas.

1 6.05 When checking answers, pause after each word to drill pronunciation.

Target vocabulary

Nouns
bravery /ˈbreɪvəri/
challenge /ˈtʃælɪndʒ/
determination /dɪtɜːmɪˈneɪʃən/
obstacle /ˈɒbstəkəl/
opportunity /ɒpəˈtʃuːnəti/

Verbs
achieve /əˈtʃiːv/
encourage /ɪnˈkʌrɪdʒ/
inspire /ɪnˈspaɪə/
overcome /əʊvəˈkʌm /
support /səˈpɔːt/

Extra vocabulary practice

2 Read out the three questions. Give students time to think about their answers before discussing them in pairs.

Vocabulary Bank SB p133

3 6.06 Ask students to look at the photos. Can they predict the challenge Bethany overcame?

Audioscript p169

Learn to learn
Tell students that if they think about the content of the questions before they listen, they will have a clearer idea about what they need to listen to, and what they don't have to pay attention to.

VOCABULARY AND LISTENING
Inspiration and challenge

She had her arm bitten off by a shark, but then went back to surfing and became a professional surfer.

1 6.05 **Read the nomination for an amazing athlete. Match the words in bold with definitions a–j.**

Send us your nominations for the most amazing athlete you know and we'll tell their story on our podcast.

- Which athlete [1]**inspires** you because they have [2]**overcome** an [3]**obstacle**?
- Did they show [4]**determination** and [5]**bravery**? How?
- How did friends or family [6]**support** and [7]**encourage** them to get on with their life?
- What was their biggest [8]**challenge**?
- What have they [9]**achieved**?
- Have they had any [10]**opportunities** to help other people?

a deal with a difficult situation successfully **2**
b finish something or reach an aim after a lot of hard work **9**
c give confidence to others and motivate them to do something **7**
d give emotional or practical help to others **6**
e make someone feel they want to do something and can do it **1**
f no fear of dangerous or difficult things **5**
g situations or chances **10**
h something which requires a lot of hard work to be done (successfully) **8**
i the ability to continue trying to do something difficult **4**
j something that stops an action or makes progress difficult or slow **3**

Use it!

2 Discuss the questions.
1 Who or what inspires you?
2 What's the biggest obstacle you or someone you know has overcome?
3 Who encourages you to do your homework?

A podcast

3 6.06 **Listen to the podcast. What big challenge did Bethany Hamilton overcome?**

LEARN TO LEARN
Listening and choosing the correct option

Read all the options, check any unknown words and cross out any options you know are not correct.

4 6.06 **Listen and circle the correct option.**
1 When she was 13 Bethany …
a learned to surf. b had an accident. c gave up surfing.
- Check you understand *gave up* (past simple of *give up* – to stop something forever.)
- Option a isn't correct as she learned to surf when she was a young child.
- Option c isn't correct as she returned to surfing soon after the accident.
- The correct answer is option b.

5 6.07 **Listen to the whole extract and circle the correct options.**
2 Bethany lost her arm … .
(a) in the sea b in hospital c three weeks after the accident
3 It was … decision to return to surfing.
(a) Bethany's b her family's c a bad
4 Bethany competes … .
a in special competitions b only in the USA (c) against other professional surfers
5 Her book and films … .
a are not true b teach people how to surf (c) inspire people to overcome challenges

Voice it!

6 What surprises you most about her story? What would you do in a similar situation?

74 NO LIMITS | UNIT 6

4 6.06 Ask students to read the three options, then focus attention on the first of the four points (i.e. the one about *give up*). After you play the recording, elicit the answer, then read through the three remaining points, which explain why option b is the correct answer.

Audioscript p169

5 6.07 Ask students to read through the options before they listen.

Audioscript p169

6 Give students time to think about their answers before they discuss them in pairs.

Class challenge
The biggest shark is the Great White Shark / Tiger Shark / **Whale Shark**.

Flipped class
Ask students to watch **Video 6.3** and do the **Video worksheet** in the *Teacher's Resource Bank*.

Homework
Workbook p51

Lesson aim: I can understand how to use the third conditional.

Warmer

▶ Play **Video 6.3** if it was not set for homework. Elicit that she is thinking about how life could have been different. She would have gone on holiday to Uluru.

1 Check students' understanding of the third conditional by asking the following questions: *Does the third conditional refer to events in the past or the present?* (the past) **2** *What tense de we use in the if clause?* (the past perfect).

2 ★ Encourage students to refer to the irregular verb list on SB p143.

3 🎧 6.08 ★ Go through the example with the class. To check students' understanding, ask *Did the girl get stuck?* (yes); *Did the team need to lift the car?* (yes).

Audioscript p170

4 ★ Elicit the beginnings of sentences 2–4 and write these on the board.

Extra grammar practice

5 Check that students form the third conditional correctly. Students can compare their sentences in pairs.

LANGUAGE IN ACTION

Third conditional

Watch video 6.3
What is she thinking about?
Where would she have gone on holiday?

¹ Imaginary situation in the past	² Possible consequence
If + **had (not)** + **past participle**	**would (not) have** + **past participle**
If they **hadn't taken** Bethany to hospital straight away, **If** that **had happened** to me,	she **would have died**. I **wouldn't have returned** to the water.
Question	
What **would** you **have done**	**if** it **had happened** to you?

1 **Complete the headings with *Possible* or *Imaginary*.**

2 **Put the words in the correct order to make third conditional sentences.**

1 had seen / she wouldn't / in the water / If Bethany / the shark / have gone
If Bethany had seen the shark, she wouldn't have gone in the water.

2 Many people wouldn't / if she / a film / have heard / hadn't made / about her bravery
Many people wouldn't have heard about her bravery if she hadn't made a film.

🎧 6.08 **3** **Complete the third conditional sentences about stories 1–3. Use the verbs in brackets. Listen and check.**

1 A girl got stuck under a car and a high school baseball team lifted the car off the girl.
a If the girl *hadn't got stuck* (not get stuck), the team *wouldn't have needed* (not need) to lift the car.
b If the team hadn't lifted (not lift) the car, the girl wouldn't have survived (not survive)

2 A 14-year-old saw a fire in his neighbour's home and went to help and saved a boy.
a If he hadn't seen (not see) the fire, he wouldn't have gone (not go) to help.
b If he hadn't gone (not go) to help, he wouldn't have saved (not save) the boy.

3 A group of teens were attacked by a bear in Alaska. One girl did first aid for nine hours until help arrived.
a If they hadn't gone (not go) to Alaska, they wouldn't have been (not be) attacked.
b If help had arrived (arrive) earlier, the girl wouldn't have done (not do) first aid for nine hours.

4 **Write a third conditional sentence for each situation.**

1 Alfie broke his leg when he went rock climbing.
If Alfie hadn't gone rock climbing, he wouldn't have broken his leg.

2 Four students got up late and missed the coach to France.
If four students hadn't got up late, they wouldn't have missed the coach to France.

3 The school cook didn't make enough food and the students were hungry.
If the school cook had made enough food, the students wouldn't have been hungry.

4 Class 4B went to Madrid and learned how to speak Spanish.
If class 4B hadn't gone to Madrid, they wouldn't have learned how to speak Spanish.

Use it!

5 **Complete the sentences about you.**

1 If I had been born in a different country ______
2 If I hadn't gone to this school ______
3 If I hadn't met my best friend ______

Finished? p123 Ex 3

UNIT 6 | NO LIMITS 75

Grammar game

Write *If …* on the board. Put students into teams and tell them they are going to add one or more words to what you have written on the board. Members of each team come to the board in turn to add words to the sentence, e.g. *If … / If I hadn't … / If I hadn't gone to the park …* Teams get a point if the words they add are correct. The team with the most points at the end of each completed sentence, wins that round.

Finished?

Fast finishers can turn to SB p123 and do Exercise 3.

Homework

Workbook p52

Lesson aim: I can encourage a friend to do something.

Warmer

In pairs, students talk about exciting activities (e.g. white-water rafting) they most enjoy doing or would most like to try.

1 6.09 ★★★ As well as listening for the activities, challenge students to listen for what Mia and Jack say about those activities.

Audioscript p170

2 6.09 When students have completed the conversation, they can practise reading it in pairs.

Useful language practice

▶ Play **Video 6.4** and encourage students to copy the intonation used by the presenter.

3 & 4 Ask students to think of situations in which they could use the phrases from the *Everyday English* box. For example,
A: *I'm going to have snowboarding lesson*
B: *Good for you!*

5 Encourage students to think of their own ideas if they are not interested in those in the box.

6 Ask students to practise the conversation, discuss what they could do better, and then practise a second time.

7 As well as answering the three questions from Exercise 4, students can give each other feedback by considering the following questions: *Did the other pair use language from the page? Was the conversation clear and easy to follow?*

SPEAKING

Encouraging a friend to do something

1 6.09 Listen to Mia and Jack's conversation. Which activities do they discuss?
Whitewater rafting and paddle boarding.

2 6.09 Complete the conversation with the phrases from the *Useful language* box. Listen and check.

MIA Are you going to come whitewater rafting this weekend?
JACK I'm not sure. It looks a little scary to me.
MIA Oh, it's not really. I had so much fun when I went. [1] You'll never know unless you try, will you?
JACK But the water is so fast! It looks seriously deep and I'm not the world's best swimmer.
MIA Relax and [2] ______ (don't worry, you'll be fine). The instructors will look after you. They don't take any risks.
JACK Mmm, I'm still not sure.
MIA: Well what about paddle boarding? That's less risky.
JACK You've got to be joking! I wouldn't dare stand up on the board in the middle of the sea. [3] What if ______ I fell in?
MIA Come on! It's easy! [4] You can do it ______! If you fall in, you just get back on the board.
JACK [5] ______ (That's easy for you to say), but I'm not like you. Water sports are a real challenge for me.
MIA Well, what if I practised with you?
JACK Hmm. That might help. OK, I'll come.
MIA Good for you! I promise [6] ______ (you'll feel really proud afterwards) and you might even have fun! Let's go on Sunday.

Useful language

Encouraging
Don't worry, you'll be fine. You can do it!
You'll feel really proud afterwards.
You'll never know unless you try …

Responding
That's easy for you to say … What if … (+ past simple)?

Watch video 6.4
Everyday English

Come on! Good for you! not really
seriously You've got to be joking!

3 Match the phrases in the *Everyday English* box with their meanings 1–5.

1 extremely seriously
2 not very not really
3 That's great! Good for you!
4 to encourage someone to do something Come on!
5 You're not serious! You've got to be joking!

4 How do you say these phrases in your language?

PLAN

5 Make notes about something you want to encourage your partner to do. Use the ideas below or your own ideas.

do an audition for a school show
try an extreme sport

SPEAK

6 Practise trying to encourage your partner. Remember to use first, second and third conditionals, vocabulary from this unit and phrases from the *Useful language* and *Everyday English* boxes.

CHECK

7 Work with another pair. Listen to their conversation and complete the notes.

What did the other students encourage each other to do? ______

Would you try the things in their conversation? ______

Class challenge

Surfing / Whitewater rafting / Paddle boarding is an Olympic sport.

Flipped class

Prepare for **Writing** (p77). Ask: *Should we take risks?* Students can think of ideas for and against taking risks.

1 Read out the questions. In pairs, students can discuss them. Encourage students to ask each other follow-up questions to develop conversations.

2 Read out the two essay titles. Before students read the essay to decide which of the titles best fits the material, elicit the ideas you might find in an essay with each of the two titles.

3 & 4 Students can work in pairs to complete both tasks. When checking answers, point out that essays are usually written in a neutral style, aim to be clear and well-organised and tend to present one idea at a time, with one paragraph dedicated to one idea.

Useful language practice

5 ★ Read out the essay title. Help students by eliciting ideas for an essay on the topic of risk. Write these ideas on the board. Give students time to prepare their essay. Monitor and help students organise their ideas as necessary.

6 Encourage students to use the essay in Exercise 1 as a model to help them write their own.

7 As well as checking their own work, encourage students to check each other's work and look for ways to improve it.

WRITING

A for and against essay

1 Think about a time when something went wrong for you. How did you feel? What did you learn?

2 Read the for and against essay. Circle the best title.

(a) Is it always bad when things go wrong? *(circled)*

b Should we try more new things?

1 There are times when things go wrong. For example, you might lose a sports match or fail an important exam. However, is it always negative when this happens?

2 On the one hand, when things go wrong we feel bad. For instance, if we fail a French exam, we might have doubts about our ability to speak the language and lose confidence. Furthermore, we might think we haven't got the skills to achieve our goals.

3 On the other hand, when we overcome a difficult situation we feel good. If we think about what went wrong, we might solve the problem in the future, such as by preparing for our next exam in a different way.

4 In conclusion, although it can feel negative when things go wrong, I personally believe that this is not always bad if we can learn something new. When we look for an opportunity to overcome the problem, we'll soon feel good again.

3 Read the essay again and discuss the questions.

1 How does the writer end the introduction? Why? **With a question. To get the reader interested.**

2 In which paragraph does the writer give their opinion? **4**

3 Which paragraph talks about the negatives? **2**

4 Which paragraph talks about the positives? **3**

4 Complete the *Useful language* box with the phrases from the essay.

Useful language

introducing a new idea: Furthermore …, [1] **On the one hand**

introducing the opposite idea: [2] **On the other hand**

giving an example: For example …, [3] **For instance**, [4] **such as**

giving an opinion: [5] **I personally believe**

introducing a conclusion: [6] **In conclusion**

Write your own for and against essay.

PLAN

5 Look at the essay title and make notes on your ideas and examples. Decide what information to include in each paragraph. Use the information in Exercise 3 to help you.

Should we take risks?

WRITE

6 Write your for and against essay. Remember to include four paragraphs, conditional tenses, vocabulary from this unit and phrases from the *Useful language* box.

CHECK

7 Do you …

- include an introduction?
- talk about the negatives?
- talk about the positives?
- have a conclusion?

Finished? p123 Ex 4

Extend it!

Ask students to read out their essays to one another. Students listen and say whether they agree with each other's opinions.

Finished?

Fast finishers can turn to SB p123 and do Exercise 4.

Homework

Workbook p53

Lesson aim: I can create a leaflet.

Project Book

For more information and activities see the Project Book p42.

1 Elicit that a leaflet is a piece of paper containing information about a service or campaign. Read out the four verbs, and either elicit or teach the meaning of each. Students can then read the leaflet and answer the question. Ask students to indicate which parts of the text led them to their answer.

2 6.10 Read through the questions with the class and ask students to underline any key words. In pairs, students can answer the questions. Once you have checked answers with the class, ask students which of the courses they would most like to go on.

3 ★★★ As well as identifying these features, students can discuss how effectively the leaflet uses them.

How to motivate yourself and your peers

Making students aware of what they can do to maintain motivation whilst doing longer tasks will help them work together and support each other during project work. Point out that self-motivation can come from making your own plan, and setting your own responsibilities and targets with others (rather than having someone else give you a task).

THE CITIZENSHIP PROJECT

A leaflet

1 Look at the leaflet. Which two things does it aim to do?

(a) inform b warn c entertain (d) persuade

2 6.10 Read the leaflet and answer the questions.

1 Who are the courses for?
2 Which activities can you do on each course?
3 On which course will you work in a team?
4 The courses are 'unplugged'. What does that mean?
5 Why might it be good to try one of the courses?

1 Teenagers from 14 to 18.
2 Outdoor survival skills: orienteering, building a fire, cooking outdoors. Water sports: surfing, paddle boarding, scuba diving, whitewater rafting. Climbing high: rock climbing, abseiling, tree-top ropes course, parkour.
3 Outdoor survival skills.
4 Participants are not allowed to take phones or other electronic devices on the courses.
5 You will feel good if you learn something new.

3 Read the leaflet again and find these features.

1 Title
2 Introduction to get readers interested
3 Details about the activities
4 Phrases to persuade people to do the course

Do you/Do you like … ?, exciting activities, If you enjoy … you will love this course, If your idea of fun is … you will get a lot out of this course, why not give them a go? One of our most popular courses is … , You will have the chance to … , you will discover that … , Just think how good you'll feel if …

How to motivate yourself and your peers

4 Match 1–4 with a–d to make tips about how to motivate yourself and your peers on a project.

1	Be clear about what you have to do.	a	All projects have problems. Find a way to solve them.
2	Don't give up when there's an obstacle.	b	Divide up the work equally.
3	Each person has a role.	c	Have confidence in yourself and your team.
4	Believe you can do the project.	d	If you don't understand something, ask.

5 6.11 Listen to students working in a team at the start of their project. Put tips 1–4 in Exercise 4 in the order you hear them.

1, 3, 2, 4

78 NO LIMITS | UNIT 6

ON COURSE TO CONFIDENCE!

title

Are you 14–18? Do you get bored in the holidays? Do you like making friends, having fun and doing lots of exciting activities? If this sounds like you, then check out our courses and choose the one for you.

introduction to get reade interested

OUTDOOR SURVIVAL SKILLS

If you enjoy adventure and being outside in the fresh air, you will love this course. It's a great way to meet new people as you will be working in teams on different activities such as orienteering, building a fire and cooking outdoors. Some of the activities are challenging and you will have to work together and support each other to complete them.

details

4 Students can do this matching task by making links between sentences 1–4 and sentences a–d. For example, 1 should be matched with d, with the link between the sentences being 'be clear' and 'if you don't understand'. Once students have completed this task, they discuss the ideas. Can they think of other ways to motivate themselves or others?

5 6.11 If necessary, play the recording a second time.

Audioscript p170

6 ★ Give students enough time to think of ideas for courses. You may need to help with this. If you have access to the internet in class, students could do some research online. Once students have come up with their ideas, make sure that you give them enough time to carry out each stage of the project, from drawing a plan of the leaflet to making it. Monitor throughout, helping students as necessary.

7 Before students present their leaflet, encourage them to check that they have included everything.

8 As well as checking one another's work, remind students to listen to each other's presentations actively, taking notes of interesting ideas they hear.

Students can collaborate digitally online and offline in the collaboration space, where teachers can set, track and assess students' work. Students can also share and showcase their work as well as comment on each other's projects.

OWN IT!

details

WATER SPORTS

If your idea of fun is spending all day in the water, you will get a lot out of this course. You will have the chance to try everything from surfing and paddle boarding to scuba diving and whitewater rafting. If you've never tried water sports before, why not give them a go? You might be surprised at how much fun you have.

details

CLIMBING HIGH

One of our most popular courses is this confidence-building one. You will have the chance to go rock climbing and then abseil down again. You'll also go on a tree-top ropes course. If you'd like to learn a different skill, you could spend a day trying parkour.

details

Remember! All of our courses are unplugged, so leave your mobiles and other electronic devices at home. From day one you will discover that you don't have to be online to have fun.

We encourage you to take risks and try new things, so if you have never tried any of these sports, one of our courses is the perfect opportunity. Just think how good you'll feel if you overcome the fear to do something you've never done before!

PLAN

6 **Work in groups. Make a list of courses for teenagers to build their confidence. Then choose two or three ideas and design a leaflet to inform and persuade people to do them. Complete the steps below.**

- Draw a plan of the leaflet.
- Decide who prepares each section.
- Prepare your section with the features in Exercise 3.
- Show your section to someone else to check.
- Listen to your classmate's ideas and improve your section.
- Work together to make your leaflet.

PRESENT

7 **Present your leaflet to your classmates. Remember to include information about the courses, the features in Exercise 3 and the tips in *How to* motivate yourself and your peers.**

CHECK

8 **Read your classmates' leaflets. Decide which activities you would like to do from their leaflets.**

Extend it!

Put students into groups to brainstorm ways to keep themselves motivated when a project becomes difficult. Elicit the ideas, write them on the board, and ask the class to choose the top three, coming up with a class action plan of how to keep going when things become difficult.

Flipped class

Prepare for the **Review** lesson (p80). Students revise the grammar and vocabulary from Unit 6.

For more work on Citizenship, students can turn to SB p139. See p155 for teaching notes.

The aim of this review page is for students to revise the grammar and vocabulary from the unit. You can either do it in class, as a timed progress test or set it for homework.

Vocabulary

1 Do this with the class as a whole. Elicit the verb that each circled word or phrase does collocate with, e.g. in number 1 – *to take risks.*

2 Put students into groups to complete the sentences. The first group to complete a sentence successfully wins a point. The group with the most points at the end wins.

Language in action

3 ★★★ Elicit definitions for each of the words in the box. Then challenge students to be the first to complete the six sentences correctly.

4 Before students complete this exercise, ask them how the first and second conditionals are formed and how they are used. Students can look back at p73 of the Student's Book to remind themselves.

5 Elicit the form and use of the third conditional and an example sentence. You may want to do the first item in the exercise to give students a model to follow. Students can then work in pairs to complete the task.

Unit quiz review

6 REVIEW

VOCABULARY

1 Circle the words which <u>don't</u> go with each verb.

1 get — *a lot out of something* / *(risks)* / *lost*
2 take — *pleasure in something* / *advantage of something* / *(doubts)*
3 have — *(on someone's nerves)* / *the chance to do something* / *fun*
4 get — *bored* / *to know someone* / *(an interest in something)*

2 Complete the sentences with the correct form of the words and phrases that don't go with the verbs in Exercise 1.

1 I had **doubts** before I went rafting because I'm not a strong swimmer.
2 It can be positive to take **risks** because we learn to make decisions.
3 My brother has started to take **an interest in** photography.
4 My sister really gets **on my nerves**. She's always taking my things.

3 Complete the sentences with the words in the box.

achieved bravery determination opportunity overcome supported

1 She was awarded a prize for her **bravery** in the fire.
2 My cousin finally **achieved** his ambition to learn how to windsurf.
3 Do students have the **opportunity** to go to music classes at your school?
4 My parents **supported** my decision to do a bungee jump for charity.
5 He passed his final exams after a lot of hard work and **determination**.
6 Since I started swimming I have **overcome** my fear of deep water.

LANGUAGE IN ACTION

4 Complete the sentences about parkour with the first or second conditional.

1 How quickly **would** I **learn** (learn) if I practised every day?
2 If you already **do** (do) regular sport or exercise, you may find it easy to learn.
3 If I **watch** (watch) parkour videos online, will I learn some techniques?
4 If you **train(ed)** (train) every day for a month, you could learn to jump over walls.

5 Join the two sentences to make one sentence in the third conditional.

1 Mozart learned music as a young child. He wrote his first symphony when he was eight or nine.
If Mozart hadn't learned music as a young child, he wouldn't have written his first symphony when he was eight or nine.
2 Emma Watson studied drama as a child. She was Hermione in the Harry Potter films.
If Emma Watson hadn't studied drama as a child, she wouldn't have been Hermione in the Harry Potter films.
3 The artist van Gogh moved to Paris. Van Gogh met his friend Paul Gauguin in Paris.
If the artist van Gogh hadn't moved to Paris, he wouldn't have met his friend Paul Gauguin.
4 J.R.R. Tolkien wrote *The Lord of the Rings*. Peter Jackson made a film trilogy of the book.
If J.R.R. Tolkien hadn't written The Lord of the Rings, Peter Jackson wouldn't have made a film trilogy of the book.

Self-assessment

I can use collocations with *get*, *take* and *have*.
I can use nouns and verbs for inspiration and challenge.
I can use the first and second conditional.
I can use the third conditional.

80 NO LIMITS | UNIT 6

Self-assessment

Encourage students to be honest about how well they have completed the tasks on the Review page. They can tell each other in pairs, and then ask you for extra homework with any of the vocabulary or grammar from Unit 6 if necessary.

Homework

Workbook pp 54–55

Learn to learn

Students should learn English outside the class as well as inside it, following their own interests and motivating themselves to improve their skills.

Warmer

Ask: *Why is it important to take responsibility for our learning?* Guide students towards the idea that we learn more when we are involved and interested in things that matter to us, and we can't expect a teacher to do work for us that we need to do for ourselves.

1 Give students time to think about the results before discussing them with a partner.

2 Ask: *Why should we all challenge ourselves to do more with our learning?* Guide students to the following idea: it is only when we challenge ourselves that we know what we are capable of and what we need to improve. Students can then read the challenges and choose the one they like the best. Ask students to work in pairs to think of a challenge of their own.

OWN IT!

3 Give students time to think about which of the extra challenges they think would most help them in their learning. In pairs, students discuss their choices. Encourage students to share any other ideas they may have about how to stretch themselves outside the classroom. This should be an ongoing task. For this reason, return to this later in the course, and find out what challenges students undertook, and whether or not they worked.

LEARN TO LEARN

LEARN TO ... TAKE RESPONSIBILITY FOR YOUR LEARNING

It's important to take responsibility for your own learning. This will help you to learn when you are outside your class as well.

1 Do the quiz and find out your score. Do you agree with what it says about you? Discuss the results with a partner.

Are you taking responsibility for your learning?

Always | Sometimes | Never

1 When you're in class, how often do you ...
- **a** pay attention to the teacher's corrections?
- **b** try to help your partner speak and write better?
- **c** use spidergrams and presentation plans?

2 When you want to learn new vocabulary, how often do you ...
- **a** write example sentences?
- **b** make and use flashcards?
- **c** use a monolingual (only English) dictionary?

3 Outside class, how often do you ...
- **a** speak in English to other people?
- **b** watch TV series or films in English?
- **c** read books or articles in English online?

4 Thinking about technology, how often do you ...
- **a** have English as the language on your phone and your apps?
- **b** use vocabulary learning apps?
- **c** listen to podcasts in English?

5 Baggage **If you were travelling in an English-speaking country, would you ...**
- **a** speak English in shops and restaurants?
- **b** try to understand signs in English?
- **c** ask for directions in English if you got lost?

Extra challenges!
- Write text messages to your friends in English.
- Send and receive voice messages with friends in English.
- Listen to music in English and look up the lyrics online.
- Read a 'graded reader' – a famous book made easier for learners.

Points: always = 2, sometimes = 1, never = 0.

0–3 points: You aren't taking much responsibility for your learning yet, but if you try more ideas from the quiz, you'll soon become a better learner!

4–7 points: You're taking some responsibility for your learning, but there's a lot more you could do if you tried. Take advantage of what you've learned in this quiz to think about how to improve.

8–10 points: You're taking lots of responsibility for your learning. That's great! Time for something new – try our extra challenges!

2 Look at the extra challenges. Which is the best idea? Write one more.

OWN IT!

3 Think about how to take more responsibility for your learning. Choose three ideas and tell your partner what you have chosen and why.

I've chosen 'read a graded reader' because I love books. If I'd known about them before, I'd have started one already!

Flipped class

Prepare for **Unit 7**. Students think about the emotions they associate with red, grey, purple and yellow.

Unit 7
Keep calm!

Lesson aim: I can talk about colours and emotions.

Warmer
Elicit the meaning of *emotion* (a strong feeling). Elicit common emotions and write these on the board, e.g. love, fear, anger, joy.

▶ Start it!

Unit quiz

1 Discuss this question with the class. Write students' ideas on the board. Possible answers are relaxed, happy, calm, peaceful.

2 Ask students to share the information about emotions and colours that they researched for homework.

3 ▶ Students can share their ideas in pairs. Then play **Video 7.1** for students to check their answers. Students can also complete the Start it! **Video worksheet** in the *Teacher's Resource Bank*.

4 If students do not wear specific colours according to how they feel, they can talk about which colours make them feel happy.

Video comprehension questions

7 KEEP CALM!

LEARNING OUTCOMES
I can ...
- understand texts about a growth mindset and reducing exam stress
- express sympathy and concern
- write an email reply
- understand gerunds and infinitives, and subject and object questions
- use adjectives that describe feelings and expressions with *heart* and *mind*
- personalise vocabulary, make gapped flashcards, and learn synonyms and antonyms.

Start it!

1 Look at the photo. How is the girl feeling?
2 Before you watch, do you associate an emotion with these colours: red, grey, purple, yellow?
3 What colour can make you feel hungry? Watch and check. yellow
4 What colours do you wear when you're happy and when you're sad?

Watch video 7.1

Language in action 7.2 p85

Language in action 7.3 p87

Everyday English 7.4 p88

Globetrotters 7.5 p90

82 KEEP CALM! | UNIT 7

Flipped class
Prepare for **Explore it!** (p83). Students find out a fact about smiling (e.g. when babies first smile, the number of muscles we use when smiling, the evolution of smiling).

Unit aims

Skills
I can ...
- understand a text about a growth mindset p84
- express sympathy and concern p88
- write an email reply p89
- understand a text about children in Denmark pp90–91

Language
I can ...
- talk about feelings p83
- understand how to use gerunds and infinitives p85
- use expressions with *heart* and *mind* p86
- understand how to use subject and object questions p87

Learn to Learn
I can ...
- remember adjectives p83
- use gapped flashcards p86
- use synonyms and antonyms p91
- give my partner useful feedback p93

Extra Resources
- *Finished?* – Student's Book p124
- *Vocabulary Bank* – Student's Book p134
- Pronunciation – Student's Book p142
- Workbook p56
- *Teacher's Resource Bank on Cambridge One* for tests package, Cambridge Exam practice, wordlists, differentiated worksheets and many other extra resources.
- *Practice Extra and Digital collaboration space*

Lesson aim: I can talk about feelings.

1 ★ Teach *emotional rollercoaster* (a situation in which you feel a variety of emotions, from excited to disappointed, very happy to very sad).

2 🎧 7.01 In pairs, students can take turns saying a word and writing it down, to practise pronunciation and spelling.

Audioscript p170

Target vocabulary
amused /əˈmjuːzd/
annoyed /əˈnɔɪd/
down /daʊn/
eager /ˈiːɡə/
glad /ɡlæd/
grateful /ˈɡreɪtfəl/
hopeful /ˈhəʊpfəl/
hurt /hɜːt/
insecure /ɪnsɪˈkjʊ/
peaceful /ˈpiːsfəl/
ridiculous /rɪˈdɪkjələs/
satisfied /ˈsætɪsfaɪd/
thrilled /θrɪld/

Extra vocabulary practice

3 🎧 7.02 Play the recording twice if necessary.

Audioscript p171

Vocabulary Bank SB p134

Learn to learn

Personalising vocabulary, by writing a sentence about an experience, is a good strategy to help students remember any new words and phrases.

4 Be prepared to help students think of contexts for each of the adjectives, e.g. *I feel peaceful when I have a bath.*

VOCABULARY
Feelings

1 Read the leaflet. Do you agree with it?

🎧 7.01 2 Match the words in **bold** in the leaflet with definitions 1–13. Listen, check and repeat.

1 happy m
2 angry d
3 unhappy b
4 very silly e
5 feeling thanks j
6 not confident c
7 enthusiastic k
8 quiet and calm i
9 in emotional pain f
10 extremely happy a
11 finding something funny g
12 positive about the future h
13 pleased to achieve something l

🎧 7.02 3 Listen and complete the sentences with one word.

1 Sally feels absolutely thrilled.
2 The boy feels annoyed.
3 Mark felt absolutely ridiculous.
4 The girl feels really hurt.
5 Monica is feeling a bit down.

LEARN TO LEARN
Remembering adjectives
Think about your personal experiences to help you remember new adjectives.

4 Do Part 1 in the Stay happy! leaflet. Think of a sentence for each adjective.
I feel amused when I watch comedy films.

5 Say your sentences. Do you have similar or different ideas?
I feel satisfied when I score a goal in football.

Use it!

6 Now do Part 2 of the leaflet. Tell your partner your plans.

STAY HAPPY!

For teenagers, life can be an emotional rollercoaster. Sometimes you're [a]**thrilled** to be alive, then you feel [b]**down** for no reason. You often feel [c]**insecure** about who you are, and [d]**annoyed** with every adult on the planet. You feel [e]**ridiculous** when you don't know something all your friends seem to know, and [f]**hurt** that nobody seems to care about what you're feeling. Of course, people do care, which is why we've created this exercise for developing positive emotions.

Part 1 For each word below (amused, etc.), think of a situation that helps you feel that emotion.

Part 2 Choose two positive emotions you want to practise. Do something which will increase those emotions every day for a week.

I feel …	This week I will …
[g]amused when my best friend tells me jokes.	ask him to tell me some every day.
[h]**hopeful** when I make a wish.	make three wishes about …
[i]**peaceful** when I walk on the beach.	
[j]**grateful** when people help me.	
[k]**eager** when I start a new art project.	
[l]**satisfied** when I've tidied my room.	
[m]**glad** when my friends are happy.	

Explore it!

Guess the correct answer.
Complete the expression *Laughter is the best …*
a communication. b exercise. (c) medicine.
Find out a fact about smiling. Write a question for your partner to answer.

UNIT 7 | KEEP CALM! 83

5 ★★★ Challenge students to use their ideas from Exercise 4 to discuss the broader issue of the link between what we do and how we feel.

Order the words to make sentences

6 ★ Point out that 'practise' a 'positive emotion' means practising an activity which will make you feel a positive emotion.

Explore it!

Students use the facts they researched about smiling.

Flipped class

Prepare for the **Reading** lesson (p84). Students research the idea of a growth mindset.

Homework

Workbook p56

Lesson aim: I can understand a text about a growth mindset.

Background information

A 'growth mindset' refers to the belief that your ability and intelligence can be improved by hard work and the willingness to learn new skills.

Warmer

Ask: *Can the way you feel about what you do have an effect on how you do it?* Discuss this question briefly with the class.

1 Encourage students to be honest at this point. If they tend to feel that there is no point trying after they do badly in an exam, they should say so.

2 7.03 Before students read the text, elicit what we would expect to read in response to each of the questions.

3 Encourage students to read through the multiple-choice questions carefully before they reread the text. Students can compare their answers in pairs, highlighting the parts of the text which gave them their answers.

4 Remind students to use the context to help them identify the words.

Complete the sentences

5 Give students time to think about the ideas before discussing them with a partner.

READING

A magazine interview

1 Read and answer the question at the beginning of the interview.

2 7.03 Read the interview and match the interviewer's questions a–d with 1–4. Listen and check.

a You had a fixed mindset?
b Malcolm, what exactly is a growth mindset?
c What advice would you give our readers?
d How can you develop a growth mindset?

3 Read the interview again and circle the correct answers.

1 Even if you have a fixed mindset, you …
  a never change.
  b are bad at maths.
  (c) can change.
  d like taking tests.
2 People with a growth mindset …
  (a) think they can get better.
  b are good at everything.
  c are scared of failing.
  d don't have to learn new skills.
3 Malcolm …
  a wanted to learn the piano.
  b played the piano for several years.
  c learned to play the guitar easily.
  (d) slowly improved his guitar playing.
4 Malcolm encourages readers to …
  (a) learn from their mistakes.
  b wait before trying new things.
  c ignore their mistakes.
  d try one thing at a time.

4 Find words in the interview that mean:

1 a feeling/opinion (question 1) **attitude**
2 not changing (question 1) **fixed**
3 without purpose (question 2) **pointless**
4 necessary (question 4) **essential**
5 not a success (question 4) **failure**

The power of 'not yet'

Imagine you've just failed an important maths test. What do you think?

a I failed this test, but I can pass the next one if I study harder.
b I'm just not good at maths. There's no point trying.

If you chose a, you have a growth mindset. People with a growth mindset are often happier and more successful. But if you chose b, don't worry – you can change. I spoke to psychologist Malcolm Adams to find out how.

1 **b** A mindset is your attitude to life. Some people have a fixed mindset. These people often avoid trying new things because they're afraid of making mistakes. They refuse to try harder, because they don't believe they can get better. On the other hand, people with a growth mindset believe they can improve with practice. They're eager to learn new skills and they're not afraid to fail sometimes. They often do well in life.

2 **d** Let me tell you a story to explain this. When I was a kid my parents made me learn the piano. I didn't like the piano and it was really difficult. I remember feeling annoyed with myself whenever I made a mistake. After about a year, I stopped trying. I thought, 'This is pointless. I don't have any musical talent.'

3 **a** Exactly. But later, at university, a friend said to me, 'If you want to be good at something, you have to believe you can do it.' So I thought, 'OK, let's try again.' I decided to learn the guitar, which I'd always adored. This time I told myself, 'You can do it!' I practised loads. It was hard, but little by little I got better. I'll never forget playing for my friends for the first time. I was thrilled! My mindset had completely changed.

4 **c** Firstly, believe in yourself. Being positive is essential. Secondly, don't worry about making mistakes. A mistake isn't failure – it's an opportunity to learn. Finally, don't forget to use the power of 'not yet'. Never say, 'I can't do this.' Always remember to tell yourself, 'I can – just not yet.'

Voice it!

5 Discuss the questions.

1 Do you like to try new things? Why / Why not?
2 Where do you think you are on the scale for the activities in the box? Why? How can you change?

doing art · doing sports · playing music and singing · speaking English

1 fixed mindset
2
3 a mixture of both
4
5 growth mindset

Finished? p124 Ex 1

84 KEEP CALM! | UNIT 7

Extend it!

Ask students to make a list of two or three well-known people who have been very successful in their own field, for example: sports, music, art, science, business, politics. Then ask them to choose a person on their list who they already know something about and to tell the rest of the class something about that person.

Finished?

Students turn to SB p124 and do Exercise 1.

Flipped class

▶ Ask students to watch **Video 7.2** and do the **Video worksheet** in the *Teacher's Resource Bank*.

Homework

Workbook p57

Lesson aim: I can understand how to use gerunds and infinitives.

Warmer

▶ Play **Video 7.2** if it was not set for homework and elicit that Claire always tries new things and isn't afraid of making mistakes. He tried doing parkour.

1 On the board, write *going* and *to go*. Elicit that *going* is a gerund and *to go* is an infinitive with *to*.

Get it right!

Encourage students to keep a record in their notebooks of which verbs take gerunds, which infinitives and which both.

2 Ask students to read through the gapped text, then ask: *What do psychologists suggest we do?* (make a list of activities that make us feel good and do one of those every day).

3 On the board, write the two sentences with *remember* from the table, but do not include the explanation in brackets. Elicit the meaning of *remember* in each case.

Extra grammar practice

4 ★★★ Give students time to think through their answers before they discuss the questions with a partner. Extend the task by challenging students to think of their own questions to ask each other with *remember*, *forget* and *stop*.

LANGUAGE IN ACTION

Gerunds and infinitives

Watch video 7.2
Why does Claire inspire him?
What did he try last summer?

Gerunds		Infinitives (with *to*)	
As the subject of the sentence	[1]Being positive is essential.	To explain purpose	[2]I spoke to Malcolm Adams to find out how.
After prepositions	[3]They're afraid of making mistakes.	After adjectives	[4]They're eager to learn new skills.
After certain verbs (*avoid, enjoy, finish, miss*, etc.)	[5]These people often avoid trying new things.	After certain verbs (*hope, refuse, would like*, etc.)	[6]They refuse to try harder.

1 **Underline the gerunds and infinitives (with *to*) in the examples in the table above.**

Get it right!

Some verbs, including *like*, *love* and *start*, can take the gerund or infinitive with no change in meaning.

He loves going/to go for walks.

You can use the gerund or infinitive after *remember*, *forget* and *stop*, but this changes the meaning.

Gerunds	Infinitives (with *to*)
I **remember feeling** annoyed. *(= I have a memory of …)*	Always **remember to tell** yourself … *(= don't forget)*
I'll never **forget playing** for my friends for the first time. *(= I won't forget that memory)*	Don't **forget to use** the power of 'not yet'. *(= don't forget to do this in the future)*
I **stopped trying**. *(= I didn't do this anymore)*	I **stopped to rest** for a few minutes. *(= I stopped what I was doing for a while)*

2 **Complete the text with the gerund or infinitive form of the verbs in the box.**

develop feel help (x2) increase ~~know~~ make say

THINK POSITIVE

You'll be glad [1] _to know_ there are steps you can take [2] _to develop_ a positive mindset. Psychologists suggest [3] _making_ a list of activities that make you feel good, and then doing one every day [4] _to increase_ your positivity. [5] _Helping_ others when they have a problem also makes us feel happier. Of course, it's important [6] _to say_ thank you to people for [7] _helping_ you. Try it! Everyone wants [8] _to feel_ more satisfied in life.

3 **Complete the questions with the gerund or infinitive form of the verbs in brackets.**

1 Do you remember _meeting_ (meet) your best friend?
2 When you're studying, how often do you stop _to take_ (take) a break?
3 What would happen if you forgot _to set_ (set) your alarm the night before an exam?
4 Would it be harder to stop _using_ (use) your phone?
5 What things do you have to remember _to do_ (do) this weekend?
6 Think of two people you'll never forget _meeting_ (meet) on your first day at school. Who are they?

Use it!

4 **Ask and answer the questions in Exercise 3.**

Finished? p124 Ex 2

UNIT 7 | KEEP CALM! 85

Grammar game

Put students into small groups. Ask students to close their books, then call out verbs from p85 (e.g. *remember, stop, finish*). Students have to decide what form of the verb follows each one and shout out 'infinitive', 'gerund' or 'both'. The first student to shout out the correct answer, wins a point.

Finished?

Fast finishers can turn to SB p124 and do Exercise 2.

Homework

Workbook p58

1 7.04 Encourage students to guess if they are not sure.

Audioscript p171

Target vocabulary

be in two minds /biː ɪn tuː maɪndz/
bear in mind /beə rɪn maɪnd/
break someone's heart /breɪk 'sʌmwʌnz hɑːt/
change your mind /tʃeɪndʒ jə maɪnd/
close to your heart /kləʊz tə jə hɑːt/
crossed your mind /krɒst jə maɪnd/
have something on your mind /hæv 'sʌmθɪŋ ɒn jə maɪnd/
learn by heart /lɜːn baɪ hɑːt/
make your mind up /meɪk jə maɪnd ʌp/
put your heart into something /pʊt jə hɑːt 'ɪntə 'sʌmθɪŋ/

Extra vocabulary practice

Learn to learn

Point out that flashcards can be a fun way of remembering vocabulary, and add variety to revision, although it can take a little extra time and effort to create them.

2 To make their flashcards, students can either use paper from their notebooks or you can give them paper or cards to use.

3 Do this with the class as a whole, eliciting sentences and writing them on the board.

Vocabulary Bank SB p134

4 ★★★ Challenge students to think of their own ways to reduce exam stress.

VOCABULARY AND LISTENING

Expressions with *heart* and *mind*

1 7.04 **Match the phrases in bold in the thought bubbles with definitions a–j. Listen, check and repeat.**

I have to [1]**learn by heart** so many facts for that exam but I don't have time!

What am I going to study at university? I have to [2]**make my mind up** soon.

I'm [3]**in two minds** about the party. I don't know many people there. Shall I go or just stay home?

[4]**I've got something on my mind** about school. Who should I talk to?

I want to become an actor, but what will Dad say? It'll [5]**break his heart** if I don't study science.

Education is a subject that's [6]**close to my heart**, but I don't know if I'd be a good teacher or not!

I need to choose my degree carefully. I can't [7]**change my mind** later.

I know if I [8]**put my heart into** this project, I'll do well, but I'm so tired!

It's just [9]**crossed my mind** that Dan might be at the party.

I must [10]**bear in mind** we can't use a pencil in the exam. I don't want to fail for something silly like that!

a	consider something important	10
b	make an effort to do something	8
c	think of something	9
d	make a decision	2
e	memorise	1
f	change a decision	7
g	unable to decide between two options	3
h	be worried about something	4
i	make someone really sad	5
j	be important to someone	6

LEARN TO LEARN

Gapped flashcards

Flashcards can help you learn expressions.

2 **Make flashcards for some of the expressions in Exercise 1, leaving a gap for *heart* or *mind*(s). Write the missing word on the back. Then test your partner.**

be in two ______ | minds

Use it!

3 **Choose six phrases in Exercise 1 and make sentences with the ideas in the box.**

clothes | friends and family | going out

When I go out in the evening, I have to bear in mind what time my parents want me to come home.

A conversation

4 **Which of these things do you think can reduce exam stress?**

1 studying late at night
2 studying with friends
3 drinking energy drinks
4 doing exercise
5 testing yourself
6 eating apples
7 making lists

5 7.05 **Listen to the conversation. Circle the things in Exercise 4 that the counsellor recommends.**

6 7.05 **Listen again and discuss the questions.**

1 Why is Gavin so stressed?
He's worried he's going to fail his exams.
2 Why does the counsellor suggest making a list? — So that he can use his time well
3 Why does the counsellor recommend eating apples and nuts? — Because they help the brain to work better.
4 Why doesn't Gavin want to go to bed early? — He thinks his brain works better at nigh
5 Why is it important for Gavin to do well in every subject? — He wants to be a primary school teacher.
6 What is Gavin going to ask his sister tonight? — To test him for his history exam
7 What was Gavin in two minds about earlier? — If he should vi the counsellor or not.

7 **Do you think the counsellor's suggestions are useful?**

86 KEEP CALM! | UNIT 7

5 7.05 Elicit that a counsellor is someone who encourages a person to talk about their problems and sometimes offers them advice.

Audioscript p171

6 7.05 ★★★ Challenge students to answer as many of the questions as they can based on their memory of the recording.

7 Encourage students to give reasons for their opinions.

Finished?

▶ Ask students to watch **Video 7.3** and do **Video worksheet 7.3** in the *Teacher's Resource Bank*.

Homework

Workbook p59

Warmer

▶ Play **Video 7.3** if it was not set for homework. Elicit that keeping a journal is a great way to stay organised and it helps you feel positive because you can see all the things you've achieved. Her friend Rena helped her in science class.

1 & 2 ★★★ Before students look at question 2, ask them if they can explain the difference between the two types of question.

Extra grammar practice

3 ★ Tell students that they shouldn't use *do* for the subject questions.

4 ★★★ Students can do this task in pairs. Ask students to explain their choice of subject or object question.

5 Encourage students to ask follow-up questions to develop longer conversations.

6 7.06 Elicit answers from the class, writing them on the board. Play the recording for students to check their answers. Students can then practise the dialogue in pairs.

Audioscript p172

7 Students can invent answers to these questions, if they wish.

Pronunciation

Students do the activities on p142 to practise initial consonant clusters with *s*.

LANGUAGE IN ACTION

Subject and object questions

Watch video 7.3
What's good about keeping a journal?
Who helped her today?

Subject questions	
Who helps you?	My sister (helps me).
[1] What makes you think that?	Everything (makes me think that)!
Object questions	
Who do you want to teach?	(I want to teach) primary school kids.
[2] What did she study?	(She studied) physics.

1 Complete the examples in the table above.

2 Circle the correct words to complete the rules.

1. The words in red are *subjects* / *objects*. The ones in green are *subjects* / *objects*.
2. *Subject* / *Object* questions always use a form of *do*.

3 Complete the present simple questions with subject or object question forms.

1. What *do you do* (do/you) at the weekend?
2. Who teaches (teach) you maths?
3. Who sends (send) you the most messages every day?
4. Which subjects do you put (put/you) your heart into?
5. Who helps (help) you with your homework?
6. What happens (happen) if you don't sleep enough?

4 Complete the past simple questions with subject or object question forms.

1. Who *taught* (teach) you English last year?
2. What did you eat (eat / you) for breakfast?
3. Who gave (give) you presents for your birthday?
4. What presents did they give (give / they) you?
5. Which TV shows did you watch (watch / you) yesterday?
6. Which country won (win) the last football World Cup?

5 Ask and answer the questions in Exercises 2 and 3.

6 7.06 Complete the dialogue with the correct subject or object question form. Listen and check.

OLAF What's that?
ROSA It's a stress ball.
OLAF What [1] *does it do* (do/it)?
ROSA It helps you relax. Look, you squeeze it like this. It was a birthday present.
OLAF Wow, that feels great! Who [2] gave (give) it to you?
ROSA My sister. She knows I get stressed out a lot so she thought it might help.
OLAF I want one.
ROSA You don't need one! You never get stressed.
OLAF That's not true. Who [3] told (tell) you that? I get stressed before exams.
ROSA Well, you could borrow this one if you like.
OLAF No, I'd prefer my own, thanks. Where [4] did your sister get (get/your sister) it?
ROSA Online, I think.
OLAF What site [5] did she use (use/she)? Do you know?
ROSA I'll ask her, but I'm sure you can get them in lots of places. They've been around for years.
OLAF Really? Who [6] invented (invent) them?
ROSA No idea. Let's look it up!

Use it!

7 Ask and answer the questions.

1. Who did you call/visit/help yesterday?
2. Who called/visited/helped you yesterday?

Pronunciation p142

Finished? p124 Ex 3

UNIT 7 | KEEP CALM! 87

Grammar game

Put students into pairs. Student A is a detective. Student B is under arrest for robbing a bank (the robbery took place at 8 pm yesterday). Student B says they were at a birthday party. Student A asks questions (e.g. *Where did you go yesterday evening? Who took you to the party? Who went to the party? Whose party was it?*) to try to find out if Student B is lying.

Finished?

Fast finishers can turn to SB p124 and do Exercise 3.

Homework

Workbook p60

1 Look at the photo with students and elicit what they can see. Then ask students to work in pairs to make a list of problems, talking about their own personal experiences where possible.

2 7.10 ★★★ Ask students to listen to but not read the conversation.

Audioscript p172

3 7.10 ★★★ Ask students to cover the *Useful language* box. Students then listen again, and complete the conversation with phrases they hear.

Useful language practice

▶ Play **Video 7.4**. Encourage students to copy the intonation used by the presenter.

4 Challenge students to think of further contexts for the phrases in the *Everyday English* box.

5 Give students time to choose and make notes on one of the problems they discussed in Exercise 1. They should choose the problem they would most like to discuss.

6 Ask students to practise their conversations until they feel comfortable enough to speak fluently without relying on their notes.

7 ★★★ Ask students to discuss the problems that they and the other pair talked about. Can they think of ways to solve these problems?

SPEAKING
Expressing sympathy and concern

1 What problems do brothers and sisters usually have?

2 7.10 Listen to the conversation. What is Jerry's problem? His brother isn't talking to him because of a broken tablet.

PAULA Hey, Jerry. What's [1]the matter? You look really down.
JERRY I am. It's my brother. He's refusing to talk to me.
PAULA Really? That's not [2] very nice ____. Why?
JERRY His tablet has stopped working. He thinks I took it without asking and broke it, but I didn't, I swear. Now when I try to talk to him he just walks away.
PAULA That's a little harsh, isn't it?
JERRY The thing is, he ought to know I wouldn't take his stuff without permission. I feel really hurt.
PAULA I [3] can imagine ____. It's horrible when someone doesn't believe you. But bear in mind he's doing his final exams at the moment. He's probably really stressed out about everything.
JERRY I guess you're right, but I hope he calms down soon.
PAULA Is there [4] anything I can do to help ?
I have an old tablet I could lend him.
JERRY That's kind of you, but you don't need to do that.
PAULA Don't mention it, but let me know if you change your mind. It'll [5] all be OK, you'll see

3 7.10 Complete the conversation with the phrases from the *Useful language* box. Listen and check.

Useful language

I can imagine.
Is there anything I can do to help?
It'll all be OK, you'll see.
That's not very nice.
What's the matter?

4 Replace the phrases in bold with the *Everyday English* phrases in the box.

1 Do I need help? No, **that's a nice thing to offer**, but I'm fine. that's kind of you ____
2 **I'm absolutely certain** my keys are here. I had them a few minutes ago. I swear ____
3 Your teacher told you off for being two minutes late? That's **not fair**. a little harsh ____
4 Of course you're **totally nervous and worried**. It's your final exams! stressed out
5 A Thanks for letting me use your desk.
B **No problem at all**. Don't mention it ____

Watch video 7.4
Everyday English

a little harsh Don't mention it. I swear stressed out That's kind of you …

PLAN

5 Make notes about one of the problems you thought of in Exercise 1.

____

SPEAK

6 Practise talking about the problem with your partner. Remember to use gerunds or infinitives, vocabulary from this unit and phrases from the *Useful language* and *Everyday English* boxes

CHECK

7 Work with another pair. Listen to their conversation and complete the notes.
What problem did they talk about? ____
How sympathetic did the conversation sound? ____

88 KEEP CALM! | UNIT 7

Extend it!
In pairs, students tell each other a problem they have (e.g. my phone is broken, I failed my maths exam, my bike was stolen). Their partner expresses sympathy and concern, and suggests a solution.

Flipped class
Prepare for the **Writing** lesson (p89). Students make a list of the most common problems that teenagers have with parents.

Warmer

Elicit the problems between teens and parents that students thought of for homework. Write these on the board. Ask: *What can be done about problems like these?*

1 After students have discussed the photo, ask them if teenagers should use social media, and if so, how often should they use it?

2 Ask students if they think the problem in the magazine is serious for the teenager, too, and if it's a problem they themselves have.

3 After students have discussed the question in pairs, put them into groups. In their groups, they can discuss the following questions: *Should parents follow their kids online? What are the pros and cons of this?*

4 Point out the phrases in the *Useful language* box are polite ways of giving someone advice.

5 After you check answers, students can practise the mini-dialogues in pairs.

Useful language practice

6 ★ Before students plan their emails, brainstorm the sort of advice you might give to someone with each of the problems in the box.

7 Monitor while students write their emails. Help as necessary.

8 Encourage students to check their partner's use of the phrases in the *Useful language* box. Have they used the phrases correctly? Does the email seem polite and helpful?

WRITING
An email reply

1 Look at the photo of a teenager and her mum. What do you think is the problem?

2 Read the email to a teenage magazine and the reply. Who is asking for advice? Who is giving it?

Janelle is asking for advice about her teenage daughter. A teenager called Abby is giving the advice.

Dear Abby,
I want to follow my daughter on social media because I'm worried about who she might become friends with, but she says I can't because it would be 'totally embarrassing' if I posted on her wall. I feel hurt by her reaction. You're a teenager – how can I change her mind?
Many thanks,
Janelle

Dear Janelle,
I'm glad you wrote. Firstly, this is a common problem, so don't feel down. However, your daughter's reaction isn't unusual. It doesn't mean she doesn't love you, but she needs space.
I would recommend telling her why you are worried. It would definitely help to talk. Why don't you suggest following, her but promise not to post on her wall? If she isn't happy with that, it might be better not to follow her at all. Whatever you do, don't get annoyed with her and don't forget to tell her that you trust her.
Good luck, and let me know how it goes.
Abby

Useful language
- It might be better (not) to …
- It would definitely help to …
- I would recommend … (+ *-ing*)
- Whatever you do, don't …
- Why don't you suggest … (+ *-ing*)?

3 How useful is Abby's advice?

4 Look at the *Useful language* box. Find and underline the phrases in Abby's email.

5 Complete the mini-dialogues with the phrases from the *Useful language* box.

1 A So the party starts at seven, does it?
B Yes, but ________, don't tell Pablo. It's a surprise. *whatever you do*

2 A My best friend is stressed about her exams.
B ________ joining a study group? *Why don't you suggest*

3 A Joe has to take his medicine.
B Yes, but ________ not to wake him. He needs to rest as well. *it might be better*

4 A What's a good way to get fit and have fun?
B ________ joining a football team. *I would recommend*

5 A Felix isn't talking to me.
B Well, ________ say sorry. *it would definitely help to*

Write an email reply to a worried parent.

PLAN

6 Imagine you are Abby. Choose one of the problems below to reply to. Think of three pieces of advice that they should or shouldn't do.

> My son never does his homework on time. His teachers are angry and I don't know what to do.
>
> My daughter refuses to help with the housework. She says she's too busy studying.

WRITE

7 Write your email reply. Remember to include the plan in Exercise 6, language from this unit and phrases from the *Useful language* box.

CHECK

8 Do you …
- say what the person should do?
- say what the person should not do?
- think the advice is useful?

Finished? p124 Ex 4

Finished?

Fast finishers can turn to SB p124 and do Exercise 4.

Flipped class

Prepare for the **Around the World** lesson (pp90–91). Students research facts about happiness.

Homework

Workbook p61

Background information

In recent years, the Danish word *hygge* (pronounced 'hoogaa'), has become well-known. An adjective to describe an atmosphere which is cosy and pleasant, it has come to signify the Danish way of life more generally, where people have been said to be among the happiest in the world.

Warmer

Ask: *How is it possible to make people in a place or a country happier?* Elicit students' ideas.

▶ The video develops the theme of happiness, looking at countries that are thought of as being particularly happy. Read through the questions with students and ask them to predict answers before playing **Video 7.5** for students to check their answers.

Video comprehension questions

1 Students can discuss this in pairs, before you extend the discussion to the whole class. Do students agree with each other?

2 7.11 Read out the five paragraph titles, making sure that students can pronounce *hygge* (see the Background information note above). Students can then work in pairs to put the titles in the correct place in the report.

AROUND THE WORLD

yes; Costa Rica – strong networks of friends, family and neighbours, Norway – short working week, voluntary work, spend time outdoors

READING

A report about schools in Denmark

Globetrotters
Watch video 7.5
Happiness around the world

- What different things can make us happy?
- Are Costa Rica and Norway considered happy countries? Why?
- What do Ecuador and Bhutan have in common?

Both countries are trying to protect the natural world.

1 **What do you think is most important in making a school a happy place? Why?**

a lots of events
b a nice building
c student clubs and sports teams
d technology in the classroom

7.11 **2** **Read the report and put the paragraph titles in the correct place 1–5. Listen and check your answers.**

a Enjoying *hygge* is for everyone
b Conclusion
c Introduction
d Understanding other people
e Learning with others builds a better society

The happiest children in the world: a report

1 c

We have written this report to describe some of the reasons why Danish children are the happiest in the world. It is part of our school project 'Happier students, happier societies'.

2 d

One of the most important reasons Danish children are so happy is that they are taught empathy from a very young age. Empathy is the ability to imagine what it must be like to be another person. At preschool, Danish children learn to do this by studying facial expressions. They are shown pictures of the faces of other children showing anger, fear, sadness, etc. The preschool children say what they think the children in the pictures are feeling, and try to imagine being them. Schoolchildren never stop learning about empathy. Even 15- and 16-year-olds continue to have one hour a week of empathy as a compulsory subject.

3 a

Danish teenagers also have 'Class time'. This is a special time when students come together to talk about any individual or group problems they are having. This could be a personal issue between two students, or even something unrelated to school. During this time, everyone bears in mind the feelings of others and avoids criticising anyone. The group tries to find a solution together. They do this in a peaceful environment, with everyone glad to take part. 'Class time' is connected to *hygge*, a Danish word that is tricky to translate into English but which means relaxed and cosy.

4 e

In Danish schools students with different strengths and weaknesses study together in mixed groups. This helps to develop their empathy by showing them that everyone has strong points, talents and positive qualities. One student might find English difficult, for example, but be good at maths. Another might find English easy but find it difficult to understand maths. In a Danish school, these two students would help each other during lessons, and often between lessons as well. The system develops teamwork, respect and collaboration. These are essential qualities for a successful, happy life both at school and in the adult world.

5 b

In summary, the main reason that Danish children are so happy is very simple: they develop empathy, and empathy increases happiness by making everyone feel included and understood. They do this in a number of different but connected ways: learning to read the feelings of others, discussing problems together, and working in mixed groups. We believe that introducing any one of these methods into our own school would be straightforward and would improve our school life a great deal. Imagine what we could achieve if we tried all three!

90 KEEP CALM! | UNIT 7

Class challenge

Denmark has over **two** / three / ten times more bicycles than cars.

Lesson aim: I can understand a text about children in Denmark.

3 Students can compare answers in pairs before you check answers with the class as a whole.

Reading comprehension questions

Learn to learn

Point out that there are few exact synonyms. As students' learn more about English, they will learn that seemingly similar words, such as *happiness*, which describes a general feeling of being happy, and *joy*, which is usually used to refer to an intense feeling of happiness such as you feel when your football team wins a tournament.

4 Tell students that they need to think about what the words in the table mean (e.g. *obligatory*) and then look in the text for a context that includes that meaning (i.e. *a compulsory subject*). Allow students to use dictionaries for this task.

5 Give students time to think of their answers to the questions before they discuss them with a partner. With the class as a whole, discuss the importance of empathy, focusing on the way it can help people form good relationships. Encourage students to consider how their actions affect the way other people feel. You can also tell them to discuss any issues or problems honestly and try to resolve them as a group.

3 Read the report again and circle the correct answers.

1 This report was written by …
a teachers.
(b) students.

2 Preschool Danish children look at pictures of …
a their classmates.
(b) children they don't know.

3 Danish teenagers …
a can study empathy if they want to.
(b) have to study empathy. — compulsory

4 In 'Class time' students talk about …
(a) all kinds of problems. — individual
b their individual problems.

5 In Danish schools, students with different abilities …
a help each other in class.
(b) help each other in and out of class.

6 To improve their own school, the writers suggest …
(a) trying all the ideas in the report.
b trying only one of the ideas.

LEARN TO LEARN

Synonyms and antonyms

Learning words with similar or opposite meanings can help you to increase your vocabulary quickly.

4 Complete the table with words from the report.

	Word(s) with a similar meaning	Word with the opposite meaning
joy	happiness	[1] *sadness*
[2] compulsory	obligatory	optional
[3] individual	single	[4] group
related	[5] connected	[6] unrelated
difficult	[7] tricky	easy
[8] strengths	strong points	weaknesses
important	[9] essential	unimportant
simple	[10] straightforward	complicated

Voice it!

5 Discuss the questions.

1 Which of the ideas in the report do you think is best for developing empathy? Why?
2 Why is empathy important in life?

Explore it!

Guess the correct answer.
Which of these can make you happier? — all of them
a smelling flowers
b the colour yellow
c being outside

Find another interesting fact about happiness. Write a question for your partner to answer.

Find it! The Culture Project — **Teacher's Resource Bank**

UNIT 7 | KEEP CALM! 91

Students can collaborate digitally online and offline in the collaboration space, where teachers can set, track and assess students' work. Students can also share and showcase their work as well as comment on each other's projects.

Culture project

See Project Book p46 for further information and activities.

Explore it!

To write their questions, students use the information they researched for homework.

Flipped class

Prepare for the **Review** lesson (p92). Students revise the grammar and vocabulary from Unit 7.

Lesson aim: I can review what I have learnt and reflect on my progress.

The aim of this review page is for students to revise the grammar and vocabulary from the unit. You can either do it in class, as a timed progress test or set it for homework.

Vocabulary

1 Turn this activity into a class competition. Put students into small groups. Elicit the answer in each case. If students get the answer right, they win a point. The first team to then explain why their answer is correct wins an extra point. The team with the most points win.

2 Before students do the task, elicit phrases with *heart* and *mind*. Put these on the board. Challenge students to be the first to complete the sentences correctly.

Language in action

3 Students can compare answers in pairs, and discuss any differences before checking answers as a class.

4 Before students complete this exercise, ask them what they know about subject and object questions. Students can look back at p87 of the Student's Book to remind themselves. After you have checked students' answers, they can practise reading the dialogue in pairs.

Unit quiz review

7 REVIEW

VOCABULARY

1 Circle the correct words.

Hi Lee,

How's it going? I've been in Turkey for a month. I'm [1] *glad* / *hopeful* I came to a town and not a city. It's more [2] *peaceful* / *grateful*. I've been practising Turkish a lot – you know me, I'm [3] *eager* / *insecure* to learn! I felt [4] *satisfied* / *ridiculous* at first, but I'm improving. I'm [5] *thrilled* / *annoyed* when people understand me, although sometimes people are [6] *hurt* / *amused* by my mistakes. Mehmet has introduced me to lots of people. I'm really [7] *grateful* / *down* to him.

Anyway, how are you? Write soon!

James

2 Complete the sentences with an expression with *heart* or *mind*.

1. I'm in two minds about the party. Should I go or not?
2. Waiter! I've changed my mind. I'll have pizza, not pasta.
3. My sister's great at learning all sorts of facts and dates by heart.
4. Pollution is an issue that's really close to my heart. That's why I don't drive.
5. It takes me ages to make up my mind what to wear in the morning. I'd prefer a school uniform!
6. Can I talk to you? I've got something on my mind. It's about my best friend.

LANGUAGE IN ACTION

3 Complete the sentences with the gerund or infinitive with *to* form of the verbs in brackets.

1. I'm not shy about giving (give) presentations.
2. I was so glad to see (see) my cousin at the party.
3. I remember feeling (feel) really insecure on my first day at school.
4. My baby brother is always amused at something. He never stops laughing (laugh).
5. Keeping (keep) notes of new vocabulary is really important when you study.

4 Complete the dialogue with the correct subject and object questions.

EMMA	Happy birthday!
YUSUF	Thanks, guys! This is amazing. Who [1] cooked (cook) the cake?
TIM	Emma did.
YUSUF	It's delicious. What [2] did you put (put/you) in it, Emma?
EMMA	Sorry – that's a secret! Anyway, what [3] do you think (think) of your birthday playlist?
YUSUF	I love it. Who [4] made (make) it?
TIM	Emma put it together.
YUSUF	Who [5] chose (choose) the song that's playing now? It's one of my favourites.
TIM	That was me!
EMMA	So tell us – what presents [6] did you get (get/you)?
YUSUF	Some clothes and this fidget spinner.
TIM	Who [7] gave (give) you that?
YUSUF	My cousin. He knows I collect them.
TIM	What [8] do you want (want/you) to drink? Some juice, some cola? We've got everything.

Self-assessment

I can use adjectives to talk about feelings.	☹ 😐 ☺
I can use expressions with *heart* and *mind*.	☹ 😐 ☺
I can use gerunds and infinitives.	☹ 😐 ☺
I can use subject and object questions.	☹ 😐 ☺

Self-assessment

Students look back through the unit in the Student's Book and the Workbook and reflect on how well they can do these things. They then discuss their opinions with a partner.

Homework

Workbook pp 62–63

Lesson aim: I can learn to give my partner useful feedback.

At this stage, students should be helping each other improve their skills. Offering useful feedback to a partner allows students to reflect on their own performance as well as their partner's.

Warmer

Ask: *What do you find most difficult about speaking English? What do you most enjoy about speaking English?* In pairs, students can discuss the questions.

1 ★★★ Challenge students to respond to the advice. Do they agree with it? Is there anything they would add to it?

2 Give students time to read the feedback on Lars' presentation. They can then discuss the feedback in pairs. With the class as a whole, decide which feedback is the most and least useful and why (it's hurtful, it's too emotional, etc.). Elicit that 1, 3 and 6 haven't followed the advice as 1 is too negative, 3 is probably exaggerated and not useful, 6 is very negative. 2, 4, 5 and 7 all followed the advice as they are generally positive and give ideas on how to improve.

3 ★ Before students prepare their talks, discuss what makes a good talk, e.g. that it has an interesting opening, that it is clear and easy to follow, that is uses humour, that you feel you learn something from it, that it isn't too long or short. Give students 15 minutes to prepare their talks.

LEARN TO LEARN

LEARN TO ... GIVE YOUR PARTNER USEFUL FEEDBACK

You can help your partner to improve their speaking by giving useful feedback. When you work together, they can help you improve too.

1 Match 1–5 with a–e to complete advice about giving feedback.

Giving your partner feedback can help them speak, but there are some important things to bear in mind.

1 Being positive is important, so always tell your partner e	a talking about personal things.
2 You don't want your partner to feel hurt, so c	b to give ideas for how your partner can improve.
3 Remember to focus on their English and avoid a	c talk about anything negative in a friendly way.
4 Feedback should be useful, so don't forget b	d better or worse than it really is.
5 Be honest. Don't say something is d	e what you liked and what they did well.

2 Look at the feedback that seven students have given Lars. Do they follow the advice in Exercise 1? Why? / Why not?

1 *You didn't speak very clearly. You sounded like a robot!*

2 *I'm glad you used lots of the new vocabulary. That was nice!*

3 *You've got a gorgeous voice!*

4 *You repeated some words a lot. I would recommend using synonyms next time.*

5 *You made some grammar mistakes, but maybe because you were nervous.*

6 *That was absolutely the most dreadful presentation in history!*

7 *I think you'll sound more natural next time if you don't learn everything by heart.*

3 Prepare a talk about a topic in the box.

a happy memory
growth mindset
how to deal with exam stress
how to stay happy

OWN IT!

4 Take turns to give your talks. While your partner is speaking, think about these things.

- What do you like about their talk?
- What language do they use well?
- How can they improve next time?

5 Give your partner useful feedback using the advice in Exercise 1. Is your partner's feedback on your own talk useful? How?

OWN IT!

4 ★ As the focus here is on receiving feedback, students may be more nervous than usual about doing their presentations. Be sensitive to this.

5 Encourage students to be honest but fair in their feedback.

Flipped class

Prepare for **Unit 8**. Students research what makes a good advert. What do advertisers have to think of? They can also make notes on their favourite adverts.

Lesson aim: I can talk about places where adverts can be seen.

Warmer

Elicit examples of current well-known TV adverts. Ask: *Do adverts ever make you want to buy something?*

▶ Start it!

Unit quiz

1 Elicit ideas about whether there is a place like this near where the students live.

2 Give students a minute to write down as many places as they can.

3 ▶ Students can discuss their ideas in pairs. Then play **Video 7.1** so that students can check their answers. They can also complete the Start it! **Video worksheet** in the *Teacher's Resource Bank*.

4 Put students into small groups to discuss this. If students do not have a favourite advert, ask them to describe the type of advert they would like to see.

Video comprehension questions

Flipped class

Prepare for **Explore it!** (p95). Students find out a fact about the tricks (clever techniques designed to influence someone, such as using music to make us feel a particular emotion) used in advertising to make a product look good.

8 ADVERTISING

LEARNING OUTCOMES

I can ...
- understand texts about online advertising and social media influencers
- recommend an online tool
- write an online product review
- understand how to use defining and non-defining relative clauses, and indefinite, reflexive and reciprocal pronouns
- talk about advertising and use Internet verbs
- understand word building (nouns and verbs) and how to answer open-ended questions
- create an advert storyboard.

Start it!

1 Look at the photo. Is there a place where you live where you can see lots of adverts like this?
2 Before you watch, think of all the different places where you can see adverts.
3 What are the four important aspects of advertising? Watch and check. — image, colour, music, humour
4 What's your favourite advert? Why?

Watch video 8.1 | Language in action 8.2 p97 | Language in action 8.3 p99 | Everyday English 8.4 p100

94 ADVERTISING | UNIT 8

Unit aims

Skills

I can ...
- understand a report about online advertising p96
- recommend an online tool p100
- write an online product review p101
- create an advert storyboard pp101–102

Language

I can ...
- talk about advertising p95
- use defining and non-defining relative clauses p97
- use internet verbs p98
- use indefinite, reflexive and reciprocal pronouns p99

Learn to Learn

I can ...
- understand wordbuilding p95
- prepare for open-ended questions p98
- work out the meaning of new words p105

Extra Resources

- *Finished?* – Student's Book p125
- *Vocabulary Bank* – Student's Book p135
- CLIL - Student's Book p140
- Pronunciation - Student's Book p142
- Workbook p64
- *Teacher's Resource Bank on Cambridge One* for tests package, Cambridge Exam practice, wordlists, differentiated worksheets and many other extra resources.
- *Practice Extra and Digital collaboration space*

Warmer

Ask: *Do you like adverts? Why? Why not?* Students can discuss this in pairs.

1 8.01 Ask students, in pairs, to take turns saying a word and writing it down, to practise pronunciation and spelling.

Audioscript p173

Target vocabulary

ad blocker /ˈædblɒkə/
advert /ˈædvɜːt/
advertise /ˈædvətaɪz/
brand /brænd/
buyer /ˈbaɪə/
influence /ˈɪnfluəns/
logo /ˈləʊgəʊ/
marketing company /ˈmɑːkɪtɪŋ ˈkʌmpəni/
product /ˈprɒdʌkt/
review /rɪˈvjuː/
seller /ˈselə/
slogan /ˈsləʊgən/

2 8.02 ★★★ Challenge students to explain their choice in each case and to say what the other word or phrase means and how it can be used.

Audioscript p173

Vocabulary Bank SB p135

Extra vocabulary practice

Learn to learn

Recording nouns and verbs together will improve students' understanding of possible spelling relationships. Encourage students to check in a dictionary to find out where the syllable stress is (recording this by underlining the syllable), as this tends to shift between noun and verb forms.

3 When going through the answers, drill the pronunciation of the nouns and verbs.

VOCABULARY

Advertising

1 8.01 **Read the story of an advert and put pictures A–F in the correct order. Listen and repeat the words in bold.**

1 A 2 F 3 C
4 B 5 D 6 E

2 8.02 **Circle the correct words. Listen and check.**

1 I love watching funny *marketing companies* / *adverts* online or on TV.
2 My dad always buys the same *brand* / *product* of toothpaste.
3 Sometimes it's not easy for *sellers* / *buyers* to decide which product they want.
4 I always look at *ad blockers* / *reviews* before I buy something new.
5 That advert *advertised* / *influenced* my decision to buy a new tablet.
6 At school we have to draw a simple design for a *logo* / *slogan* competition.

LEARN TO LEARN

Wordbuilding: nouns and verbs

When you learn a noun, check the verb form and record them in a table.

3 **Complete the table.**

Noun	Verb
advert	1 advertise
product	2 produce
3 buyer	buy
review	4 review
5 ad blocker	block (an ad)
6 market	market
influencer	7 influence
seller	8 sell

4 **Close your books. One person says a noun from the table and the other says the matching verb.**

ADVERTISING A PRODUCT

First, a company makes something to sell. This is the **product**. Then, they create a **brand** to represent the product – this is a name and design that creates a product's identity. It is usually represented by a symbol or **logo**. There is often a **slogan** (a short phrase that is easy to remember) linked to a brand.

Next an **advert** is made to **advertise** the product. This could be a poster in the street or a short film on the television or online that shows what the product is like. It is made by a **marketing company** to encourage or **influence** people to buy the product.

When the product goes on sale the customer or **buyer** buys the product from a **seller**. Buyers sometimes write their opinions about the product in an online **review**. People who don't want to see online adverts use an **ad blocker**, a computer programme that stops adverts appearing on the screen.

Use it!

5 **Read the questions and make notes.**

1 Do you think ad blockers are a good idea? Why?
2 Do online reviews influence people to buy a product?
3 Which brand slogans or logos can you remember?

6 **Ask and answer the questions in Exercise 5.**

Explore it!

Guess the correct answer.

When you see a glass of milk in an advert, it probably isn't milk. What is it?

a paint b glue c yoghurt

Find out some tricks that are used in adverts to make products look good. Write a question for your partner to answer.

UNIT 8 | ADVERTISING 95

4 ★★★ Challenge students to put each verb their partner elicits into a sentence.

5 Read out the questions. Give students time to note down some thoughts.

6 Give students three minutes to discuss the questions. Encourage students to ask follow-up questions to develop their conversations.

Explore it!

Students share the facts about advertising tricks that they researched for homework.

Quiz questions

Flipped class

Prepare for the **Reading** lesson! (p96). Students find out about social-media influencers.

Homework

Workbook p64

Lesson aim: I can understand a report about social-media influencers.

Warmer

Ask: *What online adverts do you like or dislike?* Put students into pairs to discuss the question.

1 8.03 Elicit students' ideas and write them on the board.

2 Put students in pairs to predict what the numbers refer to before they read the text.

3 Do this task with the whole class. Read out each sentence, eliciting the type of advertising it refers to.

4 ★★★ Point out that the target words are located in the sections of the text shown in brackets after each item. Challenge students to write their own sentences using this new vocabulary. Monitor and help as necessary.

Vocabulary practice

5 Give students time to think about their answers, and make notes, before they discuss the questions in pairs.

Pronunciation

Students do the activities on p142 to practise pronouncing the letters *-tion*.

READING

A report

Influencers make videos of themselves talking about products and then share them on social media to promote the products.

1 8.03 What can you see in the photos? What do you think people do with the videos? Read the report and check your ideas.

2 Read the report again. What do the numbers refer to?

1 31% — people influenced by blogs
2 74% — people who say conversations on social media give the best information
3 +600 million — people using ad blockers

3 Which type of advertising do the sentences refer to: *I* (influencer), *UGC* (user-generated content) or *N* (native)?

1 Customers can win prizes. UGC
2 Customers share photos of themselves. UGC
3 It doesn't look like advertising. N
4 People buy the products to copy someone else. I
5 Products are promoted by famous people. I
6 There is a word that tells you it's an advert. N

4 Find words in the report that mean:

1 people who follow someone online (I) followers
2 a planned series of activities to advertise a product (UGC) campaign
3 something that has your name on (UGC) personalised
4 to stop (N) block
5 paid advertising (N) sponsored

Voice it!

5 Discuss the questions.

1 Do you have a favourite social media influencer or vlogger?
2 Where have you seen native ads on social media?

Online advertising

Social media influencers

One of the most successful types of advertising on social media is influencer advertising. Brands choose social media stars who have thousands of followers on their blog, YouTube channel or Instagram to advertise their products. The stars talk positively about the products in a natural, personal way, which is different to the slogans in traditional adverts. They might talk about a beauty product, play a song, or wear certain clothes in their videos, photos or blogs. Many fans, who want to copy their favourite social media stars, go and buy the same products when they see them.

What influences us to buy a product?
Shop websites – 56%, Brand websites – 34%, Blogs – 31%

User-generated content

Another technique used is user-generated content, or UGC. You may know a soft drinks company whose advertising campaign put everyday names on their drinks bottles. Buyers took photos of themselves with their personalised bottle and shared them on social media. With UGC the buyer becomes the person who advertises the brand so, for example, they upload photos of themselves wearing clothes with the brand logo. Sometimes companies have competitions where you can win a prize for the best photo, and of course, it's free advertising for the brand.

Who gives you the best product information?
(Traditional media) TV – 34%, radio – 37%, newspapers – 44%,
(UGC) social networking – 50%, reviews – 68%, conversations with friends – 74%

Native advertising

Have you ever used an ad blocker so you don't see so many adverts online? Ad blockers block some adverts, but not native advertising. It's a type of advertising that you can't see because it looks exactly the same as a social platform or website. For example, on Facebook a native ad looks like a normal post with like, share and comment buttons, or it could be a photo or video on Instagram. However, if you look closely, you will see the words 'sponsored' or 'paid post' next to it. The good thing about native advertising is that users don't feel like their favourite social media channels are full of adverts, but some people don't like the idea of hidden adverts.

Fact: +600M people use ad blockers

Pronunciation p142

Finished? p125 Ex 1

Extend it!

Ask students to make a list of different ways shoppers can be influenced to buy products. Encourage them to use their own experiences when writing their lists.

Class challenge

Talkomatic, the first computer system which allowed people to chat together online, was created in **1973** / 1997 / 2007.

Finished?

Students turn to SB p125 and do Exercise 1.

Flipped class

Ask students to watch **Video 8.2** and do the **Video worksheet** in the *Teacher's Resource Bank*.

Homework

Workbook p65

Lesson aim: I can use defining and non-defining relative clauses.

Warmer

▶ Play **Video 8.2** if it was not set for homework. Elicit that he's giving advice about how to manage time online (e.g. turn off or mute the social media alerts on your phone when you need to study or put your phone in another room).

1 Focus students on the words in bold. Elicit that they are relative pronouns and that such words are used to either define the subject of a sentence or add extra information.

2 ★ Before students do this task, elicit what the relative pronouns mean (*which/that* = things, *who* = people, *whose* = possession, *where* = place, *when* = time).

Extra grammar practice

3 Do the first part of this task with the class as a whole, eliciting the correct relative pronoun and writing it on the board. Students can then complete the sentences with their own ideas.

4 ★ Focus on the example, showing how one sentence is formed from two. Help students by highlighting which word in items 2 and 3 the relative pronoun in brackets will refer to. (In item 2 *where* will connect to *beach*, in number 3 *which* will connect to *phone*).

5 & 6 Before students ask questions, check that they have formed them correctly.

Watch video 8.2
What is he giving advice about?
What should you do with your phone?

LANGUAGE IN ACTION

Defining and non-defining relative clauses

Defining relative clauses
With UGC the buyer becomes the person [1] who / **that** advertises the brand.
It's a type of advertising **which** / [2] that you can't see.
Sometimes companies have competitions [3] where you can win a prize for the best photo.
Many fans buy the same products [4] when they see them.
You may know a soft drinks company [5] whose advertising campaign put everyday names on their drinks bottles.
Non-defining relative clauses
The stars talk positively about the products in a natural, personal way, [6] which is different to the slogans in traditional adverts.
Many fans, [7] who want to copy their favourite social media stars, go and buy the same products when they see them.

1 **Complete the examples in the table above. Use the report on page 96 to help you.**

2 **Circle the correct relative pronouns.**

1. The online advertising *who* / *which* most teens prefer is made by social media influencers. (which)
2. Influencers *that* / *whose* channels have the most followers advertise lots of products. (whose)
3. Some influencers *who* / *where* advertise products are paid lots of money. (who)
4. Many teens ignore adverts *which* / *when* they see them on social networking sites. (when)
5. Marketing companies look for sites online *which* / *where* they can advertise products. (where)

Use it!

3 **Complete the sentences with the relative pronouns in the box and your own ideas.**

when which whose

1. A time when I feel happy is ______.
2. Someone whose videos I have watched is ______.
3. The apps which I use most are ______.

4 **Join the two sentences with a relative pronoun.**

1. Jo has got her own vlog. Jo is older than me. (who)
   Jo, who's older than me, has got her own vlog.
2. We're going on holiday to the beach. Katia's family have got a house at the beach. (where)
   We're going on holiday to the beach, where Katia's family have got a house.
3. My phone takes excellent photos. My phone is really old. (which)
   My phone, which is really old, takes excellent photos.

Use it!

5 **Think of six quiz questions about facts you have read in this book. Use a relative clause.**

What was the name of the person who … ?

6 **Ask and answer your questions.**

Finished? p125 Ex 2

UNIT 8 | ADVERTISING 97

Grammar game

In pairs students write two defining and two non-defining relative clauses, gapping the relative pronoun in each of the sentences. Their partner then has to complete the sentences using the correct relative pronoun.

Finished?

Fast finishers can turn to SB p125 and do Exercise 2.

Homework

Workbook p66

Warmer

Ask: *How much time do you spend online each day? What are your favourite things to do online?* Put students in pairs to discuss the questions.

2 8.06 Ask students to compare their answers in pairs, before you check answers with the class as a whole.

Audioscript p173

Target vocabulary
build up /ˈbɪld ʌp/
comment on /ˈkɒment ɒn /
delete /dɪˈliːt/
follow /ˈfɒləʊ/
post /pəʊst/
shut down /ʃʌt daʊn/
subscribe to /səbˈskraɪb tuː/
switch off /swɪtʃ ɒf/
switch on /swɪtʃ ɒn/
vlog /vlɒg/

Extra vocabulary practice

2 Give students time to make notes on the information in the box before asking the questions in pairs.

Vocabulary Bank SB p135

3 8.07 Elicit ideas from the class about the order of events before listening. Then play the recording for students to check.

Audioscript p173

Learn to learn

The point here is to encourage students to identify the content they need to listen out for, in order to make the task of listening easier and more focused.

VOCABULARY AND LISTENING

Internet verbs

1 8.06 **Match words 1–10 with definitions a–j. Listen and repeat the words in bold.**

- I [1]**subscribe to** a YouTube channel about parkour. They [2]**post** some awesome videos on it.
- If your Internet doesn't work, [3]**switch it off** and then [4]**switch it on** again.
- My sister didn't [5]**build up** many followers on Twitter so she [6]**shut down** her account.
- You should [7]**follow** Zoella. She [8]**vlogs** about loads of interesting things and I love her recipes.
- If people [9]**comment on** the post and it isn't very nice, we [10]**delete** it.

a choose to see the things someone uploads on social media 7
b close or stop something 6
c increase the number of something 5
d make and share videos online 8
e put a message or image on social media 2
f remove something 10
g start something working 4
h stop something working 3
i write your opinion online 9
j agree to regularly receive an online service or information about it 1

Use it!

2 **Ask and answer questions. Find three things you have in common.**

commented on something   deleted something
followed someone   posted something
subscribed to a channel   vlogged about something

Have you ever followed someone on social media?
Yes, of course!
Who do you follow?
I follow all my friends and some celebrities online.

An interview

3 8.07 **Jerome is an influencer. Put the events in the order you think he did them. Listen to the interview and check your answers.**

a He tried out and reviewed products. 5
b He commented on other posts. 1
c He got 10,000 followers. 4
d He posted videos every day. 3
e He set up his own YouTube channel. 2

LEARN TO LEARN

Open-ended questions

Read open-ended questions before you listen and think of possible answers. As you listen, make notes of important words, (names, numbers, etc.).

4 **Discuss the questions in Exercise 5. Think of possible answers for each question.**

Jerome wanted to talk about a hobby, teach people about something or show people how to make something.

5 8.07 **Listen again and answer the questions.**

1 Why did Jerome start a YouTube channel?
Because he wanted to talk about gaming.
2 Why did he delete his videos at first?
Because he didn't think they were good enough.
3 What did his followers like about his vlogs?
He was someone just like them who was talking honestly about gaming so his followers could relate to his comments.
4 Why did he nearly shut down his account?
Because his followers started arguing with one anot[her].
5 How did he solve the problem?
He turned off the comments so that the followers couldn't talk to each other.
6 When did companies send him new games?
When he reached around 10,000 followers.
7 What advice does he give?
Try to be different to everyone else and connect with your followers.

6 **Would you like to be an influencer? Why? / Why not?**

98 ADVERTISING | UNIT 8

4 Find out if students can remember enough about the recording to answer any of the questions in Exercise 5.

5 8.07 Ask students if they would be interested in following Jerome online.

6 Ask: *Why do young people follow influencers online?* You can also broaden the discussion to include the question of why social media is so popular and whether that is a problem or not.

Flipped class

Ask students to watch **Video 8.3** and do the **Video worksheet** in the *Teacher's Resource Bank*.

Homework

Workbook p67

▶ Play **Video 8.3** if it was not set for homework. Elicit that micro-influencers have under 10,000 followers. Micro-influencers are more like ordinary people and they are easier to relate to.

1 Explain that the table shows three different types of pronoun. Then play audio 8.07 again so students can complete the gaps.

Get it right!

Introduce some other verbs in English that are commonly used reflexively, e.g. *behave, cut, enjoy, hurt*.

2 Read out the example. Elicit why *anybody* is the correct indefinite pronoun (the question requires a pronoun which means a person or people). Ask students to complete the task in pairs, giving reasons for their choices.

3 ★ Tell students to first read the sentence and highlight the word that will lead them to the correct reflexive pronoun, which, in number 1, is *she*.

4 Point out that *one another* is a more formal alternative to *each other*.

5 🎧 8.08 Tell students to read through the text quickly first, then ask: *Which product is referred to?* (shampoo).

Audioscript p174

Extra grammar practice

6 Encourage students to think of more than one sentence in each case. Ask two or three students to tell the class what they found out about their partner.

LANGUAGE IN ACTION

Indefinite, reflexive and reciprocal pronouns

Watch video 8.3
How many followers do micro-influencers have? Why are they better than celebrity influencers?

Indefinite pronouns
Give your followers **something** new.
No one is interested in your selfies.
Have you got any advice for **anyone**?
There weren't any comments from [1] anyone / anybody.
I think that's why **everyone** likes it so much.
Reflexive pronouns
I tried the game out **myself**.
People are interested in [2] themselves.
Reciprocal pronouns
Some followers started arguing with **each other / one another**.

Get it right!

They looked at ***themselves*** *in the mirror.*
(Each person looked at himself/herself.)
They looked at ***each other****.*
(They looked at the different people in the group.)

1 Complete the examples in the table above.

2 Circle the correct indefinite pronouns.

1 Has *anybody* / *nobody* seen this funny video?
2 I've looked *everywhere* / *somewhere* for my mobile, but I can't find it *anywhere* / *somewhere*.
3 *Anyone* / *No one* commented on *anything* / *everything* she said.
4 We're going *everywhere* / *somewhere* in the centre of town for *everything* / *something* to eat.
5 Are you doing *anything* / *everything* special for your birthday?

3 Complete the sentences with reflexive pronouns.

1 She taught herself how to set up a website.
2 We really enjoyed ourselves at the party.
3 He's selfish. He only thinks about himself.
4 I love taking selfies of myself.

4 Match 1–4 with a–d. Then make sentences with *each other / one another*.

1 My brother lives in the USA so we talk to — d with a webcam.
2 We talk a lot. We're always sending — c messages.
3 We haven't seen — b for ages.
4 They don't understand — a and argue all the time.

1 My brother lives in the USA so we talk to each other / one another with a webcam.
2 We talk a lot. We're always sending each other / one another messages.
3 We haven't seen each other / one another for ages.
4 They don't understand each other / one another and argue all the time.

🎧 8.08 **5 Circle the correct words to complete the text. Listen and check.**

Ads are [1]*everywhere* / *anywhere*, but have you ever asked [2]*ourself* / *yourself* how advertising works? Marketing companies use techniques to make us buy things we don't even want. [3]*Everything* / *Nothing* is more effective than making us think that we are missing out on [4]*something* / *anything* that [5]*everyone* / *no one* else has and that we will be happier if we buy [6]*ourselves* / *themselves* something new. They also make us compare [7]*myself* / *ourselves* to others. For example, in a typical shampoo ad, two women look at [8]*themselves* / *each other*. One of them asks herself, 'Why is her hair so beautiful?' When they talk to [9]*one another* / *themselves* she discovers the secret: The incredible shampoo!

Use it!

6 Complete the sentences so they are true for you.

1 I have taught myself to ____________.
2 I never go anywhere without ____________.

Finished? p125 Ex 3

Grammar game
Put students in small groups. Write incorrect sentences on the board, e.g. *Everywhere likes chocolate. / He enjoyed herself at the party.* The first group to correct each sentence wins a point.

Finished?
Fast finishers can turn to SB p125 and do Exercise 3.

Homework
Workbook p68

Lesson aim: I can recommend an online tool.

Warmer

On the board, write *online tool* and elicit that this is an app that allows someone to make videos, films, music, blogs, etc. What online tools do students know and use?

1 8.09 After students have listened to the recording and answered the question, find out if they have ever used a video-creation tool.

Audioscript p174

2 8.09 ★★★ Ask students to cover the *Useful language* box. Students then listen, and fill in the conversation with the phrases they hear.

Useful language practice

▶ Play **Video 8.4**. Encourage students to copy the intonation used by the presenter.

3 ★★★ After students have completed the task, challenge them to think of further contexts for the phrases in the *Everyday English* box. Give students two minutes to do this. Elicit their ideas, check they are right, then write those ideas on the board.

4 Give students time to choose an online tool from the box. Monitor and help as necessary.

5 Ask students to practise the conversations until they feel comfortable enough to speak fluently and not rely on their notes. Encourage them to improvise a little.

Niall needs to make a video for his school technology project and doesn't know how to do it. Ginny recommends using an online video creation tool.

SPEAKING

Recommending an online tool

1 8.09 Listen to the conversation. What problem does Niall have? What does Ginny recommend?

2 8.09 Complete the conversation with the phrases from the *Useful language* box. Listen and check.

GINNY What's up, Niall?
NIALL I've got to make a video for my technology project to advertise something and I don't have a clue what to do. [1]*I don't know where to start*! Can you think of anything?
GINNY [2] ______ (You really ought to) use a video creation tool. [3] ______ (It's the best thing) to make videos. I've used some great ones. There are loads of options online.
NIALL That sounds like a plan. What do I need to know?
GINNY Well, a video creation tool [4] would be ideal because it would provide you with a ready-made template.
NIALL [5] ______ (Is it easy to use)?
GINNY Yeah, you can teach yourself to do it, no problem.
NIALL Excellent! So I add my own text and images, do I?
GINNY Well, you need to write your own text, but most video creation tools have a ready-made image bank, which is handy.
NIALL Great, I can use their images.
GINNY Yep and you can add music and a voiceover. [6] ______ (I can't recommend them enough)!
NIALL Sounds like a no-brainer. I'll check out the options online. Thanks, Ginny!

Useful language

I can't recommend it/them enough!
I don't know where to start!
Is it easy to use?
It's the best thing …
(It) would be ideal …
You really ought to …

3 Match the *Everyday English* phrases with the meanings 1–4. How do you say these phrases in your language?

1 useful ______ handy
2 I have no idea. ______ I don't have a clue.
3 What's the matter? / How are you? ______ What's up?
4 obviously the right choice ______ no-brainer

Watch video 8.4
Everyday English

handy I don't have a clue. no-brainer What's up?

PLAN

4 Make notes about an online tool you want to recommend. Use the ideas below or your own ideas.

an app a comic maker a music video creator a presentation tool

______
______
______

SPEAK

5 Practise recommending the tool to your partner. Remember to use language from this unit and phrases from the *Useful language* and *Everyday English* boxes.

CHECK

6 Work with another pair. Listen to their conversation and complete the notes.

What tool did they talk about? ______

Did they give a good recommendation? ______

---

6 As well as answering the two questions students can give each other feedback by considering the following questions: *Did the other pair use language from the page? Was their recommendation helpful?*

Extend it!

Students write up their recommendations in about 100 words.

Lesson aim: I can write an online product review.

1 Check students' understanding of the features in the box. Encourage them to scan the text when looking to see which features are mentioned, rather than reading word for word.

2 ★★★ Extend the activity by asking students if they ever read online reviews and if reviews can be trusted.

3 Ask students to discuss the questions in pairs before reading the article again to check.

4 Ask students to think of other ways to finish these sentences, e.g. *Batteries are (not) included*. *It's designed to be used by children.*

Useful language practice

5 Brainstorm products to review with the class, then ask students to select one of these products to focus on.

6 Encourage students to use the review in Exercise 1 as a model to follow when they are writing their own.

7 Ask students to review each other's work. Then tell them to discuss the question of using stars in reviews. Are they useful? Why? Why not

HOME | STORIES | PHOTOS

Star rating ★★★★★

1 b **Sounds Around** is a great new product. If you're looking for a wireless speaker with a cool design, which is compact in size but big in sound quality, this is for you.

2 c **Sounds Around** is designed to be used outside. You can take it everywhere, to the beach, camping or to a pool party. It has all the features you need, it looks great and is extremely tough. One of its best features is that it's waterproof. It also allows you to connect two devices at the same time, so you can choose to play music from either of them. The charging cable is included, but the one thing that's missing is a microphone, so you can't record yourself. However, the battery lasts for 10 hours, which is more than other wireless speakers offered by other brands.

3 a **Sounds Around** offers the buyer an excellent range of features at an amazing price. In my opinion it's one of the best low-cost speakers. I can't recommend it enough!

WRITING
An online product review

1 **Look at the picture. Which of the features in the box do you think the speaker has? Read the review and check.**

compact size good price good sound
lightweight long-lasting battery
microphone waterproof wireless

The speaker has all the features in the box apart from a microphone and the weight of the speaker isn't mentioned.

2 **Read the review again. Match titles a–c with paragraphs 1–3.**

a Opinion
b Short description of the product
c Design and specific features

3 **Discuss the questions.**

1 Where does the reviewer suggest taking the speaker? Everywhere outside, the beach, camping or a pool party.
2 What's the advantage of connecting to two devices at the same time? You can play music on two devices.
3 What doesn't the reviewer like about the speaker? There isn't a microphone.
4 Why is the battery better than that of other brands? Because it lasts for up to 10 hours, which is more than other speakers.

4 **Read the review again and complete the phrases in the *Useful language* box.**

Useful language

[1] The charging cable is included. It allows you to [2] connect two devices at the same time
It is designed to be used [3] outside
One of its best features is [4] that it's waterproof
The one thing that's missing is [5] a microphone

Write your own online product review.

PLAN

5 **Choose a product to review. Make notes.**
short description of the product
design and specific features
your opinion

WRITE

6 **Write your product review. Remember to include three paragraphs, language from this unit and phrases from the *Useful language* box.**

CHECK

7 **Do you ...**
- give a star rating?
- say what you like and don't like?
- say whether you would buy it?

Finished? p125 Ex 4

Extend it!
In pairs, students make lists of the pros and cons of online shopping. Ask them to think of at least three ways in which it is better than traditional shopping, and three ways in which it is worse. Then compare as a class. Are there any points which everybody has in common?

Class challenge
Amazon began by selling **books** / clothes / computers online.

Finished?
Fast finishers can turn to SB p125 and do Exercise 4.

Homework
Workbook p69

Warmer

Ask: *What do advertisers have to think about when coming up with a new advert?* Students can discuss this question in pairs. You can then ask students to share their ideas with the class.

Project Book

For more information and activities see the Project Book p50.

1 Elicit students' ideas about the product that is being advertised.

2 8.10 Ask students to work in pairs to imagine the dialogue for each image. Remind them that the images are for an advert, so it's trying to sell something. Give them about ten minutes to write their dialogues for each picture (students should write no more than 50 words in total).

Audioscript p174

3 8.10 Read out the example, then ask students to read through the rest of the questions. Play the recording. Students can do the activity individually and then compare their answers in pairs.

How to give feedback

Encourage students to give each other specific feedback, saying what they liked or disliked about a piece of work, as well as making practical suggestions for ways to improve it. Refer students back to the Learn to Learn section on p93, which focused on giving feedback.

THE ART AND DESIGN PROJECT

An advert storyboard

1 Look at the pictures from an advert. What product does it advertise? a backpack

2 8.10 Work in pairs. Look at the pictures and guess the dialogue for each one. Listen and check.

3 8.10 Listen again and complete the table.

	Advert features	Example
1	What's the problem?	*Katia has a backpack that isn't waterproof. When it rains everything gets wet.*
2	What's the solution?	The Funpack is waterproof so nothing gets wet.
3	What are the special features of the product?	Lots of pockets. Special pockets for phones and tablets. A charger pocket to charge phones and tablets.
4	Who are the characters in the story?	Two teenage girls, one called Katia.
5	What information does the narrator give?	Information about available colours, designs which you can personalise yourself for free and the Funpack's special features.
6	What's the slogan?	Funpack. Packed full of fun!

How to give feedback

4 Feedback should be positive and useful. Complete the feedback phrases with the words in the box.

best how idea maybe positive work

The thing I liked [1] best was …
Some [2] positive things were …
I really liked [3] how you …
… is a great [4] idea.
[5] Maybe you could …
… might [6] work too.

4 Students can work in pairs to complete the sentences. Point out that the phrases are useful for giving constructive feedback and that students will have the opportunity to use these in Exercise 7, after they have looked at each other's storyboard presentations.

Lesson aim: I can create an advert storyboard.

Background information

Before production, the creators of an advert often begin with a storyboard. This is a simple line drawing of the key scenes in the advert, together with the script, the cast and the props.

5 Read out the products in the box, then give students a few minutes to decide, in groups, which of the products they want to produce an advert storyboard for. Once students have chosen their product, ask them to work through the five steps of the process. Give students thirty minutes to complete the steps, telling them it is their responsibility to manage their time properly.

6 ★ Before students present their adverts, encourage them to check their work one final time. Have they included the right information and is everything clear and easy to follow? Is their advert persuasive enough? Is there anything they want to add or take away? Help each group by asking them to do a bit of their presentation in front of you. Offer any tips you think will help each group improve its presentation.

7 Encourage students to be honest in their feedback. If they think that something didn't work in the other group's storyboard presentation, they should say so, explaining their view and suggesting a way to improve the presentation.

OWN IT!

B

D

PLAN

5 **Work in groups. Choose a product from the box or your own idea.**

sunglasses with headphones
personalised trainers
a new flavour of soft drink
a new perfume

Make a list of its features and the good things about its design. Then create an advert storyboard to advertise the product. Complete the steps below.

- Copy the table in Exercise 3 and complete it with information about your product.
- Write a dialogue and narrator's voiceover.
- Decide how to present the storyboard (act it out, video, poster, slide presentation).
- Work together to prepare your storyboard.
- Practise your presentation.

PRESENT

6 **Present your storyboard to your classmates. Remember to use information in Exercises 3 and 5.**

CHECK

7 **Look at your classmates' storyboard presentations. Give them motivating feedback with the phrases in the *How to* give feedback section. Which advert is your favourite?**

UNIT 8 | ADVERTISING 103

Students can collaborate digitally online and offline in the collaboration space, where teachers can set, track and assess students' work. Students can also share and showcase their work as well as comment on each other's projects.

For more work on Art and Design, students can turn to SB p140. See p156 for teaching notes.

Flipped class

Prepare for the **Review** lesson (p104). Students revise the grammar and vocabulary from Unit 8.

Lesson aim: I can review what I have learnt and reflect on my progress.

The aim of this review page is for students to revise the grammar and vocabulary from the unit. You can either do it in class, as a timed progress test or set it for homework.

Vocabulary

1 Put students into pairs. Challenge the pairs to be the first to complete the advertising facts correctly.

2 Do this task with the class as a whole. Ask students to explain their choice of word in each case. Elicit example sentences with the words not circled. Write these sentences on the board.

Language in action

3 Before students do this task, elicit the difference between defining and non-defining relative clauses. Students can look back at p97 to remind themselves.

4 Students can compare answers in pairs, and discuss any differences before checking answers as a class.

Unit quiz review

Self-assessment

After completing the checklist, encourage students to select their own homework from the Workbook, based on the areas they think they need to improve on.

Homework

Workbook pp70–71

8 REVIEW

VOCABULARY

1 Complete the advertising facts with the words in the box.

ad blocker advert advertise brand buyer influence logo marketing company product review seller slogan

Advertising facts

An [1] advert or ad is a short film, song or picture that tries to make you buy a [2] product.

When you [3] advertise something you tell people about it to try to sell it.

A [4] brand is the name you call a product. It is often represented by a symbol or [5] logo.

A [6] buyer buys something from a [7] seller. They sometimes give their opinions about the product in a [8] review.

When you [9] influence someone, you change how they think about something.

An [10] ad blocker is a computer programme that stops adverts appearing on screen.

A [11] marketing company is a business that encourages people to buy things.

A [12] slogan is a short phrase used in an advert that is easy to remember.

2 Circle the correct words.

1 Are you going to *post* / *vlog* those photos online? (post)
2 If you don't like comments, you can *subscribe to* / *delete* them. (delete)
3 How many people do you *build up* / *follow* online? (follow)
4 We have to *switch off* / *shut down* our phones at school. (switch off)

LANGUAGE IN ACTION

3 Join the sentences to make one sentence with a defining or non-defining relative clause.

1 Pablo is Eva's cousin. Pablo does voiceovers.
Pablo, who is Eva's cousin, does voiceovers.
2 She lent me a book. It didn't have the last page.
The book which she lent me didn't have the last pag
3 The film was about Corfu. We went to Corfu on holiday.
The film was about Corfu, where we went on holiday last year.
4 Ali is a friend. His wife is an influencer.
Ali is a friend whose wife is an influencer.

4 Complete the comments with the words in the box.

each other everyone everything myself ourselves themselves

1 Sometimes images in ads make me feel bad about myself.
2 When we see an ad, we should tell ourselves that it's not the real world.
3 Everyone sees adverts, but that doesn't mean they believe everything they see.
4 Many ads show people enjoying themselves.
5 Some online ads encourage users to tell each other about new products.

Self-assessment

I can use words to talk about advertising.	☹	😐	☺
I can use verbs to talk about the Internet.	☹	😐	☺
I can use defining and non-defining relative clauses.	☹	😐	☺
I can use indefinite, reflexive and reciprocal pronouns.	☹	😐	☺

104 ADVERTISING | UNIT 8

Lesson aim: I can learn to work out the meaning of new words.

As students' understanding of English develops, they should make use of what they already know to help them with words they don't understand. Point out that they don't need to have every word they come across as part of their active vocabulary, but they do need to develop strategies for dealing with words they don't understand.

Warmer

Ask: *What do you do when you read an English word that you don't understand?* Elicit students' ideas and write them on the board.

1 Give students time to read the text. Then discuss the question with the class as a whole. Encourage students to give reasons for their opinions.

2 Students work alone to match the definitions with the words in bold in the text. They can then work in pairs to compare. Students should not use dictionaries until Exercise 5.

3 In groups, students decide whether they agree with the definitions in Exercise 2 or whether they want to change or add to them. Elicit students' ideas and then agree definitions with the class as a whole.

OWN IT!

4 ★ Read out the four questions. To give students a model to follow, choose one of the other words in bold in the text and elicit answers from the class.

LEARN TO LEARN

LEARN TO … WORK OUT THE MEANING OF NEW WORDS

You can work out the meaning of new words and phrases by using clues from the rest of the text.

1 Read the text quickly, ignoring the words in bold if you don't understand them. Do you think space advertising is a good idea?

Space advertising

Imagine this. It's 2030 and you're **gazing** up at the night sky. The stars are **twinkling** and the moon is bright, but these days they're **no longer** alone. They've been joined by lots of huge signs in the **darkness**, like the **billboards** you see at the sides of a road, advertising everything from soft drinks to holidays. This might sound like science fiction, but space adverts will be with us **sooner or later**. In fact, a Russian company is already developing the technology to make it possible, and wants to send up its first ads in the next few years.

They will be created by special **satellites**, like the ones that send and receive TV and internet signals, only smaller. These satellites, **arranged** in groups to make the shapes of words or logos, will **reflect** light from the sun and will be **visible** at night from anywhere on Earth. For companies eager to advertise their products to buyers **around the globe**, this might seem like a dream come true. But ask yourself this: shouldn't we keep somewhere free from advertising? After all, ad blockers won't work in space.

2 Three students are working out the meaning of the words in bold. Which ones are they talking about?

1 *OK, it's a noun. They must be a kind of advertising sign, because it says you see them at the sides of a road. What else? Well, I know 'board' from 'whiteboard'…*

billboard ______

2 *I think this phrase must be about when the ads will be sent up. I know 'soon' and 'late'. They're both about time and they're opposites …*

sooner or later ______

3 *It's a verb, something that stars do. I think it's connected to their light, because the sentence also says 'and the moon is bright'.*

twinkling ______

3 What do you think the words mean?

1 ______
2 ______
3 ______

OWN IT!

4 Choose five of the other words or phrases in bold. Answer the questions to try to work out their meaning.

1 What is it? A verb, a noun, an adjective or a phrase?
2 What does the rest of the sentence tell you about it?
3 Do you understand part(s) of the word or phrase?
4 What do you think it means?

5 Check the meanings in a dictionary or with your teacher. Were you correct? Did the questions in Exercise 4 help you?

UNIT 8 | ADVERTISING 105

5 As well as checking answers, discuss with the class whether they found the questions in Exercise 4 useful.

Flipped class

Prepare for **Unit 9**. Students think about why we like stories and what impact Hollywood films have had on storytelling.

▶ Start it!

Unit quiz

1 Elicit the type of story that the girl on the right might be telling the girl on the left. You would expect students to say that the story being told is funny because the girl on the left is smiling.

2 & 3 ▶ Students share the ideas they were asked to think of for homework. Then play **Video 7.1** for students to check their answers. Students can also complete the Start it! **Video worksheet** in the *Teacher's Resource Bank*.

4 Elicit that a *moral* is a message that you take away from a story, e.g. be kind to others. Students can discuss this question with a partner.

Video comprehension questions

Flipped class

Prepare for **Explore it!** (p107). Students find out a fact about something famous or valuable.

9

HAVE YOU HEARD THE NEWS?

LEARNING OUTCOMES

I can ...

- understand a newspaper story and a news report
- tell an anecdote
- write a news story
- understand how to use reported statements, commands and questions
- use reporting verbs and adverbs of time and manner
- tell stories to remember new verbs, compare notes to improve listening, learn irregular adjective and noun pairs, and practise summarising.

Start it!

1 Look at the photo. What do you think the children are telling each other?
2 Before you watch, why do people like stories?
3 How have Hollywood films and the Internet changed storytelling? Watch and check.
4 Do you like stories with a moral? Why / Why not?

We expect stories to be more fast-moving, more exciting and with an obvious hero, and the internet allows us to share stories around the world.

Watch video 9.1 | Language in action 9.2 p109 | Language in action 9.3 p111 | Everyday English 9.4 p112 | Globetrotters 9.5 p114

106 HAVE YOU HEARD THE NEWS? | UNIT 9

Unit aims

Skills

I can ...

- understand a newspaper story p108
- tell an anecdote p112
- write a news story p113
- understand a story pp114–115

Language

I can ...

- use reporting verbs p107
- understand how to report statements and commands p109
- use adverbs of time and manner p110
- use reported questions p111

Learn to Learn

I can ...

- tell stories to remember new words p107
- compare notes to improve listening p110
- learn irregular adjectives and noun pairs p115
- ask for help when I don't understand p117

Extra Resources

- *Finished?* – Student's Book p126
- *Vocabulary Bank* – Student's Book p136
- Pronunciation – Student's Book p142
- Workbook p72
- *Teacher's Resource Bank* on *Cambridge One* for tests package, Cambridge Exam practice, wordlists, differentiated worksheets and many other extra resources.
- *Practice Extra* and *Digital collaboration space*

Lesson aim: I can use reporting verbs.

Warmer
Put students into pairs to discuss these questions: *Do you pay attention to the news? Where do you get your news? What type of news stories interest you most?*

1 Either elicit answers to this question from the class as a whole, or ask students to discuss it with a partner.

2 9.01 ★★★ After you have checked answers, challenge students to write four sentences using the new verbs.

Audioscript p174

Target vocabulary
admit /əd'mɪt/
announce /ə'naʊns/
apologise /ə'pɒlədʒaɪz/
claim /kleɪm/
complain /kəm'pleɪn/
confirm /kən'fɜːm/
deny /dɪ'naɪ/
discover /dɪ'skʌvə/
insist /ɪn'sɪst/
promise /'prɒmɪs/
refuse /rɪ'fjuːz/
suggest /sə'dʒest/

Extra vocabulary practice

Learn to learn
Using new words, by either saying or hearing them, will help students remember vocabulary. The more they use or experience the word, the more memorable it becomes.

3 Before students do this activity, tell them to read through the stories in Exercise 1 again so that they can remind themselves of what they are about.

VOCABULARY
Reporting verbs

1 Read news stories A–D. Which one is most interesting? Why?

9.01 **2** Match the words in **bold** in the news stories with definitions (a–l). Listen, check and repeat.

A A woman in Georgia, USA [1]**claimed** that she had thrown away jewellery worth $100,000 into the rubbish. The rubbish collection company agreed to look through nearly ten tonnes of rubbish to try and find a black bag with the jewellery. After three hours, they [2]**announced** that they had found it.

a told people officially 2
b said something was true even if it might not be 1

B A curator at a university in Australia who [3]**insisted** that he should open an old box in a store room [4]**discovered** that it contained an Egyptian mummy that he believes is 2,500 years old. Experts [5]**have confirmed** that the body is an adult and [6]**suggest** that it might be an important woman from ancient Egyptian society.

c have shown that something is true 5
d found something, especially for the first time 4
e said something firmly 3
f mention an idea for others to consider 6

C A family [7]**have complained** that their neighbours have stolen their cat. However, the neighbours [8]**deny** that they stole the cat and say that it was homeless and hungry, so they gave it food and a home. The neighbours say that the family [9]**refuses** to believe that the cat prefers to live with them!

g say something is not true 8
h say you will not do something 9
i have told someone that something is wrong 7

D A school in the north of England [10]**has apologised** for leaving a teenage student in London after a school trip to the capital city. The school [11]**admitted** that they made a mistake and [12]**promised** that it will never happen again.

j agreed that something was true 11
k has said sorry for something someone has done 10
l told someone you will certainly do something 12

LEARN TO LEARN
Telling stories to remember new words
Use reporting verbs in stories to remember what they mean.

3 Work in pairs.
Student A: Tell your partner one of the stories in Exercise 1. Use reporting verbs, but change one fact.
Student B: Listen to your partner tell the story. What did they change?

Use it!

4 Read the options. Make notes on your answers.
Think of a time when you … something.
1 admitted to ______
2 denied ______
3 promised to do ______
4 apologised for ______
5 refused to do ______

5 Compare your answers. Which situations were the most difficult? Which were the easiest?

Explore it!
Guess the correct answer.
In 2014 a French family found a Caravaggio painting in their house. Experts suggested it could be worth … million.
a €20 b €80 (c) €120
Find an interesting fact about something famous or valuable. Write a question for your partner to answer.

Pronunciation p142

4 Monitor while students make notes, helping as necessary.

5 Give students a few minutes to discuss their answers. Encourage students to ask follow-up questions to develop their conversations.

Tell stories using the prompts

Vocabulary Bank SB p136

Pronunciation
Students do the activities on p142 to practise pronouncing the letters *cia*.

Explore it!
Students share the facts that they researched for homework.

Class challenge
Someone who presents the news on TV is called a news teller / **newsreader** / news director.

Homework
Workbook p72

Lesson aim: I can understand a newspaper story.

Warmer

Write *twins* on the board and elicit the meaning. Ask: *Would like to have a twin?* If any students do have a twin brother or sister, ask them to explain what it's like.

1 9.04 Read out the three titles. Elicit the sort of report you would expect to read under each title. Students can then read the report quickly and choose the best title.

2 Tell students to read the options carefully before they do the task. They should highlight the part of the text that gives them their answers, then compare their answers in pairs before you check with the class.

Reading comprehension questions

3 Refer students back to what they learned about working out the meaning of new words in the *Learn to learn* on p105.

4 Read out the four questions. Give students time to think about their answers, and make notes, before they discuss the questions in pairs.

Extend it!

Write *nature* and *nurture* on the board. Elicit that your 'nature' is determined by your DNA, while 'nurture' refers to your background, environment and upbringing. In small groups, students discuss the question of which is the most important in forming our identities.

READING

A newspaper story

1 9.04 **Read the newspaper story. Circle the best title.**

a The twins who have never met.
b The twins who have never spent a day apart.
(c) International twins!

2 Read the newspaper story again and circle the correct answers.

1 Jonas and Santiago have …
 a nothing in common.
 b the same adoptive parents.
 (c) lots in common.
 d the same school friends.
2 The orphanage … the boys …
 (a) said … weren't twins.
 b took … to Spain.
 c gave … a blue sweatshirt.
 d suggested … were twins.
3 The twins see each other …
 a every day.
 (b) as often as possible.
 c only in the USA.
 d only on social media.
4 The boys were filmed …
 a only in Spain.
 b only in the USA.
 (c) in Spain and the USA.
 d separately.

3 Find words in the story that mean:

1 exactly the same (paragraph 1) **identical**
2 a home for children whose parents cannot care for them (paragraph 2) **orphanage**
3 taken into a different family and looked after (paragraph 2) **adopted**
4 from the same family (paragraph 3) **related**

1 **Identical twins Jonas and Santiago look similar, sound similar and even love the same things. But they live separate lives in different parts of the world and very nearly didn't discover that each other existed.**

2 In 2004, Jonas and Santiago were left at an orphanage in Ghana, Africa when they were babies. A few months later both boys were adopted but by different families; Jonas by a couple from New York and Santiago by a Spanish family. Fortunately, both families went to collect their baby son at the adoption agency in Ghana on the same day and both had bought a new blue sweatshirt for him to wear. A woman at the adoption agency suggested that the babies looked extremely similar and when the parents saw the two baby boys together in their blue sweatshirts they agreed that they were exactly the same. The parents then discovered that the boys shared the same birthday, but the orphanage denied that they were twins.

3 The four adoptive parents couldn't believe that the boys weren't related and insisted that they were going to do a DNA test, which confirmed that the boys were in fact identical twins. The parents promised to keep in touch and said that they would meet as soon as they could, which wasn't easy because Santiago lived in a small village in northern Spain and Jonas on the other side of the world in New York.

4 However, in 2010 they finally met and although they couldn't speak the same language, there was a deep connection between the brothers.

A twin 'can understand you when most people don't,' Jonas said. 'Like in weird situations when you feel a certain way, most people are like, 'What?' But your twin is like, 'Oh, yeah. Yeah, I get that.' I am like, 'Thank you, someone finally gets me.'

5 Since then, they have seen each other several times and speak online regularly. In an interview, Jonas explained that he had learned some Spanish phrases, such as how to ask for directions, and that Santiago's English had improved dramatically. In 2012 a Spanish film director offered to make a film to tell the boys' story. He suggested filming the boys together in both Spain and the USA. He told the boys to act naturally while he filmed them, so we get to see the boys playing football in the Spanish countryside and going skateboarding and to the cinema in the USA. Jonas admitted that being in a film was 'a bit strange' but 'really fun', especially with his twin brother by his side.

Voice it!

4 Discuss the questions.

1 What is the most amazing thing about their story?
2 What would be difficult about living in a different country to your twin?
3 What would you ask Jonas or Santiago if you met them?
4 Would you like to be a twin? Why / Why not? (If you are a twin, what do / don't you like about it?)

Finished? p126 Ex 1

108 HAVE YOU HEARD THE NEWS? | UNIT 9

Finished?

Students turn to SB p126 and do Exercise 1.

Flipped class

▶ Ask students to watch **Video 9.2** and do the **Video worksheet** in the *Teacher's Resource Bank*.

Homework

Workbook p73

Warmer

▶ Play **Video 9.2** if it was not set for homework. Elicit that they complained because there was a dog in the lion's cage. The zoo claimed it was a zoo employee's dog they had put in the cage while the lion was out.

1 Elicit what students know about the difference between reported speech and direct speech (e.g. tense changes, pronoun changes).

Get it right!

Test students' understanding of this by giving them a direct sentence to report, e.g. Mark (to me): *Go to the pool. Mark told me to go to the pool.*

2 Ask students to compare answers in pairs before checking answers with the class.

3 ★ Read out the example, eliciting the changes that have been made to the reported sentence, e.g. *will* ⟶ *would*, *my* ⟶ *his*.

4 ★ Elicit the difference between an offer (something someone says they can do for you) and a suggestion (an idea for something to do).

Extra grammar practice

5 & 6 Elicit which sentences are offers or suggestions. Elicit that we use the infinitive with *to* after *offer*, and the *-ing* form of the verb after *suggest*.

LANGUAGE IN ACTION
Reported statements and commands

Watch video 9.2 Why did the visitors to the zoo complain? What did the zoo claim?

Statements
The orphanage **denied** (that) they **were** twins.
The parents **insisted** (that) they [1] were **going to do** a DNA test.
The parents **said** (that) they [2] would **meet**.
The parents **promised to keep** in touch.
Jonas **explained** (that) Santiago's English [3] had **improved** dramatically.
Orders / Commands
He [4] told the boys **to act** naturally.
He **told** me **not to worry**.

1 Complete the examples in the table above. Use the story on page 108 to help you.

Get it right!
After ***tell***, we use words like *the boys*, *me*, etc. and the *to* infinitive.
*She **told him (not) to go.***

2 Circle the correct words.

The director has agreed [1] *that he makes* / *to make* another film about twins Jonas and Santiago. He explained that the new film [2] *had been* / *would be* about their lives as teenagers and he told us that the boys [3] *were* / *had been* more independent now and that they [4] *were starting* / *to start* to travel between the USA and Spain without their parents. He said that Jonas [5] *lived* / *had been living* with Santiago in Spain and [6] *to go* / *had been* to school with his brother.

3 Complete the reported statements and commands.

1 'I'll do my homework when the film has finished.'
He explained that he …
would do his homework when the film had finished.

2 'I'm going to play your song.'
He promised me that he was going to play my song.

3 'I didn't take my dad's tablet!'
She denied that she had taken her dad's tablet.

4 'Don't watch this video!'
He told me not to watch that video.

5 'We will come and meet you at the park.'
They said that they would come and meet me/us at the park.

Reported offers and suggestions
A Spanish film director **offered** [1] to make (make) a film to tell the boys' story.
He **suggested** [2] filming (film) the boys together in both Spain and the USA.

4 Complete the examples in the table above with the correct form of the verbs in brackets. Use the story on page 108 to help you.

Use it!

5 Read the dialogue. Write offers and suggestions in reported speech.

SOFIA Shall we go to the cinema?
PAULA OK. Let me see what's on.
SOFIA What about *Horror Fair*?
PAULA Sounds good.
SOFIA Shall we go at six o'clock?
PAULA Sure. I can buy the tickets online.

Sofia suggested going to the cinema later.
Paula offered to see what was on.
Sofia suggested watching Horror Fair.
Sofia suggested going at six o'clock.
Paula offered to buy the tickets online.

6 Tell each other the offers and suggestions that Sofia and Paula made.

Finished? p126 Ex 2

Grammar game

Put students in groups of three. Student A says something to Student B, which Student B then reports to Student C. Students continue like this until each student has had the chance to report a few sentences.

Finished?

Fast finishers can turn to SB p126 and do Exercise 2.

Homework

Workbook p74

Lesson aim: I can use adverbs of time and manner.

1 Elicit the meaning of *headline* (the title of a news story). Elicit ideas for what the three stories could be about.

2 9.05 ★ Before students listen, elicit vocabulary you would expect to feature in each story.

Audioscript p175

Learn to learn

Point out that collaborating is part of the learning process. Encourage students to work together and share ideas wherever possible.

3 Find out what students found difficult about the listening in Exercise 2. Was it the pronunciation, the intonation, the speed at which the two people spoke?

4 9.05 ★★★ Challenge students to answer as many of the questions as they can before they listen again.

5 Students can discuss the question with a partner.

Target vocabulary

after a while /ˈɑːftə ə waɪl/
eventually /ɪˈventʃuəli/
fluently /ˈfluːəntli/
gradually /ˈɡrædʒuəli/
nowadays /ˈnaʊədeɪz/
occasionally /əˈkeɪʒənəli/
patiently /ˈpeɪʃəntli/
regularly /ˈreɡjələli/
secretly /ˈsiːkrətli/
surprisingly /səˈpraɪzɪŋli/

6 9.06 When playing the recording, pause after each word or phrase to drill the pronunciation.

Audioscript p176

LISTENING AND VOCABULARY

A news report

1 Look at headlines a–c. What do you think the stories are about?

a Sock horror in girl's bedroom
b **The bird that came back speaking another language**
c Emergency in the kitchen!

2 9.05 Listen and put the stories in Exercise 1 in the order you hear them.

1 b 2 c 3 a

LEARN TO LEARN

Collaborative listening

Talking about what you understood with a partner before listening a second time can help you find out what you missed.

3 Tell your partner what you remember about each story. Do you remember the same information?

4 9.05 Listen again and answer the questions. Did talking to your partner in Exercise 3 help you?

1 Where had the parrot been?
With a Guatemalan family (also in California).
2 Why did Darren decide not to keep the parrot after he was found?
Because the Guatemalan grandfather was missing it.
3 What mistake did the girls make?
They didn't put any water in the pot to cook the pasta.
4 What was the emergency?
It started a fire.
5 Why did the English family make a phone call?
They thought there was a (terrifying) lizard under the girl's bed.
6 Why didn't the specialist touch the 'lizard' immediately?
Because they/everybody thought it might be dangerous.

Adverbs of time and manner

5 Read the blog. Which of the two news stories in the blog do you think was invented? the story about the robot

If you read my blog **regularly**, you'll know I **occasionally** write about 'unbelievable' news stories, like the one about the parrot that spoke Spanish **fluently**. **Nowadays**, there's so much information on the Internet that it's difficult to know if something is true or not. The other day, I was reading a story about a boy who had invented a robot to do his homework. It said he'd been **secretly** developing the technology in his bedroom, **patiently** trying out different designs. Cool idea, right? But the story got **gradually** more ridiculous. It said that one day the robot had offered to go to school, telling the boy he could stay in bed. **After a while**, I began to think, 'This can't be true.' **Eventually**, I realised it was a joke. It's **surprisingly** easy to believe 'fake news'!

6 9.06 Match the adverbs in **bold** in the blog with their definitions. Listen, check and repeat.

1 little by little *gradually* M
2 these days nowadays T
3 sometimes but not often occasionally T
4 in the end eventually T
5 in an unexpected way surprisingly M
6 without telling anyone secretly M
7 often regularly T
8 in a patient way patiently M
9 easily and well fluently M
10 after some time after a while T

7 Are the adverbs in Exercise 6 adverbs of time (*T*) or manner (*M*)?

Use it!

8 Think of situations when people do things in these ways. Can your partner guess the verb and adverb?

gradually: get better, move
regularly: go to bed late, not eat, practise
patiently: listen, sit, wait
secretly: gesture, speak, write

This happens before you play an important football match.
You practise regularly?
Yes!

110 HAVE YOU HEARD THE NEWS? | UNIT 9

7 Elicit answers from the class. Put the adverbs on the board in two lists, one headed *Adverbs of Manner*, the other *Adverbs of Time*.

Extra vocabulary practice

8 Before students do this task, give them time to think of situations.

Vocabulary Bank SB p136

Extend it!

On the board, write *How can we believe what we read online?* In pairs, students discuss the question.

Flipped class

▶ Ask students to watch **Video 9.3** and do the **Video worksheet** in the *Teacher's Resource Bank*.

Homework

Workbook p75

Lesson aim: I can use reported questions.

Warmer

▶ Play **Video 9.3** if it was not set for homework. Elicit that the two friends wanted to see their favourite band who were being interviewed on a radio show. They showed the guard the webpage that they had created.

1 Elicit the words needed to complete the table, then focus on the changes to the sentence in the reported question.

2 9.07 Students can compare answers in pairs before you check with the class.

Audioscript p176

3 9.08 ★ Read out the example. Elicit the changes that have been made to the reported question. Then ask students to work in pairs to complete the task.

Audioscript p176

Extra grammar practice

4 Give students time to think of their questions. Ask some students to report one of their partner's questions to the class and find out if any students were asked the same question.

LANGUAGE IN ACTION

Reported questions

Watch video 9.3
What did the two friends want to see? How did they get into the radio studio?

Direct questions	Reported questions
***Wh-* questions**	
'What **are** your favourite stories?'	Last week, one of our listeners asked us [1] what our favourite stories **were**.
'Where **did** you **leave** the other sock?'	Everybody asked her [2] where she**'d left** the other sock.
***Yes/No* questions**	
'**Can** we have the parrot back?'	The Guatemalan family asked Darren if they **could** have the parrot back.
'**Have** you ever **cooked** anything before?'	Their Italian friends asked them [3] if they**'d** ever **cooked** anything before.

1 Complete the examples in the table above.

2 9.07 **Put the words in the correct order to make sentences. Listen and check.**

1. the boy / had / his homework / done / the teacher / if / asked / he
The teacher asked the boy if he had done his homework.
2. doing / Laura / what / she / Jack / later / asked / was
Jack asked Laura what she was doing later.
3. me / ended / asked / my sister / how / the story / had
My sister asked me how the story had ended.
4. left / the assistant / any tickets / were / I / there / asked / if /
I asked the assistant if there were any tickets left.
5. we / where / the station / an old man / was / asked
We asked an old man where the station was.
6. arrive / Tom / me / would / I / asked / what time
Tom asked me what time I would arrive.

3 9.08 **Rewrite the sentences as reported questions. Listen and check.**

1. 'Who's the hero of the story?' Mikhail asked his sister.
Mikhail asked his sister who the hero of the story was.
2. 'Do you prefer comedy or drama?' Elena asked me.
Elena asked me if I preferred comedy or drama.
3. Ruben asked his friend, 'Where did you hear that?'
Ruben asked his friend where they had heard that.
4. 'Will it rain later?' she asked.
She asked if it would rain later.
5. 'Can we still get tickets?' I asked the receptionist.
I asked the receptionist if we could still get tickets.
6. 'What are you reading?' Sally asked me.
Sally asked me what I was reading.

Use it!

4 Think of five questions someone asked you last week. Write the names and tell your partner the questions. Can they guess who asked what?

my maths teacher, my dad, my best friend Rachel, my sister, my cousin

This person asked me if I had cleaned my room.

Your dad asked you if you had cleaned your room.

No, try again!

Finished? p126 Ex 3

Extend it!

Draw three columns on the board, headed *say*, *tell* and *ask*. Say the following words for students to decide which verb they go with: *hello, good morning, sorry* (say); *a joke, a lie, a story* (tell); *a question, a favour, for information* (ask).

Grammar game

Put students in groups of three. Student A asks Student B a question about school, hobbies, holidays, friends. Student B reports it and C checks B reported it correctly. Students then swap roles.

Finished?

Fast finishers can turn to SB p126 and do Exercise 3.

Homework

Workbook p76

1 9.09 Ask students if they have ever been bowling and what they thought of it. Then elicit ideas about what happened to the boy in the photo and play the recording for students to check.

Audioscript p176

2 9.09 Ask students to read along with the conversation as they complete it with the phrases. With a partner, students can then act out the conversation.

Useful language practice

▶ Play **Video 9.4**. Encourage students to copy the intonation used by the presenter.

3 Students can complete the task in pairs, and then think of situations in which they could use phrases from the *Everyday English* box. For example, *A: You don't believe what happened to me at the park? B: Let me guess.*

4 Point out that an anecdote is a short (often amusing) story about a real incident. Give students time to make notes. Students can invent stories if they wish.

5 Give students five minutes to plan their anecdotes. If appropriate, they can use their smartphones to record themselves telling their anecdotes, listening back to check they're using the language from the unit.

6 Encourage each pair to give each other feedback. In what ways could they be improved?

SPEAKING

Telling an anecdote

1 9.09 Look at the photo. What happened at the bowling alley? Listen to the conversation and check.

Jamie fell over while he was bowling.

2 9.09 Complete the conversation with the phrases from the *Useful language* box. Listen and check.

JAMIE [1] You'll never guess what happened to me last night.
ESMA No, what? Tell me.
JAMIE [2] It was so embarrassing!
[3] Basically, what happened was, my new classmates asked me if I wanted to go bowling with them. I said yes and when we got there, they asked me how well I could bowl.
ESMA You didn't say you were any good, did you?
JAMIE Well, you know I'm a show-off! So I said, 'Just watch me!'
ESMA But you're terrible at bowling! I've seen you.
JAMIE Hey! I'm not that bad! So [4] anyway, I picked up the ball, put my fingers in the holes, went to bowl …
ESMA Let me guess. Your fingers got stuck.
JAMIE Completely! I swung the ball back carefully and then swung it forward and just sort of went flying with it. The next [5] thing I knew, I was flat on my back!
ESMA What a fantastic first impression!
JAMIE And to make matters worse, I couldn't get my fingers out.
ESMA Oh, Jamie!

Useful language

Basically, what happened was …
It was so (+ *adjective*)
So anyway, …
The next thing I knew …
You'll never guess what happened …

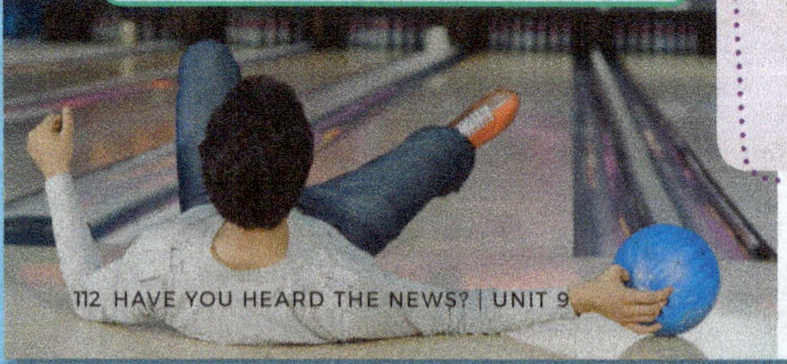

Watch video 9.4
Everyday English

Hey! Let me guess.
show-off sort of to make matters worse

3 Match the words in the *Everyday English* box with the words and phrases 1–5.

1 I disagree! Hey!
2 to make the situation even more unpleasant to make matters worse
3 someone who tries to make other people look at them show-off
4 in a way sort of
5 I think I know what you're going to say. Let me guess.

PLAN

4 Make notes on something embarrassing, funny, etc. that has happened to you.

Introduce the anecdote
Decide which details are the most important
End the anecdote

SPEAK

5 Practise telling the anecdote to your partner. Remember to use reported statements, commands and questions, vocabulary from this unit and phrases from the *Useful language* and *Everyday English* boxes.

CHECK

6 Work with another pair. Listen to their conversation and complete the notes.

What kind of anecdote was it? ______
What were the important details? ______
How did the anecdote end? ______

Extend it!

On the board, write *What's the best way to tell a story?* In small groups, students discuss the question, thinking of how to start, how much information to include and how to keep listeners interested.

Warmer

Elicit popular flavours of ice cream. Students can then say whether they like ice cream, which flavours they tend to eat, and when they tend to eat it.

1 After students have checked with the story, ask them to give their opinion of it.

2 Students can discuss the questions in pairs.

3 Read out the questions. Give students time to think of their answers before discussing ideas with a partner.

Choose the function of the sentences

4 Point out that a range of reporting verbs can be used in stories (not just news stories) rather than always using formulations such as 'he said' or 'they told'.

5 Point out that the news story should answer the questions *What happened?*, *Who did it happen to?*, *Where did it happen?* and *When did it happen?*. If students can't go online, they can work in groups to discuss the topic of birthday celebrations and generate ideas. Alternatively, students can invent their own news story.

6 Give students up to 15 minutes to write their news story. Monitor and help as necessary.

7 Ask students to read and offer feedback on each other's work.

Free ice cream, anyone?

Most of us expect to receive presents on our birthday. However, Jimmy Teng or 'Uncle Jimmy' is different. The ice cream man from Singapore regularly gives away free ice cream on his birthday. He started the tradition on his 70th birthday when he offered to give away 700 free ice creams.

This year Uncle Jimmy announced that he was going to give away 1,000 free ice creams. Surprisingly, some customers insisted that they would pay for the ice cream. When asked why he did it, Mr Teng explained that nowadays everyone in Singapore was stressed and he wanted to make them feel happy. He also admitted that sharing ice cream made him feel good too. 'I'm so happy,' he said. 'I wouldn't be this happy if I won the lottery!'

Uncle Jimmy, who has been an ice cream man for over 15 years, has lots of customers. When asked what his favourite flavour was, he answered 'Sweetcorn' and he explained that ice cream in Singapore was sometimes served with bread rather than a cone.

WRITING
A news story

1 Why would someone give away free ice cream? Read the news story and check. to make people happy

2 Read the news story again and answer the questions.

1 Who is the story about? Jimmy Teng, an ice cream man.
2 What happens? He regularly gives away free ice cream.
3 When does it happen? Every year on his birthday.

3 Discuss the questions about the structure of the story.

1 What does the headline tell us about the story? What doesn't it tell us? *It tells us about free ice cream but doesn't give any more information.*
2 What is the aim of the first sentence? *To get the reader interested in the story and want to read more.*
3 What do we learn in the first paragraph of the story? *Who the story is about, what happens, when and where it happens and when it started.*
4 When do we learn why the story happened? *In the second paragraph.*
5 Is the information in the third paragraph necessary or extra? *He's been an ice cream man for over 15 years, his favourite flavour is sweetcorn and ice cream in Singapore is sometimes served with bread. These facts are extra information.*
6 What effect does the direct speech have in the story? *It brings us closer to the man in the story.*

4 Complete the phrases in the *Useful language* box with details from the news story.

Useful language

A man from [1] Singapore regularly gives away free ice cream ...
He announced/explained/admitted that [2] he was going to give away 1,000 free ice creams.
[3] 'I'm so happy ,' he said.
Surprisingly/Nowadays etc., [4] everyone in Singapore was stressed and he wanted to make them happy.
When asked ... he answered/explained/said [5] sweetcorn' and he explained that ice cream in Singapore was sometimes served with bread rather than a cone.

Write your own news story.

PLAN

5 Make notes on something special that someone has done to celebrate their birthday or find an interesting news story online.

WRITE

6 Write a news story about your idea in Exercise 5. Remember to include three paragraphs, language from this unit and phrases from the *Useful language* box.

CHECK

7 Do you ...

- include an interesting headline?
- include some extra details in the third paragraph?
- include some direct speech?

Finished? p126 Ex 4

Extend it!

Ask students to close their books and, in pairs, to take turns telling the news story in Exercise 1. They count how many different reporting verbs their partner uses.

Finished?

Fast finishers can turn to SB p126 and do Exercise 4.

Flipped class

Prepare for **Around the World** (pp114–115). Students research traditional stories from their country.

Homework

Workbook p77

Lesson aim: I can understand a Maori story.

Warmer

Elicit traditional stories from the students' country. Ask: *Why are some stories passed down from one generation to the next?* Elicit that such stories can be used to teach important lessons and to link the past with the present.

▶ The video develops the theme of traditional stories. Read through the questions with students and ask them to predict answers before playing **Video 9.5** for students to check their answers.

Video comprehension questions

AROUND THE WORLD

READING
A story

1 Look at pictures A–D. What is happening in each one? Put them in order to make a story.

2 9.10 Were your ideas correct? Read the introduction about Maori storytelling and the story 'How Maui slowed the Sun'.

3 Read the introduction and the story again. Write *T* (true) or *F* (false).

1 The Maori have always written down their stories. F
2 It was impossible for the villagers to finish their work each day. T
3 Maui had never done anything impressive before. F
4 Only Maui's brothers helped to make the ropes. F
5 The Sun saw Maui and his brothers coming closer. F
6 Maui hit the Sun more than once with the bone. T
7 The Sun stopped moving completely. F

Globetrotters
Watch video 9.5
Stories on stage

- Where do you think opera comes from? Where is it popular? Italy. It is now popular throughout Europe.
- What is *jingju* and what does it involve? It is Beijing opera and it combines music, dance and acrobatics.
- What different skills do *jingju* performers need to have? song, speech, dance-acting, acrobatics, play-fighting with swords

A 2

B 1

MAORI STORYTELLING

Storytelling is an essential part of the culture of the Maori people, the first inhabitants of Aotearoa (New Zealand). They didn't use to have a written language, so they learned stories by heart to remember their history. The Maori people still tell their stories, often in a traditional meeting place called a* marae*. The stories are accompanied by dance, songs and chants. Here is one for you to enjoy.

How Maui slowed the Sun

Long ago, the Sun used to move so quickly across the sky that the days were too short for people in the village to do all their work. The villager Maui, however, had a plan. He gathered his four brothers and said, 'Why should the Sun control us? Let's catch him and make him go more slowly.'

The brothers were worried. They asked Maui if it was really possible to get safely near the Sun. 'The heat and flames will burn us!' they said. 'We might die!' Maui held his grandfather's bone high, and said, 'I have achieved many things which you thought were impossible. I have brought fire to the people, I have caught the greatest fish in the world. With this bone, and with your help, I will catch the Sun.'

Everyone agreed to help him. Over the next five days they made strong ropes to catch the Sun. When they were ready, the brothers set off to the east, where the Sun rises. They travelled during the night so that the Sun wouldn't see them approaching. Eventually, they arrived at an enormous deep hole in the ground. This was where the Sun slept.

While the Sun was still asleep, the brothers built a wall around the hole and hid behind it, waiting patiently. Maui told his brothers not to throw the ropes until he said so. After a while, the ground began to shake. The Sun was waking up! First came his burning hair, then his fiery eyes and his white-hot teeth.

114 HAVE YOU HEARD THE NEWS? | UNIT 9

1 Elicit students' ideas about what they think is happening in each picture and then ask students to work in pairs to order the pictures. Answers: Picture A shows a line of men walking with a long rope on their shoulders. Picture B shows a group of villagers watching the sun go down behind a hill. Picture C shows the same villagers and the sun now high in the sky and being held by ropes. Picture D shows the men throwing ropes over the sun.

2 9.10 Set students a three-minute time limit to skim read the story. Tell them not to worry about unknown vocabulary at this point. In pairs, ask students to try to summarise the story.

3 Ask students to underline key words in the questions to help them find the relevant information in the text. Students can work individually before comparing in pairs. Ask students to explain why sentences are false.

Match the words to the meanings

Lesson aim: I can understand a Maori story.

Students will be aware that many adjective and noun pairs follow regular forms, for example, *health, healthy; colour, colourful; belief, believable*. However, there are irregular forms, and these should be recorded together to help students remember the form and meaning.

4 Encourage students to try to complete the table with the correct adjectives and nouns before they check with the text. When students have completed the table, drill the pronunciation of the words, focusing on the nouns in particular.

5 ★ Elicit that the way to summarise is to focus on the important parts of a story, namely, what happens, and miss out the supporting detail. Tell students to look back at the text to help them complete this ordering task.

6 Give students time to think of their answers to the questions before they discuss them with a partner. After students have finished their discussion, say: the story is about working together. Ask: *Why is cooperation and teamwork important?* Discuss this question with the class.

Students can collaborate digitally online and offline in the collaboration space, where teachers can set, track and assess students' work. Students can also share and showcase their work as well as comment on each other's projects.

C 4

D 3

'Now!' cried Maui. The brothers threw the ropes over the Sun. They tangled in his hair and trapped his huge, hot body. The men pulled on the ropes as strongly as they could.

'What are you doing?' the Sun cried angrily.

Maui jumped on the wall and lifted up his grandfather's bone. He smashed it with all his strength down on the head of the Sun, who screamed in pain.

'Are you trying to kill me?'

'No, but you must go more slowly,' said Maui.

The Sun tried hard to escape, but again and again Maui hit him with the bone. The Sun gradually grew weaker, until at last he could only move slowly across the sky.

And that is why the days are now long enough for all our work, and why sometimes, if you look carefully, you can still see the ropes that connect the Sun to the Earth – shining through the clouds.

LEARN TO LEARN

Irregular adjective and noun pairs

Learn adjectives and their related nouns to increase your vocabulary.

4 Complete the table with words from the story.

Adjective	Noun
wide	width
1 high	height
hot	2 heat
3 long	length
strong	4 strength
5 deep	depth

Summarising

Sometimes we need to tell a shorter version of a longer story. Summarising can help us to do this.

5 Put the sentences in order to make a summary of the story.

a The brothers travelled by night to where the Sun slept. 4
b You can still see the ropes that hold the Sun to the Earth. 8
c Maui hit the Sun with the bone. 6
d Maui, his brothers, and the villagers made strong ropes. 3
e People didn't use to have enough time to do everything because the Sun moved too quickly across the sky. 1
f The Sun eventually started to move more slowly. 7
g When the Sun woke up, the brothers trapped him. 5
h Maui had a plan to control the Sun. 2

Voice it!

6 Discuss the questions.

1 Without Maui, could the brothers have trapped the Sun?
2 Talk about a story from your culture. What does it mean?

Explore it!

Guess the correct answer.

Aotearoa, the Maori name for New Zealand, means land of …

a the perfect sky.
b the long white cloud.
c the towering mountains.

PUSH IT! The Culture Project Teacher's Resource Bank

Explore it!

Elicit the answer, then ask students if they know of nicknames for other countries or cities, e.g. Japan is known as 'The Land of the Rising Sun', New York is called 'The Big Apple'.

Class challenge

Traditional stories are often called **folk tales** / people tales /person tales.

Culture project

See Project Book p54 for further information and activities.

Flipped class

Prepare for the **Review** lesson (p116). Students revise the grammar and vocabulary from Unit 9.

Lesson aim: I can review what I have learnt and reflect on my progress.

The aim of this review page is for students to revise the grammar and vocabulary from the unit. You can either do it in class, as a timed progress test or set it for homework.

Vocabulary

1 ★★★ Extend the challenge by asking students to test each other on their understanding of the verbs in the box. For example, Student A says, 'OK, it's true, I ate your chocolate bar.' Student B says, 'You admitted that you ate my chocolate bar'.

2 Put students into small groups and turn this task into a class competition. The first group to complete the sentences correctly wins.

Language in action

3 Ask students to work alone to complete the sentences. Then they can compare answers in pairs.

4 Students can work in pairs to write the direct questions. They can then discuss the first two questions.

Unit quiz review

Self-assessment

Ask students to reflect on how well they can do the things in the self-assessment box. Encourage them to ask you for extra homework on the language they had the most problems with.

9 REVIEW

VOCABULARY

1 Match the reporting verbs in the box with the definitions.

admit apologise complain deny discover promise

Which reporting verb do we use to …

1 say that something is not true? deny
2 tell someone you're sorry? apologise
3 find out information for the first time? discover
4 agree that something is true? admit
5 tell someone formally something is wrong? complain
6 tell someone you will certainly do something? promise

2 Complete the sentences with the adverbs in the box.

eventually fluently gradually nowadays regularly secretly surprisingly

1 I eventually finished reading the book you recommended but it took me ages.
2 I speak French regularly, mostly with my Canadian cousin – once a week.
3 Mike's family planned his birthday party secretly. He was very surprised!
4 The exam was surprisingly easy. I finished it really quickly.
5 My best friend speaks English fluently.
6 Nowadays I get on with my brother, but we didn't use to.
7 My English is improving gradually but I need to learn more vocabulary.

LANGUAGE IN ACTION

3 Complete the second sentences.

1 'I'll help you with your homework.' Ayaz offered to help me with my homework.
2 'Send me a message when you get there.' Shaun told me to send him a message when I got there.
3 'Why don't we meet at the new café?' Ada suggested meeting at the new café.
4 'I promise I'll give you a lift.' She promised to give me a lift.

4 Rewrite the direct questions as reported questions.

1 'Do you often read the news online?' my sister asked me.
My sister asked me if I often read the news online.
2 'How can I improve my English?' Zehra asked her teacher.
Zehra asked her teacher how she could improve her English.
3 'Have you seen what's happened in London?' Ian asked Jake.
Ian asked Jake if he had seen what had happened in London.
4 'Will the museum be open tomorrow?' the tourist asked.
The tourist asked if the museum would be open tomorrow / the next day.

Self-assessment

I can use reporting verbs.
I can use adverbs of time and manner.
I can use reported statements and commands.
I can use reported questions.

116 HAVE YOU HEARD THE NEWS? | UNIT 9

Homework

Workbook pp78–79

Lesson aim: I can learn to ask for help when I don't understand.

Tell students that there is nothing wrong with admitting that they don't know something. Explain that nobody knows everything and that learning a language is a continuous process.

Warmer

Ask: *What do you do if you don't understand what an English speaker has said to you?* In pairs, students discuss the question.

1 Read out the introduction, then give students time to read and discuss the problems. Encourage students to think of any other problems they have had with understanding people speaking English.

2 After students complete the matching task, they can practise reading the conversations in pairs.

OWN IT!

3 Read out the topics, then give students time to plan the explanation of their chosen topic. Encourage students to not explain their topic clearly or to speak too quickly when explaining it. This will allow their partner to make use of the phrases in bold in Exercise 2.

LEARN TO LEARN

LEARN TO … ASK FOR HELP WHEN YOU DON'T UNDERSTAND

There are different ways to ask English speakers for help and check you understand what they've said.

1 Read the problems people have understanding someone in English. Then discuss the questions.

We asked six language learners what problems they'd had understanding people in English. This is what they told us.

1. For me, it's usually that the other person speaks too fast.
2. The worst thing is when people use lots of difficult words I don't know
3. I usually understand more or less, but I don't understand all of the details.
4. Sometimes I think I've understood someone, but then I realise I haven't at all!
5. My problem is that when I don't understand I'm too shy to say. I just say 'yes' a lot!

Have you had any of these problems? How did you solve them?

2 Read the conversations. Match phrases 1–5 with phrases with similar meanings a–e.

a Could you repeat from the beginning? 4
b I want to make sure I've understood correctly. 5
c What's the meaning of that word? 2
d I didn't hear the last thing you said. 3
e What were your instructions? 1

1

BEN Sorry, Miss. I didn't understand. [1]**What did you say I had to do?**
TEACHER I told you to compare the two pictures and discuss how similar they are.
BEN [2]**What does 'similar' mean?**

2

ALISON Excuse me, can you tell me how to get to the post office, please?
MAN IN Sure. Go straight until you see a big building. It's opposite that …
ALISON [3]**I didn't catch that.** The big what?
MAN IN Building.

3

GISELLE Bea thought Juan had promised he would bring the food, but he hadn't! After a while, someone said-
JO Wait, wait, wait! [4]**Can you start again, please?** I'm lost!
GISELLE Sorry, sorry. What happened was that …

4

VLAD Which bus do I need for Oxford Park?
WOMAN You need two, actually. Take the 147 fromhere to Austen Square, cross the road and then take the 29 from in front of the bank.
VLAD OK, [5]**let me check I've got this right.** First, I take 147 to Austen Square?
WOMAN That's right.

OWN IT!

**3 Student A: choose one of the topics in the box and explain it to Student B.
Student B: use the phrases from the conversations in Exercise 2 to help you understand. Then swap roles.**

how to get from your school to your house
the story of how Maui slowed the Sun
the rules of a sport

FINISHED? ANSWER KEY

The aim of these pages is to allow students who have already finished the lesson to practise the target language for the corresponding Student's Book page in a game-like way.

Unit 1 SB p118

1 2 spotted 3 striped 4 tight 5 checked
6 flat 7 high-heeled 8 long-sleeved

2 1 c 2 d 3 a 4 b

3 2 extremely 3 really 4 totally 5 fairly
6 pretty 7 quite 8 rather 9 a lot 10 a little
11 a bit
Students' own answers

4 2 match 3 fit 4 wear out 5 suit 6 hang up
7 fold 8 do up 9 undo
Mystery expression: go out of fashion

Unit 2 SB p119

1 Across: 3 without 5 back 6 end 7 signed
Down: 1 went 2 moved 4 turned

2 **Possible answers:**
… he used to … live in the city / have hair / be poor / play football (every day).
… he didn't use to … have much money / have a beard / wear glasses.
… he would play football every day.

3 Students' own answers

4 2 ~~sandal~~ handle 3 ~~hug~~ plug 4 ~~Swiss play~~ display 5 ~~pens~~ lens 6 ~~map~~ strap

Unit 3 SB p120

1 roast, chop, overcook, grill, season, peel, slice, fry, bake, spread, grate, heat

2 1 What are you doing this evening?
2 What are you going to do next summer?
3 How do you think people will travel in the future?
4 What's the weather going to be like tomorrow?

3 Students' own answers

4

H	A	N	D	F	U	L	T	G	F	D
V	Y	D	B	E	H	E	E	D	G	X
S	P	R	I	N	K	L	E	C	C	O
L	K	R	I	C	O	I	C	K	E	W
E	A	S	A	W	U	S	V	I	A	E
E	J	P	D	F	B	P	I	E	C	E
P	Q	O	F	V	S	L	L	C	H	J
O	I	O	V	C	K	A	W	E	U	K
P	J	N	E	D	A	S	I	O	N	R
C	H	F	C	W	Y	H	N	D	K	N
Q	R	U	J	H	Q	B	G	G	R	T
W	S	L	I	C	E	H	T	I	O	M

Unit 4 SB p121

1 1 clouds 2 a pear 3 (a) ringtone(s)

2 Students' own answers
It's a durian.

3 Students' own answers

4

R	U	Z	D	H	S	W	I	D	D	T	L
C	O	L	M	S	H	A	R	P	F	R	U
H	G	U	J	T	I	C	Y	L	S	A	F
N	T	X	G	H	N	A	B	U	M	V	R
S	V	O	D	H	Y	L	Q	S	E	U	U
M	K	L	O	D	E	F	E	B	L	H	O
O	I	P	R	M	K	M	U	Z	L	E	L
O	F	H	Z	G	S	P	I	C	Y	F	O
T	A	S	O	U	R	O	W	J	A	C	C
H	D	R	M	V	P	A	S	I	L	J	E
T	N	E	R	A	P	S	N	A	R	T	H
O	S	Q	U	G	A	T	V	Z	N	I	F

Unit 5 SB p122

1 2 collect, produce 3 deliver, measure
4 communicate, supply 5 create, solve
6 connect, attract

2 1 **c** At first, his heart rate will be measured by Nurse Evans.
2 **a** Next, the anaesthetic will be given by Dr Sanna.
3 **f** The first part of the operation will be done by Dr Lansbury.
4 **b** The second part of the operation will be done by Dr Rees.
5 **e** Until he is completely better, he will be visited in hospital by Dr Jones.
6 **d** Finally, he will be taken home by Nurse Simms.

3 Students' own answers

4

F	E	T	D	E	A	F	E	N	I	N	G
R	A	N	E	E	F	R	L	J	A	B	P
E	H	S	O	R	A	F	L	Q	M	O	U
E	D	S	C	R	R	U	I	J	Q	I	N
Z	R	W	T	I	M	I	A	U	J	L	D
I	E	J	J	U	N	O	F	F	I	I	Q
N	A	V	X	X	N	A	U	Y	R	N	B
G	D	V	F	Y	O	N	T	S	I	G	V
D	F	F	C	S	W	I	I	I	K	N	A
B	U	M	L	R	X	N	X	N	N	E	G
V	L	M	A	T	B	T	E	C	G	G	H
M	A	R	V	E	L	L	O	U	S	Z	D
A	B	L	Z	G	O	R	G	E	O	U	S

Unit 6 SB p123

1 Across 2 fun 5 out 7 bored 9 interest
11 lost 12 chance
Down 1 advantage 3 nerves 4 doubts
6 pleasure 8 risks 10 know

2 1 b 2 e 3 d 4 a 5 c

3 Students' own answers

4 2 bravery 3 determination 4 opportunity
5 obstacle 6 support 7 encourage
8 overcome 9 achieve 10 inspire

Unit 7 SB p124

1 3 e 4 a 5 l 6 t 7 h 8 y 9 m 10 i 11 n 12 d
a healthy mind is as important as a healthy body

2 Alex never stops talking in class. / Megan refuses to speak during most lessons.
Berat hopes to stay in the city forever. / Mira misses living in the countryside.
Charlie always forgets to put his notebook in his bag. / Sara always remembers to take all her books to class.
Jacob doesn't mind getting up early. / Olivia would love to get up late every day if she could.

3 Possible answers:
Who built the Pyramids? The Ancient Egyptians.
What did the Ancient Egyptians build? The Pyramids.
Who wrote the Harry Potter stories? J.K. Rowling.
What did J.K. Rowling write? The Harry Potter stories.
Who invented the iPhone and the iPod? Steve Jobs.
What did Steve Jobs invent? The iPhone and the iPod.
Who discovered gravity? Isaac Newton.
What did Isaac Newton discover? Gravity.
Who invented pizza? The Italians.
What did the Italians invent? Pizza.

4 blue: something crossed my (mind), red: close to my (heart), brown: change my (mind), pink: learn by (heart), orange: break somebody's (heart), purple: bear in (mind), green: in two (minds).
There are four *heart* expressions and four *mind* expressions.

Unit 8 SB p125

1 2 Which logos do you know?
3 Do you ever write reviews?
4 Do you use ad blockers?
5 What influences you to buy a product?
6 Which slogans can you remember?

2 1 when, grateful
2 which/that, fun
3 where, peaceful
4 which/that, fascinating
5 who, annoyed
6 whose, seller

3 1 myself
2 anyone
3 someone
4 something
5 nothing
Students' own answers

4

K	W	G	B	I	C	B	K	A	A	N	N	P
S	H	U	T	D	O	W	N	Y	V	K	O	I
O	T	E	B	I	R	C	S	B	U	S	T	W
G	Y	F	S	B	D	R	M	U	N	F	N	O
G	O	N	F	E	U	T	S	O	P	O	E	Q
J	Z	L	L	O	A	I	H	Y	D	L	M	Y
W	S	E	V	E	H	C	L	E	M	L	M	E
Y	T	H	X	X	T	C	H	D	Y	O	O	Y
E	U	S	R	I	X	Q	T	C	U	W	C	Y
E	X	N	W	N	H	L	M	I	Z	P	E	A
E	S	S	T	N	I	R	P	R	W	X	D	B
D	H	X	K	Q	S	H	K	H	X	S	G	C
P	Y	P	W	C	K	R	O	S	U	B	C	F

Unit 9 SB p126

1 deny, apologise, announce, confirm, complain, admit, insist, suggest, refuse, promise

2 Students' own answers

3 Students' own answers

4 2 secretly 3 after a while 4 surprisingly
5 patiently 6 eventually 7 fluently
8 gradually 9 regularly
Adverb in the boxed letters: occasionally

VOCABULARY BANK ANSWER KEY

The aim of the Vocabulary Bank pages is to offer students more practice of the unit vocabulary, and can be set as homework, as a class test, or as further tasks for fast finishers.

Starter Unit SB p127

1 1 False 2 False 3 True 4 False 5 True

2 1 greeted 2 smiling 3 describe 4 shouts 5 shake hands

3 Students' own answers

Unit 1 SB p128

1 2 Incorrect 3 Correct 4 Incorrect 5 Correct

2 1 go with 2 fit 3 wear out 4 Hang it up 5 suits you

3 Putting clothes away: hang up, fold
Ways of saying that clothes look good: go with, match, suit me
Reasons not to wear clothes: fit, wear out, goes out of fashion
Putting on and taking off clothes: undo, do up

Unit 2 SB p129

1 1 move to 2 turn down 3 look forward to 4 try out 5 settle down

2 1 lens 2 button 3 cover 4 cable 5 display
Mystery word: strap

3 1 key: keyboard, laptop
2 handle: vacuum cleaner, saucepan, door
3 lid: jam jar, laptop, saucepan, shoe box
4 plug: laptop, vacuum cleaner

Unit 3 SB p130

1 1 heat 2 Peel 3 chop 4 season 5 Roast 6 overcook

2 1 a 2 d 3 e 4 b 5 c

3 Students' own answers

Unit 4 SB p131

1 1 fresh bread 2 stone 3 delicious 4 a train 5 icy

2 1 c 2 d 3 b 4 e 5 a

3 Students' own answers

Unit 5 SB p132

1 1 b 2 e 3 a 4 d 5 c

2 1 freezing 2 deafening 3 enormous 4 dreadful 5 fascinating

3 Students' own answers

Unit 6 SB p133

1 1 I'd like to get to know her better.
2 Simon got a lot out of the course.
3 Did you have fun at the picnic?
4 Some of my classmates get on my nerves.

2 2 happiness 3 salary 4 disappointment

3 2 oOo 3 ooOoo

Unit 7 SB p134

1 1 grateful 2 insecure 3 ridiculous 4 eager 5 peaceful

2 1 broke my heart 2 make your mind up 3 put his heart into it 4 in two minds

3 Students' own answers

Unit 8 SB p135

1 1 buyer 2 reviews 3 adverts 4 product 5 influence

2 1 follow 2 subscribe 3 vlog 4 post 5 comment on

3 1 e 2 d 3 a 4 c 5 b

Unit 9 SB p136

1 **1** admitted **2** complained **3** promised **4** refused **5** apologised

2 **1** patiently **2** eventually **3** surprisingly **4** after a while **5** gradually

3 Students' own answers

Lesson aim: I can understand a text about history.

Background information

Many citizens of the USA can trace their family history back to a European country such as Ireland or Italy. Such Americans often describe themselves as being Irish American or Italian American.

Warmer

Write *migration* on the board. Elicit the meaning (the movement of people to a new city, town or country in search of work and a better life).

1 Read out the two questions. After students have discussed the questions, compare ideas with the class as a whole.

2 ★★★ Encourage students to respond more fully to the text by asking: *What problems can immigrants have in the country they move to? How can immigrants improve life in the countries they move to?*

3 Ask students to do the exercise in pairs. Encourage them to highlight the part of the text which gives them the answer to the rest of the items in the exercise.

4 ★ You want to do this with the class as a whole, guiding students to such ideas as getting a better job, escaping war or poverty, finding freedom, marrying someone from another country.

5 If students don't know the words in bold, encourage them to guess their meaning from the context.

2 HISTORY

1 Look at the title and picture and discuss the questions.

1 When do you think this picture was taken?

2 Where are the people and what are they doing?

2 Read the text. Check your answer to question 2 in Exercise 1. 2.14 The people are migrating to the United States.

STARTING AGAIN

Between 1880 and 1910, 17 million Europeans made the decision to move to the United States and start a new life. Many of them never went back to their country of birth. This was part of what is known as the Great Atlantic **Migration**. It started in the 1840s and it is the largest migration in history.

For many people, it was the first time they had ever left their hometown. The two-week journey was very unpleasant, and on larger ships up to 2,000 people were **crammed** into the lower **decks**. It was dark, there was little fresh water, and the air was **rancid**. So why choose to go through such a difficult experience?

One major reason was hunger. For example, in Ireland in the 1840s, people used to depend on potatoes for food. When the potato crop failed for three years in a row, there was not enough to eat and around one million people died. After this, half of the Irish population decided to move to the United States. They were nervous about the journey, but they looked forward to a better life.

> I am exceedingly well pleased at coming to this land of plenty.
>
> *Letter from an Irish immigrant to* The Times, *London, 1850*

Immigrants from all over Europe had their own story to tell. Although they had never experienced life in the United States before, they arrived ready to **settle** in a new culture. Immigrants helped build the United States into the country it is today. Like all migrations, the Great Atlantic Migration is the story of people making difficult decisions for the chance to start again.

3 Read the text again. Write *T* (true), *F* (false) or *DS* (doesn't say).

1 Most immigrants to the United States eventually returned to their country of birth. F

2 There wasn't much room on board the ships. T

3 Poverty was a major reason for migration. DS

4 Irish immigrants felt hopeful about their future. T

5 Immigrants from all over Europe moved for the same reasons as the Irish. DS

6 They made a positive contribution to American society. T

4 Discuss other possible causes of migration throughout history and up to the present day.

5 Complete the definitions with the words in bold in the text.

1 migration (n) the act of moving from one place to another

2 decks (n) the floors of a ship

3 settle (v) to make a home

4 crammed (v) to be filled with something so there is no more room

5 rancid (adj) having a very bad smell (or taste)

Explore it!

Guess the correct answer.

How many people live in a country different to the one they were born in?

a over 50 million

b over 150 million

c over 250 million

Find another interesting fact about migration. Write a question for your partner to answer.

UNIT 2 | CLIL 137

Explore it!

Elicit the answer to the question from the class as a whole. If appropriate, students can then go online to research a question about migration for their partner. Or students can come up with a question in groups.

Extend it!

Have a class discussion about the history of migration to the students' country.

Lesson aim: I can understand a text about science.

Warmer

On the board, write *bats* and *dolphins*. What do students know about these animals? Elicit students' ideas.

1 ★★★ Read out the questions. Challenge students to answer them before they look at the text. Do not confirm students' answers at this point.

2 🎧 4.10 After students have read the article, elicit the answers to the two questions in Exercise 1, asking students to refer to the specific parts of the text which gave them their answers. You can then drill the pronunciation of the word *echolocation* /ˈɛkə(ʊ)lə(ʊ)ˌkeɪʃ(ə)n/.

3 Students can work in pairs to complete the table.

4 Give students a minute to look at the words in bold in context in the article. Then read out the gapped text, asking students to complete each gap as you come to it. You could then turn this into a class competition by putting students into groups and giving a point to the first group to complete the gap correctly.

Explore it!

Elicit the answer to the question from the class as a whole. If appropriate, students can then go online to research a question about bats, whales or echolocation for their partner to answer. Or students can come up with a question in groups.

Extend it!

Ask students if they know anything about how other animals (e.g. cats, horses) communicate with each other or with humans.

4 SCIENCE

Echolocation

Imagine you are walking with a torch through a forest at night. Suddenly, the light goes out and you cannot see a thing. You feel a branch brush your face and smell the leaves on the trees. You need to go home, but how can you find your way?

If you were a bat, you would use echolocation. Echolocation is a technique used by some animals to move around in the dark. It helps them identify friends and enemies and 'see' where they are going. Here are two examples of how animals use it.

Dolphins

To identify objects in deep, dark waters, dolphins produce high-frequency **clicks**. These create sound waves that **bounce back** as echoes. This information helps dolphins work out the distance, direction of travel, speed and size of things.

Bats

To hunt for insects in the dark, bats make a **high-pitched** call as they fly, then listen for the returning **echo**. They calculate how far away something is by how long it takes the echo to return. A bat can **detect** an insect in the dark from a distance of five metres!

But you don't have to be a bat or a dolphin to echolocate. You might be surprised to learn that some humans can echolocate too. One such person is Daniel Kish. Daniel is completely blind, so he gets information about what is around him by clicking his tongue and listening to the echo. This technique allows him to safely ride a bike or go hiking in the wild. He also trains other blind people to echolocate. Amazing, isn't it?

1 Discuss the questions.

1 What special skills do the animals in the pictures have? They both use echolocation.

2 What do they use these skills for? Moving around in the dark.

2 🎧 4.10 **Read the article. Check your answers to Exercise 1.**

3 Complete the table with information from the article.

	Sound	How it helps
Bat	1 high-pitched call	4 They can calculate how far something is by how long the echo takes to return.
Dolphin	2 high-frequency clicks	5 They create sound waves. The echoes help them work out distances, direction of travel, speed and size.
Daniel Kish	3 clicking his tongue	6 He gets information about what is around him and can ride a bike and go hiking.

4 Complete the text with the words in bold in the article.

Whales, like dolphins, produce [1] clicks to work out an object's distance, direction, speed and size. These sounds can be low- or [2] high-pitched. The sounds hit an object and [3] bounce back to the whale's throat. The time it takes the [4] echo of these sounds to return to the whale helps the animal to [5] detect, or sense, what is around it.

Explore it!

Guess the correct answer.

Some bats have a scream as loud as a …

a jet engine 30 metres away.
b very loud opera singer.
c machine that breaks rocks.

Find another interesting fact about bats, whales or echolocation. Write a question for your partner to answer.

138 CLIL | UNIT 4

Lesson aim: I can understand a text about citizenship.

Warmer

Remind students of what citizenship (being a citizen of a particular country) means. Ask: *What rights and responsibilities should people have as citizens of a country?*

1 Read out the questions. You can then elicit answers to the questions or ask students to discuss them in pairs.

2 6.12 After students have read the article, elicit the answers to the two questions in Exercise 1, asking students to refer to the specific parts of the text which gave them their answers.

3 Check students' understanding of the nine themes in the box before you put students in pairs to complete the table.

4 Give students a few minutes to read the article again and to consider their answers. They can then discuss in groups.

5 ★★★ Challenge students to define the words in bold in the text by looking at the context in which those words are used. They can then use the words to complete the sentences.

6 CITIZENSHIP

1 Discuss the questions.

1. What is digital citizenship?
2. How can the way we use technology affect our relationships with people?

2 6.12 **Read the article. Check your answers to Exercise 1.**

3 Read the nine themes of digital citizenship and mark (✓) the ones that apply to each case study. Some apply to both and some to neither.

Nine Themes of Digital Citizenship	CS1	CS2
1 Have equal access to technology.	✗	✗
2 Buy and sell safely online.	✗	✗
3 Share information safely.	✓	✗
4 Learn how to use technology appropriately.	✓	✓
5 Follow an ethical code of conduct.	✓	✓
6 Use technology lawfully.	✗	✗
7 Act responsibly.	✓	✓
8 Promote physical and psychological well-being.	✓	✗
9 Protect online safety.	✓	✗

4 Discuss the questions in the case studies in the article.

5 Complete the sentences with the words in bold in the article.

1. That is a very flattering photo. You look great!
2. You cannot trust some websites to be safe. You should check your online privacy.
3. Please don't ignore me. Turn off your phone and listen to what I am saying.
4. I am going to monitor how often I use social media. I want to use it less.
5. He is always very polite and respectful when he sends messages.

Digital citizenship: case studies

Today's citizens can make the most of living, learning, and working in a digital world. However, this brings responsibilities as well as opportunities, as these digital citizens need to act in a safe, legal, and ethical way. Digital citizenship is similar to traditional citizenship in that it means being kind, **respectful** and ready to take part in activities that make the world a better place.

If teens take risks with the way they use digital devices, it could lead to problems. These case studies illustrate some common situations.

Case study 1

Some friends are having fun at the beach. Later, one of them posts photos of the others online. She does not ask permission and some of the pictures are not very **flattering**. If you had been in possession of these pictures, what would you have done?

Case study 2

A group of friends are sitting in a café. One of them gets a call on his phone. He answers the call, **ignores** his friends, and has a loud, personal conversation in front of them. How would you feel if you were in the group?

The way these people use technology raises serious questions about **trust**, friendship and social relationships.

Digital citizenship involves many things, from sharing information safely to acting responsibly online. If we want to get the best out of a fast-changing world, we should **monitor** our digital habits. In this way we can meet the challenge of becoming good digital citizens.

Explore it!

Guess the correct answer.

In an average lifetime, people will spend … on social media.

a one year and two months
b three years and five months
c five years and four months

Find another interesting fact about the digital world. Write a question for your partner to answer.

UNIT 6 | CLIL 139

Explore it!

Elicit the answer to the question from the class as a whole. If appropriate, students can then go online to research a fact about the digital world. Or students can come up with a question in groups.

Extend it!

Discuss with the class the question of bad online behaviour, e.g. people posting unkind messages or posting photos of other people without getting their permission. Ask: *How can we encourage people to be good digital citizens?*

Lesson aim: I can talk about art and design.

Warmer

Ask students to brainstorm things that make an attractive, interesting advert (e.g. slogans, logos, colours, etc.) Write students' ideas on the board.

1 Read out the questions and check understanding of *elements* (parts of something). Students can discuss them in pairs.

2 8.11 After students have checked their answers, find out if they were surprised by anything they learnt.

3 Read out the four incomplete sentences. Check students' understanding of *marketing companies* and *brand's image*. Give students time to think about the sentences and how they might complete them. Monitor and help as necessary. Students can then work in pairs to share their ideas.

4 Before students do this task, ask: *What makes a good headline for an advert?* Elicit students' ideas. Put students into groups to come up with their headlines for one of the two products. Groups can then present their ideas to the class, which can vote on the best headline.

5 Encourage students to use the context around each word in bold to help them complete the task.

8 ART AND DESIGN

1 Discuss the questions.

1 Where do you see print adverts? everywhere
2 How do print adverts communicate their messages? with an attention grabbing headline, subhead, image and an effective layout
3 What are the main elements of a print advert?

2 8.11 Read the article. Check your answers to Exercise 1.

How to design an effective print advert

We are surrounded by print adverts. When we walk down the street, there are slogans, logos and images everywhere. Think about how many adverts you have seen today. How many of them can you actually remember?

Marketing companies, which are responsible for advertising campaigns, charge a lot of money for their services. Therefore, a printed message needs to effectively communicate a brand's image. In fact, the person who creates an advert is a communicator more than a designer. So how is an **effective** print advert designed?

The **headline** is the most important element. An advert has approximately two seconds to catch the reader's eye, so the headline needs to be clear and focus on one idea. A **subhead**, which still needs to be brief, can then give more information.

Next is the image. Sometimes an image can become the centre of attention and distract from the message of a print advert. The headline and image need to work well together and it is essential that the image is relevant to the product. Also, advertising research shows men and women respond to images differently. Many advertisers use brighter colours in adverts for women and darker shapes in adverts for men.

Once an advert has these features, it is time to decide on a final **layout**. The top-to-bottom layout in the picture, which is widely used, is very effective. Most adverts influence potential buyers with the most important information at the top.

A good advert tells us we need things that previously we didn't even know existed. Next time you walk down a street full of print adverts, think about how effective they are.

3 Complete the sentences with your own ideas.

1 Marketing companies need to effectively communicate a brand's image because … they charge a lot of money for their services.
2 A headline is the most important element of a print advert because … it has to catch the reader's e
3 An image should not be the main focus of a print advert because … it can distract fr the message.
4 Different images are used for men and women in print adverts because … they respond to images differently.

4 Choose an idea and turn it into a headline of three or four words for an advert.

1 This toothpaste will leave your mouth fresh and clean and your teeth white.
2 You must buy these jeans because they are more comfortable and cheaper than others.

5 Complete the definitions with the words in bold in the article.

1 layout (n) the design of something
2 headline (n) the title written in big letters
3 subhead (n) heading that comes after the headline
4 effective (adj) successful

Explore it!

Guess the correct answer.

More than … a year is spent on advertising.

a $6 billion b $60 billion c $600 billion

Find another interesting fact about advertising. Write a question for your partner to answer.

140 CLIL | UNIT 8

Explore it!

Elicit the answer to the question from the class as a whole. If appropriate, students can then go online to research a fact about advertising. If students do not have access to the internet, set this task for homework.

Extend it!

Have a class discussion about adverts that are specially designed to attract children and teenagers. Ask: *Should such adverts be allowed? Why? Why not?*

PRONUNCIATION ANSWER KEY

Unit 1 SB p141

1 Students' own answers

2

/eə/	/e/	/iː/	/eɪ/
pear	head	clean	break
	heaven	peach	great
	weather	please	

3 Students' own answers

Unit 2 SB p141

1 Students' own answers

2 No, they aren't.

3 **1** He used to have a lot of free time.
2 They used to live in Italy.
3 I used to like horror films but I don't now.
4 Jack used to go ice-swimming.

4 & 5 Students' own answers

Unit 3 SB p141

1 Students' own answers

2

/ʃ/	/tʃ/	/k/
moustache	check	chemistry
parachute	reach	chorus
	search	headache
	touch	mechanic

3 Students' own answers

Unit 4 SB p141

1 Students' own answers

2 **2** We have to leave early tomorrow.
3 You ought to study more for your exams.
4 Do you need to make a phone call?

3 & 4 Students' own answers

Unit 5 SB p141

1 Students' own answers

2 **2** I haven't got any debts.
3 He hurt his thumb with a hammer.
4 I saw a sheep with two lambs.

3 Students' own answers

Unit 6 SB p142

1 Students' own answers

2 **2** Wednesday **3** business **4** category
5 chocolate **6** secondary **7** vegetable
8 memorable

3 **2** Wednesday **3** business **4** category
5 chocolate **6** secondary **7** vegetable
8 memorable

4 Students' own answers

Unit 7 SB p142

1–3 Students' own answers

Unit 8 SB p142

1 Students' own answers

2 **2** digestion 2 **3** contribution 1 **4** vacation 1
5 connection 1 **6** question 2 **7** indigestion 2

3 & 4 Students' own answers

Unit 9 SB p142

1–3 Students' own answers

4 **1** sociable
2 mathematician
3 beneficial
4 musician
5 artificial
6 magician

STUDENT'S BOOK AUDIOSCRIPTS

Starter Unit

S.01
1 sightseeing
2 trip
3 holiday resort
4 accommodation
5 tourist attractions
6 backpacking

S.02
A Where did you go on holiday this summer?
B London. It's a great city for sightseeing because there are so many tourist attractions. My favourite was Big Ben.
C To a holiday resort in Greece. The accommodation was amazing – a beautiful hotel right next to the beach.
D I went backpacking in Mexico this summer – just me, my bag, and a paper map. It was the best trip of my life.

S.03
1 rehearsal 3 lines 5 audience
2 show 4 part 6 scene

S.05
1 Mike goes sightseeing every year.
2 Amalia didn't learn her lines until the night before the first show.
3 A Where's Harry? B He's reading in his room.
4 You didn't like the play, did you, Emir? You were sleeping during it!
5 I'm so happy we weren't staying in that holiday resort last week when the terrible storm came.
6 Ana's not at the rehearsal because she's not feeling well right now.

S.06
1 shake hands 4 smile 7 greet
2 whisper 5 shout 8 post
3 wave 6 translate 9 describe

S.07
1 [The sound of two people whispering to each other.]
2 Look at the camera and show me those lovely teeth! Say cheese!
3 [A group of children shouting at each other.]
4 RITA Hi, Al! How are you?
AL Oh hello, Rita. I'm fine. How are you?
5 A So I'm looking for something, but I can't remember the word. It's for a pencil, you know when the pencil doesn't write and you turn it like this and then you can write with it …
B Ahh … you mean this … a pencil sharpener!
A Yes, that's it!

S.08
MATEO Hi, everyone. So, last year I did this tourism course and I've been at university now for three months studying translating. And before that, I was lucky enough to spend six months in London, but a lot of the things that helped me learn English you can use too.
ALICE Did you go to a language school in London?
MATEO No, I didn't, I stayed with a family with two children. Erm, they were really friendly, but difficult to understand at first because they spoke so fast and the kids shouted a lot … and at the same time! Also, I was really shy at first because I didn't want them to hear my bad English, so I just talked really quietly so that they couldn't hear my mistakes!! But the kids said to me, 'Why are you always whispering? We can't understand you!' and they were right and because they didn't care if I made a mistake, I just started talking … and talking … and talking … and I haven't stopped since I was there! You know, if I don't know a word, I just describe it with other words, or translate it and make an English word that's similar to the Spanish word and sometimes that works!
ALICE What was the most different thing about living in London?
MATEO Erm … probably the times people eat … and the food. They eat a lot of different food from different countries, which is great. And things like shaking hands when you meet new people! But it's important to learn the everyday things people do in other cultures, especially if you want to be a translator.
LIAM And the best thing?

MATEO Oh, definitely the people. I met so many interesting people and I've stayed in contact with lots of them … and I watched a lot of TV in English, I think I've watched every episode of *The Big Bang Theory*. That's another great way to learn!

5.09
A Have you ever been to a music festival?

B Yeah, I went to one this summer. It was great.

A Where was it?

B Near the town where we went on holiday. We've stayed in the town lots of times but this was our first time at the festival.

A What did you like best?

B The Night Owls had some amazing dancers and sounded incredible.

A I've never heard of them.

B Oh, they're great! I've liked them for ages.

Unit 1

1.01
1 tight jeans
2 plain cotton T-shirt
3 denim skirt
4 striped T-shirt
5 checked shirt
6 flowery dress
7 long-sleeved dress
8 high-heeled boots
9 baggy trousers
10 flat shoes
11 spotted shoes

1.02
ROSA So, come on, Juan, have you decided?

JUAN I don't know. I quite like this striped T-shirt, but they haven't got my size. But there's this checked shirt, which is also quite nice. What do you think?

ROSA Yeah, I like it. Are you getting some jeans too?

JUAN Mmm, there are these ones, but they're too tight. I don't like tight jeans.

ROSA Well, what about some trousers?

JUAN Yeah, maybe. Do you like these ones?

ROSA Yeah, they're really nice.

JUAN Not too baggy?

ROSA No, I like baggy trousers.

JUAN OK, that's me. Now what about you? Have you chosen something?

ROSA Nearly, I mean I like this denim skirt, but I really wanted to get a dress.

JUAN What about this one?

ROSA Mmm, no I don't think so, I don't like flowery clothes.

JUAN Or this one?

ROSA Yeah, but it's short-sleeved and I think I might get cold. Do you like this one? It's got long sleeves and it's my favourite colour!

JUAN Yeah, that's nice.

ROSA Cool. I'm going to get these flat shoes to go with it. What do you think?

JUAN Perfect. Let's go and pay.

1.04
Recently, I've been trying to learn how to knit. It's really difficult! I've been watching lots of videos online, but I haven't been practising very much. I've been making a scarf for a few days now, but it's full of holes and looks awful. My mum has been helping me too, but she's been working all week and hasn't really got much free time.

1.05
1 How long has he been designing clothes?
2 Have you ever learned to knit?
3 She has never worn high-heeled shoes.
4 I have been walking in these shoes all morning and my feet really hurt!

1.06
1 fit
2 go out of fashion
3 wear out
4 suit
5 go with
6 match
7 do up
8 undo
9 hang up
10 fold

1.07
INTERVIEWER So, Carla, how long have you been interested in fashion?

CARLA I've been totally obsessed with fashion since I was a child. Even when I was quite young, about 10 or 11, I loved trying on different outfits and deciding what went with what or what suited me.

INTERVIEWER A true follower of fashion! And when did you know you wanted to be a fashion designer?

CARLA Well, I've always been extremely interested in art and when I was about 12, I started reading fashion blogs and got lots of ideas for creating my own designs and upcycling.

INTERVIEWER I've heard of recycling, but not upcycling. What is it exactly?

CARLA It's when you create something new from something that already exists. So, I take clothes I don't wear any more, or second-hand clothes and change them into something totally different. I've changed leggings into tops or denim jeans into skirts. I've made bags out of denim jeans too.

INTERVIEWER That sounds fun!

CARLA It is, and recently I've been printing my own designs onto plain T-shirts and tops. They look pretty good.

INTERVIEWER You must be really creative. Tell me about your designs. What are they like?

CARLA Well, they're all individual. So, I talk to the person and find out what makes them feel good and try and match my design with their personality.

INTERVIEWER That's so cool. I like the idea of wearing something that no one else has. It's not like fast fashion, where people buy the same clothes from stores anywhere in the world!

CARLA Absolutely! I'm trying to avoid fast fashion as much as possible. I know the clothes are cheap, but I think we buy far more clothes than we need and then when they go out of fashion we just throw them away. It's really worrying how many clothes we throw away each year!

INTERVIEWER That's true. I've never really thought about that before. But not everyone can make their own clothes.

CARLA No, but we can buy fewer clothes and take the clothes we don't wear any more to second-hand shops. Some clothing companies are now thinking a lot more about the people who make the clothes and the materials they use, which is extremely important.

INTERVIEWER Do you mean ethical fashion?

CARLA Yeah, these clothes are a bit more expensive, but they last a lot longer.

INTERVIEWER I agree, I think all clothes stores should make ethical fashion. Can I look at some of your designs?

CARLA Absolutely!

1.10 Making materials like cotton or denim can be extremely damaging for the environment. That's why it's absolutely essential we create new materials from natural products that are a lot better for the planet. Some materials like bamboo have been fairly successful. Others are still being developed, like a material from the rice plant, which is quite similar to cotton, and one made from chicken feathers, which is pretty warm, like wool. Technology has also made it far easier to recycle materials like plastic bottles into clothes such as leggings and T-shirts, which is really good news for the environment!

1.11 **DIEGO** Hey, Dana. How's it going?

DANA Hi, Diego. I've been shopping all morning. I've bought some great stuff. Do you want to see?

DIEGO Yeah, sure.

DANA I got this striped jacket from Zaps, that new store they've just opened.

DIEGO Oh right. Wow! That's … err… different!

DANA I know! It's totally out there!

DIEGO Mmm, I'm not a huge fan of yellow and blue together, but the blue matches the colour of your eyes.

DANA Thanks! And check out these trousers.

DIEGO Flowery trousers! Wow! Very retro!

DANA I know! They fit really well. What do you think?

DIEGO Well, they're not exactly my style, but I can see why you like them.

DANA Do you think they suit me?

DIEGO Yes, I guess so.

DANA I think I might wear them to go out later, with the jacket.

DIEGO Mmm, I don't know if I'd wear them together. I think maybe the trousers would go better with a plain top.

DANA No, patterns are totally in this year.

DIEGO You're such a fashion victim, Dana!

Unit 2

2.01

1 look forward to	7 settle down
2 do without	8 go back
3 end up	9 sign up
4 go through	10 turn down
5 move out	11 turn out
6 try out	12 move to

2.02

1 WOMAN … or we have one for beginners on Mondays and Wednesdays …

MR SMITH Hmm … Well, I studied it a bit at school, and I've been to Paris a few times, so Beginners is probably too easy. What's the next level?

WOMAN Pre-intermediate. Students learn how to have simple conversations, talk about family, hobbies, that sort of thing.

MR SMITH Ooh, yes. I'd like to join that one, please.

WOMAN Very good, Mr Smith. So, please write down your name here.

2 MOLLY Hi, Ben, on Saturday my uncle's taking me to a baseball game. I'm really excited. Why don't you come with us?

BEN I'd love to, Molly – I haven't been to a game in ages, but I can't this weekend. It's my sister's 18th birthday party.

MOLLY Are you sure? Last chance!

BEN I'm sure, but thanks for asking me. You guys have fun!

MOLLY Thanks, I can't wait!

3 SHARON Are you OK, Tom? You look a bit sad.

TOM No, I'm just tired. My brother's in hospital at the moment. I'm visiting him every day. I've also been really stressed because I changed school last month.

SHARON Oh no! Is your brother going to be OK?

TOM Yeah, he had an accident on his bike but the doctors say he'll be fine. But the last few weeks haven't been easy at all. At least I'm happy now in my new school.

SHARON Oh, you poor thing!

4 ED It's really easy. First, click here. That takes you to the home page. Then, at the bottom it says, 'Find out more'. Click there and … Jo? Jo? Are you listening?

JO Sorry, Ed, I was checking my phone.

ED You haven't heard a word I said!

JO Sorry, can you start again?

ED OK … first, click here. That takes you to the home page. Then …

5 RACHEL … but we always have the same thing. Pasta, pizza, pasta, pizza …

MARTA OK, OK. Something different. What do you suggest?

RACHEL There's that Japanese place in the town centre. I've never been there but everybody says their sushi is delicious.

MARTA Oh, I've never had Japanese food before. Let's go there.

6 LEILA I was really nervous because I'd never had a party before.

ERIC You worry too much, Leila!

LEILA I kept thinking, 'What if nobody comes?' and 'What if nobody has a good time?'

ERIC I'm sure in the end it was fine, wasn't it?

LEILA Oh yes. Lots of people came. It was a brilliant evening.

2.08

1 lens	5 plug	9 lid
2 button	6 cable	10 handle
3 key	7 strap	
4 display	8 cover	

2.09 1 When you carry a backpack, do you use one strap or both? Why?

2 Do you always put the lid back on the toothpaste after using it?

3 How often do you clean the lens of the camera on your phone?

4 Without looking, can you remember what is on the cover of this book?

5 Can you name six objects that have an on/off button?

6 Do you take your phone charger cable with you when you go out?

2.10

QUIZ MASTER Welcome, everybody, to this week's Retro Mystery Object Quiz. Today we have Joey and Nicola in the studio. Joey, Nicola – are you ready to play?

JOEY Yep.

NICOLA Absolutely.

QUIZ MASTER OK, fingers on buzzers. Our first object has –

MAN 1 Wait, Joey, wait! I hadn't started yet.

JOEY Sorry, I'm just really excited!

QUIZ MASTER OK, OK. Let me go back. Our first object has a plastic strap.

NICOLA A watch!

QUIZ MASTER It is a watch, but it can do other things too. It has a display and some really small buttons.

JOEY I know this time! The thing that tells you how many steps you've walked and stuff like that. A – what's it called? – a sports watch?

QUIZ MASTER No, sorry, Joey, not a sports watch. We're talking about things that were popular long before anyone had seen a Fitbit! OK, a final clue. It has a calculator.

NICOLA It's a digital watch!

QUIZ MASTER Correct, Nicola! It is! That's ten points to you. Well done!

NICOLA It wasn't really a guess. I knew because my grandfather used to show me his watch all the time. He couldn't live without it!

QUIZ MASTER He sounds like a cool guy! OK, object number two. Now, this one is a kind of machine. You could send messages on it. There used to be one in almost every office.

NICOLA Like a phone?

QUIZ MASTER Not exactly. The machine had a phone, but people didn't use to use it for speaking. Another clue: the messages were printed out on paper.

JOEY Is it a printer?

MAN 1 Nope, this was before anyone had ever heard of printers. One more clue. These days, companies usually have a telephone number, a website and an email address. In the past, companies would have two numbers – a telephone number and a special number for this machine. Joey, Nicola – any idea what it might be? No? It's a fax machine. Here's a picture of one.

JOEY Oh, OK! I'd heard of fax machines before but I'd never seen one. I didn't know that's what they were. I thought it was like a USB stick!

QUIZ MASTER Nothing like a USB stick, sorry! OK, it's ten points to Nicola so far. Time for our final object. This one has a cable and a plug, and it's made of glass. There's colourful liquid inside and when you switch it on, the liquid changes shape.

JOEY Is it an … a … Oh, sorry, I thought I knew the answer.

QUIZ MASTER OK, they'd already gone out of fashion by the time you were born, but they were popular in the 90s and around the year 2000. People would use them as decorations in their bedrooms and living rooms.

NICOLA A lava light!

QUIZ MASTER It's actually called a lava lamp, but I'll give you that. That's another ten points to you, Nicola, making twenty in total. Joey, I'm afraid you have zero points today, I'm sorry.

JOEY Oh well, I guess I wasn't very good at this game in the end!

QUIZ MASTER … which means tonight's winner is Nicola! Well done, Nicola!

NICOLA Thanks!

2.11 Last year I went on an exchange to Moscow. I had never travelled alone before, so I felt nervous at first. Before I went, I had already learned to read the Russian alphabet, although I hadn't practised speaking Russian. By the time I left, I had improved a lot. Everybody in Moscow was really kind and friendly, but it wasn't easy to deal with the cold weather. I hadn't packed enough warm clothes, so I had to buy some after I arrived. Anyway, I can't wait to go back. I hadn't expected to enjoy it much before I actually got there, but in the end I really did!

2.12 **YUSUF** What's that? Is it some kind of computer?

MERI No, it's my granddad's old typewriter.

YUSUF Where's the display?

MERI There isn't one, and there's no plug or cable.

YUSUF That's so old-school! How did it work?

MERI The paper would move as you typed. What you do is, you press the keys hard, but not too fast or they get stuck. Try it out!

YUSUF Like this, you mean?

MERI That's it. Just imagine – people used to type books on these things!

YUSUF No way! I can't even find the letters I want.

MERI You need to sign up for typing classes! They're in the same place as an ordinary keyboard.

YUSUF Oh no! I've messed it up. How do I go back? There's no 'delete' key.

MERI You'll have to start all over again.

YUSUF No, thanks! Anyway, how come your granddad had this?

MERI He used to need it for work, but after a while he ended up buying a computer.

YUSUF I'm not surprised! I'm glad they'd invented computers by the time I started school! I'd hate to do my homework on this!

Unit 3

3.01

1 bake	**5** grill	**9** slice
2 chop	**6** overcook	**10** spread
3 fry	**7** roast	**11** peel
4 grate	**8** season	**12** heat

3.02 Peel the tomatoes and chop them. Then heat them in a pan and season with salt and pepper. Grill some bread. Then spread the tomatoes on the bread and grate some cheese on top. Bake in the oven, but only for a few minutes – you don't want to overcook it!

3.06 a cup of cereal

some pieces of strawberry

some slices of banana

some chunks of pineapple

a handful of blueberries

a packet of nuts

a pinch of cinnamon

a sprinkle of brown sugar

a spoonful of yoghurt

a splash of milk

3.07 **PRESENTER** Welcome to *Next Great Chef*. Today's theme is 'Something different' and our chefs will be cooking not one, but two dishes today using ingredients we are less familiar with. They only have 45 minutes to create their delicious dishes, so they're going to be busy. Our chefs today are Anton, Mei and Lara. Let's find out what they're going to cook. Hi, Anton. So, what will you be making today and why?

ANTON OK, I'll be making two dishes inspired by bugs. I really believe that we need to eat more insects, because by 2030 the world population will have grown to 8.5 billion people. There just won't be enough food for everyone, so we need to look for alternatives. Lots of cultures already eat bugs, but they're still quite unusual for us here in Europe, so we need to learn how to cook and eat them.

PRESENTER I see! Erm, can you tell us about your recipes?

ANTON Well, first I'll be making a pear smoothie, but instead of adding milk or yoghurt for protein, I'll be using cricket flour.

PRESENTER Cricket flour? OK, not your typical smoothie then! How will you make it?

ANTON It's very simple. I'll be mixing together a handful of ice, a cup of orange juice, some pieces of chopped pear and a large spoonful of cricket flour. Then I'm going to add extra chunks of mango and pineapple and a splash of lime juice to increase the fruit flavour.

PRESENTER Interesting. And what else will you be making?

ANTON I'm going to make ant tacos.

PRESENTER I'm sorry. Did you say <u>ant</u> tacos?

ANTON Yeah, I'll be using ant larvae as the main ingredient, but also typical ingredients you find in tacos like chilli, coriander and tomatoes, of course. So, I'll be frying half a cup of ant larvae in butter and then adding a cup of chopped tomatoes and a handful of chopped chillies. Then, when it's soft, I'll season it with a pinch of salt and pepper and a sprinkle of chopped coriander and mix it all together. I'm also going to bake some tacos. They take a while to bake so I need to make them first to make sure they'll have cooked in time.

PRESENTER Right, thanks, Anton! I'll be very interested to see how these dishes turn out. Now let's go and find out what Mei will be making today … Thanks, chefs, for explaining your recipes. I can safely say that by the end of today's competition we'll have seen and tasted some very unusual dishes. It's very exciting. So, Anton, Mei and Lara, are you ready? Your 45 minutes starts … now!

3.08 **ZOE** How will restaurants have changed by 2030?

SAM I think they will have become more automatic. Instead of human chefs, machines will be cooking your food and human waiters won't be serving the tables, robots will.

ZOE So humans won't be working in restaurants?

SAM That's right, but I think we will have designed robots that look like humans by then.

3.09 **ROB** Can you give me the recipe for your yummy Spanish omelette? I'm going to make it for the picnic tomorrow. It won't take ages, will it?

EVA No, it's a piece of cake! You'll need half a kilogramme of potatoes, five eggs, salt, oil and an onion.

ROB OK. Is that it?

EVA Yep, so start by peeling and slicing the potatoes. Once that's done, chop the onion.

ROB OK. Then what?

EVA Heat a cup of oil in a pan and fry the potatoes and onions.

ROB That's a fair amount of oil!

EVA Yeah, I know! While that's frying, mix the eggs in a bowl. Then put everything together and add a pinch of salt. Heat a spoonful of oil in a smaller pan and pour in the mixture. Once the bottom part has cooked, don't forget to flip the omelette with a plate and cook the other side.

ROB OK, I'll try.

EVA It's delicious! Your friends will all be asking for the recipe! Will you still be there at four?

ROB Yeah, but we'll have finished the omelette by then!

Unit 4

4.02
1 This drink must have lots of sugar in it. It tastes really sweet.
2 Don't touch that snake! It might be poisonous.
3 This milk must be really old. It smells disgusting.
4 It looks like a painting by Monet, but it can't be. It was painted after he died.

5 A What instrument is that? It sounds like a violin.

B Maybe, or it could be a viola.

6 This jacket must be very warm in winter. It feels like a blanket!

4.03

OMER What are you listening to? It's so loud!

BRIONY It's Beethoven. I think it's beautiful.

OMER You must be joking! I thought you hated classical music.

BRIONY Well, that's because I hadn't really listened to any before. Did you know Beethoven became deaf when he was still quite young?

OMER Wow, that can't be easy for anyone, but it must be absolutely terrible for a musician. You should turn it down, though. The neighbours might be home.

BRIONY They can't be. The lights are off and their car's not there. Anyway, I'm sure they'd prefer Beethoven to the heavy metal you always play. They must hate that! Every time you put it on they start banging on the wall. They must hate that! Every time you put it on they start banging on the wall.

4.04

1 sharp
2 transparent
3 colourful
4 smooth
5 spicy
6 rough
7 sour
8 shiny
9 smelly
10 faint

4.05

INTERVIEWER Hello, listeners. What does this sound like? You might be thinking it's a horse, but actually it's a sound effect, and the person who's making it is James Ford, our artist of the week. Hello, James.

JAMES Hi.

INTERVIEWER So, James, how were you making that sound?

JAMES With the two halves of a coconut. You hit them together like this.

INTERVIEWER Brilliant! Now, you're a Foley artist, aren't you? What exactly is that?

JAMES A person who makes the sound effects for movies.

INTERVIEWER You must make a lot of effects for one movie.

JAMES Oh, thousands! Even when there's no speaking or music or anything, there are always faint sounds in the background and they must sound natural. In fact, you can't ever have complete silence. That sounds strange.

INTERVIEWER Do you have to work hard?

JAMES Well, we need to experiment a lot. We have to use ordinary things to make hundreds of different effects.

INTERVIEWER Can you give us another example?

JAMES OK. I'll play you some recordings.

INTERVIEWER Well, that sounds like a person walking on grass, but I guess it must be newspaper, mustn't it?

JAMES That's right! It's just bits of old newspaper in a plastic bag. Do you want to listen to more?

INTERVIEWER Oh, yes, can we hear another one? That sounds like a fire burning!

JAMES Yes, it sounds like a fire, but in fact it's cellophane.

INTERVIEWER Cellophane? The transparent plastic you can make gift bags from?

JAMES Yep. You just make it into a ball and squeeze it with your hands.

INTERVIEWER Wow, that's amazing. I imagine your work must have changed a lot since people started to use computers.

JAMES Yes, that's true. In the past, Foley artists had to create all the effects in a movie. These days, we don't have to because the sound engineers create many of them on computers. However, there are still sound effects that a computer can't make. For example, I've just finished working on an action film. There were lots of loud crashes – I didn't have to make those sounds –

INTERVIEWER	Uh-huh.
JAMES	But, there was a scene where a man breaks his leg. A sound like that has to be very natural, so I had to create it.
INTERVIEWER	A leg breaking? What did you use for that?
JAMES	Sticks of celery – you know, the long green vegetable. You just have to break them. Easy!
INTERVIEWER	I see! Now, James, how do you become a Foley artist?
JAMES	Well, you don't need to have any formal training. But you ought to be a creative person, with the ability to listen really well. You need to find similarities between the sounds that different things make.
INTERVIEWER	Like celery and bones!
JAMES	Exactly!
INTERVIEWER	I think we should listen to one more effect before we go.
JAMES	Sure.
INTERVIEWER	It sounds like rain, but it can't be, can it?
JAMES	No, it's someone pouring rice from a bag onto a metal tray.
INTERVIEWER	That's wonderful! Thank you, James.

4.08

1 She didn't have to study hard for the exam because she's really good at English.

2 I didn't have to wear a uniform at my last school but I do at the one I go to now.

3 Billy didn't have to get up early this morning because it's a holiday.

4 Mia had to go to the dentist because she had toothache.

5 I got all the answers wrong so I had to do the exercise again.

4.09

AIDAN	Hey, do you want to see something cool?
ZOE	Sure, why not? Wow! What are those?
AIDAN	They're called *tabi*. They're from Japan. Guess what they are.
ZOE	Well, they're definitely some kind of clothing. They look like gloves, but they can't be, can they?
AIDAN	Nope. They're definitely not gloves.
ZOE	They're in the shape of an 'L', so I guess they must be socks.
AIDAN	Bingo!
ZOE	But why is the big toe separate from the other toes?
AIDAN	I'm not telling you. Try and work it out yourself.
ZOE	Hmm … Perhaps it's something traditional. Maybe Japanese people wear rings on their big toes.
AIDAN	No, that's not it. Guess again.
ZOE	No, I give up!
AIDAN	It's so that they can wear them with sandals with straps. The strap goes between the big toe and the others.
GIRL 1	Oh, that's a clever idea! They must be nice and warm to wear.
ZOE	I guess so. I haven't tried them on yet.

Unit 5

5.01

measure	attract
communicate	produce
collect	connect
deliver	waste
supply	solve
create	develop

5.03 A I was reading a blog that said in the future many jobs will be done by robots.

B Really? Like what?

A Well, food will be served by them in restaurants, houses will be built by them – and in some schools, classes will be taught by them.

B Robot teachers! That will be strange. But will all humans be replaced by robots?

A I don't think so. The blog said most operations won't be done by robots – human doctors and surgeons will still do those.

B What about sports? Will human football players be replaced completely?

A I don't think so, but who knows?

B I hope not, because that's what I want to be in the future!

5.04 **LAURA** What are we doing today, Miss?

SIMON We don't have a test, do we?

TEACHER No, Simon, no test today. We're going to use the virtual reality glasses for your geography lesson.

SIMON Cool!

LAURA Great! I love virtual reality!

TEACHER You'll enjoy this then. We're going to visit some places that were recently voted the New Seven Wonders of Nature. So, let's put our glasses on. Ready?

LAURA Ready.

TEACHER OK, what are you looking at?

SIMON I'm looking at the sea, a city … and there's a mountain behind the city. Where is it, Miss? It isn't Sydney, is it?

TEACHER It's not Sydney, no.

LAURA It's Cape Town in South Africa, isn't it?

TEACHER That's right.

LAURA The 2010 World Cup was held there. That's how I know.

SIMON Who was that won by?

LAURA By Spain!

TEACHER Does anyone know the name of the mountain in Cape Town?

LAURA No.

TEACHER Well, look at its shape. What does it look like?

LAURA It looks like a bed to me. Or a table.

SIMON Oh, I know. Is it Table Mountain?

TEACHER Exactly. The flat part is three kilometres from side to side and there are often clouds on top. It's very beautiful, isn't it?

LAURA It's stunning. Can we go up to the top?

TEACHER Sure. Ready? Here we go!

SIMON Now I can't see a thing!

LAURA We must be in the clouds.

TEACHER OK, let's turn around and go forward a little.

SIMON Be careful!

TEACHER There, we're out of the clouds now. That's Cape Town below us.

LAURA It's so pretty. Where are we going to next, Miss?

WOMAN 1 You'll see. Ready? Three, two, one …

SIMON Argh! What's that?! A crocodile? Where are we?

TEACHER This is Komodo Island, one of Indonesia's 13,000 or so islands and that's a type of lizard, called the Komodo dragon.

SIMON It looks terrifying!

LAURA What are you scared of? We're not really there! You won't be eaten, will you?

TEACHER Well, they can be dangerous, Laura. Only a few years ago, a man was killed by two of them.

LAURA By two of them? That's dreadful! But why are they called dragons?

TEACHER Well, when they were discovered, people thought they could breathe fire.

LAURA: They can't though, can they?

TEACHER: Of course not. But they're fascinating animals. They're the largest lizards in the world. They can grow up to three metres long.

SIMON: That's enormous!

TEACHER: They can also eat 80% of their own body weight in one meal, plus they're excellent swimmers.

LAURA: Are there many of them on the island?

TEACHER: There are about 1,700. Komodo Island is protected, because they're so special. OK, now we're going to see a very famous waterfall in South America. Ready?

SIMON: Oh, I know where we are! I've been here. It's Iguazu Falls.

TEACHER: Well done! Can you tell us something about it?

SIMON: Sure. It's between Argentina and Brazil. It was created by a volcanic eruption, and it's actually a combination of 275 waterfalls. Together, they're the largest waterfalls in the world. The sound of the water in real life is deafening. From the top to the bottom the falls are a maximum height of 82 metres.

TEACHER: Look, everyone – a rainbow!

SIMON: Wow, that's gorgeous.

LAURA: The world is marvellous, isn't it, Miss?

TEACHER: It is, Laura. Back to the classroom now, though, I'm afraid. We'll visit some more places next time.

5.05 The Sahara Desert looks stunning. I've been learning about it in class. It's fascinating. At 9.2 million km squared, it's enormous. The sand dunes are gorgeous. It would be marvellous to visit it one day, but it would be terrifying to get lost there without water. During the day it's boiling, but at night it can be freezing. Sometimes there are sandstorms with deafening winds. It must be dreadful to be caught in one.

5.06 ANGELA: So, Ryan, how was your trip to Rome?

RYAN: Oh, man, you should go. It's absolutely stunning. There's so much history and so many amazing buildings there. I loved it.

ANGELA: Where was your favourite place?

RYAN: I'd say it was the Coliseum.

ANGELA: That's where the gladiators used to fight, isn't it?

RYAN: Got it in one. Sometimes they would fight with animals, too. Bears, lions, elephants.

ANGELA: You can't be serious. With animals?

RYAN: Yep. On one occasion over 10,000 animals were killed in a single day.

ANGELA: Are you kidding me? That's dreadful!

RYAN: And they used to have sea battles there.

ANGELA: I find that hard to believe. How was that done?

RYAN: They would fill the stadium with water from the aqueducts. There were real ships and everything.

ANGELA: Seriously? That's fascinating.

RYAN: Wanna see a photo of me dressed as a gladiator outside?

ANGELA: OK, go on. Wow! Is that you? I can't believe you actually wore that!

RYAN: I look terrifying, don't I?

ANGELA: Er, not exactly. You look sweaty. It must've been really hot there.

RYAN: It was. It was boiling.

Unit 6

6.01

a People who are unpredictable sometimes get on my nerves. Get on my nerves.

b I get bored when I watch a film I've seen before. Get bored .

c I don't like to take risks and would never do extreme sports. Take risks.

d I don't have fun on theme park rides. They scare me! Have fun.

e I take an interest in all kinds of fun activities, like going on theme park rides. Take an interest in.

f I have doubts about trying new foods I've never eaten before. Have doubts.

g I take pleasure **in** watching films a second or third time. Take pleasure in.

h I try new foods whenever I have the chance. Have the chance.

i I never walk around new places by myself in case I get lost. Get lost.

j I get a lot out of extreme sports like skiing or waterskiing. Get a lot out of.

k I like getting to know people who are exciting and unpredictable. Getting to know.

l I like taking advantage of being in unknown places by myself to explore. Taking advantage of.

6.06–7 **PRESENTER** Today we have a story of incredible determination and bravery and here to tell us about it is surfing fan Martin Short. So, Martin, tell us about this amazing athlete.

MARTIN Her name's Bethany Hamilton and she's a fantastic surfer from Hawaii. She's lived there all her life and has been surfing since she was a young child.

PRESENTER I've had the chance to try surfing and it's quite difficult. So, what's special about Bethany?

MARTIN Well, when she was 13, she went surfing one morning with her best friend and her friend's parents. There were lots of turtles in the sea and they were just relaxing on their boards in the water chatting and watching the turtles when suddenly a huge tiger shark attacked her.

PRESENTER Oh my goodness! Was she OK?

MARTIN Well, no she wasn't. Unfortunately, the shark bit off her arm.

PRESENTER What … her whole arm?

MARTIN I'm afraid so, she lost all of it. Her friend's parents rushed to the hospital and when she got there she had already lost 60% of her blood. If they hadn't taken her to hospital straight away, she would have died.

PRESENTER Poor girl!

MARTIN However, just a few weeks after the accident, she made a very important decision. She decided to go back to the water.

PRESENTER To return to surfing?

MARTIN That's right! She got so much out of the sport that she was determined to start surfing again as soon as she could. Her family totally supported her decision and encouraged her to do what she loved.

PRESENTER Wow! That's a brave decision. I can't imagine doing that. I mean, what would you have done if it had happened to you?

MARTIN I really don't know, I think most people would never have gone back in the water again!

PRESENTER So, she taught herself to surf again with just one arm?

MARTIN She did, and since the age of 16 she's been competing as a professional surfer. It isn't easy, because there are many obstacles she has to deal with that the other surfers don't. Her arm has to work twice as hard, as she has to kick hard with her feet to get out into the waves, and she has to use a special handle on the front of her board to help her with certain moves. But she competes against professional surfers around the world and has had top results in Brazil, Australia and the USA.

PRESENTER Incredible! And she's also a mother, isn't she?

MARTIN That's right, she has two young boys. Bethany is an incredibly positive person and she wanted to share her story and inspire other people to overcome difficult challenges. She's written her autobiography and some films have also been made about her life.

PRESENTER She sounds like an inspiration to us all and a great example of how anyone can overcome challenges and achieve their goals with lots of hard work and determination.

MARTIN And a positive attitude!

6.08

1 A girl got stuck under a car and a high school baseball team lifted the car off the girl.

- a If the girl hadn't got stuck, the team wouldn't have needed to lift the car.
- b If the team hadn't lifted the car, the girl wouldn't have survived.

2 A 14-year-old saw a fire in his neighbour's home and went to help and saved a boy.

- a If he hadn't seen the fire, he wouldn't have gone to help.
- b If he hadn't gone to help, he wouldn't have saved the boy.

3 A group of teens were attacked by a bear in Alaska. One girl did first aid for nine hours until help arrived.

- a If they hadn't gone to Alaska, they wouldn't have been attacked.
- b If help had arrived earlier, the girl wouldn't have done first aid for nine hours.

6.09

MIA Are you going to come whitewater rafting this weekend?

JACK I'm not sure. It looks a little scary to me.

MIA Oh, it's not really. I had so much fun when I went. You'll never know unless you try, will you?

JACK But the water is so fast! It looks seriously deep and I'm not the world's best swimmer.

MIA Relax and don't worry, you'll be fine. The instructors will look after you. They don't take any risks.

JACK Mmm, I'm still not sure.

MIA Well what about paddle boarding? That's less risky.

JACK You've got to be joking! I wouldn't dare stand up on the board in the middle of the sea. What if I fell in?

MIA Come on! It's easy! You can do it! If you fall in, you just get back on the board.

JACK That's easy for you to say, but I'm not like you. Water sports are a real challenge for me.

MIA Well, what if I practised with you?

JACK Hmm. That might help. OK, I'll come.

MIA Good for you! I promise you'll feel really proud afterwards and you might even have fun! Let's go on Sunday.

6.11

A So, before we start, let's check we're all clear about what to do.

B It says here that we have to design a leaflet about confidence-building courses for teenagers.

C How many courses do we have to talk about?

A Mr Jones said two or three. It depends how much detail we give about each one, I suppose.

B OK, so we know what to do, but who is going to do what?

C Well I think we should all look for information online and then write about one course each.

A That's a good idea, so we'll look for information online and then I'll write the text for the leaflet and someone else can be in charge of designing the leaflet. Gabby, you're very creative, I think you'd be good at that.

C OK. What about Tom?

A Maybe Tom can prepare the presentation. What we're going to say to the class.

B Good idea, but there are a couple of problems.

A What?

B I don't have a printer and … I hate speaking in front of the class.

C You can give the leaflet to me on a USB stick and I'll print it, so that's not a problem.

A And we'll practise the presentation together. You can do it! We'll help you. You'll be great!

B OK. I'll do it if you both help me practise. And if you present some of it too so I'm not the only one talking.

C Absolutely! We'll all do a bit. We're going to do a great job!

A I agree! We make a good team!

Unit 7

7.01

1 glad	8 peaceful
2 annoyed	9 hurt
3 down	10 thrilled
4 ridiculous	11 amused
5 grateful	12 hopeful
6 insecure	13 satisfied
7 eager	

7.02

1 Hi, James, it's me, Sally. How are you? Listen, I've just had some amazing news. Do you remember I entered that art competition? That's right. I painted a picture of the mountains. Well, guess what! I won first prize. I know! It's fantastic!

2 Todd, can you please go and play that stupid game somewhere else? I'm trying to study and I can't concentrate with all the noise.

3 **A** Well, I thought it was going to be a fancy-dress party, so I dressed up and went as a giant chicken.

B And it wasn't?

A No, it was just an ordinary party. When I got there, everybody was wearing normal clothes. T-shirts, jeans …

B Oh no, Mark! Did everyone laugh?

A They couldn't stop laughing! One guy said, 'Look – the food's arrived!' I felt … well, you can imagine how I felt!

4 I don't understand it, Ben. Why didn't Elaine invite me to the picnic? She invited you and everyone else. I thought we were friends.

5 **A** What's up, Monica? Have you been crying?

B A little bit. I've just been looking at some photos of our old house. I miss it. I really liked living in the countryside. I wish we could go back sometimes. I don't like the city very much.

7.04

a bear in mind
b put my heart into
c crossed my mind
d make my mind up
e learn by heart
f change my mind
g in two minds
h I've got something on my mind
i break his heart
j close to my heart

7.05

COUNSELLOR Hi, Gavin, come in, take a seat. How are you?

GAVIN I'm OK.

COUNSELLOR Really? You look a bit down. What do you want to talk about?

GAVIN I don't know. Maybe it's nothing.

COUNSELLOR Well, you must have something on your mind. What's worrying you? Trouble with friends? Something at home?

GAVIN No, it's nothing like that. It's just … I'm really stressed.

COUNSELLOR Oh dear. What about?

GAVIN Exams. I'm worried I'm going to fail everything!

COUNSELLOR I'm sure you're not. What makes you think that?

GAVIN Everything! I have too many subjects to study for, and I don't have enough time, and if you fail your exams you can't get into university!

COUNSELLOR OK, Gavin, first stop panicking! Exams aren't everything. And it's normal to feel stressed about them, but there are things you can do to reduce the stress.

GAVIN Like what?

COUNSELLOR Well, first of all, make a list of what you have to do. Then you can put everything in order. First, what's essential. Next, what's important and last, what can wait. Do the essential things first. That way you'll use your time well.

GAVIN OK. I'll try that.

COUNSELLOR Also, remember to do some exercise and to eat some brain food.

GAVIN Brain food?

COUNSELLOR Something healthy that helps your brain to work better, especially when you're studying or before an exam. Like apples.

GAVIN Apples can make me do better in an exam?

COUNSELLOR Yes, or nuts, for example.

GAVIN Wow, OK.

COUNSELLOR Also, you must go to bed early.

GAVIN But my brain works better at night!

COUNSELLOR It doesn't. There's no point studying with a tired brain, Gavin. You need to rest it. And that means no energy drinks. You need to go to bed early and sleep well. Drink water if you're thirsty.

GAVIN OK, OK.

COUNSELLOR And don't try to do everything alone. Ask someone at home to help you.

GAVIN I already do.

COUNSELLOR That's good? Who helps you?

GAVIN My sister. She's really intelligent. She's just graduated from university.

COUNSELLOR Really? What did she study?

GAVIN Physics. She wants to be a teacher. Me too, one day.

COUNSELLOR I didn't know that. Who do you want to teach?

GAVIN Primary school kids. That's why I have to study hard. I have to pass every subject with excellent grades.

COUNSELLOR Well, it's great that your sister helps you with your homework, but maybe she can help you study for exams as well. She could give you little tests, for example.

GAVIN Actually, that's not a bad idea. Like, for the history exam, I have to learn a lot of dates by heart. She could test me. I'll ask her tonight.

COUNSELLOR Ah! Something else just crossed my mind! Do you know Jack Wellwood from class B7? You two could be study buddies.

GAVIN I know him, but what's a study buddy?

COUNSELLOR It's a friend you study with. Jack came to see me yesterday and said he wanted someone to study with. It can be fun to study with someone else.

GAVIN Thanks, Miss. I'll talk to him.

COUNSELLOR Great. Are you feeling a bit better now?

GAVIN Yeah, I'm feeling much calmer, actually. You know, I was in two minds about coming to see you. In fact, this morning I decided not to but then I changed my mind. I'm glad I did!

7.06

OLAF What's that?

ROSA It's a stress ball.

OLAF What does it do?

ROSA It helps you relax. Look, you squeeze it like this. It was a birthday present.

OLAF Wow, that feels great! Who gave it to you?

ROSA My sister. She knows I get stressed out a lot so she thought it might help.

OLAF I want one.

ROSA You don't need one! You never get stressed.

OLAF That's not true. Who told you that? I get stressed before exams.

ROSA Well, you could borrow this one if you like.

OLAF No, I'd prefer my own, thanks. Where did your sister get it?

ROSA Online, I think.

OLAF What site did she use? Do you know?

ROSA I'll ask her, but I'm sure you can get them in lots of places. They've been around for years.

OLAF Really? Who invented them?

ROSA No idea. Let's look it up!

7.10

PAULA Hey, Jerry. What's the matter? You look really down.

JERRY I am. It's my brother. He's refusing to talk to me.

PAULA Really? That's not very nice. Why?

JERRY His tablet has stopped working. He thinks I took it without asking and broke it, but I didn't, I swear. Now when I try to talk to him he just walks away.

PAULA That's a little harsh, isn't it?

JERRY The thing is, he ought to know I wouldn't take his stuff without permission. I feel really hurt.

PAULA I can imagine. It's horrible when someone doesn't believe you. But bear in mind he's doing his final exams at the moment. He's probably really stressed out about everything.

JERRY I guess you're right, but I hope he calms down soon.

PAULA Is there anything I can do to help? I have an old tablet I could lend him.

JERRY That's kind of you, but you don't need to do that.

PAULA Don't mention it, but let me know if you change your mind. It'll all be OK, you'll see.

Unit 8

8.01

product	marketing company
brand	influence
logo	buyer
slogan	seller
advert	review
advertise	ad blocker

8.02

1 I love watching funny adverts online or on TV.

2 My dad always buys the same brand of toothpaste.

3 Sometimes it's not easy for buyers to decide which product they want.

4 I always look at reviews before I buy something new.

5 That advert influenced my decision to buy a new tablet.

6 At school we have to draw a simple design for a logo competition.

8.06

1 subscribe to	5 build up	9 comment on
2 post	6 shut down	10 delete
3 switch off	7 follow	
4 switch on	8 vlog	

8.07

INTERVIEWER Social media influencers focus on everything from fashion to gaming. But what qualities do you need to become an influencer and what are some of the pros and cons of the job? Today were talking to Jerome to find out. Hi, Jerome. Tell us about how you became an influencer.

JEROME Well, a few years ago I was following lots of different YouTubers and commenting a lot on other people's posts. One day a friend said I should set up a social media channel myself, because I knew more about gaming than most other YouTubers.

INTERVIEWER So tell me exactly how you started.

JEROME I started recording and uploading videos, but deleted most of them because I didn't think they were good enough. Then I read somewhere that if you want to learn something new you just have to try and see what works and what doesn't. So, I started posting regularly, about once a day and soon got the hang of what followers liked and what they didn't.

INTERVIEWER That's interesting! And what did your followers like best?

JEROME Well, I think basically that I was someone just like them talking honestly about gaming. They could relate to my comments and pretty soon I'd built up a huge number of followers.

INTERVIEWER I've heard that people can post some pretty harsh comments. Did you get negative comments from anyone?

JEROME I did get a few, but nothing unusual. The thing that became a real problem was that some followers started arguing with one another in the comments.

INTERVIEWER That's pretty normal though, isn't it?

JEROME Yes, but it got so bad that I nearly shut down the account. However, I just switched off the comments on my channel so that they couldn't talk to each other instead.

INTERVIEWER And what happened?

JEROME Oh, it made everything so much better. There weren't any comments from anyone, but I focused on what my followers wanted and produced the best vlogs I could.

INTERVIEWER So, is that when the marketing companies started to contact you?

JEROME Yeah, when I reached around 10,000 followers, they started to send me new games to vlog about. I tried out the game myself and then gave my opinion about it in my videos.

INTERVIEWER Sounds like you're pretty good at it! Have you got any advice for anyone who wants to start their own YouTube channel?

JEROME The main thing is that you need to be different. No one is interested in your selfies, but people are interested in themselves. Connect with your followers and give them something new. On my channel I don't give the typical walkthroughs or game reviews like other channels. I share unforgettable gaming moments in a funny, entertaining way and I also vlog with my friends and my family. I think that's why everyone likes it so much.

8.08 Ads are everywhere, but have you ever asked yourself how advertising works? Marketing companies use techniques to make us buy things we don't even want. Nothing is more effective than making us think that we are missing out on something that everyone else has and that we will be happier if we buy ourselves something new. They also make us compare ourselves to others. For example, in a typical shampoo ad, two women look at each other. One of them asks herself, 'Why is her hair so beautiful?' When they talk to one another she discovers the secret The incredible shampoo!

8.09 GINNY What's up, Niall?

NIALL I've got to make a video for my technology project to advertise something and I don't have a clue what to do. I don't know where to start! Can you think of anything?

GINNY You really ought to use a video creation tool. It's the best thing to make videos. I've used some great ones. There are loads of options online.

NIALL That sounds like a plan. What do I need to know?

GINNY Well, a video creation tool would be ideal because it would provide you with a ready-made template.

NIALL Is it easy to use?

GINNY Yeah, you can teach yourself to do it, no problem.

NIALL Excellent! So I add my own text and images, do I?

GINNY Well, you need to write your own text, but most video creation tools have a ready-made image bank, which is handy.

NIALL Great, I can use their images.

GINNY Yep and you can add music and a voiceover. I can't recommend them enough!

NIALL Sounds like a no-brainer. I'll check out the options online. Thanks, Ginny!

8.10 A

A Oh no! Not again!

B What's wrong, Katia?

A Oh, everything in my backpack's wet! My books, my tablet, even my phone. Do you have the same problem?

B No! My Funpack's waterproof, so nothing gets wet. It's also got loads of pockets. There's even a special one for my tablet and another for my phone. Look!

B

A Oh no! I haven't got a phone charger!

B With the Funpack you don't need one, look! This pocket is a charger so I can charge my phone or tablet anytime, anywhere.

A Oh wow! That's fantastic! Can I see?

C

Find your Funpack on www.funpack.com. Choose from a wide range of colours and designs, which you can personalise yourself for free. All packs are waterproof and include a special charger pocket to charge when you are out and about.

D

B Hey, Katia! How's it going?

A Great! I love my Funpack. It's the best!

B Funpack. Packed full of fun!

Unit 9

9.01
a – 2 announced
b – 1 claimed
c – 5 have confirmed
d – 4 discovered
e – 3 insisted
f – 6 suggest
g – 8 deny
h – 9 refuses
i – 7 have complained
j – 11 admitted
k – 10 has apologised
l – 12 promised

9.05

SAM Hello, everyone, and welcome to *That's News to Me!* I'm Sam.

DAN And I'm Dan.

SAM And we've got a special show today, haven't we, Dan?

DAN That's right. Last week one of our listeners asked us what our favourite news stories were. Well, we occasionally hear some very strange stories, and we've chosen three of the strangest to tell you today. Where shall we start, Sam? The parrot?

SAM Why not? This is about a parrot that used to live with a British man called Darren in California and then disappeared one day. He was gone for four whole years, right?

DAN Yes, but Darren eventually found him again. The thing is, before he disappeared, he'd spoken with a British accent – 'It's a piece of cake! I can't believe it!' – that sort of thing, but by the time he came home, he'd learned Spanish.

SAM Wow! Was he speaking fluently?

DAN No, but he was saying things like *Qué ha pasado? Qué ha pasado?* which means 'What's happened' in Spanish. It turns out he'd been living with a Guatemalan family in a different city in California. This family really loved him, especially the grandfather, who spoke to him in Spanish.

SAM But then he disappeared again!

DAN This parrot likes to travel! Well, somebody found him and gave him to a vet. The vet identified him and returned him to Darren, but then the Guatemalan family asked him if they could have the parrot back. The grandfather was missing him, you see. Darren said yes, so now the parrot lives with them.

SAM What a sweet story! Shall we tell the listeners about the pasta disaster next?

DAN Yes, now this one is unbelievable.

SAM Yes it is pretty weird. So, three young American women who were on a student exchange in Florence, Italy didn't know that water was necessary for cooking pasta. They bought a packet of pasta, put the pasta in a pot – without a single drop of water – and put the pot on the stove to cook. After a while, a fire started and the women had to call the fire brigade.

DAN Talk about burning your food! Fortunately, nobody was hurt, right?

SAM That's right, but I imagine their Italian friends asked them if they'd ever cooked anything at all before!

DAN Well, a local chef has offered to give them free cooking lessons. I don't think I'd go to one of their dinners though. It doesn't sound like they cook very regularly.

SAM No, nor me, but I think I'd rather go to one of their dinners than visit the bedroom of the girl in our last story.

DAN Same here. A family in England called an organisation that looks after animals because they had discovered – well, they thought they had discovered – a terrifying lizard under their teenage daughter's bed.

SAM Yes, so a specialist went to the family home and very carefully approached the lizard. It was about 18 cm long, and wasn't moving at all. Everybody thought it might be dangerous. But it wasn't, was it?

DAN Not at all, no. It was actually a dirty old pink stripy sock.

SAM How disgusting!

DAN Of course, everybody immediately asked her where she'd left the other one!

SAM I hope she's cleaned her room since then.

9.06

1 gradually	6 secretly
2 nowadays	7 regularly
3 occasionally	8 patiently
4 eventually	9 fluently
5 surprisingly	10 after a while

9.07

1 The teacher asked the boy if he had done his homework.

2 Jack asked Laura what she was doing later.

3 My sister asked me how the story had ended.

4 I asked the assistant if there were any tickets left.

5 We asked an old man where the station was.

6 Tom asked me what time I would arrive.

9.08

1 Mikhail asked his sister who the hero of the story was.

2 Elena asked me if I preferred comedy or drama.

3 Ruben asked his friend where he had heard that.

4 She asked if it would rain later.

5 I asked the receptionist if we could still get tickets.

6 Sally asked me what I was reading.

9.09

JAMIE You'll never guess what happened to me last night.

ESMA No, what? Tell me.

JAMIE It was so embarrassing! Basically, what happened was, my new classmates asked me if I wanted to go bowling with them. I said yes and when we got there, they asked me how well I could bowl.

ESMA You didn't say you were any good, did you?

JAMIE Well, you know I'm a show-off! So I said, 'Just watch me!'

ESMA But you're terrible at bowling! I've seen you.

JAMIE Hey! I'm not that bad! So anyway, I picked up the ball, put my fingers in the holes, went to bowl …

ESMA Let me guess. Your fingers got stuck.

JAMIE Completely! I swung the ball back carefully and then swung it forward and just sort of went flying with it. The next thing I knew, I was flat on my back!

ESMA What a fantastic first impression!

JAMIE And to make matters worse, I couldn't get my fingers out.

ESMA Oh, Jamie!

WORKBOOK ANSWER KEY

Starter Unit pp4–7

VOCABULARY AND READING

1 2 sightseeing 3 backpacking
4 tourist attractions 5 holiday resort
6 accommodation

2 Students' own answers

3 2 lines 3 rehearsals 4 show
5 audience 6 scene

4 a

5 1 He stayed in a hotel.
2 It was amazing.
3 He saw an Italian opera.
4 Because there were subtitles.

LANGUAGE IN ACTION AND VOCABULARY

1 2 They weren't listening to music.
3 Was I making a lot of noise?
4 Beth usually played football on Saturday.
5 They didn't live in a flat.
6 Did Michael eat meat?

2 2 enjoyed 3 did you do 4 visited
5 were having 6 was helping

3 Students' own answers

4 post, shout, whisper, describe, smile, translate, shake hands, greet, wave

5 1-4: describe, shake hands, greet, wave
5-10: shout, whisper, describe, smile, translate, greet

6 2 post 3 shout 4 describe 5 smile
6 whisper 7 wave 8 greet; shake hands

LISTENING AND GRAMMAR

1 1 b 2 c 3 a

2 Japan

3 a 6 b 4 c 3 d 5 e 2 f 1

4 Students' own answers

5 2 since 3 ever 4 for 5 never 6 's

6 2 Have you ever climbed 3 's liked 4 haven't done 5 phoned 6 've been

7 2 arrived 3 hasn't got 4 've done 5 went
6 've eaten 7 made 8 haven't felt

WRITING

1 a and c

2 1 D 2 B 3 C 4 A

3 1 Present perfect (to describe actions when exact time is not important) and past simple (to describe actions done at a particular time)

4 a 5 b 3 c 1 d 4 e 2

5, 6 and 7
Students' own answers

Unit 1 pp8–15

VOCABULARY

1 2 baggy 3 checked 4 flat 5 striped
6 long-sleeved

2 2 flowery 3 cotton 4 checked 5 denim
6 high-heeled

3 2 cotton 3 flowery 4 spotted 5 long-sleeved

4 2 a plain denim skirt
3 tight white cotton trousers
4 a baggy red denim jacket
5 a tight brown and blue striped cotton T-shirt
6 flat brown and white spotted leather shoes

5 Students' own answers

EXPLORE IT!

b

READING

1 1 blog post
2 how often to wash jeans

2 2 harm 3 research 4 brand 5 claim 6 turn out

3 2 F She says 'I don't know about that!' 3 T
4 F Freezing them won't eliminate bacteria, skin cells and natural oils. 5 T 6 T

4 Students' own answers

LANGUAGE IN ACTION

1 2 d 3 e 4 a 5 f 6 c

2 2 've been doing 3 has been visiting
4 Have they finished 5 hasn't been speaking
6 has had

3 2 answered 3 gone 4 been making
5 you bought 6 Have you been revising

4 2 Finally I've finished my school project! / I've finally finished …
3 Nick has been wearing the same clothes all week.
4 Have you ever been to France?
5 I've been trying to contact you all day!
6 Jan hasn't decided what to do.

5 2 Have you found 3 've been shopping 4 've tried on 5 haven't bought 6 've been waiting

6 Students' own answers

VOCABULARY AND LISTENING

1 2 hang 3 undo 4 go out of fashion
5 go with 6 suit

2 2 fit 3 go with 4 suit 5 fold 6 hang (them) up

3 Students' own answers

4 a 3 b 2 c 1

5 2 a 3 c 4 b 5 c

LANGUAGE IN ACTION

1 2 b 3 b 4 a 5 b 6 a

2 2 F 3 T 4 F 5 T 6 F

3 2 far 3 quite 4 far 5 really 6 fairly

4 2 c 3 a 4 b 5 a 6 c

5 Students' own answers

WRITING

1 1 Five ways to spend less money on clothes.
2 Sonya has bought clothes online. Aidan has been to second-hand clothes shops

2 1 to be honest; in my opinion 2 for emphasis
3 for emphasis

3 2 decided 3 post, sharing 4 no idea 5 Since

4 Students' own answers

5 **Sample answer**
Great post! Thanks for sharing! Since reading your post, I've decided to only buy clothes in the sales. As a result, I've been spending A LOT less money and A LOT less time clothes shopping! TBH I think that I was almost addicted to it before, but I had no idea! IMO there are far better ways to spend your weekend! At first, it's a bit difficult to change your habits, but after a while it gets pretty easy. For example, I've started to do canoeing on Saturdays instead and I feel A LOT happier!

6 Students' own answers

REVIEW

1

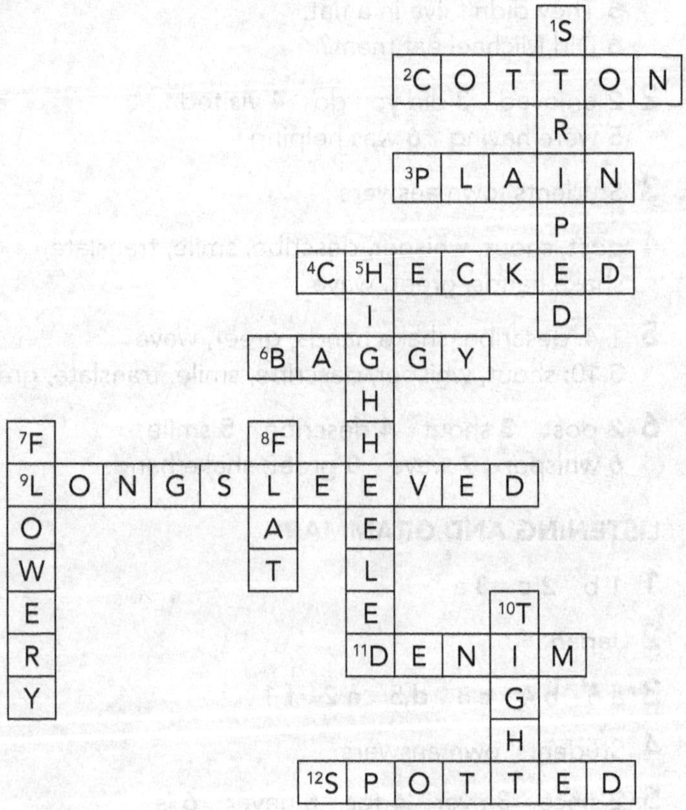

2 1 go out of fashion 2 do up 3 fit 4 match 5 suit 6 fold; hang (them) up 7 go with 8 undo 9 wear (them) out

3 1 haven't seen 2 has been trying 3 've lost 4 has never played 5 've finished; 've been waiting 6 Have we bought

4 1 pretty 2 absolutely 3 a little 4 quite 5 far 6 totally

5 1 a 2 c 3 c 4 b 5 a 6 c 7 b 8 c 9 a 10 b 11 c 12 a

Unit 2 pp16–23

VOCABULARY

1 2 looking 3 up 4 try 5 going 6 down

2 2 turn out 3 move out 4 end up 5 do without 6 go back

3 2 turn out 3 going through 4 sign up 5 try out 6 look forward to 7 move to 8 do without

4 Students' own answers

5 Students' own answers

EXPLORE IT!

18

READING

1 b

2 2 keen 3 surrounded 4 law 5 plenty of 6 lecture

3 1 no information
2 She means that you have to make new friends because your old friends aren't with you.
3 Because she's meeting lots of new people.

4 **Studying at school**
2 ask questions and discuss things with teachers
3 no information
Studying at university
1 lectures with over 100 students 2 just take notes
3 only 12 hours of lectures

5 Students' own answers

LANGUAGE IN ACTION

1 2 used to have 3 didn't use to like 4 didn't use to go 5 Did you use to play 6 Did Matt use to be

2 2 In the past, did your granddad use to ride a bike to work? 3 People used to go to the cinema more often before the Internet. 4 Clothes didn't use to wear out so quickly (before). 5 not possible 6 Did there use to be a castle in this town (before)?

3 **Possible answers:**

1 People used to wash clothes by hand. / People didn't use to have washing machines.
2 People didn't use to have mobile phones. / People used to make calls with landline phones.
3 People used to send postcards on holiday. / People didn't use to post messages about their holidays on social media.
4 People didn't use to use technology to find a place. / People used to use maps in books to find a place.

4 2 wouldn't 3 would 4 wouldn't 5 wouldn't 6 would

5 2 I would often arrive late for school when I was younger. 3 Did you use to wear glasses before? 4 My grandma would always go for a walk after breakfast. 5 My dad would often swim in the sea when he lived in Cádiz. 6 My mum used to be a nurse.

6 1 Did you use to have 2 did 3 would / used to 4 decided 5 didn't 6 did you / did you use to

VOCABULARY AND LISTENING

1

b	o	l	s	l	e	n	s
h	b	u	t	t	o	n	o
a	t	h	r	o	o	s	p
n	r	c	a	b	l	e	l
d	i	m	p	l	a	y	u
l	l	c	o	v	e	r	g
e	i	h	k	e	y	o	u
t	d	i	s	p	l	a	y

2 2 display 3 lens 4 handle 5 lid 6 plug 7 key 8 cover 9 cable

3 Students' own answers

4 2✓ 3✓ 4✓ 6✓

5 2 Her gran thinks that young people spend too much time using 'technological things'.
3 Katie's gran didn't use a calculator at school.
4 There weren't many programmes on TV before.
5 Katie thinks that life before sounds fun.
6 When her gran was at school, each student had a small blackboard to write on.

6 2 F 3 T 4 T 5 F 6 F

7 Students' own answers

LANGUAGE IN ACTION

1 2 My sister had already got married by the time she was 20. **3** Dan wasn't happy because I had turned down his invitation. **4** By the time the match finished, we had scored five goals!
5 We had walked a very long way by the time we found the river.

2 2 e **3** b **4** d **5** a

3 2 (Jack) had come back by then.
3 (Had) you already woken up when I rang you?
4 (Before) last year I had never been abroad.
5 (Had) you ever seen a snake before then?

4 2 Had Sean ever made **3** had already started; arrived
4 left; had learned **5** had never felt; saw
6 Had everyone already gone; started

5 2 had been **3** had already settled **4** became
5 was **6** had always wanted **7** received
8 had never got

6 Students' own answers

WRITING

1 No

2 1 B and C **2** gives their opinion
3 repeats their opinion

3 2 Therefore / This means that **3** Secondly
4 In addition **5** Therefore / This means that
6 In conclusion

4 1 in the old days **2** more favourable **3** position
4 examine

5 *used to*; *would*

6 Students' own answers

7 Sample answer:
It's more important to speak English today than in the past.

Nowadays, everyone, or nearly everyone, wants to learn English. In my opinion, there are good reasons for this because knowing English has never been so important.

Firstly, if you want to get a good job, you will almost certainly need to speak English. In the old days, some companies wouldn't ask about your level of English when they interviewed you. However, things have changed a lot! This means that speaking English has become essential.

Secondly, a lot of the most interesting content on the Internet is in English. Therefore, if you don't know English, you won't be able to enjoy it. Of course, in the past this didn't use to be a problem because we didn't have the Internet. In addition, if you want to travel, you'll need to speak English because it's the international language. Before, people wouldn't travel abroad a lot, so English wasn't so important.

In conclusion, it's much more important to speak English today than in the past. So, if you can't speak it, now is the time to learn!

REVIEW

1 1 go back to **2** (really) looking forward to
3 do without a shower **4** turn down your invitation
5 settling down well **6** going through
7 moved to **8** try out this new

2

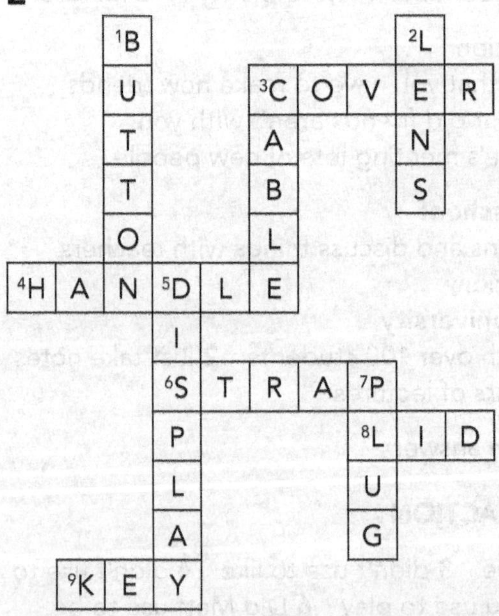

3 1 got
2 followed / used to follow / would follow
3 used to explore / would explore
4 used to fight / would fight
5 didn't come 6 was 7 put up

4 1 B 2 A 3 A 4 B 5 B 6 A

5 1 a 2 b 3 c 4 b 5 c 6 b 7 c 8 a 9 c
10 b 11 a 12 a 13 b

Unit 3 pp24–31

VOCABULARY

1

c	h	o	p	o	p	e	e	l
r	o	v	g	r	i	l	l	d
i	s	e	a	s	o	n	s	i
s	p	r	e	a	d	o	l	h
h	o	c	r	a	m	f	i	e
a	r	o	a	s	t	f	c	a
r	e	o	v	e	r	r	e	t
b	a	k	e	r	y	y	o	t
o	m	u	g	r	a	t	e	e

2 2 heat 3 peel 4 roast 5 spread 6 slice
7 fry 8 overcook

3 2 Chop 3 bake 4 grill 5 Season 6 spread

4 2 spread 3 Grate 4 heat 5 fry 6 overcook
7 Season

5 Students' own answers

6 **-ed ending**

grated	sliced
peeled	fried
baked	overcooked
heated	**other**
seasoned	roast
chopped	

(*spread* doesn't have an adjective form)

EXPLORE IT!

c

1 It is a dish made with the leftover vegetables from a roast dinner.

2 At breakfast time

READING

1 1 B 2 A 3 D 4 C

2 2 sensible 3 melt 4 hiking 5 freezing
6 highlight

3 2 a 3 f 4 b 5 d 6 c

4 Students' own answers

LANGUAGE IN ACTION

1 2 b 3 a 4 c 5 b 6 a

2 2 starts 3 is going to learn 4 're meeting
5 'm going to make 6 has 7 'm going to get
8 're going

3 Students' own answers

4 1 b 2 c 3 a

5 2 might come 3 will love 4 isn't going to cost
5 will have 6 may / might not finish

6 2 will get 3 may / might make 4 are you doing / are you going to do 5 'm going / 'm going to go
6 starts

7 Students' own answers

VOCABULARY AND LISTENING

1 2 a pinch of 3 a spoonful of 4 a piece of
5 a sprinkle of 6 chunks of

2 **Possible answers:**

Sugar
a cup of
a handful of
a packet of
a pinch of
a spoonful of
a sprinkle of

Milk
a cup of
a splash of

Cheese
a piece of
a slice of

3 Students' own answers

4 1 F 2 T 3 T 4 F

5 2 seventy 3 good 4 sit 5 young 6 office
7 customers 8 check / taste

6 Students' own answers

LANGUAGE IN ACTION

1 **2** 'll be listening **3** won't be lying
4 won't be working **5** Will we be eating
6 Will Aidan be cooking

2 **2** won't be doing
3 'll be starting
4 Will Chloe be playing; Yes, she will.
5 will she be having; She'll be having it / her dance class on Wednesday.

3 **2** 'll **3** won't **4** 'll **5** No, I won't.

4 **2** I won't (have) **3** will have arrived
4 'll have sliced **5** won't have fried
6 will you have grilled **7** I won't (have)
8 won't have had

5 **2** this time tomorrow **3** by the end of this month
4 By the end of this year **5** in five minutes

6 Students' own answers

WRITING

1 Five future fashion trends

2 2 T 3 F 4 F 5 T

3 **2** Smart clothes will be the norm.
3 What could be more exciting than being a fashion designer?
4 T-shirts are here to stay. / T-shirts will be around forever. / T-shirts aren't going anywhere.

4 Students' own answers

5 **Possible answer:**
Five ways my life will be different in 20 years' time

1 I'll probably be married.
I imagine that in 20 years I'll have settled down and I'll have got married if everything turns out well!

2 I might have children!
I hope I'll have some children by then, too. I mean, starting a family – what could be better than that?

3 I'll be working as an engineer – I hope!
My dad's an engineer and he really enjoys his job, so that's what I want to do, too. It's a good career because engineers aren't going anywhere. We're always going to need them.

4 I might be abroad!
I've always wanted to live in another country for a while, so perhaps I'll be living abroad in 20 years' time. Also, I think that moving to another country will be the norm for many people as they look for a better job.

5 New friends … and old friends
I hope I'll make lots of new friends in the next 20 years. But I'm certain that I'll always stay in contact with the friends I have now. I'm 100% sure of that prediction!

6 Students' own answers

REVIEW

1

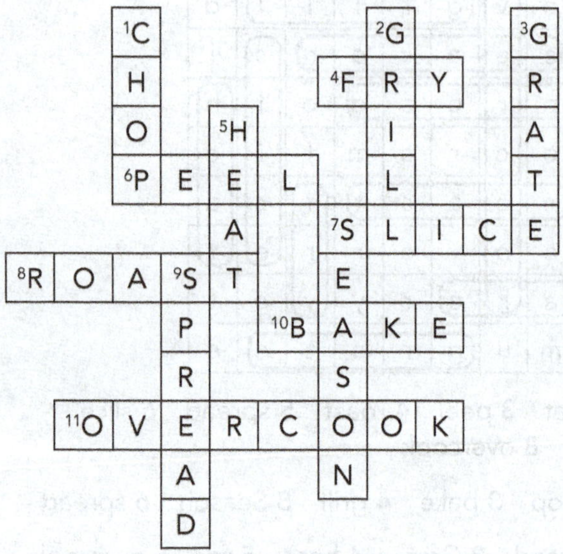

2 **1** sugar **2** chocolate **3** cake **4** cheese
5 nuts **6** crisps **7** pepper **8** grated cheese
9 olive oil **10** vinegar

3 **1** does **2** 'm going to **3** Are you going
4 might **5** will eat **6** is staying

4 **1** will have discovered **2** will be living
3 won't have hit **4** will be going
5 won't have found **6** will be planning

5 **1** b **2** a **3** c **4** b **5** a **6** b **7** a **8** c **9** b
10 c **11** a **12** b **13** c

Unit 4 pp32–39

VOCABULARY

1 2 C 3 A 4 D 5 B

2 2 tastes 3 look like 4 feels 5 smell
6 sound like 7 tastes like 8 looks

3 Students' own answers

4 Students' own answers

EXPLORE IT!

c

Students' own answers

READING

1 b

2 2 flavours 3 background 4 accurately
5 does for a living 6 challenge

3 2 c 3 b 4 a 5 b

4 Students' own answers

LANGUAGE IN ACTION

1 1 b 2 c 3 a

2 could, may

3 2 can't 3 must 4 might 5 must 6 might

4 2 can't 3 might 4 must 5 can't 6 might
7 must

5 2 That can't be the right answer.
3 You must need good exam results to do medicine at university.
4 This might / could be the worst film I've seen!
5 It can't take a long time to make that dish.

6 **Possible answers:**
2 It can't be daytime.
3 The battery might need charging.
4 There must be fireworks in the sky.

VOCABULARY AND LISTENING

1 2 rough 3 shiny 4 faint 5 colourful 6 sour
7 smooth 8 sharp 9 smelly

2 2 smelly 3 smooth 4 sour 5 sharp 6 colourful

3 2 spicy 3 sour 4 faint 5 smooth 6 shiny 7 rough

4 Students' own answers

5 b

6 2 c 3 a 4 b 5 b

7 Students' own answers

LANGUAGE IN ACTION

1 2 mustn't 3 ought to 4 need to 5 should
6 shouldn't 7 don't need to

2 2 c 3 a 4 c 5 b 6 b 7 a 8 b

3 2 You mustn't walk on the grass.
3 We don't have to watch the match.
4 Jack didn't have to give me a present.
5 We need to contact him.
6 You shouldn't be in the sun without a hat.

4 Students' own answers

WRITING

1 Marlee is deaf, so her hearing is damaged.

2 2 she acted for the first time
3 a deaf woman who refuses to speak because the rest of the world refuses to learn sign language
4 an enthusiastic worker for many charities
5 she doesn't always need to use an interpreter
6 there wouldn't be any opportunities for deaf people in films / as actors

3 2 was born 3 including 4 at the age of
5 According to 6 known as

4–6 Students' own answers

REVIEW

1 1 smell 2 sound like 3 looks like
4 sounds like 5 smells like 6 feels like
7 tastes 8 look; feel; taste

2

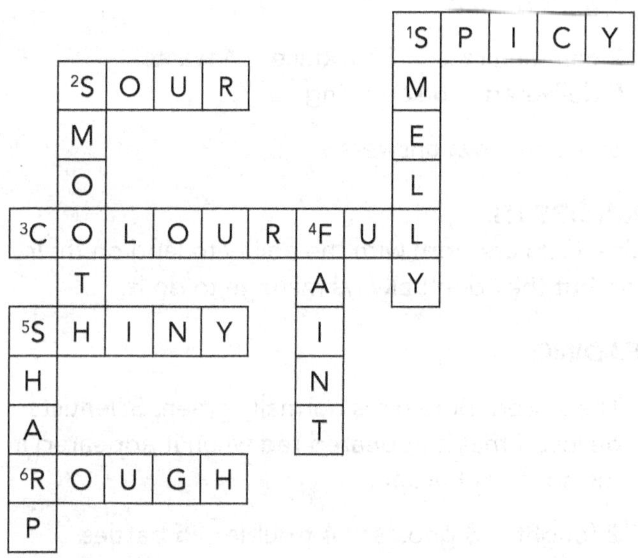

3 1 must 2 might 3 can't 4 must 5 might
6 can't 7 might 8 must

4 1 mustn't 2 had to 3 should 4 don't need to 5 Did you have to 6 should 7 don't have to 8 Do we need / have to

5 1 c 2 b 3 a 4 c 5 a 6 c 7 b 8 b 9 c 10 a 11 b 12 a 13 b

Unit 5 pp40–47

VOCABULARY

1

C	O	P	R	O	D	U	C	E	P	Z	C
M	E	A	S	U	R	E	G	V	C	Q	O
E	S	C	S	U	P	P	L	Y	R	M	M
B	R	T	I	D	E	L	I	V	E	R	M
Z	A	R	O	E	Y	U	I	D	A	C	U
N	S	I	C	V	C	O	L	E	T	O	N
C	O	N	N	E	C	T	O	P	E	L	I
H	L	O	T	L	O	I	L	L	O	L	C
T	V	P	G	O	L	B	N	Z	G	E	A
E	E	X	V	P	A	T	T	R	A	C	T
W	Y	G	I	U	V	K	W	A	S	T	E

2 measure 3 supply 4 deliver / develop 5 connect / communicate / collect / create 6 attract 7 waste 8 communicate / collect / connect / create 9 create / communicate / collect / connect 10 develop / deliver 11 collect / connect / communicate / create 12 solve

2 1 a 2 b 3 c

3 2 communicate 3 produce 4 waste 5 delivered 6 supplying

4 Students' own answers

EXPLORE IT!

False. Cats are born with the ability to land on their feet, but they don't always manage to do it.

READING

1 The Aurora Borealis is normally green. Scientists believed that it appeared red when it appeared in the south of Europe.

2 2 fought 3 ghosts 4 trouble 5 battles 6 creator

3 2 F Stories about it are found in many cultures. 3 T 4 F They believed they were ghosts trying to communicate with the living. 5 T 6 T

4 Students' own answers

LANGUAGE IN ACTION

1 2 was 3 will be 4 wasted 5 was 6 were

2 2 was built 3 were used 4 were measured 5 will be collected 6 are attracted

3 2 was; created 3 is measured 4 were; produced 5 will be delivered

4 **Possible answers:**
1 Mobile phones are made of plastic.
2 Some are produced in China.
3 The iPhone was produced in 2007.
4 Apps are downloaded when you go to a store.
5 They'll be used to do everything.

VOCABULARY AND LISTENING

1 2 marvellous 3 dreadful 4 gorgeous 5 freezing 6 deafening 7 fascinating 8 enormous

2 2 deafening 3 terrifying 4 fascinating 5 enormous 6 boiling 7 marvellous 8 gorgeous 9 stunning

3 Students' own answers

4 2 e 3 d 4 a 5 b

5 2 100 years 3 Architect and engineer 4 At Eiffel's factory 5 A work of art

6 Students' own answers

LANGUAGE IN ACTION

1 2 c 3 a 4 f 5 b 6 e

2 2 haven't they 3 doesn't she 4 won't you 5 can't she 6 has he

3 2 about 3 to 4 for 5 of 6 from

4 2 can 3 will 4 for / at 5 does 6 by / for

5 2 Where do you come from?
3 What is it made of?
4 You're coming with us, aren't you? / You'll come with us, won't you?

6 Students' own answers

WRITING

1 4–The food

2 **2** Its size **3** Next to the Thames, near Westminster Bridge **4** 135 metres **5** Because it has so many incredible places to visit

3 **2** the highlight **3** (London) deserves to win **4** I'm absolutely certain **5** Without a doubt

4–6 Students' own answers

REVIEW

1 **1** freezing **2** create **3** waste **4** deafening **5** solve **6** measure **7** dreadful **8** gorgeous

2 **1** connected **2** fascinating **3** terrifying **4** delivered **5** collected **6** marvellous; stunning **7** attracted **8** enormous

3 **1** were collected **2** were delivered **3** were (all) created **4** were measured **5** is pulled **6** is dropped **7** will be made **8** will be cut **9** will be brought

4 **1** isn't it **2** can we **3** has she **4** did he **5** won't they **6** does she **7** haven't they **8** don't they

5 **1** c **2** d **3** c **4** c **5** c **6** b **7** b **8** a **9** d **10** d **11** b **12** a **13** c **14** c

Unit 6 pp48–55

VOCABULARY

1

get	have	take
lost	doubts	advantage of
bored	fun	an interest in
on my nerves	the chance	pleasure in
to know		risks
a lot out of		

2 **2** e **3** b **4** f **5** d **6** c

3 **2** in **3** gets **4** know **5** had **6** of **7** have **8** doubts

4 Students' own answers

EXPLORE IT!

a

READING

1 Essex and Ecuador.

2 **2** hut **3** ridiculous **4** tribe **5** admits **6** rainforest

3 **2** b **3** c **4** a

4 Students' own answers

LANGUAGE IN ACTION

1 **2** c **3** a **4** e **5** b

2 **2** didn't take **3** got **4** if it gets **5** If you play

3 **2** 'll give **3** put **4** won't eat **5** don't like **6** 'll put / might put **7** made **8** wouldn't use **9** 'll help **10** took **11** would ask

4 **2** <u>won't</u> → wouldn't **3** <u>won't</u> → don't **4** <u>might be</u> → might **5** <u>don't try</u> → try **6** <u>you would</u> → would you

5 Students' own answers

VOCABULARY AND LISTENING

1

E	N	C	O	U	R	A	G	E	I	D	G
N	F	A	P	T	X	C	N	I	R	E	D
I	N	S	P	I	R	E	T	A	S	T	C
B	E	R	O	B	S	T	A	C	L	E	H
X	O	B	R	A	V	E	R	Y	B	R	A
Q	V	T	T	O	R	Z	T	T	O	M	L
P	E	F	U	U	T	Y	B	G	O	I	L
U	R	C	N	R	G	U	D	V	Y	N	E
A	C	H	I	E	V	E	W	O	R	A	N
L	O	T	T	P	V	I	S	A	E	T	G
V	M	W	I	P	L	D	A	Q	W	I	E
B	E	X	E	R	W	A	U	X	D	O	K
R	U	S	S	U	P	P	O	R	T	N	E

2 **2** encourage **3** obstacle **4** support **5** inspire **6** challenge **7** determination **8** overcome **9** opportunities **10** achieve

3 Students' own answers

4 a 5 b 3 c 6 d 1 e 4 f 2

5 **2** c **3** b **4** c **5** b

LANGUAGE IN ACTION

1 2 b 3 a 4 c

2 2 would have been 3 wouldn't have got 4 had sent 5 hadn't jumped 6 wouldn't have broken 7 hadn't come 8 wouldn't have brought

3 2 wouldn't have 3 would have tasted 4 hadn't broken 5 have turned

4 Students' own answers

WRITING

1 Against

2 2 On 3 instance 4 such 5 other 6 Furthermore 7 In 8 believe

3 1 the most dangerous place in the world
2 do something dangerous
3 to have a quiet life
4 take risks (or) stay alive

4 1 second para (C) 2 last para (D) 3 first para (A) 4 third para (B)

5–8 Students' own answers

REVIEW

1 1 get 2 take 3 have 4 take 5 get 6 have 7 take 8 get 9 take 10 get 11 get 12 have

2 1 support 2 challenge 3 opportunities 4 encouraged 5 bravery 6 determination 7 inspired 8 overcome; obstacles 9 achieve

3 1 If I didn't know the answer, I'd ask the teacher.
2 If you have any doubts, you'll have to ask Peter.
3 If I get bored, I'll send you a message.
4 Unless you try harder, you'll never achieve your dreams.
5 If I thought it was risky, I wouldn't do it.
6 You'll never achieve anything unless you overcome this obstacle.

4 1 had got; wouldn't have arrived
2 would have done; had encouraged
3 wouldn't have said; hadn't got
4 wouldn't have been; hadn't saved,
5 hadn't sat; would have heard

5 1 b 2 a 3 c 4 c 5 b 6 a 7 d 8 d 9 a 10 c 11 a 12 b

Unit 7 pp56–63

VOCABULARY

1 2 grateful 3 hurt 4 down 5 glad 6 peaceful 7 insecure 8 amused 9 eager 10 annoyed 11 hopeful 12 thrilled 13 satisfied

Positive: grateful, glad, peaceful, amused, eager, hopeful, thrilled, satisfied

Negative: ridiculous, hurt, down, insecure, annoyed

2 2 annoyed 3 insecure 4 eager 5 satisfied 6 thrilled

3 2 glad 3 peaceful 4 down 5 amused 6 hopeful

4 Students' own answers

EXPLORE IT!

a and c

READING

1 False

2 2 senses 3 technique 4 studies 5 powerful 6 reduce

3 2 the present 3 control our feelings
4 we sometimes make ourselves
5 can teach people to understand their feelings
6 not difficult to learn

4 Students' own answers

LANGUAGE IN ACTION

1 2 to take 3 cooking 4 to check 5 to wear 6 losing

2 2 to try 3 to learn 4 breathing 5 to hold 6 doing 7 Learning 8 trying 9 to practise 10 to tell

3 2 winning 3 hearing 4 to write 5 looking 6 to bring

4 1 a 2 b 3 d 4 c

5 Students' own answers

VOCABULARY AND LISTENING

1 2 heart 3 mind 4 heart 5 mind

2 2 in 3 crosses 4 change 5 bear

3 Students' own answers

4 Become a singer in a band.

5 2 She does athletics / running and jumping.
3 It gets her out of the house to do something different from studying. It's good for her.
4 She plays the guitar.
5 She felt a bit ridiculous.
6 Because he can't sing well.

6 Students' own answers

LANGUAGE IN ACTION

1 2 What 3 What 4 Who 5 Who

2 2 What crossed your mind when you saw the drone?
3 Who did you decide to go shopping with?
4 Who is going to get bored at a football match?
5 What did you get so annoyed with?

3 a 4 b 2 c 5 d 3

4 2 What made you change your mind?
3 Who (has) supported you in the difficult times?
4 Who inspires / has inspired you?
5 What does it feel like?
6 What gets on your nerves?

5 Students' own answers

WRITING

1 buy an expensive guitar

2 2 b 3 e 4 a 5 c

3–5 Students' own answers

REVIEW

1

R	B	E	A	G	E	R	F	O	L	P	S
I	V	S	N	L	C	V	U	H	U	R	T
D	G	A	N	A	Y	A	I	N	H	V	H
I	R	T	O	D	O	W	N	N	O	P	R
C	A	I	Y	F	R	B	S	J	P	K	I
U	T	S	E	D	T	V	E	U	E	Q	L
L	E	F	D	P	E	A	C	E	F	U	L
O	F	I	A	F	Y	E	U	W	U	K	E
U	U	E	S	C	H	F	R	R	L	J	D
S	L	D	A	M	U	S	E	D	F	U	P

2 1 break 2 cross 3 two 4 close 5 make 6 learn 7 put; into 8 have 9 bear 10 change

3 1 I 2 G 3 I 4 G 5 G 6 I

4 1 learning 2 to help 3 feeling 4 going 5 Wasting 6 to see

5 1 When did you start playing basketball?
2 Who taught you how to play?
3 Who gave you your first basketball?
4 Who is your favourite player?
5 What makes you feel insecure?
6 Where do you practise?

6 1 d 2 b 3 a 4 c 5 c 6 b 7 d 8 a 9 b 10 a

Unit 8 pp64–71

VOCABULARY

1

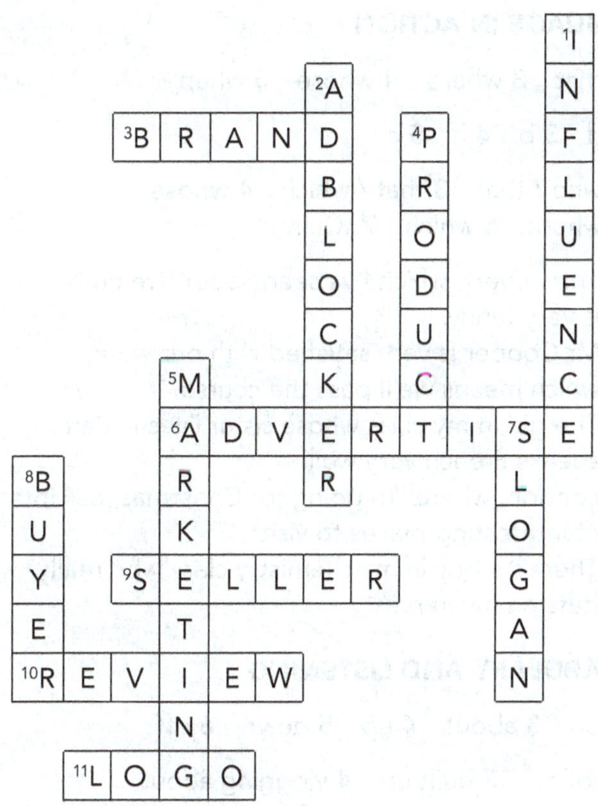

2 2 reviewed 3 advertised 4 to market 5 is selling 6 are produced 7 doesn't influence 8 to block

3 2 reviewer 3 advert 4 marketing 5 seller 6 producer 7 influencer 8 blocker

EXPLORE IT!

c

READING

1 Companies can find out what we search for, the people we are following and the photos we are looking at. They also know where we are through GPS. Shopping and music sites can also see what we like to watch.

2 2 browsing 3 gather 4 update 5 data 6 give away

3 2 T 3 T 4 F Information is gathered for users to give them a better service. 5 F Today we generate 50,000 GB of data in one second. In 1992 we only generated 100 GB in a day. 6 T

4 Students' own answers

LANGUAGE IN ACTION

1 2 that 3 where 4 whose 5 when

2 2 d 3 b 4 a 5 e

3 2 who / that 3 that / which 4 whose 5 where 6 which 7 when

4 2 This advert, which I've seen about five times, is very funny.
3 Mr Cooper is very satisfied with our work, which means we'll pass the course.
4 The girl in my class whose sister lives in Paris speaks French very well.
5 London, where I'm going for Christmas, has lots of interesting places to visit.
6 There's a boy in my chemistry class who really gets on my nerves.

VOCABULARY AND LISTENING

1 2 on 3 about 4 up 5 down 6 off

2 2 follow 3 built up 4 vlogging about 5 comment on 6 post 7 switch on 8 deleted 9 shut down

3 2 over 1 billion 3 50 million 4 5 billion

4 Students' own answers

5 2 T 3 F We love product reviews. 4 T

LANGUAGE IN ACTION

1 2 anybody 3 anything 4 anybody 5 no one 6 nothing

2 2 nothing 3 anything 4 someone 5 something 6 someone 7 something 8 nothing

3 2 yourself 3 myself 4 each other 5 ourselves 6 one another

4 2 Anna taught **herself** how to vlog about video games.
3 Phil and I are really good friends. We talk to **each other / one another** about everything.
4 There isn't **anything** you can do about adverts on TV except switch them off.
5 It's nothing serious – I just cut **myself** with a knife.
6 I don't know **anyone** at this party. Is there anyone you know here?

5 2 everything 3 herself 4 anyone / anybody 5 herself 6 nothing 7 each other 8 someone / somebody

WRITING

1 1 The voice message feature with famous voices.

2 2 allows 3 features 4 missing 5 included

3 2 A 3 B 4 B 5 C

4–6 Students' own answers

REVIEW

1 1 product 2 brand 3 slogan 4 logo 5 advert 6 advertise 7 marketing 8 influenced 9 buyer 10 seller 11 ad-blocker 12 review

2 1 e 2 d 3 a 4 h 5 g 6 c 7 f 8 b

3 1 that / which 2 which 3 whose 4 which 5 who 6 where

4 1 yourself 2 himself 3 herself 4 each other 5 yourself

5 1 someone 2 anyone 3 nothing 4 Everything 5 anything 6 someone

6 1 d 2 b 3 c 4 a 5 b 6 c 7 b 8 d 9 a 10 c

Unit 9 pp72-79

VOCABULARY

1

R	E	F	D	E	N	Y	U	R	S	E
C	L	A	I	M	O	F	A	E	U	A
O	I	N	S	I	S	T	D	F	G	N
N	O	U	C	S	I	E	M	U	G	N
F	A	P	O	L	O	G	I	S	E	O
I	C	W	V	G	G	E	T	E	S	U
R	F	K	E	E	R	Z	I	U	T	N
M	V	P	R	O	M	I	S	E	D	C
C	O	M	P	L	A	I	N	F	O	E

2 **2** confirm **3** insist **4** suggest **5** refuse
6 complain

3 **2** announced **3** claimed **4** promised
5 discovered **6** admit

4 Students' own answers

EXPLORE IT!

a

READING

1 c

2 **2** mysterious **3** pianist **4** wandering
5 useless **6** beautifully

3 **2** Because he drew a picture of a piano.
3 He pointed to Oslo on a map.
4 Because they couldn't get any useful information (from the public).
5 His parents came from Germany and took him home.
6 It's an ending that is usually good and happy for everyone.

4 Students' own answers

LANGUAGE IN ACTION

1 **2** S **3** S **4** S **5** C **6** C

2 **2** My brother complained that he always had to do the washing-up.
3 David denied that he had sent the message.
4 Mia refused to talk to Ryan.
5 The teacher announced that there was going to be an exam the next / following day.
6 The doctor told me to go home and lie down and (that) I would be fine in a few hours.

3 **2** S **3** O **4** O **5** S **6** S

4 **2** Tim suggested checking online to see if there were any good films on.
3 Ayaz offered to lend me a nice shirt.
4 She offered to hold my bag while I tried on the sweater.
5 The teacher suggested meeting after class to discuss my progress.
6 Ada offered to ask her dad if he would give them a lift.

5 Students' own answers

VOCABULARY AND LISTENING

1 **2** occasionally **3** secretly **4** surprisingly
5 after a while; gradually; eventually
6 fluently; regularly

2 **2** regularly / occasionally
3 Occasionally / After a while
4 surprisingly **5** secretly **6** fluently
7 After a while / Eventually **8** gradually
9 eventually

3 It makes us laugh.

4 **2** three **3** the end **4** popular **5** great tips
6 clever

5 Students' own answers

LANGUAGE IN ACTION

1 **2** who **3** was **4** if / whether **5** had **6** could

2 **2** Who are you chatting to?
3 What's your favourite sport?
4 Do you want something to eat?
5 Did you go to the party last Friday?
6 Can I come to your house to watch the match later?

3 **2** My dad asked me where I'd been.
3 Paul asked me if I could help him fix his bike.
4 She didn't ask me if I was going to school tomorrow.
5 Brooke / Marco asked me when I'd seen Marco / Brooke.

4 **1 b** what had been his favourite subject at school
2 a why he had started playing the guitar
3 c if he was happy with his latest album
4 e when his next tour was
5 d if he would play a song for them

5 Students' own answers

WRITING

1 Children are brought up speaking the women's language. When boys get older, they learn to speak like the men. Nowadays, most children are learning English.

2 **2** B **3** A / C **4** A **5** B

3 **2** asked **3** insisted **4** said **5** Nowadays

4–6 Students' own answers

REVIEW

1 **1** suggested **2** admitted **3** claims
4 promised **5** complaining **6** denied
7 announced **8** apologised **9** discovered
10 insisted **11** refusing **12** confirmed

2 **1** secretly **2** occasionally **3** patiently
4 fluently **5** gradually **6** Nowadays **7** regularly
8 after a while **9** surprisingly **10** eventually

3 **1** e **2** c **3** a **4** f **5** d **6** b

4 **1** if / whether I could **2** Josh had said
3 if / whether I would / to **4** where I was
5 how we knew **6** if / whether we needed

5 **1** d **2** c **3** b **4** a **5** d **6** b **7** c **8** d **9** a
10 b **11** c **12** d

EXAM PRACTICE pp80–85

LISTENING SKILLS pp80–81

1 **1** A **2** B **3** A **4** B **5** A **6** B

2 **1** F **2** F **3** T **4** F **5** T **6** F

3 **1** Yes **2** Yes **3** No

4 B

READING SKILLS pp82–83

1 **1** C **2** B **3** A

2 **1** cook in the oven **2** lived as a child **3** cook in oil
4 will possibly **5** think **6** cut into pieces

3 A and C

4 **1** Sam is interested in both quick and complicated recipes. Nathan is mainly interested in quick recipes.
2 Sam doesn't eat fried food. Nathan likes fried food.
3 Sam doesn't eat food with a very strong flavour. Nathan likes spicy food.

LISTENING SKILLS pp84–85

1 **1** a number **2** a time **3** a price

2 **1** 49 **2** 10.15 **3** 2.50
Other numbers: 30, 35, 38, 11.30, 20, 10.30, 1 o'clock, £12, £5

3 **A** uncle
B robotdesigners
C class
D 300

4 **1** day **2** name of food **3** time
4 a type of clothing **5** subject **6** number

5 **1** Tuesday **2** chicken **3** 5.30 **4** T-shirt
5 Marketing **6** 100

LANGUAGE REFERENCE & PRACTICE

Starter Unit p87

1 **2** Are you going **3** happens **4** was listening; saw
5 don't need **6** Did you buy

2 **2** 'm/am trying **3** do you normally leave **4** put
5 did you have **6** had **7** arrived **8** was talking
9 remember **10** went **11** looked / 've looked
12 didn't find **13** Were you wearing **14** left

3 **2** sang **3** 've/have told **4** 've/have (just) painted
5 didn't (you) laugh **6** hasn't played

4 **2** I didn't know you liked playing tennis.
3 You have taken a long time to finish your essay.
4 We didn't answer all the questions in the exam.
5 Why did you decide to come with us?
6 We haven't heard any news from Julia.

Unit 1 p89

1 **2** 's/has waited **3** Has (Jane) told
4 haven't played **5** has organised

2 **2** Have (you) been running **3** 's/has been raining **4** 's/has been wearing **5** has been tidying

3 **2** folded **3** sent **4** been painting **5** read **6** ordered

4 **2** have you been doing **3** 've been studying **4** 've always found **5** haven't even started **6** 've been trying **7** haven't finished **8** 've written **9** 've done **10** 've copied / copied

5 **2** really; quite **3** totally; rather **4** a bit

6 **2** c **3** d **4** a **5** f **6** b

Unit 2 p91

1 **2** used to eat **3** didn't use to look **4** used to win **5** didn't use to have **6** didn't use to give

2 **2** Did there always use to be a cinema here? / Was there always a cinema here?
3 Did your dad use to have a bike when he was a teenager? / Did your dad have a bike when he was a teenager?
4 Did you hear what happened yesterday?
5 What sort of music did you use to listen to when you were younger? / What sort of music did you listen to when you were younger?

3 **2** both **3** a **4** a

4 **2** already **3** the time **4** already **5** by then **6** never

5 **2** By **3** had already **4** then **5** already **6** had

6 **2** By the time we got there, our team had scored.
3 She had tried to apologise to him the week before, but by then it was too late.
4 Until last week, Camilla had never spoken in English.
5 When you arrived, Dennis had already found his keys.

Unit 3 p93

1 **2** 's going to **3** will **4** 'll **5** is going to **6** may not

2 **2** 'll pass / 're going to pass **3** is Tim meeting / is Tim going to meet **4** 'm not going to buy **5** might/may not have **6** 'm going to order

3 **2** 'm going to buy **3** starts **4** might / may need

4 **2** won't be wearing **3** won't be teaching **4** 'll be enjoying **5** 'll be writing **6** 'll be preparing

5 **2** will have spent **3** will (probably) have seen **4** will have laughed **5** will have eaten **6** will (probably) have drunk

6 **2** In 20 years, we'll ~~be~~ **have** built robots to do the cooking for us. **3** By ~~the~~ **this** time tomorrow, I'll have finished all my exams. **4** I ~~be not~~ **won't be / 'm not** doing anything later so call me.
5 Will ~~have you~~ **you have** started the dinner when I get home? **6** What will ~~be you~~ **you be** wearing to Chloe's party?

Unit 4 p95

1 **2** can **3** could **4** can't **5** must **6** might

2 **2** Freya might be in bed. **3** You might need to sit down. **4** That can't be Freddie. **5** He might/may not arrive on time for his first class. **6** It must be very smelly.

3 **2** N **3** A **4** A **5** O **6** O

4 **2** need to pack / mustn't forget **3** have to take **4** ought to buy **5** don't have to worry **6** mustn't forget / need to pack

5 **2** shouldn't call **3** had to go **4** don't have/needn't **5** mustn't run **6** can't be

Unit 5 p97

1 **2** were solved **3** Are (phone batteries) produced **4** will be wasted **5** was chopped **6** isn't connected

2 **2** Why are flies attracted to the smell of food?
3 How were these images created?
4 Where will we be collected after the museum visit?
5 How was the meat cooked?
6 When will a time machine be developed?

3 **2** Your grades will be communicated to you in a week.
3 The ingredients were measured very carefully.
4 The fish is grilled over a fire.

4 **2** was developed **3** are attracted **4** was completed **5** was opened **6** is planned **7** will be connected

5 2 don't 3 will 4 was

6 2 didn't he 3 don't they 4 can they
5 does she 6 will you

7 2 What was the class about?
3 Who did Logan bake a cake for?
4 Who was the food delivered by?
5 Who is your dad angry with?

Unit 6 p99

1 2 c 3 b 4 f 5 a 6 d

2 2 won't understand; get 3 won't have; joins
4 wastes; 'll be 5 won't be; connect

3 2 went; wouldn't 3 could; 'd work
4 would you; found 5 didn't; 'd

4 2 If animals could communicate with humans, what would they say?
3 Would you go to Mars if you had the chance?
4 What would you do all day if you lived on a desert island?

5 2 wouldn't have got; hadn't told
3 would have finished; had encouraged
4 wouldn't have missed; hadn't fallen
5 would have happened; had pressed

6 2 would (you) have gone 3 would have given
4 would (you) have bought 5 would have looked
6 hadn't hurt 7 wouldn't have had

Unit 7 p101

1 2 to help 3 Being 4 to sell 5 listening 6 flying

2 2 going 3 using 4 to play 5 Taking; driving
6 to solve

3 2 to come 3 to tell 4 to send 5 to practise
6 travelling 7 seeing 8 to hear

4 2 to do 3 listening 4 to eat 5 winning 6 to set

5 2 Which class is going to the National Museum tomorrow?
3 Who sent you a message on your birthday?
4 What fell on your dad's car?

6 2 does your sister study 3 is going 4 happened
5 can we ask 6 did you beat

Unit 8 p103

1 2 f 3 a 4 d 5 c 6 e

2 2 where 3 whose 4 that/which 5 where

3 2 This fish, which we bought ~~it~~ in the supermarket, was very expensive.
3 Maya, ~~who's~~ whose dad comes from Australia, works in marketing.
4 Theo's review of the film, ~~that~~ which Lucas sent me, was hilarious.
5 Dublin, ~~which~~ where Mike has lived since he was five, is the capital of Ireland.
6 My friend, ~~which~~ who I was following on social media, has blocked me.

4 2 everything 3 everywhere 4 Everyone / Everybody
5 someone / somebody; no one / nobody
6 anywhere

5 2 themselves 3 himself 4 nobody 5 anything
6 each other 7 anywhere 8 someone

Unit 9 p105

1 2 They told us (that) they wouldn't waste any more time.
3 Joshua said (that) he could help me to make lunch.
4 Andy said to Amy (that) he hadn't bought her Christmas presents yet.
5 You told me (that) Heidi was moving to Australia next week.

2 2 me not to 3 to tell them 4 told me not

3 2 to collect 3 not telling 4 to help 5 switching

4 2 Maria asked me what would make me change my mind.
3 I asked my friend if / whether they / he / she had ever been to Vienna.
4 Leah asked the teacher when the next exam was.
5 Jake asked her if / whether she changed her mind often / often changed her mind.

5 2 ~~hadn't I~~ – I hadn't
3 ~~where it does hurt~~ – where it hurt
4 ~~could she~~ – she could
5 ~~what did happen~~ – what (had) happened

6 2 was 3 going out 4 had seen 5 not to forget